McGRAW-HILL'S

CONQUERING SAT MATH

SECOND EDITION

Robert Postman

Professor of Mathematics and Education
Mercy College, New York

Ryan Postman

Mathematics Department
Pascack Hills High School, New Jersey

McGRAW-HILL

New York / Chicago / San Francisco / Lisbon / London / Madrid / Mexico City
Milan / New Delhi / San Juan / Seoul / Singapore / Sydney / Toronto

McGRAW-HILL's Conquering SAT Math

1234567890 QPD/QPD 0987

ISBN-13: 978-0-07-149341-3
ISBN-10: 0-07-149341-7

Printed and bound by Quebecor World.
Copyright images reproduced with permission from Texas Instruments.

McGraw-Hill books are available at special quantity discounts to use as premiums and sales promotions or for use in corporate training programs. For more information, please write to the Director of Special Sales, Professional Publishing, McGraw-Hill. Two Penn Plaza, New York, NY 10121-2298. Or contact your local bookstore.

ACKNOWLEDGMENTS

This book shows you how to get your highest possible score on the New SAT: Mathematics Test. Hundreds of high school students, just like you, field tested this book. Much of what is here reflects these students' opinions about what was most helpful to them. The book has also been reviewed by many high school teachers and college faculty, and it incorporates many of their suggestions about what will be most helpful to you.

This book has over 600 realistic SAT problems with explained answers. Many of those problems are in five SAT Math Practice Tests. The rest of the problems are in the chapters that review all of the mathematics concepts on the new SAT. These review chapters have hundreds more examples and practice exercises to help you sharpen your mathematics skills.

Special thanks go to Judy Brendel, Mathematics Supervisor, who supported the development of this book. Particular thanks go to John Uhl, Janet Telesmanich, Charleen Martinelli, Kevin Killian, and Michelle Gaeta. These talented mathematics teachers reviewed the SAT Math Practice Tests. Thanks are due also to the hundreds of high school students who reviewed every part of this book. Thanks are also due to Texas Instruments for permission to use images of their calculators.

CONTENTS

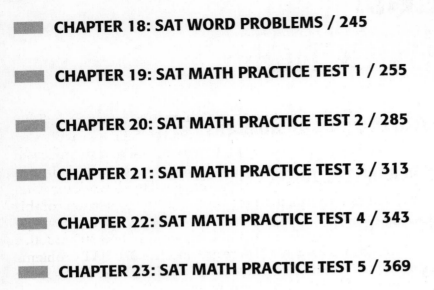

CHAPTER 1

INTRODUCTION

Conquering the New SAT Math covers all the mathematics topics and all the problem types on the new version of the SAT. It is the SAT you will take. Every page in this book was field tested by high school students and reviewed by experienced high school math teachers. We listened very carefully to student and teacher recommendations to create a book that will work for you.

You learn mathematics by doing mathematics. The review sections of this book contain hundreds of examples and practice problems. The review sections also feature worked-out model SAT problems—more than 300 practice SAT problems with explained answers. There are another 270 SAT problems with explained answers in five SAT Mathematics Practice Tests. That's more than 600 worked-out SAT practice problems in all.

We review each of the 17 major areas on the SAT in 17 separate chapters. Each chapter begins with a clear review and practice with answers. Next come several worked-out SAT problems to show you how to apply the mathematics concepts to the SAT format. Then comes a whole set of practice SAT problems in each chapter, with explained answers. The problems generally increase in difficulty.

The five mathematics practice tests follow the review chapters. Each test reflects the mix of mathematics problems you will find on the real SAT. The tests are deliberately a little more difficult than the actual SAT. You will get an estimated mathematics score range for each test you complete.

We show you strategies for answering SAT multiple choice and "grid-in" math questions. However, the most important strategy is to think mathematically, just like the people who make up the test do. These test writers always have particular mathematics skills and concepts in mind as they write an item. Knowing how to spot those concepts is usually the secret to getting a high score. You'll learn that from this book.

You Decide How Much Review You Need

This book is designed to help you no matter how much SAT mathematics preparation you need. Which type of student are you?

✓ I need mathematics review.
✓ I need to practice SAT problems.
✓ I need to take practice SAT Tests.

Work through the review chapters and then take the practice tests.

✓ I need to practice SAT problems.
✓ I need to take practice SAT Tests.

Skip the teaching and practice in the review chapters and go directly to the Model Problems in each chapter. Complete the practice problems in each chapter and take the practice tests.

✓ I just need to take practice SAT Tests.

Skip the review chapters and go to the practice tests.

MATHEMATICS TEST OVERVIEW

There are two types of SAT mathematics problems, multiple choice and student response (grid-in). Here is an overview of the Math sections of the SAT

Two 25-minute test sections
One 20-minute test section
Total 70 minutes

Multiple-choice items	44 items
Grid-ins	<u>10 items</u>
Total	54 items

Math Is Not my Favorite Subject

OK, we understand that. Most of the other parts of the SAT reflect things you might do in a normal week—reading, understanding, and writing. The only time most people do SAT mathematics problems is on the mathematics SAT. But, that's the way it is. If things ever change, we'll be the first to tell you. Until then, we'll show you the way to your highest possible score.

MATHEMATICS TEST STRATEGIES

There are different strategies for each problem type. Let's take them in order.

Multiple Choice

Remember, a multiple choice item always shows you the correct answer. Each multiple choice item has five answer choices. SAT scoring deducts 1/4 point for each incorrect answer. That means that, on average, you'll lose a small fraction of a point if you just guess an answer. However, if you are sure that one or more of the answers are wrong, on average, you will gain if you guess. It's just simple mathematics.

Eliminate and Guess

If you know the answer, fill in that oval on the answer sheet. If you don't know the answer, and you can definitely eliminate at least one answer, cross off the answers you know are incorrect right in the test booklet. Then guess from among the remaining answers.

Use the Test Booklet

The test booklet is yours. Do your work in the test booklet. Cross off incorrect answers in the test booklet. Draw diagrams—whatever you like.

Darken the Correct Oval

The machine that scores multiple choice tests does not know if you are right or wrong. The machine just "knows" if you have filled in the correct oval, so it is possible to know the correct answer but be marked wrong.

The fewer times your eyes go from the test sheet to the answer sheet, the less likely you are to make a recording error. We recommend this practice. Write all the answers next to the problem for a two-page spread of questions. Then transfer the answer to the Answer Sheet.

2. In which of the following choices would the symbol > create an incorrect statement?

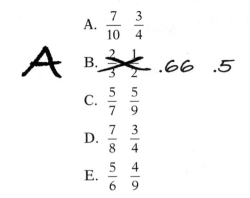

A. $\dfrac{7}{10}$ $\dfrac{3}{4}$

B. $\dfrac{2}{3}$ $\dfrac{1}{2}$ .66   .5

C. $\dfrac{5}{7}$ $\dfrac{5}{9}$

D. $\dfrac{7}{8}$ $\dfrac{3}{4}$

E. $\dfrac{5}{6}$ $\dfrac{4}{9}$

Estimate

Estimate the answer. An estimate may lead you to the correct answer or it may enable you to cross off some answers you know are incorrect.

Work From the Answers

You know that one of the answers must be correct. You may be able to find the correct answer by substituting answers in the problem.

Grid-ins

The answer format for grid-in items is shown below. Write your answer in the four spaces at the top of the grid. But the scoring machine just reads the ovals you fill in. You must fill in the correct oval to receive credit.

You may enter the digits and symbols shown in each column. The symbols represent the fraction line and the decimal point. These choices put some natural limits on the answers. You'll read about those limits in this section.

How to Grid-in an Answer

Here are some examples of grid-in answers. Remember, you must fill in the ovals to receive credit.

Here's how to enter the fraction $\dfrac{5}{13}$ in the grid. Notice that we entered the numerator and the denominator separated by the slash, and then we filled in the corresponding ovals.

Say that your answer is $\frac{3}{5}$. There are several ways to fill in the grid.

You can grid in $\frac{3}{5}$.   You can grid in the decimal equivalent. 0.6

If your answer is 197, you can fill in the grid two different ways.

The fraction $\frac{2}{3}$ is equivalent to the repeating decimal 0.666 . . . You can grid-

in $\frac{2}{3}$, or .666 or .667.

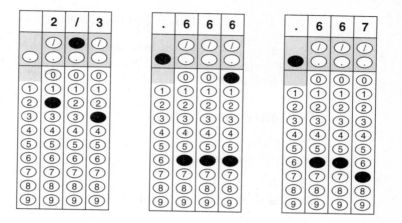

The Grid Can Help You Determine if Your Answer Is Incorrect

An answer can never be less than 0 or larger that 9999. That means you can never have a negative number as an answer.

The numerator or denominator of a fraction can never have more than two digits.

A decimal can extend only to the thousandths place.

If You Can't Grid-in Your Answer, Then Your Answer Is Incorrect

The answer has to fit in the four spaces at the top of the grid. You must be able to select the digits and symbols from the column below each digit or symbol you enter. If you can't do that, your answer is not correct.

Not Sure of an Answer? Skip It and Come Back Later

Skip any question that just seems too difficult. Circle the number of the question in your test booklet and come back later.

THE CALCULATOR

You should bring a calculator when you take the SAT. Most people do. A calculator helps you avoid answering questions incorrectly because you make an arithmetic error. However, many students bring calculators that can graph equations. That graphing capability will help with a limited number of SAT questions, but every question counts.

We discuss some calculators below. You should only bring a calculator you know how to use. Don't go out just before the test to buy the latest high-powered calculator; stick with what you know. However, if you know how to use one of the calculators we discuss below, well, so much the better.

Key Entry Errors

We all have a tendency to trust answers that appear on a calculator. However, if you press the wrong keys you'll get an incorrect answer. If the answer is part of a chain of calculations, you probably won't catch it. There are two ways to avoid key entry errors.

Use a Calculator with a Two-Line Display

Most scientific and graphing calculators have at least two lines in the display. That means your entries appear on one line and your answer appears on the other line.

Estimate Before You Calculate

Estimate an answer before you calculate. Something is wrong if your calculated answer is significantly different from your estimate.

Decide When to Use a Calculator

Use a calculator as you need it to find the answer to a question. Do you need to compute, find a graph, solve an equation? There's a good chance the calculator will help. There are many SAT questions when one person will use a calculator and another person will not. There are many other SAT problems when a calculator will not be helpful to anyone. Using a calculator for these problems will just slow you down and cause problems.

Every question on the SAT can be answered without a calculator. You should reach for your calculator only when it will help you.

Calculator Choices

You will probably take a Texas Instruments calculator to the SAT. We discuss two calculators you might take to the SAT test. There are other choices, but you should take a calculator that is similar to one of the two calculators we discuss below.

TI 83 (Plus) Graphing Calculator

The TI 83 (Plus) is the calculator of choice for most SAT test takers. However, you may buy the TI-84, which is replacing the TI-83. It has all the capability you will need for the SAT. You don't need a more advanced calculator, unless that more advanced calculator is your calculator of choice.

The TI-83 and the TI-84 have one significant shortcoming. They do not directly display the answer to fraction problems. You have to know how to go through the complicated procedure to see the fraction representation. Direct calculation of fractions is available on the very advanced TI-89 calculator. Direct calculation of fractions is also available on the TI-34II Explorer Plus and several other TI scientific calculators.

TI-34II Explorer Plus Scientific Calculator

If you don't want to use a graphing calculator, a scientific calculator such as the Explorer Plus will get you through the SAT just fine.

Reproduced with permission.
Copyright © Texas Instruments Incorporated.

The Explorer Plus, and other scientific calculators, offer direct calculation of fractions and a scrolling two line display. The Explorer Plus is an excellent calculator choice for students who are unfamiliar with a graphing calculator.

Calculators You Can't Use

Here is a list of the calculators and devices you can't bring to the SAT.

You can't bring a computer, even a hand-held computer, and you can't bring a calculator with a typewriter keyboard (QWERTY). That means you can't bring the TI-92.

You can't bring a PDA, a writing pad, or an electronic pen device.

You can't bring a talking or noisy calculator, one that prints answers, or one that needs to be plugged in to an electrical outlet.

OK, Let's Do Some Math.

This is the secret. The more math you do, the better you'll get at it. Let's go.

CHAPTER 2

NUMBERS AND OPERATIONS ON NUMBERS

There are several operations that can be applied to numbers. We are most familiar with multiplication, division, addition, and subtraction. We use these operations to simplify expressions and to create numerical patterns called sequences. A calculator usually helps with these problems. Union and intersection can be applied to sets of numbers. Begin with the mathematics review and then complete and correct the practice problems. There are 2 Solved SAT Problems and 17 Practice SAT Questions with answer explanations.

NUMBERS

Numbers can represent quantities, amounts and positions on a number line. The counting numbers (1, 2, 3, 4, 5 . . .) are the numbers we use most often. A prime number is evenly divisible by itself and 1; 2, 3, 5, 7, and 11 are examples of primes. All other numbers are composite, except 1, which is neither prime nor composite.

SAT questions in this category may also be about signed numbers, decimals, and fractions, including adding, subtracting, multiplying, and dividing these numbers. The SAT questions may also ask you about reciprocals, to compare fractions and decimals, and to convert among fractions, improper fractions, mixed numbers, and decimals. We do not specifically review these topics in this section.

SIMPLIFYING EXPRESSIONS

When working with numbers and addition, subtraction, multiplication, division and powers be sure to use the correct order of operations: **P**arentheses, **E**xponents, **M**ultiplication/**D**ivision, **A**ddition/**S**ubtraction (PEMDAS). Some people use the phrase "**P**lease **E**xcuse **M**y **D**ear **A**unt **S**ally" to remember this order.

Example:

Simplify the expression: $(-5 + 7^2)[3 - (-6)^3] + (-11 - 2)(8 - 12)$.

$(-5 + 49)[3 - (-216)] + (-11 - 2)(8 - 12)$

$= (44)(219) + (-13)(-4)$

$= 9{,}636 + 52 = 9{,}688.$

Example:

Simplify $\left(\dfrac{3}{2} - \dfrac{2}{5}\right) \div \left(\dfrac{1}{3} + \dfrac{3}{4}\right)$

First, find common denominators for each set of fractions and add fractions:

$$\left(\frac{3\times5}{2\times5}-\frac{2\times2}{5\times2}\right)\div\left(\frac{1\times4}{3\times4}+\frac{3\times3}{4\times3}\right)=\left(\frac{15}{10}-\frac{4}{10}\right)\div\left(\frac{4}{12}+\frac{9}{12}\right)=\frac{11}{10}\div\frac{13}{12}.$$

When dividing fractions we must multiply reciprocals:

$$\frac{11}{10}\div\frac{13}{12}=\frac{11}{10}\times\frac{12}{13}=\frac{11\times12}{10\times13}=\frac{11\times6}{5\times13}=\frac{66}{65}=1\frac{1}{65}.$$

SETS

The **Intersection** of two sets X and Y is the set of elements common to X and Y. An element has to be in both sets to be in the intersection. Intersection is written $X\cap Y$.

The **Union** of two sets X and Y is the set of all elements in either set X or set Y, with no element repeated twice. An element that is in one set or both sets is in the union. Union is written $X\cup Y$.

Example:

Say that X is the set of all prime numbers less than 10, and Y is the set of all odd numbers less than 10. What is the union and intersection of sets X and Y?

$X=\{2,3,5,7\}$ and $Y=\{1,3,5,7,9\}$,

$X\cup Y=\{1,2,3,5,7,9\}$,

$X\cap Y=\{3,5,7\}$.

SEQUENCES

Sequence—a list of numbers in a specified pattern. Here are some examples of sequences.

Arithmetic Sequence—a sequence in which each term is a constant difference d from the previous term.

Find the next three terms in the sequence: 3, 6, 9, . . . In this sequence 3 is the common difference (d). Therefore, the next three terms in the sequence are 12, 15, 18.

The formula $a_n=a_1+d\cdot(n-1)$ can be used to find the nth term of an arithmetic sequence. In the example above, $a_1=3$, and $d=3$. We can use the formula to find terms in the sequence.

First term: $a_1=3+3(1-1)=3+3\cdot0=3$.

Fourth term: $a_4=3+3(4-1)=3+3\cdot3=3+9=12$.

Geometric Sequence—a sequence such that each term is given by a constant multiple r of the previous one.

Example:

Find the next three terms in the sequence: 3, 6, 12. In this sequence $r = 2$. Therefore, the next three terms in the sequence are 24, 48, 96.

The formula $a_n = a_1 \cdot r^{(n-1)}$ can also be used to find the nth term of the sequence. In this problem $a_1 = 3$ and $r = 2$, therefore we can see that

$$a_1 = 3 \cdot (2)^{(1-1)} = 3 \cdot 2^0 = 3 \cdot 1 = 3.$$

$$a_6 = 3 \cdot (2)^{(6-1)} = 3 \cdot 2^5 = 3 \cdot 32 = 96.$$

Other Sequences. There are other types of sequences.

Example:

Find the next three terms in the sequence: 3, 8, 5, 10, 7, 12. The sequence is not an arithmetic sequence, nor a geometric sequence. Inspect the sequence to find the pattern.

3		8,		5,		10,		7,		12		9		14		11
	+5		**−3**		**+5**		**−3**		**+5**		**−3**		**+5**		**−3**	

The pattern is add 5, subtract 3. The next three terms are 9, 14, 11.

Practice Questions

Write the correct answer.

1. Simplify the following expression:

    $(13 - 5) - [8^3 + (-20)] + [7 - (-14)^2](-12 - 6).$

2. Simplify the following expression: $\left(\dfrac{7}{5} - \dfrac{2}{3}\right) \div \left(\dfrac{2}{9} + \dfrac{1}{3}\right).$

3. Let the set X be all the positive composite numbers less than 10 and the set Y be all positive even numbers less than 10. Find $X \cup Y$ and $X \cap Y$.

4. Order the fractions $\dfrac{7}{13}, \dfrac{8}{15}$, and $\dfrac{9}{17}$ from least to greatest.

5. Find the next three terms in the sequence: 7, 11, 15.
6. Find the next three terms in the sequence: 5, 15, 45.

Practice Answers

1. 2,918 Remember to use the correct order of operations.

2. $\dfrac{33}{25} = 1\dfrac{8}{25}$ Add or subtract inside parentheses, then divide.

3. Write the sets. $X = \{4, 6, 8, 9\}$ $Y = \{2, 4, 6, 8\}$.
    Find the union and the intersection.

    $X \cup Y = \{2, 4, 6, 8, 9\}$ $X \cap Y = \{4, 6, 8\}$.

4. $\dfrac{9}{17} < \dfrac{8}{15} < \dfrac{7}{13}$.

It is easiest to use a calculator to convert the fractions to decimals and then compare the decimals.

5. 19, 23, 27.   The constant difference is 4.

6. 135, 405, 1,215.   The constant multiple is 3.

SOLVED SAT PROBLEMS

1. In a certain geometric sequence, 5 is the first term and 45 is the 3rd term. What term is 3,645?

Solution: **7**

Use the formula $a_n = a_1 \cdot r^{(n-1)}$.

Find the value of r.

$a_3 = 45 = 5 \cdot r^{(3-1)} \Rightarrow 45 = 5 \cdot r^2 \Rightarrow 9 = r^2 \Rightarrow 3 = r$.

Therefore,

$a_n = 3{,}645 = 5 \cdot 3^{(n-1)} \Rightarrow 729 = 3^{(n-1)}$.

Use your calculator and just keep multiplying by 3 to determine that $729 = 3^6$.

This means that $n - 1 = 6 \Rightarrow n = 7$.

3,645 is the 7th term.

2. $X = \{-7,-3,2,1,5,8\}$ and $Y = \{-8,-3,-1,2,5,8,9\}$.

Which of the following is equal to the sum of the elements of $X \cap Y$?

A. 0
B. 4
C. 6
D. 12
E. 16

Answer: **D**

Find the intersection of X and Y $X \cap Y = \{-3,2,5,8\}$.

Add the elements of the intersection $-3 + 2 + 5 + 8 = 12$.

NUMBERS AND OPERATIONS ON NUMBERS
PRACTICE SAT QUESTIONS

ANSWER SHEET

Choose the correct answer.
If no choices are given, grid the answers in the section at the bottom of the page.

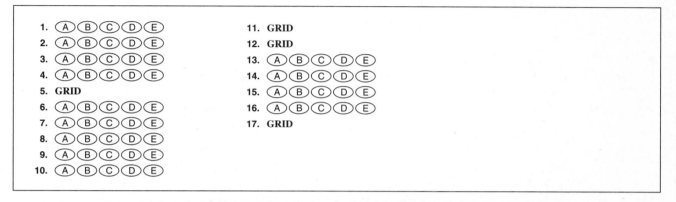

Use the answer spaces in the grids below if the question requires a grid-in response.

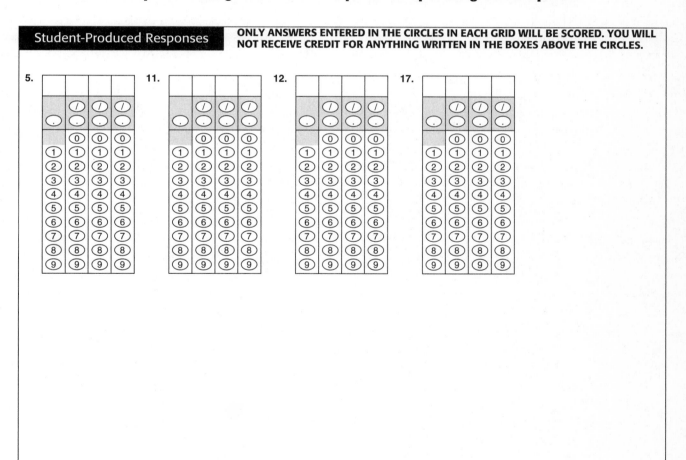

PRACTICE SAT QUESTIONS

1. Which of the following is not equal to $\frac{5}{9}$?

   A. $\frac{10}{18}$

   B. $\frac{20}{36}$

   C. $\frac{30}{45}$

   D. $\frac{35}{63}$

   E. $\frac{50}{90}$

2. In which of the following choices would the symbol > create an incorrect statement?

   A. $\frac{1}{4}$ $\frac{3}{10}$

   B. $\frac{2}{3}$ $\frac{1}{2}$

   C. $\frac{4}{7}$ $\frac{5}{9}$

   D. $\frac{7}{8}$ $\frac{3}{4}$

   E. $\frac{5}{6}$ $\frac{7}{9}$

3. $(17 - 3) \div 7 - 2\,(-4 - 8) =$

   A. -20
   B. -2
   C. 26
   D. 31
   E. 34

4. $\dfrac{\frac{3}{4}}{\frac{3}{8}} =$

   A. $\frac{9}{32}$

   B. $\frac{1}{2}$

   C. $\frac{32}{9}$

   D. 2

   E. $\frac{3}{2}$

5. What is the next term in the sequence: 2,8,32,128 . . . ?

6. If $3^{x+2} = 81$, then $x =$

   A. 5
   B. 4
   C. 3
   D. 2
   E. 1

7. Which of the following has the smallest result?

   A. $\frac{2}{3} + \frac{5}{6} - \frac{1}{2}$

   B. $\frac{3}{4} - \frac{3}{2} + \frac{2}{3}$

   C. $\frac{5}{8} + \frac{1}{2} - \frac{5}{4}$

   D. $\frac{4}{7} - \frac{9}{14} + \frac{5}{2}$

   E. $\frac{3}{5} + \frac{7}{5} + \frac{2}{5}$

8. What is the difference between the largest and smallest number in the set below?

   $$\left\{ \frac{3}{7}, \frac{5}{8}, \frac{7}{9}, \frac{2}{5} \right\}$$

   A. $\frac{11}{56}$

   B. $\frac{11}{72}$

   C. $\frac{9}{40}$

   D. $\frac{1}{35}$

   E. $\frac{17}{45}$

9. Set $X = $ *even integers* and Set $Y = $ *odd integers.*
   Therefore $X \cap Y = $

   A. prime numbers
   B. integers
   C. empty set
   D. composite numbers
   E. whole numbers

10. Which of the following number sets has the property that the sum of any two numbers in the set is also in the set?
    I. Even integers
    II. Odd integers
    III. Composite numbers

    A. I
    B. II
    C. III
    D. I and II
    E. I and III

11. $\left(\dfrac{3}{5} + \dfrac{1}{3}\right) \div 1\dfrac{2}{5} = $

12.

8	8
5	5
a	b
+4	+4
24	36

    What is the value of $b - a$

13. The first term in a geometric sequence is 3 and the 4th term is 81. What is the 10th term of the sequence?

    A. 177,147
    B. 59,049
    C. 19,683
    D. 6,561
    E. 2,187

14. Multiplying a number by $\dfrac{4}{5}$ and then dividing by $\dfrac{2}{5}$ is the same as doing what to the number?

    A. Dividing by 4
    B. Multiplying by $\dfrac{1}{2}$
    C. Multiplying by 2
    D. Dividing by 5
    E. Multiplying by 5

15. Which of the following choices could be equal to set Z if

    $X = \{2,5,6,7,9\}$ and $Y = \{2,5,7\}$

    $X \cup Y \cup Z = \{1,2,3,4,5,6,7,8,9\}$

    $X \cap Z = \{2,6\}$

    $Y \cap Z = \{2\}$

    A. $Z = \{1,4,8\}$
    B. $Z = \{1,3,8\}$
    C. $Z = \{1,3,4,8\}$
    D. $Z = \{1,2,3,4,6,8\}$
    E. $Z = \{1,2,3,5,6,8\}$

16. For which of the following values of x is $x^3 < x$ not a true statement?

    A. -3
    B. -2
    C. $-\dfrac{1}{2}$
    D. $\dfrac{1}{3}$
    E. $\dfrac{1}{2}$

17. The first term in a geometric sequence is 2, and the common ratio is 3. The first term in an arithmetic sequence is 3, and the common difference is 3. Let set X be the set containing the first six terms of the geometric sequence and set Y be the set containing the first six terms of the arithmetic sequence. What is the sum of the elements in $X \cap Y$?

■ EXPLAINED ANSWERS

1. *Answer:* **C**

   Use the calculator: $\dfrac{5}{9} = 0.55\overline{5}$.

   Every other choice is equal to $0.55\overline{5}$ except for $\dfrac{30}{45} = 0.66\overline{6}$.

2. *Answer:* **A**

   Write a fraction as a decimal.

   $\dfrac{1}{4} = 0.25 < \dfrac{3}{10} = 0.3$

3. *Answer:* **C**

   Use the correct order of operations.

   $(17 - 3) \div 7 - 2(-4 - 8) =$
   $14 \div 7 - 2(-12) =$
   $2 + 24 =$
   26

4. *Answer:* **D**

   Multiply by the reciprocal.

   $\dfrac{\tfrac{3}{4}}{\tfrac{3}{8}} = \dfrac{3}{4} \times \dfrac{8}{3} = \dfrac{3 \times 8}{4 \times 3} = 2$

5. *Answer:* **512**

   Multiply by 4 to find the next term in the sequence.
   Therefore, $128 \times 4 = 512$.

6. *Answer:* **D**

   Use the rules of exponents.
   $81 = 3^4$ so $3^4 = 3^{x+2}$

   Therefore, $x + 2 = 4 \Rightarrow x = 2$.

7. *Answer:* **C**

   Using your calculator you can add each set of fractions and get the following results.

   A. $\dfrac{2}{3} + \dfrac{5}{6} - \dfrac{1}{2} = 1$

   B. $\dfrac{3}{4} - \dfrac{3}{2} + \dfrac{2}{3} = -0.083\overline{3}$

   C. $\dfrac{5}{8} + \dfrac{1}{2} - \dfrac{5}{4} = -0.125$

   D. $\dfrac{4}{7} - \dfrac{9}{14} + \dfrac{5}{2} \approx 2.42857$

   E. $\dfrac{3}{5} + \dfrac{7}{5} + \dfrac{2}{5} = 2.4$

8. *Answer:* **E**

   Use your calculator. Divide the numerator of each fraction by the denominator to find the decimal equivalent. You will be able to determine that $\dfrac{7}{9}$ is the largest number and $\dfrac{2}{5}$ is the smallest number.

   $$\frac{7}{9} - \frac{2}{5} = \frac{35}{45} - \frac{18}{45} = \frac{17}{45}$$

9. *Answer:* **C**

   When two sets have nothing in common, we refer to their intersection as the empty set. There are two appropriate ways to denote the empty set

   $$X \cap Y = \{\ \} \text{ or } X \cap Y = \phi$$

10. *Answer:* **A**
    I.   Correct. The sum of two even numbers is always an even number.
    II. Not correct because the sum of two odd integers is always an even number. For example, $7 + 5 = 12$, which is even.
    III. Not correct because there are several examples in which the sum of two composite numbers is a prime number. For example, $20 + 9 = 29$.

11. *Answer:* $\dfrac{2}{3}$

    Evaluate the expression

    $$\left(\frac{3}{5} + \frac{1}{3}\right) \div 1\frac{2}{5} =$$

    $$\left(\frac{9}{15} + \frac{5}{15}\right) \div \frac{7}{5} =$$

    $$\frac{14}{15} \times \frac{5}{7} =$$

    $$\frac{14 \times 5}{15 \times 7} =$$

    $$\frac{70}{105} = \frac{14}{21} = \frac{2}{3}$$

12. *Answer:* **12**

    Because all the numbers being added in both columns are the same except for the a and b. Therefore, the difference in the two sums must be the difference between a and b.

    Therefore, $b - a = 36 - 24 = 12$.

13. *Answer:* **B**

    $$a_n = a_1 \cdot r^{(n-1)} \Rightarrow a_4 = 81 = 3 \cdot r^{(4-1)} \Rightarrow 81 = 3 \cdot r^3 \Rightarrow 27 = r^3 \Rightarrow 3 = r$$

    Therefore,

    $$a_{10} = 3 \cdot 3^{(10-1)} = 3 \cdot 3^9 = 59,049.$$

14. *Answer:* **C**

Divide $\dfrac{4}{5}$ by $\dfrac{2}{5}$.

$$\dfrac{\dfrac{4}{5}}{\dfrac{2}{5}} = \dfrac{4}{5} \times \dfrac{5}{2} = 2$$

The result is the same as multiplying by 2.

15. *Answer:* **D**

We know that:

$X = \{2,5,6,7,9\}$ and $Y = \{2,5,7\}$
$X \cup Y \cup Z = \{1,2,3,4,5,6,7,8,9\}$

This tells us that Z must contain $\{1,3,4,8\}$ because these elements are in the union of X, Y, and Z but not in set X and not in set Y.

We also know that

$X \cap Z = \{2,6\}$
$Y \cap Z = \{2\}$

This tells us that Z must also contain $\{2,6\}$.

Only choice D contains all these elements.

$Z = \{1,2,3,4,6,8\}$

16. *Answer:* **C**

Find the cube (x^3) of each answer choice.

A. $(-3)^3 = -27 < -3$
B. $(-2)^3 = -8 < -2$

C. $\left(-\dfrac{1}{2}\right)^3 = -\dfrac{1}{8} > -\dfrac{1}{2}$. The cube is not less than the answer.

D. $\left(\dfrac{1}{3}\right)^3 = \dfrac{1}{27} < \dfrac{1}{3}$

E. $\left(\dfrac{1}{2}\right)^3 = \dfrac{1}{8} < \dfrac{1}{2}$

17. *Answer:* **24**

Geometric sequence   Arithmetic sequence
$X = \{2,6,18,54,162,456\}$ and $Y = \{3,6,9,12,15,18\}$
$X \cap Y = \{6,18\} \Rightarrow 6 + 18 = 24$

CHAPTER 3

FACTORS AND MULTIPLES

Factors and multiples deal with dividing and multiplying positive integers {1,2,3,4, . . .}. In this chapter you will work with such concepts as Greatest Common Factor (GCF) and Least Common Multiple (LCM). You will use the factors and multiples of a number to help you solve a variety of SAT Problems. You will see this as you review the 2 Solved SAT Problems, complete the 15 Practice SAT Questions and review the answer explanations.

FACTORS

A **factor** of a whole number divides the number, with no remainder.

Example:

Is 6 a factor of 50?

$$\begin{array}{r} 8 \\ 6\overline{)50} \\ 48 \\ \hline 2 \end{array}$$ Because 6 divides into 50 eight times with remainder 2, 6 is not a factor of 50.

The answer to the division problem above can be rewritten as $8\frac{2}{6} = 8\frac{1}{3} = 8.33\overline{3}$.

Example:

Is 7 a factor of 63?

$$\begin{array}{r} 9 \\ 7\overline{)63} \\ 63 \\ \hline 0 \end{array}$$ Because 7 divides into 63 nine times without a remainder, 7 is a factor of 63.

PRIMES AND COMPOSITES

A **prime** number is a positive integer that has exactly two factors, 1 and itself
A **composite** is a positive integer that has more than two factors

Example:

Is 20 a prime or composite number? The factors of 20 are {1,2,4,5,10,20}. Therefore, 20 is a composite number.

Example:

Is 17 a prime or composite number? The factors of 17 are {1,17}. Therefore, 17 is a prime number.

The **GREATEST COMMON FACTOR (GCF)** of two numbers is the largest factor the two numbers have in common.

Example:

What is the GCF of 16 and 36?

The factors of 16 are {1,2,4,8,16}, and the factors of 36 are {1,2,3,4,6,9,12, 18,36}. Therefore, the GCF is 4.

PRIME FACTORIZATION is a positive integer written as a product of prime numbers.

Example:

What is the prime factorization of 72?

$72 = 2^3 \cdot 3^2$

The **MULTIPLES** of a given number are those numbers created by successive multiplication. The given number divides the multiple without a remainder.

Example:

List the first five multiples of 3 and the first five multiples of 6.

The multiples of 3 are {3,6,9,12,15}, and the multiples of 6 are {6,12,18, 24,30}.

The **LEAST COMMON MULTIPLE (LCM)** is the smallest multiple two numbers have in common

Example:

What is the LCM of 3 and 6?

Answer: 6

Look at the list of multiples shown above.
Notice that 6 is the smallest multiple these numbers have in common.

Practice Questions

1. List the factors of the following numbers and then identify the greatest common factor.

   A. 34
   B. 52

2. State whether the following numbers are *prime* or *composite*.

   A. 31
   B. 45
   C. 63
   D. 59

3. Write the prime factorization for each number.

   A. 44
   B. 195

4. List the first eight multiples of each number and then identify the least common multiple of the two numbers.

   A. 5
   B. 7

Practice Answers

1. A. {1,2,17,34}
   B. {1,2,4,13,26,52}

The GCF is 2.

2. A. Prime
   B. Composite
   C. Composite
   D. Prime

3. A. $2^2 \cdot 11$
   B. $3 \cdot 5 \cdot 13$

4. A. {5,10,15,20,25,30,35,40}
   B. {7,14,21,28,35,42,49,56}

The least common multiple is 35.

SOLVED SAT PROBLEMS

1. What is the LCM of the numbers that satisfy these conditions?

   factor of 48

   multiple of 8

   Answer: **8**

   The factors of 48 are {1,2,3,4,6,8,12,16,24,48}. Of these numbers {8,16,24,48} are also multiples of 8.

   8 is the LCM of these numbers.

2. If a, b, and c are distinct integers such that

$a < b < c$, $b < 0$, and $c = a \cdot b$, then which of the following must be true?

A. c is a positive number.
B. $-a$ is a prime number.
C. b is a prime number.
D. c is a factor of a.
E. c is a prime number.

Answer: **A**

Because $a < b < c$ and $b < 0$, both a and b are negative integers.

$c = a \cdot b$, so c is a positive integer. The product of two negative integers is a positive integer.

FACTORS AND MULTIPLES
PRACTICE SAT QUESTIONS

ANSWER SHEET

Choose the correct answer.
If no choices are given, grid the answers in the section at the bottom of the page.

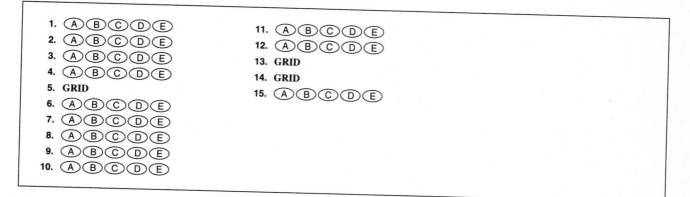

1. Ⓐ Ⓑ Ⓒ Ⓓ Ⓔ
2. Ⓐ Ⓑ Ⓒ Ⓓ Ⓔ
3. Ⓐ Ⓑ Ⓒ Ⓓ Ⓔ
4. Ⓐ Ⓑ Ⓒ Ⓓ Ⓔ
5. GRID
6. Ⓐ Ⓑ Ⓒ Ⓓ Ⓔ
7. Ⓐ Ⓑ Ⓒ Ⓓ Ⓔ
8. Ⓐ Ⓑ Ⓒ Ⓓ Ⓔ
9. Ⓐ Ⓑ Ⓒ Ⓓ Ⓔ
10. Ⓐ Ⓑ Ⓒ Ⓓ Ⓔ

11. Ⓐ Ⓑ Ⓒ Ⓓ Ⓔ
12. Ⓐ Ⓑ Ⓒ Ⓓ Ⓔ
13. GRID
14. GRID
15. Ⓐ Ⓑ Ⓒ Ⓓ Ⓔ

Use the answer spaces in the grids below if the question requires a grid-in response.

Student-Produced Responses ONLY ANSWERS ENTERED IN THE CIRCLES IN EACH GRID WILL BE SCORED. YOU WILL NOT RECEIVE CREDIT FOR ANYTHING WRITTEN IN THE BOXES ABOVE THE CIRCLES.

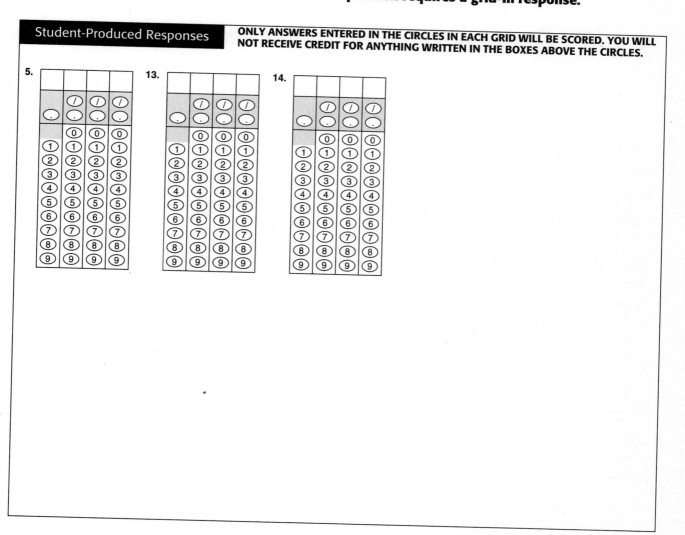

PRACTICE SAT QUESTIONS

1. What is the sum of all the factors of 24?
   A. 46
   B. 49
   C. 50
   D. 60
   E. 66

2. What is the greatest number of 3s that can be multiplied together and still have a result less than 250?
   A. 3
   B. 4
   C. 5
   D. 6
   E. 7

3. Which of the following must be true about the sum of all the prime numbers between 20 and 30?
   A. It is a prime number.
   B. It is an odd number.
   C. It is a factor of 156.
   D. It is a multiple of 5.
   E. It is a factor of 10.

4. At a dinner party each table can seat eight people. If 100 people attend the party, what is the minimum number of tables that are needed?
   A. 12
   B. 13
   C. 14
   D. 15
   E. 16

5. What is the greatest integer that evenly divides both 48 and 64?

6. Let P be a prime number greater than 4. How many distinct prime factors does $9 \cdot P$ have?
   A. 2
   B. 3
   C. 4
   D. 5
   E. 6

7. When x is divided by 8, the remainder is 3. What is the remainder when $4x$ is divided by 8?
   A. 1
   B. 2
   C. 3
   D. 4
   E. 5

8. Let x, y, and z be positive integers such that y is a multiple of x and z. All of the following statements are true except for:
   A. $y \cdot z$ is a multiple of x.
   B. x is a factor of y.
   C. $x \cdot z$ is a factor of y.
   D. z divides evenly into y.
   E. x divides evenly into $y \cdot z$.

9. When a two-digit number is divided by 5 the remainder is 2. Which of the following statements must be true about the two-digit number?
   A. The sum of all the digits is odd.
   B. The digit in the one's place is odd.
   C. The number is prime.
   D. The number is odd.
   E. The digit in the one's place is prime.

10. The sum of 3 consecutive integers is 15. How many distinct prime factors does the product of these three numbers have?
    A. 2
    B. 3
    C. 4
    D. 5
    E. 6

11. If a, b, and c are all integers greater than 1 and $a \cdot b = 21$ and $b \cdot c = 39$, then which of the following choices gives the correct ordering of the numbers?
    A. $b < a < c$
    B. $c < a < b$
    C. $a < b < c$
    D. $b < c < a$
    E. $a < c < b$

12. How many positive integers less than 20 have an odd number of distinct factors?

    A. 12
    B. 10
    C. 8
    D. 6
    E. 4

13. In the repeating decimal 0.714285714285 . . . , what is the 50th digit to the right of the decimal point?

14. How many distinct composite numbers can be formed by adding 2 of the first 5 prime numbers?

15. A rope is 13 feet long. How many ways can the rope be cut into more than one piece so that the length of each piece is a prime number?

    A. 4
    B. 5
    C. 6
    D. 7
    E. 8

EXPLAINED ANSWERS

1. *Answer:* **D**

   The factors of 24 are {1,2,3,4,6,8,12,24}.

   $1 + 2 + 3 + 4 + 6 + 8 + 12 + 24 = 60$

2. *Answer:* **C**

   $3^5 = 3 \times 3 \times 3 \times 3 \times 3 = 243$.

3. *Answer:* **C**

   23 and 29 are the only prime numbers between 20 and 30.

   $23 + 29 = 52$.

   $52 \cdot 3 = 156$.

   This shows that 52 is a factor of 156.

4. *Answer:* **B**

   Divide the number of people at the party by the number of seats around each table.

   $100 \div 8 = 12.5$.

   Thirteen tables will be needed to seat all 100 people.

5. *Answer:* **16**

   The largest integer that evenly divides both 48 and 64 is the GCF of the two numbers.

   The factors of 48 are {1,2,3,4,6,8,12,16,24,48}.

   The factors of 64 are {1,2,4,8,16,32,64}.

   The GCF is 16.

6. *Answer:* **A**

   Because P is a prime number, the prime factorization of $9 \cdot P$ is $3^2 \cdot P$. Therefore, 3 and P are the two distinct primes of $9 \cdot P$.

7. *Answer:* **D**

   Try an example. Choose 3 for x.

   3 divided by 8 leaves a remainder of 3.

   Multiply $3 \times 4 = 12$.

   12 divided by 8 leaves a remainder of 4.

8. *Answer:* **C**

   Note that this item asks for the choice that is NOT true.

   We know y is a multiple of x and z. That means y times any number is also a multiple of x, so choice A must be true.

   Also, because we know y is a multiple of x and z, this means that x and z divide evenly into y, so choices B, D and E are true.

   The process of elimination leaves choice C.

   Use an example to check this. Let $x = 3$, $y = 12$, and $z = 6$. y is a multiple of x and z, but $x \cdot z = 18$ is not a multiple of $y = 12$.

9. ***Answer:*** **E**

    The two-digit numbers that have a remainder of 2 when divided by 5 are

    $\{12,17,22,27,32,37,42,47,52,57,62,67,72,77,82,87,92,97\}$.

    Only choice E is always true, the one's digit is prime.

    Don't be fooled because some of the answers are true sometimes.

    For example, in choice (A) the sum of all digits is odd.

    This is true if the two-digit number is 32.

    The sum of the digits $3 + 2 = 5$ is odd.

    But choice (A) is not always true.

    If the two digit number is 42, the sum of the digits $4 + 2 = 6$ is not odd.

10. ***Answer:*** **B**

    The numbers must be 4, 5, and 6.

    $4 + 5 + 6 = 15 \quad$ and $\quad 4 \cdot 5 \cdot 6 = 120 = 2^3 \cdot 3 \cdot 5$

    2,3, and 5 are the three distinct prime factors.

11. ***Answer:*** **A**

    The question states that *a, b,* and *c* are integers greater than 1. That means *b* is an integer greater than 1 that divides evenly into both 21 and 39.

    That means that *b* must be 3.

    Divide.

    a must be 7, $7 \cdot 3 = 21$. *c* must be 13, $3 \cdot 13 = 39$.

    $3 < 7 < 13$

    $b < a < c$

12. ***Answer:*** **E**

    The only positive integers less than 20 that have an odd number of factors are the squares 1, 4, 9, and 16. That is because these numbers, alone, have a factor that is multiplied by itself. The factors for each are as follows:

Number	Factors
1:	{1}
4:	{1,2,4}
9:	{1,3,9}
16:	{1,2,4,8,16}

13. ***Answer:*** **1**

    In the repeating decimal 0.714285714285 . . . , 5 is the 6th, 12th, 18th, 24th, 30th, 36th, 42nd, and 48th digit.

    7 is the 49th digit and 1 is the 50th digit.

    You might also realize that there are 6 digits that repeat, divide 50 by 6, and get a remainder of 2. Therefore the 2nd of the 6 digits that repeat, which is 1, will be the 50th digit.

14. *Answer:* **7**

The first 5 prime numbers are {2,3,5,7,11}.

Add pairs of primes.

2 + 3 = 5

2 + 5 = 7   3 + 5 = 8

2 + 7 = 9   3 + 7 = 10   5 + 7 = 12

2 + 9 = 11   3 + 11 = 14   5 + 11 = 16   7 + 11 = 18

5, 7, and 11 are prime numbers.

8, 9, 10, 12, 14, 16, and 18 are composite numbers.

15. *Answer:* **E**

Try a diagram.

The different possibilities are

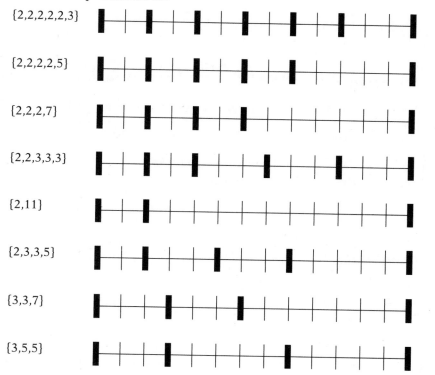

{2,2,2,2,2,3}

{2,2,2,2,5}

{2,2,2,7}

{2,2,3,3,3}

{2,11}

{2,3,3,5}

{3,3,7}

{3,5,5}

CHAPTER 4

RATIOS AND PROPORTIONS

Ratios show the relationship between two numbers. Proportions are most useful to find an unknown value when the ratio between the two values is known. Begin with the mathematics review and then complete and correct the practice problems. There are 2 Solved SAT Problems and 20 Practice SAT Questions with answer explanations.

A **Ratio** is a comparison of two quantities that can be expressed in three ways.

$$2 \text{ to } 3 \qquad \frac{2}{3} \qquad 2:3$$

A **Proportion** is a statement that two ratios are equal. $\frac{56}{136}$ and $\frac{7}{17}$ form a proportion (are proportional) because $\frac{56}{136} = \frac{\cancel{8} \times 7}{\cancel{8} \times 17} = \frac{7}{17}$. A common technique for checking if two ratios are proportional is to cross multiply. If both answers are the same, then the two ratios form a proportion, $\frac{56}{136} \underset{}{\overset{}{\times}} \frac{7}{17} = \frac{952}{952}$.

The cross products are equal so the ratios are equal.

When **Solving a Proportion**, cross multiply and solve for the unknown value.

Example:

Solve the proportion $\frac{x}{8} = \frac{7}{2}$.

$$\frac{x}{8} = \frac{7}{2} \Rightarrow 2x = 56 \Rightarrow x = 28.$$

Example:

Sam's printer can print 4 pieces of paper in 15 seconds. How long will it take to print 25 pieces of paper?

Write a proportion and solve.

$$\frac{4}{15} = \frac{25}{x} \Rightarrow 4x = 375 \Rightarrow x = 93.75 \text{ sec.}$$

The **Average Rate of Speed** is the total distance traveled divided by the total time of the trip.

Example:

Jim is driving home for spring break, a 335-mile trip. He travels an average of 70 miles per hour for the first 140 miles, and then he travels an average of 65 miles per hour for the last 195 miles. What is Jim's average velocity for the entire trip?

We must first calculate the total time for the trip.

$$D = R \times T \Rightarrow T = \frac{D}{R} \Rightarrow T = \frac{140}{70} + \frac{195}{65} = 2 + 3 = 5 \text{ hours.}$$

Then divide to find the velocity.

$$D = R \times T \Rightarrow R = \frac{D}{T} = \frac{335}{5} = 67 \text{ miles per hour.}$$

Practice Questions

1. A computer store sells 3 computer CDs for $2. How much would 15 computer CDs costs?
2. When Drew goes to the grocery store for every 2 oranges he buys, he purchases 3 peaches and 1 apple. Drew bought 8 oranges. How many peaches and how many apples did Drew buy?
3. Jason ran for 5 miles. He ran the first 3 miles at an average rate of 8 miles per hour, and then he ran the final 2 miles at an average rate of 6 miles per hour. What is Jason's average speed for the entire 5 miles?

Practice Answers

1. $10
2. 12 peaches and 4 apples
3. approximately 7.0588 miles per hour

SOLVED SAT PROBLEMS

1. On a school trip there must be 2 chaperones for every 25 students. How many chaperones need to be on a trip if 180 students are on the trip?

   A. 12
   B. 13
   C. 14
   D. 15
   E. 16

   Answer: **D**

   Write a proportion and solve.

   $$\frac{2}{25} = \frac{x}{180} \Rightarrow 25x = 360 \Rightarrow x = 14.4.$$

   Therefore, the 180 students require more than 14 chaperones, so round the answer to 15.

2. Jordan swam 4 laps. Each lap is 100 meters. Jordan's average speed for the first $\frac{3}{4}$ of his swim was 40 meters per minute, and for the rest of his swim he averaged 35 meters per minute. What is Jordan's average rate for the entire 4 laps, rounded to the nearest whole number?

   Answer: 39 meters per minute

   $$D = R \times T \Rightarrow T = \frac{D}{R} \Rightarrow T = \frac{300}{40} + \frac{100}{35} \approx 10.357 \text{ minutes}$$

   Therefore, the 400 meters took approximately 10.357 minutes to complete. Don't round yet.

   Jordan's average rate of speed was

   $$D = R \times T \Rightarrow R = \frac{D}{T} \Rightarrow R = \frac{400}{10.357} \approx 38.621 \text{ meters per minute.}$$

   That's 39 meters.

RATIOS AND PROPORTIONS
PRACTICE SAT QUESTIONS

ANSWER SHEET

Choose the correct answer.
If no choices are given, grid the answers in the section at the bottom of the page.

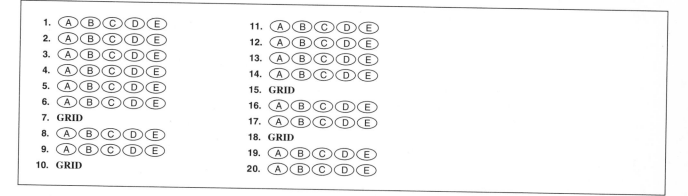

Use the answer spaces in the grids below if the question requires a grid-in response.

Student-Produced Responses   ONLY ANSWERS ENTERED IN THE CIRCLES IN EACH GRID WILL BE SCORED. YOU WILL NOT RECEIVE CREDIT FOR ANYTHING WRITTEN IN THE BOXES ABOVE THE CIRCLES.

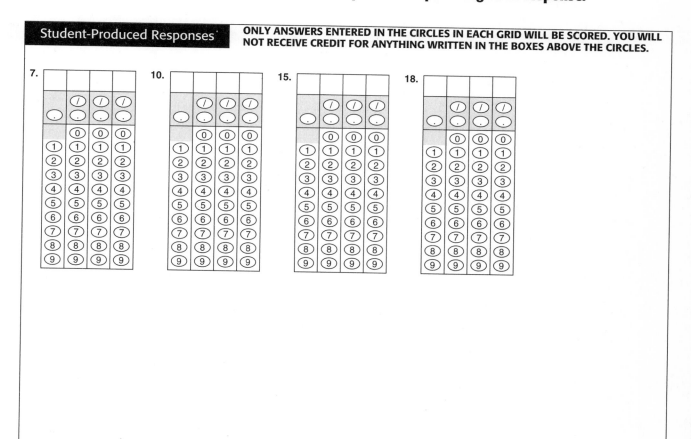

PRACTICE SAT QUESTIONS

1. $7:4 = 21:x$; what is the value of x?
   A. 12
   B. 10
   C. 8
   D. 6
   E. 4

2. Julie drinks 4 bottles of water every day. How many bottles of water does she drink in a week?
   A. 20
   B. 22
   C. 24
   D. 26
   E. 28

3. Two iced lattes cost $5. How much does it cost for seven iced lattes?
   A. $16.5
   B. $17
   C. $17.5
   D. $18
   E. $19.5

4. On a certain map, 10 miles is represented by 1.5 centimeters. What is the distance on the map that represents 40 miles?
   A. 4 centimeters
   B. 5 centimeters
   C. 6 centimeters
   D. 7 centimeters
   E. 8 centimeters

5. Dave and Chad took a 3,000-mile trip from New Jersey to Oregon. Chad Drove $\frac{3}{4}$ of the total distance. How many miles did Dave drive?
   A. 2,500 miles
   B. 2,250 miles
   C. 1,500 miles
   D. 750 miles
   E. 500 miles

6. 3 gallons of paint are needed for a wall that is 100 ft². How many gallons of paint must be purchased at the store for 480 ft² of wall space?
   A. 14 gallons
   B. 15 gallons
   C. 16 gallons
   D. 17 gallons
   E. 18 gallons

7. In a pet store there are 12 dogs and 10 cats. The ratio of dogs to cats is proportional to the ratio of hamsters to guinea pigs. How many hamsters are there in the store if there are 15 guinea pigs?

8. The ratio of a person's weight on the moon to his or her weight on Earth is $\frac{1}{6}$. If a person weighs 180 pounds on Earth, how much does he or she weigh on the moon?
   A. 30 pounds
   B. 180 pounds
   C. 360 pounds
   D. 1,080 pounds .
   E. 1,800 pounds

9. Jerry went for an 18-mile bike ride and got a flat after he completed $\frac{2}{9}$ of his trip. How many more miles of of the trip does Jerry have to complete after he fixes his flat?
   A. 4 miles
   B. 9 miles
   C. 12 miles
   D. 14 miles
   E. 18 miles

10. Dan is preparing for a 10-mile race. He will run the first 5 miles at an average speed of 6 miles per hour, the next 3 miles at an average speed of 8 miles per hour, and the final 2 miles at an average speed of 10 miles per hour. How many hours, rounded to the nearest hundredth of an hour, will it take Dan to run the race if he follows his plan?

11. In a classroom of 25 students, 10 of the students are females. What is the ratio of males to females in the classroom?
    A. 5:2
    B. 2:5
    C. 5:3
    D. 2:3
    E. 3:2

12. A car tire rotates 3,360 times every 4 miles. How many times will the car tire rotate in 50 miles?

A. 42,000 rotations
B. 84,000 rotations
C. 100,000 rotations
D. 168,000 rotations
E. 672,000 rotations

13. A baseball team has a total of 18 pitchers. The ratio of right-hand pitcher to total number of pitchers is 5:6. How many left-hand pitchers does the team have?

A. 18
B. 15
C. 13
D. 5
E. 3

14. An airplane traveled at a speed of 600 miles per hour for 90 minutes. How far did the airplane travel?

A. 54,000 miles
B. 12,000 miles
C. 900 miles
D. 600 miles
E. 450 miles

15. Company A, Company B, and Company C are the top three cell phone providers in a certain area of the country. The ratio of subscribers of A to B to C is 5:4:3. If Company A has 1,000 subscriptions, what is the total number of subscribers between Company A, Company B, and Company C?

16. If Greg lost 20 pounds, then the ratio of Ted's weight to Greg's weight would be $\frac{4}{3}$. If Ted weighs 180 pounds, what was Greg's initial weight?

A. 115 pounds
B. 125 pounds
C. 135 pounds
D. 145 pounds
E. 155 pounds

17. A company produces baseballs at 3 different plants: Plant A, Plant B, and Plant C. Doubling Plant A's production is equal to $\frac{1}{3}$ of the company's total production. Doubling Plant B's production is equal to the company's total production. Tripling Plant C's production is equal to the company's total production. What is the ratio of Plant A's production to Plant B's production to Plant C's production?

A. 1:3:2
B. 3:1:2
C. 2:1:3
D. 1:2:3
E. 3:2:1

18. A person running an 800-meter race averages 130 meters per minute for the first $\frac{3}{4}$ of the race. The average speed for the remainder of the race is 145 meters per minute. What is the person's average speed for the entire 800 meters rounded to the nearest whole number?

19. Company A, Company B, and Company C are three Internet providers in a certain area of the country. The ratio of subscribers of A to B to C is 2:5:6. If there are a total of 65,000 subscriptions, how many of the 65,000 use Company A and Company C?

A. 55,000
B. 40,000
C. 35,000
D. 30,000
E. 25,000

20. Store A, Store B, and Store C sell soccer balls. The ratio of the number of soccer balls sold of A to B is $\frac{7}{4}$. The ratio of the number of soccer balls sold of B to C is $\frac{5}{3}$. If Store C sold 36 soccer balls, how many soccer balls did Store A sell?

A. 75
B. 90
C. 95
D. 105
E. 110

EXPLAINED ANSWERS

1. *Answer:* **A**

   Write a proportion and solve.

   $$7:4 = 21:x \Rightarrow \frac{7}{4} = \frac{21}{x}$$

   $$7x = 84 \Rightarrow x = 12$$

2. *Answer:* **E**

   Just think, $4 \times 7 = 28$.

   Or you can write a proportion.

   $$\frac{B}{7} = \frac{4}{1} \Rightarrow B = 28$$

3. *Answer:* **C**

   Just think: $5 for 2 iced lattes is $2.50 for 1.
   $7 \times \$2.50 = \$17.50$.

   Or you can write a proportion.

   $$\frac{C}{7} = \frac{5}{2} \Rightarrow 2C = 35 \Rightarrow C = \$17.50.$$

4. *Answer:* **C**

   Just think, each mile is 1.5 centimeters. $4 \times 1.5 = 6$.

   Or write a proportion.

   $$\frac{D}{40} = \frac{1.5}{10} \Rightarrow 10D = 60 \Rightarrow D = 6 \text{ centimeters}$$

5. *Answer:* **D**

   Just think: Dave drove $\frac{1}{4}$ of the distance, $\frac{1}{4} \times 3{,}000 = 750$.

   Or write a proportion.

   $$\frac{C}{3{,}000} = \frac{3}{4} \Rightarrow 4C = 9{,}000 \Rightarrow C = 2{,}250 \text{ miles}$$

   $3{,}000 - 2{,}250 = 750$ miles

6. *Answer:* **B**

   Write a proportion and solve.

   $$\frac{G}{480} = \frac{3}{100} \Rightarrow 100G = 1{,}440 \Rightarrow G = 14.4 \text{ gallons}$$

   Therefore, 15 gallons of paint must be purchased.

7. *Answer:* **18**

   Write a proportion and solve.

   $$\frac{H}{15} = \frac{12}{10} \Rightarrow 10H = 180 \Rightarrow H = 18 \text{ hamsters}$$

8. *Answer:* **A**

   Write a proportion and solve.

   $$\frac{M}{180} = \frac{1}{6} \Rightarrow 6M = 180 \Rightarrow M = 30 \text{ pounds}$$

9. *Answer:* **D**

   Jerry will travel $\frac{7}{9}$ of the trip after he fixes the flat.

   $$\frac{D}{18} = \frac{7}{9} \Rightarrow 9D = 126 \Rightarrow D = 14 \text{ miles}$$

10. *Answer:* **1.41**

    Use the formula $D = R \times T$ written $T = \frac{D}{R}$ to represent the time for each part of the race. Then add.

    It will take Dan $T = \frac{5}{6} + \frac{3}{8} + \frac{2}{10} \approx 1.41$ hours to finish the race with his plan.

11. *Answer:* **E**

    Because there are a total of 25 students, including 10 females, there must be $25 - 10 = 15$ males. So the ratio of males to females is $\frac{15}{10} = \frac{3}{2}$.

12. *Answer:* **A**

    Write a proportion and solve.

    $$\frac{R}{50} = \frac{3,360}{4} \Rightarrow 4R = 168,000 \Rightarrow R = 42,000 \text{ rotations}$$

13. *Answer:* **E**

    The ratio $\frac{5}{6}$ in this problem means $\frac{5}{6}$ of the pitchers are right-handed.

    Just multiply $\frac{5}{6} \times 18 = 15$, or write a proportion.

    $$\frac{R}{18} = \frac{5}{6} \Rightarrow 6R = 90 \Rightarrow R = 15 \text{ right-hand pitchers}$$

    Therefore, there are $18 - 15 = 3$ left-hand pitchers.

14. *Answer:* **C**

   Just think, 90 minutes is 1.5 hours, and multiply $1.5 \times 600 = 900$.

   Or, write a proportion.

   $$\frac{D}{1.5} = \frac{600}{1} \Rightarrow D = 900 \text{ miles}$$

15. *Answer:* **2,400**

   Write proportions, and then add. A, B, and C represent the three cell phone providers.

   $$\frac{5}{4} = \frac{1,000}{B}$$

   $$5B = 4,000 \Rightarrow B = 800$$

   $$\frac{5}{3} = \frac{1,000}{C}$$

   $$5C = 3,000 \Rightarrow C = 600$$

   $$A + B + C = 1,000 + 800 + 600 = 2,400$$

   Therefore, there is a total of 2,400 subscribers.

16. *Answer:* **E**

   Write a proportion and solve.

   $$\frac{4}{3} = \frac{T}{G-20} \Rightarrow \frac{4}{3} = \frac{180}{G-20}$$

   $$4(G - 20) = 540$$

   $$G - 20 = 135$$

   $$G = 155 \text{ pounds.}$$

17. *Answer:* **A**

   Write equations to show the relationship between each plant's production and the total production.

   $$2A = \frac{1}{3}T \Rightarrow A = \frac{1}{6}T \quad \text{and} \quad 2B = T \Rightarrow B = \frac{1}{2}T \quad \text{and} \quad 3C = T \Rightarrow C = \frac{1}{3}T$$

   Therefore, $A:B:C = \frac{1}{6}T:\frac{1}{2}T:\frac{1}{3}T = \frac{1}{6}:\frac{1}{2}:\frac{1}{3}$.

   Now, by multiplying each number in the ratio by 6 we see that $A:B:C = 1:3:2$.

18. *Answer:* **133**

   Using the formula $D = R \times T$, written $T = \frac{D}{R}$, it will take

   $T = \frac{600}{130} \approx 4.615$ minutes to finish the first 600 meters of the race and $T = \frac{200}{145} \approx 1.379$ minutes to finish the last

   200 meters of the race. Therefore, using the formula $D = R \times T \Rightarrow R = \frac{D}{T}$ the average speed for the runner is

   $R = \frac{800}{4.615 + 1.379} = \frac{800}{5.994} \approx 133.467$ meters per minute.

19. *Answer:* **B**

Find three numbers that add up to 65,000 and have a 2:5:6 ratio.

$2x + 5x + 6x = 65,000 \Rightarrow 13x = 65,000 \Rightarrow x = 5,000$

The ratio of A to B to C is

$2 \cdot 5,000 : 5 \cdot 5,000 : 6 \cdot 5,000 = 10,000 : 25,000 : 30,000$

Therefore, Company A and Company C have a total of $10,000 + 30,000 = 40,000$ subscribers.

20. *Answer:* **D**

We must find A. We know that $C = 36$. $\dfrac{A}{B} = \dfrac{7}{4}$ and $\dfrac{B}{C} = \dfrac{5}{3}$.

$\dfrac{B}{C} = \dfrac{5}{3} \Rightarrow \dfrac{B}{36} = \dfrac{5}{3} \Rightarrow 3B = 180 \Rightarrow B = 60$

$\dfrac{A}{B} = \dfrac{7}{4} \Rightarrow \dfrac{A}{60} = \dfrac{7}{4} \Rightarrow 4A = 420 \Rightarrow A = 105$

CHAPTER 5
PERCENTS

A percent shows the ratio of a number to 100. Just finding what percent one number is of another is usually not enough. You will also be asked to find how much a value has increased or decreased, or the new amount of a value after it has increased or decreased. Begin with the mathematics review and then complete and correct the practice problems. There are 2 Solved SAT Problems and 21 Practice SAT Questions with answer explanations.

PERCENT

Percent is a part of a whole represented in hundredths, 0.01 = 1%. The formula

$$Percent = \frac{Part}{Whole} \Rightarrow Part = Percent \times Whole$$

can be used to solve for the Percent, Part, or Whole.

Example:

What percent of 50 is 42?

$$Percent = \frac{Part}{Whole} = \frac{42}{50} = 0.84 = 84\%$$

Example:

30% of 60 is what number?

$$Part = 0.30 \times 60 \Rightarrow Part = 18$$

Example:

15% of what number is 12?

$$12 = 0.15 \times Whole \Rightarrow 80 = Whole$$

PERCENT INCREASE AND PERCENT DECREASE

$$Percent\ Increase = \frac{Part}{Whole} = \frac{Change\ in\ Amount}{Original\ Amount} = \frac{New\ Amount - Original\ Amount}{Original\ Amount}$$

$$Percent\ Decrease = \frac{Part}{Whole} = \frac{Change\ in\ Amount}{Original\ Amount} = \frac{Original\ Amount - New\ Amount}{Original\ Amount}$$

Example:

In a science experiment, 18 ounces of water were placed in a bottle. During the experiment some of the water in the bottle evaporated, leaving 15 ounces of water in the bottle. How much did the water in the bottle change from the original amount?

$$Percent\ Decrease = \frac{18-15}{18} = \frac{3}{18} = 0.166\overline{6} = 16.66\overline{6}\% = 16\frac{2}{3}\%$$

Calculator Tip

Here is how to use a graphing calculator to convert $0.166\overline{6}$ to $16\frac{2}{3}\%$.

1. Multiply 0.1666666667 by 100, which equals 16.66666667.
2. Then subtract 16 from 16.66666667, equaling .66666667.
3. Then press the keys that display Ans ▶ Frac on your calculator. The result is 2/3.
4. Therefore, $0.166\overline{6} = 16.66\overline{6}\% = 16\frac{2}{3}\%$

A display of 0.1666666667 means 6 is repeating; 7 is the last digit because the calculator is programmed to round the last digit.

When a value is increasing:

New Amount = (1 + *Percent Increase*) × *Original Amount*

When a value is decreasing:

New Amount = (1 − *Percent Decrease*) × *Original Amount*

Example:

A certain stock started the day at $35 a share. By the end of the day the stock had increased by 20%. What is the new price of the stock?

New Amount = (1 + 0.2) × 35 = 1.2 × 35 = $42

Practice Questions

1. Jack is 30 years old and Alice is 35 years old. What percent of Alice's age is Jack, rounded to the nearest tenth of a percent?
2. 90% of the students in a high school have a cell phone. If there are 750 students in the school, how many of the students have cell phones?
3. Richard's car cost 70% of Brian's car. If Richard's car cost $17,500, what is the price of Brian's car?
4. A jacket went on sale. The original price was $24, and the sale price was $18. At what percent was the jacket discounted?
5. Over the summer Jason grew from 70 inches to 73.5 inches. What percent has Jason's height increased?

6. Last season a certain basketball player averaged 25 points a game. This season the basketball player increased her average by 12%. What is the basketball player's new scoring average?

7. The cost of grapes at a grocery store is normally $2.99 a pound. There was a sale on grapes for 65% off the normal price. What is the sale price of the grapes to the nearest cent?

Practice Answers

1. 85.7%
2. 675 students
3. $25,000
4. 25%
5. 5%
6. 28 points per game
7. $1.05 per pound

SOLVED SAT PROBLEMS

1. In a 20-game season a certain basketball player scores at least 15 points in 60% of the first 10 games, 40% of the next 5 games, and 20% in the last 5 games. In what percent of all 20 games did this player score less than 15 points?

   A. 40%
   B. 45%
   C. 50%
   D. 55%
   E. 60%

   Answer: **D**

   Multiply and add to find the number of games in which the player scored at least 15 points.

   $0.6 \cdot 10 + 0.4 \cdot 5 + 0.2 \cdot 5 = 9$

   The player scored at least 15 points in 9 games, which means that the player scored less than 15 points in 20 − 9 = 11 games.

   $\frac{11}{20} = 0.55 = 55\%$ of the games the player scored less than 15 points.

2. 45% of 80 equals what percent of 60?

   A. 60%
   B. 55%
   C. 50%
   D. 45%
   E. 40%

Answer: **A**

Find 45% of 80.

$0.45 \times 80 = 36$

Find what percent 36 is of 60.

$$\frac{36}{60} = 0.60 = 60\%$$

PERCENTS
PRACTICE SAT QUESTIONS

ANSWER SHEET

Choose the correct answer.
If no choices are given, grid the answers in the section at the bottom of the page.

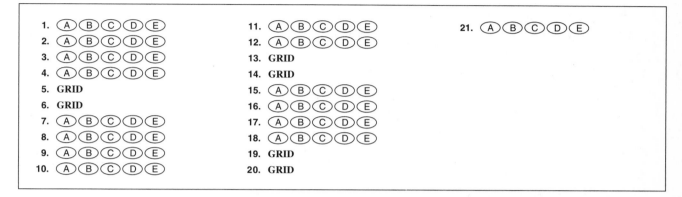

1. Ⓐ Ⓑ Ⓒ Ⓓ Ⓔ
2. Ⓐ Ⓑ Ⓒ Ⓓ Ⓔ
3. Ⓐ Ⓑ Ⓒ Ⓓ Ⓔ
4. Ⓐ Ⓑ Ⓒ Ⓓ Ⓔ
5. GRID
6. GRID
7. Ⓐ Ⓑ Ⓒ Ⓓ Ⓔ
8. Ⓐ Ⓑ Ⓒ Ⓓ Ⓔ
9. Ⓐ Ⓑ Ⓒ Ⓓ Ⓔ
10. Ⓐ Ⓑ Ⓒ Ⓓ Ⓔ

11. Ⓐ Ⓑ Ⓒ Ⓓ Ⓔ
12. Ⓐ Ⓑ Ⓒ Ⓓ Ⓔ
13. GRID
14. GRID
15. Ⓐ Ⓑ Ⓒ Ⓓ Ⓔ
16. Ⓐ Ⓑ Ⓒ Ⓓ Ⓔ
17. Ⓐ Ⓑ Ⓒ Ⓓ Ⓔ
18. Ⓐ Ⓑ Ⓒ Ⓓ Ⓔ
19. GRID
20. GRID

21. Ⓐ Ⓑ Ⓒ Ⓓ Ⓔ

Use the answer spaces in the grids below if the question requires a grid-in response.

Student-Produced Responses ONLY ANSWERS ENTERED IN THE CIRCLES IN EACH GRID WILL BE SCORED. YOU WILL NOT RECEIVE CREDIT FOR ANYTHING WRITTEN IN THE BOXES ABOVE THE CIRCLES.

5.   6.   13.   14.   19.

20.

PRACTICE SAT QUESTIONS

1. 15% of what number is 18?

   A. 102
   B. 110
   C. 112
   D. 120
   E. 125

2. What percent of 60 is 14?

   A. 23%
   B. 23.3%

   C. $23\frac{1}{3}\%$

   D. 23.6%

   E. $23\frac{2}{3}\%$

3. 13 of the 18 players on the varsity soccer team are seniors. What percent of the players on the team are not seniors?

   A. $27\frac{7}{9}\%$

   B. $27\frac{5}{9}\%$

   C. 27.7%

   D. $27\frac{1}{7}\%$

   E. 27.8%

4. What is 12% of 70?

   A. 8.4
   B. 8.5
   C. 8.6
   D. 8.7
   E. 8.8

5. What percent of 42 is 25% of 56?

6. Erin received a raise at her job from $14 per hour to $17 per hour. What is the percent increase of her raise?

7. There are 15 students on a yearbook committee. 40% of the students are females. How many students on the committee are males?

   A. 6
   B. 9
   C. 12
   D. 13
   E. 15

8. A camping tent went on sale from $80 to $60. A camping chair that originally cost $20 was discounted by the same percent. What is the new price of the camping chair?

   A. 25
   B. 20
   C. 15
   D. 10
   E. 5

9. Jerry, Will, and Al all work at the same company. Jerry earns 80% of Will's salary, and Will earns 75% of Al's salary. What percent of Al's salary is equal to Jerry's salary?

   A. 80%
   B. 75%
   C. 70%
   D. 65%
   E. 60%

10. 60% of the students at the high school play sports. 14% of the students who play sports play baseball. What percent of the students in the school play baseball?

   A. 4.6%
   B. 4.8%
   C. 6.4%
   D. 8.4%
   E. 10.6%

11. Alex weighs 185 pounds. If he decreases his weight by 10%, what will be his new weight?

   A. 160 pounds
   B. 166.5 pounds
   C. 170 pounds
   D. 170.5 pounds
   E. 175.5 pounds

12. A house was appraised at $300,000. One year later the house was appraised at $335,000. At what percent did the appraised price of the house increase?

   A. $11\frac{2}{3}\%$

   B. $11\frac{1}{3}\%$

   C. 11%

   D. $13\frac{2}{3}\%$

   E. $13\frac{1}{3}\%$

13. 16% of s equals t. 10% of t equals 40. What is the value of $s - t$?

14. Below is a table showing the classes that Mr. Lipton taught and the number of students in each class. If no student was enrolled in more than one class, what percent of the students in Mr. Lipton's classes did not take Statistics?

Algebra	Statistics	Calculus
35	55	10

15. If x percent of 80 is 12, then x percent of what number is 18?

   A. 112
   B. 115
   C. 117
   D. 118
   E. 120

16. The percent increase from 8 to 14 is equal to the percent decrease from 35 to x. What is the value of x?

   A. 7.5
   B. 7.75
   C. 8.25
   D. 8.5
   E. 8.75

17. On the first day of a two-day fishing trip, George caught 9 trout; $33\frac{1}{3}\%$ of the trout are rainbow trout.

   By the end of the fishing trip, George caught 6 more trout, but none are rainbow trout. What percent of all the trout that George caught are rainbow trout?

   A. $33\frac{1}{3}\%$

   B. 33%

   C. $22\frac{2}{9}\%$

   D. 20%
   E. 15%

18. A television set is on sale for 15% off the original price. If the sale price is $340, what was the original price of the televisions set?

   A. $340
   B. $370
   C. $400
   D. $440
   E. $470

19. Dan needs to gain 8% of his current body weight to wrestle in weight Class A. Dan needs to lose the same percent of his current weight to wrestle in weight Class B. What percent of Dan's Class A weight, to the nearest tenth, does he need to lose to get to his Class B weight?

20. During last year's baseball season, a certain player has 625 at bats and gets a hit 32% of the time. This season the player increased the at bats by 12%, and got a hit 34% of the time. What is the percent increase in the number of hits?

21. Mike has a goal to bench press 220 pounds. When he started working out, Mike was able to lift 150 pounds. He has currently increased that amount by 20%. What percent of his current lifting amount must Mike increase to reach his goal of 220 pounds?

   A. $22\frac{1}{2}\%$

   B. 22%

   C. 22.22%

   D. $22\frac{2}{9}\%$

   E. $22\frac{2}{11}\%$

EXPLAINED ANSWERS

1. *Answer:* **D**

   Part = Percent × Whole

   $18 = 0.15x$

   $18 / 0.15 = x$

   $x = 120$

   15% of 120 is 18.

2. *Answer:* **C**

   $Percent = \dfrac{Part}{Whole} = \dfrac{14}{60} = .233\overline{3} = 23.33\overline{3}\% = 23\dfrac{1}{3}\%$

   $23\dfrac{1}{3}\%$ of 60 is 14.

3. *Answer:* **A**

   $Percent = \dfrac{Part}{Whole} = \dfrac{18 - 13}{18} = \dfrac{5}{18} = .277\overline{7} = 27.77\overline{7}\% = 27\dfrac{7}{9}\%$

4. *Answer:* **A**

   $Percent \times Whole = Part = 0.12 \times 70 = 8.4$

5. *Answer:* **33.3**

   Use the formula $Percent = \dfrac{Part}{Whole} = \dfrac{14}{42} = 0.33\overline{3} \approx 33.3\%$.

   Notice that no percent sign is used to record the final answer.

6. *Answer:* **21.4**

   $Percent\ Increase = \dfrac{Change\ in\ Amount}{Original\ Amount} = \dfrac{17 - 14}{14} = \dfrac{3}{14} \approx 21.4\%$

7. *Answer:* **B**

   Because 40% of the members are females, 60% of the members are males.

   $Percent \times Whole = Part = 0.60 \times 15 = 9$

8. *Answer:* **C**

   Use percent formulas.

   $Percent\ Decrease = \dfrac{Change\ in\ Amount}{Original\ Amount} = \dfrac{80 - 60}{80} = \dfrac{20}{80} = 25\%$

   $New\ Amount = \left(1 - Percent\ Decrease\right) \times Original\ Amount = \left(1 - 0.25\right) \times 20 = 0.75 \times 20 = \$15$

9. *Answer:* **E**

   $J = 0.8W$ and $W = 0.75A$

   Substitute $0.75A$ for W.

   $J = 0.8 \times 0.75A = 0.6A$

   Therefore, 60% of Al's salary is equal to Jerry's salary.

10. *Answer:* **D**

    14% of the 60% play baseball so $0.14 \times 0.60 = 0.084 = 8.4\%$ of the students in the school play baseball.

11. *Answer:* **B**

    $New\ Amount = (1 - Percent\ Decrease) \times Original\ Amount =$

    $(1 - 0.1) \times 185 = 0.90 \times 185 = 166.5$ pounds

12. *Answer:* **A**

    $Percent\ Increase = \dfrac{Change\ in\ Amount}{Original\ Amount} = \dfrac{335,000 - 300,000}{300,000} = \dfrac{35,000}{300,000} =$

    $0.11666\overline{6} = 11.66\overline{6}\% = 11\dfrac{2}{3}\%$

13. *Answer:* **2,100**

    Find t and s.
    Then subtract.

    $0.10t = 40 \Rightarrow t = 400$

    $0.16s = t \Rightarrow 0.16s = 400 \Rightarrow s = 2,500$

    $s - t = 2,500 - 400 = 2,100$

14. *Answer:* **45**

    $Percent = \dfrac{Part}{Whole} = \dfrac{45}{100} = 0.45 = 45\%$

15. *Answer:* **E**

    $Percent = \dfrac{Part}{Whole} \Rightarrow x = \dfrac{12}{80} = 15\%$

    $18 = 0.15 \times Whole \Rightarrow 120 = Whole$

    x percent of 120 is 18.

16. *Answer:* **E**

    $Percent\ Increase = \dfrac{Change\ in\ Amount}{Original\ Amount} = \dfrac{14 - 8}{8} = \dfrac{6}{8} = 75\%$

    Therefore, 35 must be decreased by 75%.

    $New\ Amount = (1 - 0.75) \times 35 = 0.25 \times 35 = 8.75$

17. *Answer:* **D**

    $Part = Percent \times Whole \Rightarrow Rainbow = Percent \times Total = \dfrac{1}{3} \times 9 = 3\ Rainbow.$

    By the end of the trip, George caught a total of 15 trout. Because no more rainbow trout were caught, there were still 3 rainbow trout.

    $Percent\ Rainbow = \dfrac{Rainbow}{Total} = \dfrac{3}{15} = \dfrac{1}{5} = 20\%$

18. *Answer:* **C**

New Amount = (1 − Percent Decrease) × Original Amount
$$340 = (1 − 0.15) × Original\ Amount$$
$$340 = 0.85 × Original\ Amount \Rightarrow \$400 = Original\ Amount$$

19. *Answer:* **14.8**

The best way to solve this problem is to choose a weight for Dan, such as 100 pounds.

Class A Weight = (1 + *Percent Increase*) × *Current Weight*
Class A Weight = (1 + 0.08) × 100 = 108 pounds

Class B Weight = (1 − *Percent Decrease*) × *Current Weight*
Class B Weight = (1 − 0.08) × 100 = 0.92 × 100 = 92 pounds

$$Percent\ Decrease = \frac{Change\ in\ Amount}{Original\ Amount} = \frac{108 − 92}{108} = 14.\overline{814}\%$$

Dan needs to lose approximately 14.8% of his Class A weight to get to his Class B weight.

20. *Answer:* **19**

Part = *Percent* × *Whole* ⇒ last season hits = 0.32 × 625 = 200

New Amount = (1 + *Percent Increase*) × *Original Amount*
this season at bats = (1 + 0.12) × 625 = 1.12 × 625 = 700

Part = *Percent* × *Whole* ⇒ this season hits = 0.34 × 700 = 238

$$Percent\ Increase = \frac{Change\ in\ Amount}{Original\ Amount} = \frac{238 − 200}{200} = 19\%$$

21. *Answer:* **D**

New Amount = (1 + *Percent Increase*) × *Original Amount* =
(1 + 0.20) × 150 = 1.2 × 150 = 180

$$Percent\ Increase = \frac{Change\ in\ Amount}{Original\ Amount} = \frac{220 − 180}{180} = 22.\overline{22}\% = 22\frac{2}{9}\%$$

CHAPTER 6

MEAN, MEDIAN, AND MODE

You will calculate the Mean, Median, and Mode of a set of numbers on the SAT. However, the SAT questions will ask you to do more. You may have to find the missing number in a set given the mean, median, or mode, or you may be asked to use the mean, median, or mode to solve another problem. Begin with the mathematics review and then complete and correct the practice problems. There are 2 Solved SAT Problems and 17 Practice SAT Questions with answer explanations.

The **Arithmetic Mean (Average), Median,** and **Mode** are used to describe a set of data when each item in the set is a number.

The **Arithmetic Mean (Average)** is the sum of the items divided by the number of items.

The **Median** is the middle number when the list is placed in order, if there is an odd number of items. If there is an even number of items the median is the mean of the middle two numbers.

The **Mode(s)** is (are) the item(s) that occur(s) most frequently. If every item appears the same number of times, then there is no mode in the set.

Example:

Find the mean, median, and mode for each set of data.

a. {5,9,4,3,5,10,6}

Mean:
$(5 + 9 + 4 + 3 + 5 + 10 + 6) \div 7 = 6$
6 is the mean.

Median:
First rewrite the items from least to greatest
{3,4,5,$\underline{5}$,6,9,10}
5 is the median.

Mode:
The mode is 5; it appears most often.

b. {63,67,54,68,76,54,87,63}

Mean:
$(63 + 67 + 54 + 68 + 76 + 54 + 87 + 63) \div 8 = 66.5$
66.5 is the mean.

Median:
First rewrite the items from least to greatest
{54,54,63,63,67,68,76,87}.

Because there are an even number of items, find the mean of the middle two numbers

$$\frac{63 + 67}{2} = 65$$

65 is the median.

Mode:

In this problem there are two modes 54 and 63. This is because both 54 and 63 occur most frequently.

Practice Questions

1. Find the mean, median, and mode for each set of data

   A. {8,2,6,8,4,2,3,4,8}
   B. {97,65,58,67,87,42,34,57}
   C. {15,13,19,17,25,13,23,18,19,17}

2. On three of the first four geometry tests Jim earned the following scores: 84, 92, and 88. If Jim's average for all four tests is 87.5, what score did Jim earn on his fourth test?

3. Mark, Danielle, Peter, and Kendra have an average height of 71 inches. What is the sum of all of their heights?

4. There are 24 students in period 1 gym class and 20 students in a Period 2 gym class. The students ran an obstacle course during gym class. The average time in period 1 was 165 seconds, and the average time in Period 2 was 180 seconds. What is the average time for the two combined gym classes?

Practice Answers

1. A. *Mean* = 5, *Median* = 4, *Mode* = 8
   B. *Mean* = 63.375, *Median* = 61.5, *Mode* = no mode
   C. *Mean* = 17.9, *Median* = 17.5, *Mode* = 13, 17, and 19

2. $\dfrac{84 + 92 + 88 + x}{4} = 87.5 \implies 84 + 92 + 88 + x = 350$

   $264 + x = 350 \implies x = 86$

3. $\dfrac{M + D + P + K}{4} = 71 \implies M + D + P + K = 284$ inches

4. $\dfrac{24 \cdot 165 + 20 \cdot 180}{44} = 171.\overline{81}$ seconds

▦ SOLVED SAT PROBLEMS

1. What is the sum of the mean, median, and mode(s) of the set {2,4,8,7,4,6,8,9}?

   A. 12.5
   B. 16.5
   C. 20.5
   D. 24.5
   E. 26.5

   Answer: **D**

   First, rewrite the set from smallest to largest {2,4,4,6,7,8,8,9}.

   Mean = $(2 + 4 + 4 + 6 + 7 + 8 + 8 + 9) \div 8 = 6$

   Median = 6.5

   Mode = 4 and 8

   The sum of mean, median, and mode is $6 + 6.5 + 4 + 8 = 24.5$.

2. What is the average (arithmetic mean) of a set of 20 numbers if the sum is 340?

   Answer: **17**

   Because the sum of the 20 numbers is 340, then the average is $\frac{340}{20} = 17$.

MEAN, MEDIAN, MODE
PRACTICE SAT QUESTIONS

ANSWER SHEET

Choose the correct answer.
If no choices are given, grid the answers in the section at the bottom of the page.

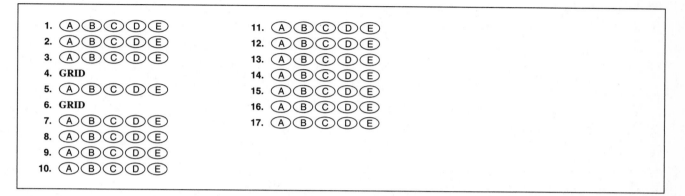

1. Ⓐ Ⓑ Ⓒ Ⓓ Ⓔ
2. Ⓐ Ⓑ Ⓒ Ⓓ Ⓔ
3. Ⓐ Ⓑ Ⓒ Ⓓ Ⓔ
4. GRID
5. Ⓐ Ⓑ Ⓒ Ⓓ Ⓔ
6. GRID
7. Ⓐ Ⓑ Ⓒ Ⓓ Ⓔ
8. Ⓐ Ⓑ Ⓒ Ⓓ Ⓔ
9. Ⓐ Ⓑ Ⓒ Ⓓ Ⓔ
10. Ⓐ Ⓑ Ⓒ Ⓓ Ⓔ

11. Ⓐ Ⓑ Ⓒ Ⓓ Ⓔ
12. Ⓐ Ⓑ Ⓒ Ⓓ Ⓔ
13. Ⓐ Ⓑ Ⓒ Ⓓ Ⓔ
14. Ⓐ Ⓑ Ⓒ Ⓓ Ⓔ
15. Ⓐ Ⓑ Ⓒ Ⓓ Ⓔ
16. Ⓐ Ⓑ Ⓒ Ⓓ Ⓔ
17. Ⓐ Ⓑ Ⓒ Ⓓ Ⓔ

Use the answer spaces in the grids below if the question requires a grid-in response.

Student-Produced Responses   ONLY ANSWERS ENTERED IN THE CIRCLES IN EACH GRID WILL BE SCORED. YOU WILL NOT RECEIVE CREDIT FOR ANYTHING WRITTEN IN THE BOXES ABOVE THE CIRCLES.

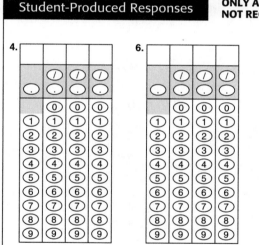

PRACTICE SAT QUESTIONS

1. The average (arithmetic mean) of three numbers is 90. The sum of two of the numbers is 150. What is the value of the third number?

    A. 90
    B. 100
    C. 110
    D. 120
    E. 130

2. Using the data set, {30,70,40,50,90,40,60}, which of the following statements is correct?

    A. Median   <mean   <mode
    B. Mode   <mean   <median
    C. Mode   <median   <mean
    D. Mean   <mode   <median
    E. Median   <mean   <mode

3. The average (arithmetic mean) of four numbers is 50. Two of the numbers are 30 and 60. What is the average of the other two numbers?

    A. 70
    B. 65
    C. 60
    D. 55
    E. 50

4. The average (arithmetic mean) of four consecutive even integers is 5. What is the median of these four numbers?

The tables below show the points scored by two different basketball players, Jay and Ed. Ed's average (arithmetic mean) for 4 games is 2 less than Jay's average for 5 games.

Use these data for Question 5 and Question 6.

Jay's points	Ed's points
20	15
16	21
25	17
15	
14	

5. How many points did Ed score during the fourth game?

    A. 12
    B. 11
    C. 10
    D. 9
    E. 8

6. Say that Ed scored 16 points in the fourth game. What should be added to Jay's median score to equal the median of Ed's scores?

7. Blaire, Chen, Erin, Liz, and Mauro all participate in a 1-mile race. The average (arithmetic mean) for the times of all girls is 6.5 minutes. If the average time for Blaire, Chen, and Erin is 6.7 minutes, what is the average time for Liz and Mauro?

    A. 6.1 minutes
    B. 6.2 minutes
    C. 6.3 minutes
    D. 6.4 minutes
    E. 6.5 minutes

8. What is the median of the modes in the dataset {−5, 4, 3, 7, 2, 1, 3, 4, 5, −1, 7, 8, −4, 2, 6}?

    A. 2
    B. 2.5
    C. 3
    D. 3.5
    E. 4

9. The average of x and y is 7, and $z = 3x + 2$. What is the average of y and z?

    A. $2x + 8$
    B. $2x - 16$
    C. $2x + 16$
    D. $x - 8$
    E. $x + 8$

10. The average of a set of n numbers is x. If each number is increased by y, then what is the average of the new set of numbers?

    A. x
    B. y
    C. $n(x + y)$
    D. $x + y$
    E. $\dfrac{x + y}{n}$

11. Mr. Jones administered a test to the students in each of his three Algebra II classes. The average (arithmetic mean) of all the students in his classes was 82.8. What is the average for his Period 8 class?

	Period 1	Period 7	Period 8
Number of students	16	19	15
Class average	85	80	?

   A. 80
   B. 81
   C. 82
   D. 83
   E. 84

12. $\dfrac{a + b + c + d}{4} = 12$. If the average of a, b, c, d, and e is 14, what is the value of e?

   A. 14
   B. 16
   C. 18
   D. 20
   E. 22

13. Frank took 4 history tests. Frank earned an 85, 92, and 89 on the first three tests. If Frank's average (arithmetic mean) for all 4 tests is 91, what did he earn on his last test?

   A. 100
   B. 99
   C. 98
   D. 97
   E. 96

14. If the average of 6 evenly spaced numbers is x, what is the median of the 6 numbers?

   A. x
   B. $2x$
   C. $\dfrac{x}{2}$
   D. $6x$
   E. $\dfrac{x}{6}$

15. a, b, and c are all positive integers such that $a + b + c = 150$, and none of these values are equal to each other. What is the smallest possible value for the median of a, b, and c?

   A. 5
   B. 4
   C. 3
   D. 2
   E. 1

16. s and t are positive integers whose average (arithmetic mean) is 9. If $s < t$, what is the median of all possible values of s?

   A. 6.5
   B. 6
   C. 5.5
   D. 5
   E. 4.5

17. The modes of a set of 9 numbers are x, y, and z, and the average (arithmetic mean) of the 9 numbers is 20. Three of the 9 numbers are $2x + 5$, $2y$, and $2z - 3$. What is the value of $4(x + y + z)$?

   A. 178
   B. 179
   C. 180
   D. 181
   E. 182

EXPLAINED ANSWERS

1. **Answer: D**

   Write an equation to represent the mean.

   $$\frac{150 + x}{3} = 90 \quad \Rightarrow \quad 150 + x = 270 \quad \Rightarrow \quad x = 120$$

   The third number is 120.

2. **Answer: C**

   First rearrange the numbers in the list from least to greatest.

   $\{30, 40, 40, 50, 60, 70, 90\}$

   Find the mode, median, and mean.

   Mode = 40

   Median = 50

   $$Mean = \frac{30 + 40 + 40 + 50 + 60 + 70 + 90}{7} \approx 54.29$$

   Write the numbers in order. 40 (*Mode*) < 50 (*Median*) < 54.29 (*Mean*)

3. **Answer: D**

   Write an equation to show the mean.

   $$\frac{x + y + 30 + 60}{4} = 50 \quad \Rightarrow \quad x + y + 90 = 200$$

   Find the mean of $(x + y)$.

   $$x + y = 110 \quad \Rightarrow \quad \frac{x + y}{2} = \frac{110}{2} = 55$$

   The mean of x and y is 55.

4. **Answer: 5**

   Write an equation for the average and an equation for the sum

   $$\underbrace{\frac{a + b + c + d}{4} = 5}_{\text{Average}} \quad \Rightarrow \quad \underbrace{a + b + c + d = 20}_{\text{Sum}}$$

   Through a guess and check process notice that the four numbers are 2, 4, 6, and 8. Therefore, the median is $\frac{4 + 6}{2} = 5$.

5. **Answer: B**

   Write an equation that shows the relationship between Ed's points and Jay's points.
   The variable x represents the missing score from Ed's points. Solve the equation.

   $$\frac{15 + 21 + 17 + x}{4} = \frac{20 + 16 + 25 + 15 + 14}{5} - 2$$

   $$\frac{53 + x}{4} = 18 - 2 \quad \Rightarrow \quad \frac{53 + x}{4} = 16$$

   $$53 + x = 64 \quad \Rightarrow \quad x = 11$$

   Ed scored 11 points in the fourth game.

6. *Answer:* **0.5**

   Ed's points are $\{15,16,17,21\}$.

   Ed's median is $\dfrac{16+17}{2} = 16.5$

   Jay's median is 16. Add 0.5 to Jay's median to equal Ed's median.

7. *Answer:* **B**

   B = Blaire's time

   C = Chen's time

   E = Erin's time

   L = Liz's time

   M = Mauro's time

   Write an equation for the mean of the five times. Then write an equation for the mean of Blaire's, Chen's and Erin's times.

   $$\frac{B+C+E+L+M}{5} = 6.5 \implies B+C+E+L+M = 32.5,$$

   $$\frac{B+C+E}{3} = 6.7 \implies B+C+E = 20.1$$

   Substitute 20.1 in for $B+C+E$:

   $$20.1 + L + M = 32.5 \quad \text{Solve for } L+M \implies L+M = 12.4 \implies \frac{L+M}{2} = \frac{12.4}{2} = 6.2$$

   The average of L and M is 6.2.

8. *Answer:* **D**

   The modes of the set $\{-5,4,3,7,2,1,3,4,5,-1,7,8,-4,2,6\}$ are $\{2,3,4,7\}$.

   The median is $\dfrac{3+4}{2} = 3.5$.

9. *Answer:* **E**

   Write an equation for the average of x and y.

   $$\frac{x+y}{2} = 7 \quad \text{Solve for } y \implies x+y = 14 \implies y = 14 - x.$$

   The problem states $z = 3x + 2$.

   Write an equation for the average of y and z.

   $$\frac{y+z}{2} = \frac{(14-x)+(3x+2)}{2} = \frac{16+2x}{2}$$

   $$\frac{2(8+x)}{2} = 8 + x = x + 8$$

10. *Answer:* **D**

    The best way to answer this question is try some examples.

    $\dfrac{2+5+11}{3} = \dfrac{18}{3} = 6$. Now add 4 to each value.

    $$\frac{(2+4)+(5+4)+(11+4)}{3} = \frac{30}{3} = 10 = 6 + 4$$

    The average of the new set of numbers is $(x + y)$. It is a fact that if every number in a set is increased by a certain value, that the mean of the set will also be increased by that same value.

11. *Answer:* **E**

    Write an equation for the mean of all the students.

    Use x to represent the Period 8 average.

    There are 50 students in all.

    $$\frac{16 \cdot 85 + 19 \cdot 80 + 15 \cdot x}{50} = 82.8 \quad \text{Solve for } x \implies 16 \cdot 85 + 19 \cdot 80 + 15 \cdot x = 82.8 \cdot 50$$

    $$1,360 + 1,520 + 15 \cdot x = 4,140 \implies 2,880 + 15x = 4,140$$

    $$15x = 1,260 \implies x = 84$$

    The average for the Period 8 class is 84.

12. *Answer:* **E**

    The average of a, b, c, and d is 12, so the sum of a, b, c, and d is four times the average, or 48.

    The sum of a, b, c, d, and e is 5 times the average, or 70.

    Subtract to find e.

    $$70 - 48 = 22, \; e = 22$$

13. *Answer:* **C**

    Write an equation for the average of the four tests. Use x for the unknown score.

    $$\frac{85 + 92 + 89 + x}{4} = 91 \quad \text{Solve for } x \implies 85 + 92 + 89 + x = 364$$

    $$266 + x = 364 \implies x = 98$$

    Frank earned 98 on the fourth test.

14. *Answer:* **A**

    In general, the mean and median of an even number of evenly spaced numbers will always be the same. Here are some examples.

    $\{1,4,7,10,13,16\}$

    $$Mean = \frac{1 + 4 + 7 + 10 + 13 + 16}{6} = 8.5$$

    $$Median = \frac{7 + 10}{2} = 8.5$$

    $\{2,6,10,14,18,22\}$

    $$Mean = \frac{2 + 6 + 10 + 14 + 18 + 22}{6} = 12$$

    $$Median = \frac{10 + 14}{2} = 12$$

15. *Answer:* **D**

    First, find the mean of $a + b + c$.

    $$a + b + c = 150 \implies \frac{150}{3} = 50$$

    Therefore the average of a, b, and c is 50. Because a, b, and c are all positive integers, the set of numbers that would create the smallest median is $\{1,2,147\}$. The median is 2.

16. *Answer:* **E**

    All the possible values for *s* and *t* are

    $$\begin{Bmatrix} s = 1, t = 17 & s = 2, t = 16 & s = 3, t = 15 & s = 4, t = 14 \\ s = 5, t = 13 & s = 6, t = 12 & s = 7, t = 11 & s = 8, t = 10 \end{Bmatrix}$$

    Therefore, the set of all possible values of *s* is {1,2,3,4,5,6,7,8}.

    The median is $\dfrac{4 + 5}{2} = 4.5$.

17. *Answer:* **A**

    There are 9 numbers, three of which are $2x + 5$, $2y$, and $2z - 3$. The modes are *x*, *y*, and *z*. There are more of each of these numbers than the other numbers. That means there must be 2 each of *x*, *y*, and *z*.

    The set of nine numbers is {$x, x, y, y, z, z, 2x + 5, 2y, 2z - 3$}. Because the average for this set of nine numbers is 20, the sum of the numbers is 180.

    Add the numbers in the set.

    $$x + x + y + y + z + z + (2x + 5) + 2y + (2z - 3) = 180$$
    $$4x + 4y + 4z + 2 = 180$$
    $$4x + 4y + 4z = 178$$
    $$4(x + y + z) = 178$$

CHAPTER 7

POWERS AND RADICALS

The secret to solving this type of problem is to know the power and root algebraic rules. The best way to do this is to apply the rules to problems. This section gives you the practice you need to learn these algebraic techniques. Begin with the mathematics review and then complete and correct the practice problems. There are 2 Solved SAT Problems and 19 Practice SAT Questions with answer explanations.

EXPONENTS

$5^4 = 5 \cdot 5 \cdot 5 \cdot 5.$

Calculator $5^4 = 5 \wedge 4$

Below are some basic rules for exponents.

$$x^0 = 1 \qquad\qquad x^a \cdot x^b = x^{a+b} \qquad\qquad \frac{x^a}{x^b} = x^{a-b}$$

$$\left(x^a\right)^b = x^{a \times b} \qquad\qquad x^{-a} = \frac{1}{x^a}$$

$$\left(x \cdot y\right)^a = x^a \cdot y^a \qquad\qquad x^{\frac{a}{b}} = \left(\sqrt[b]{x}\right)^a = \sqrt[b]{x^a}$$

$$\sqrt{a \times b} = \sqrt{a} \times \sqrt{b} \qquad \sqrt{\frac{a}{b}} = \frac{\sqrt{a}}{\sqrt{b}}$$

Use the rules of exponents.

Example:

$x^2 \cdot x^b = x^9, b =$

$\qquad x^2 \cdot x^b = x^{2+b} = x^9 \Rightarrow 2 + b = 9 \Rightarrow b = 7$

Example:

$\left(2^3\right)^b = 64, b =$

$\qquad \left(2^3\right)^b = 2^{3 \times b} = 64 = 2^6 \Rightarrow 3 \times b = 6 \Rightarrow b = 2$

Example:

$\dfrac{a^3 b^7 c^{11}}{a^{10} b^8 c^4} =$

$\dfrac{a^3 b^7 c^{11}}{a^{10} b^8 c^6} = a^{-7} b^{-1} c^5 = \dfrac{c^5}{a^7 b}$

Example:

$3^{-a} = 81, a =$

$3^4 = 81 \Rightarrow a = -4$

Example:

$x^{\frac{3}{2}} = 8, x =$

$x^{\frac{3}{2}} = 8 \Rightarrow \left(x^{\frac{3}{2}}\right)^{\frac{2}{3}} = 8^{\frac{2}{3}} \Rightarrow x^{\frac{3}{2} \times \frac{2}{3}} = 8^{\frac{2}{3}}$

$x = 8^{\frac{2}{3}} = \left(\sqrt[3]{8}\right)^2 = 2^2 = 4 \Rightarrow x = 4$

Simplify radicals.

Example:

$4\sqrt{50} - 3\sqrt{32} =$

$4\sqrt{50} - 3\sqrt{32} = 4\sqrt{25 \times 2} - 3\sqrt{16 \times 2} = 4 \times \sqrt{25} \times \sqrt{2} - 3 \times \sqrt{16} \times \sqrt{2} =$
$4 \times 5 \times \sqrt{2} - 3 \times 4 \times \sqrt{2} = 20\sqrt{2} - 12\sqrt{2} = 8\sqrt{2}$

Example:

$\dfrac{9\sqrt{24}}{2\sqrt{27}} =$

$\dfrac{9\sqrt{24}}{2\sqrt{27}} = \dfrac{9\sqrt{4 \times 6}}{2\sqrt{9 \times 3}} = \dfrac{9 \times 2\sqrt{6}}{2 \times 3\sqrt{3}} = \dfrac{18\sqrt{6}}{6\sqrt{3}} = 3\sqrt{2}$

Example:

$7\sqrt{x} + 14 = 42, x =$

$7\sqrt{x} + 14 = 42 \Rightarrow 7\sqrt{x} = 28 \Rightarrow \sqrt{x} = 4 \Rightarrow x = 16$

Practice Questions

1. $\dfrac{x^a}{x^{15}} = \dfrac{1}{x^{-5}}, a =$

2. $(a^2)^4 = 6{,}561, a =$

3. $\dfrac{a^{14}b^8c^6}{a^5b^{13}c^{15}} =$

4. $27^{\frac{5}{3}} = x^5, x =$

5. $7\sqrt{45} + 5\sqrt{180} =$

6. $\dfrac{3\sqrt{60}}{2\sqrt{20}} =$

7. $8\sqrt{x} - 37 = -21, x =$

Practice Answers

1. $a = 20$
2. $a = 3$
3. $a^9 b^{-5} c^{-9} = \dfrac{a^9}{b^5 c^9}$
4. $x = 3$
5. $51\sqrt{5}$
6. $\dfrac{3\sqrt{3}}{2}$
7. $x = 4$

SOLVED SAT PROBLEMS

1. $16y = 2^{4+x}$, $y =$
   A. 2^x
   B. $2x$
   C. 2
   D. 4
   E. 16

   Answer: **A**

   Use the rules of exponents.

   $16y = 2^{4+x} = 2^4 \cdot 2^x = 16 \cdot 2^x$

   That means $16y = 16 \cdot 2^x \Rightarrow y = 2^x$.

2. $\sqrt{-a} - 1 = 7, a =$

    A. −64
    B. 64
    C. 49
    D. 36
    E. −36

Answer: **A**

Use the rules of exponents.

$\sqrt{-a} - 1 = 7 \Rightarrow \sqrt{-a} = 8$

We know $\sqrt{64} = 8$.

That means $-a = 64$ and $a = -64$.

POWERS AND RADICALS PRACTICE SAT QUESTIONS

ANSWER SHEET

Choose the correct answer.
If no answer choices are given, grid the answers in the section at the bottom of the page.

1. GRID
2. GRID
3. Ⓐ Ⓑ Ⓒ Ⓓ Ⓔ
4. Ⓐ Ⓑ Ⓒ Ⓓ Ⓔ
5. Ⓐ Ⓑ Ⓒ Ⓓ Ⓔ
6. Ⓐ Ⓑ Ⓒ Ⓓ Ⓔ
7. GRID
8. Ⓐ Ⓑ Ⓒ Ⓓ Ⓔ
9. Ⓐ Ⓑ Ⓒ Ⓓ Ⓔ
10. GRID
11. Ⓐ Ⓑ Ⓒ Ⓓ Ⓔ
12. Ⓐ Ⓑ Ⓒ Ⓓ Ⓔ
13. Ⓐ Ⓑ Ⓒ Ⓓ Ⓔ
14. Ⓐ Ⓑ Ⓒ Ⓓ Ⓔ
15. Ⓐ Ⓑ Ⓒ Ⓓ Ⓔ
16. GRID
17. Ⓐ Ⓑ Ⓒ Ⓓ Ⓔ
18. Ⓐ Ⓑ Ⓒ Ⓓ Ⓔ
19. Ⓐ Ⓑ Ⓒ Ⓓ Ⓔ

Use the answer spaces in the grids below if the question requires a grid-in response.

Student-Produced Responses

ONLY ANSWERS ENTERED IN THE CIRCLES IN EACH GRID WILL BE SCORED. YOU WILL NOT RECEIVE CREDIT FOR ANYTHING WRITTEN IN THE BOXES ABOVE THE CIRCLES.

1.

	/	/	/
.	.	.	.
	0	0	0
1	1	1	1
2	2	2	2
3	3	3	3
4	4	4	4
5	5	5	5
6	6	6	6
7	7	7	7
8	8	8	8
9	9	9	9

2.

	/	/	/
.	.	.	.
	0	0	0
1	1	1	1
2	2	2	2
3	3	3	3
4	4	4	4
5	5	5	5
6	6	6	6
7	7	7	7
8	8	8	8
9	9	9	9

7.

	/	/	/
.	.	.	.
	0	0	0
1	1	1	1
2	2	2	2
3	3	3	3
4	4	4	4
5	5	5	5
6	6	6	6
7	7	7	7
8	8	8	8
9	9	9	9

10.

	/	/	/
.	.	.	.
	0	0	0
1	1	1	1
2	2	2	2
3	3	3	3
4	4	4	4
5	5	5	5
6	6	6	6
7	7	7	7
8	8	8	8
9	9	9	9

16.

	/	/	/
.	.	.	.
	0	0	0
1	1	1	1
2	2	2	2
3	3	3	3
4	4	4	4
5	5	5	5
6	6	6	6
7	7	7	7
8	8	8	8
9	9	9	9

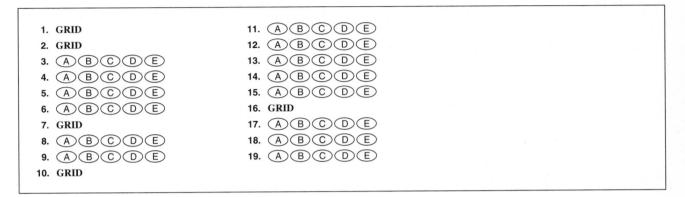

PRACTICE SAT QUESTIONS

1. $9^3 \times 27^2 = 3^n$, $n =$

2. $x^{-3} = \dfrac{1}{8}$, $x =$

3. $4^{-a} = 64$, $a =$
   A. 4
   B. −4
   C. 3
   D. −3
   E. 2

4. $5\sqrt{8} + 7\sqrt{32} =$
   A. $18\sqrt{2}$
   B. $38\sqrt{2}$
   C. $23\sqrt{4}$
   D. $33\sqrt{3}$
   E. $38\sqrt{3}$

5. $4\sqrt{18} \times 11\sqrt{12} =$
   A. $12\sqrt{6}$
   B. $34\sqrt{6}$
   C. $264\sqrt{6}$
   D. $264\sqrt{3}$
   E. $264\sqrt{2}$

6. $y^{-5} = 1{,}024$, $y =$
   A. 5
   B. 4
   C. 3
   D. $\dfrac{1}{5}$
   E. $\dfrac{1}{4}$

7. $2^{-n} = \dfrac{1}{256}$, $n =$

8. $\sqrt{x} = 4a^2bc^3$, $x =$
   A. $16a^4b^2c^9$
   B. $16a^4b^2c^6$
   C. $16a^2bc^3$
   D. $8a^4b^2c^6$
   E. $2ab^{\frac{1}{2}}c^{\frac{3}{2}}$

9. $8^{12} = 2^x$, $x =$
   A. 4
   B. 12
   C. 24
   D. 36
   E. 42

10. $c^{\frac{2}{5}} = 4$, $c =$

11. $\dfrac{9^{4x}}{27^{3x}} =$
    A. 9^x
    B. $\dfrac{1}{3^x}$
    C. $\dfrac{1}{9^x}$
    D. 3^x
    E. $\dfrac{1}{4^x}$

12. Which of the following is equal to 5^{8x}?
    I. $(5^{4x})^4$
    II. $(5^{4x})^2$
    III. $(5^{4x})(5^{4x})$

    A. I
    B. II
    C. III
    D. I and II
    E. II and III

13. $n^3 \geq n^2$ for which of the following?
    I. $n = 1$
    II. $n = 0$
    III. $n = -1$

    A. I
    B. II
    C. III
    D. I and II
    E. II and III

14. $\dfrac{a^2b^{-6}c^{11}d^{-4}}{a^{-5}b^{-2}c^7d^9} =$

A. $\dfrac{a^3b^4}{c^4d^{13}}$

B. $\dfrac{a^7b^8}{c^4d^{13}}$

C. $\dfrac{a^7c^4}{b^4d^{13}}$

D. $\dfrac{c^7d^4}{a^4b^{13}}$

E. $\dfrac{a^3c^4}{b^8d^{13}}$

15. $27^{\frac{4}{x}} = 81, x =$

A. 2
B. 3
C. 4
D. 5
E. 6

16. $3\sqrt{x} - 7 = 5, x =$

17. $9\sqrt{x} - 7\sqrt{x} - 36 = -16, x =$

A. 5
B. 10
C. 20
D. 50
E. 100

18. $x = 2, y = x^2, \left(y^2 - x^3\right)^{\left(\frac{x^2}{3y}\right)} =$

A. 2
B. 3
C. 4
D. 5
E. 6

19. $\sqrt{x} + c\sqrt{y} = d\sqrt{y}, \dfrac{x}{y} =$

A. $d - c$
B. $\sqrt{d - c}$
C. $c - d$
D. $(d - c)^2$
E. $\sqrt{c - d}$

▇▇ EXPLAINED ANSWERS

1. ***Answer:* 12**

   Rewrite left side of equation using rules of exponents.

   $$9^3 \times 27^2 = \left(3^2\right)^3 \times \left(3^3\right)^2 = 3^6 \times 3^6 = 3^{12}$$

   so $n = 12$

2. ***Answer:* 2**

   Solve the equation using rules of exponents.

   $$x^{-3} = \frac{1}{8} \Rightarrow \frac{1}{x^3} = \frac{1}{8} \Rightarrow x^3 = 8 \Rightarrow x = 2$$

3. ***Answer:* D**

   Write 64 as 4^3, and solve the equation.

   $$4^{-a} = 64 = 4^3 \Rightarrow -a = 3 \Rightarrow a = -3$$

4. ***Answer:* B**

   Simplify radical expression.

   $$5\sqrt{8} + 7\sqrt{32} = 5\sqrt{4 \times 2} + 7\sqrt{16 \times 2} =$$
   $$10\sqrt{2} + 28\sqrt{2} = 38\sqrt{2}$$

5. ***Answer:* C**

   Simplify radical expression.

   $$4\sqrt{9 \times 2} \times 11\sqrt{4 \times 3} = 12\sqrt{2} \times 22\sqrt{3} = 264\sqrt{6}$$

6. ***Answer:* E**

   Solve the equation.

   Remember, $x^{-n} = \dfrac{1}{x^n}$ and $x^{(1/n)} = \sqrt[n]{x}$

   $$y^{-5} = 1{,}024 \Rightarrow y = 1{,}024^{\left(\frac{1}{5}\right)}$$

   $$= \frac{1}{1{,}024^{(1/5)}} = \frac{1}{4}.$$

7. ***Answer:* 8**

   Solve the equation.

   $$2^{-n} = \frac{1}{256} \Rightarrow \frac{1}{2^n} = \frac{1}{256} \Rightarrow 2^n = 256 \Rightarrow n = 8$$

8. ***Answer:* B**

   Solve the equation.

   $$\sqrt{x} = 4a^2bc^3 \Rightarrow x = \left(4a^2bc^3\right)^2 \Rightarrow x = 16a^4b^2c^6$$

9. *Answer:* **D**

Rewrite left side of equation using rules of exponents.

$$8^{12} = 2^x \Rightarrow (2^3)^{12} = 2^x$$

$$2^{36} = 2^x \Rightarrow x = 36$$

10. *Answer:* **32**

Solve the equation.

$$c^{\frac{2}{5}} = 4 \Rightarrow c = 4^{\frac{5}{2}} = 32$$

11. *Answer:* **B**

Rewrite expression using rules of exponents.

$$\frac{9^{4x}}{27^{3x}} = \frac{(3^2)^{4x}}{(3^3)^{3x}} = \frac{3^{8x}}{3^{9x}} =$$

$$3^{8x-9x} = 3^{-x} = \frac{1}{3^x}$$

12. *Answer:* **E**

I. $(5^{4x})^4 = 5^{16x}$ NO
II. $(5^{4x})^2 = 5^{8x}$ YES
III. $(5^{4x})(5^{4x}) = 5^{4x+4x} = 5^{8x}$ YES

13. *Answer:* **D**

Make a table

	n^3	n^2
$n = 0$	0	0
$n = 1$	1	1
$n = -1$	-1	1

$n^3 \geq n^2$ when $n = 0$ (I) and $n = 1$ (II).

14. *Answer:* **C**

Solve the equation.

$$\frac{a^2 b^{-6} c^{11} d^{-4}}{a^{-5} b^{-2} c^7 d^9} = a^{2-(-5)} b^{-6-(-2)} c^{11-7} d^{-4-9} =$$

$$a^7 b^{-4} c^4 d^{-13} = \frac{a^7 c^4}{b^4 d^{13}}$$

15. *Answer:* **B**

Rewrite left side of equation using rules of exponents.

$$27^{\frac{4}{x}} = 81 \Rightarrow (3^3)^{\frac{4}{x}} = 3^4$$

$$3^{\frac{12}{x}} = 3^4 \Rightarrow \frac{12}{x} = 4$$

Solve for x. $12 = 4x \Rightarrow 3 = x$

16. *Answer:* **16**

    Solve the equation.

    $$3\sqrt{x} - 7 = 5 \Rightarrow 3\sqrt{x} = 12$$

    $$\sqrt{x} = 4 \Rightarrow x = 16$$

17. *Answer:* **E**

    Solve the equation.

    $$9\sqrt{x} - 7\sqrt{x} - 36 = -16 \Rightarrow 2\sqrt{x} - 36 = -16$$

    $$2\sqrt{x} = 20 \Rightarrow \sqrt{x} = 10 \Rightarrow x = 100$$

18. *Answer:* **A**

    Substitute. Evaluate the expression.

    $$x = 2 \text{ and } y = x^2 = 2^2 = 4$$

    $$\left(y^2 - x^3\right)^{\left(\frac{x^2}{3y}\right)} = \left(4^2 - 2^3\right)^{\left(\frac{2^2}{3\times4}\right)} = \left(16 - 8\right)^{\left(\frac{4}{12}\right)} = 8^{\frac{1}{3}} = \sqrt[3]{8} = 2$$

19. *Answer:* **D**

    Solve for $\dfrac{x}{y}$.

    $$\sqrt{x} + c\sqrt{y} = d\sqrt{y} \Rightarrow \sqrt{x} = d\sqrt{y} - c\sqrt{y} \Rightarrow \sqrt{x} = \sqrt{y}\left(d - c\right)$$

    $$\frac{\sqrt{x}}{\sqrt{y}} = \left(d - c\right) \Rightarrow \sqrt{\frac{x}{y}} = \left(d - c\right) \Rightarrow \frac{x}{y} = \left(d - c\right)^2$$

CHAPTER 8

BASIC ALGEBRA

This section reviews the fundamental algebra skills of multiplying, simplifying, factoring, and problem-solving that you need to succeed on the SAT. Some SAT problems simply ask you to apply this knowledge in a straightforward way. Other times these skills are only a part of what is necessary to solve the problem. Begin with the mathematics review and then complete and correct the practice problems. There are 2 Solved SAT Problems and 24 Practice SAT Questions with answer explanations.

SIMPLIFYING POLYNOMIALS

Multiply each term in one polynomial to each term in the other polynomial. Finally, add and subtract like terms to complete the process.

Example:

Multiply terms.

$(4x^2 + 5x - 3)(x + 5) - (2x + 7)(x - 4) =$
$(4x^3 + 20x^2 + 5x^2 + 25x - 3x - 15) - (2x^2 - 8x + 7x - 28) =$

Combine like terms in parentheses.

$(4x^3 + 25x^2 + 22x - 15) - (2x^2 - x - 28) =$

Distribute the negative.

$4x^3 + 25x^2 + 22x - 15 - 2x^2 - (-x) - (-28) =$

Group like terms.

$4x^3 + (25x^2 - 2x^2) + [22x - (-x)] + [-15 - (-28)] =$

Combine like terms.

$4x^3 + 23x^2 + 23x + 13$

FACTORING POLYNOMIALS

When factoring polynomials, check first to see if there is a common factor to all the terms. When factoring is complete, check the answer by multiplying the polynomial.

Difference of Squares

The difference of squares follows a standard form.

$(a^2 - b^2) = (a - b)(a + b)$

Example:

Simplify $3x^2 - 27 = 3(x^2 - 9) = 3(x - 3)(x + 3)$

Square of Binomial

The square of a binomial follows a standard form.

$(a + b)^2 = a^2 + 2ab + b^2$

Example:

Simplify $(8x^2 + 24xy + 18y^2) = 2(4x^2 + 12xy + 9y^2) = 2(4x^2 + 2 \cdot 2x \cdot 3y + 9y^2)$

$(4x^2 + 12xy + 9y^2)$ is the square of $(2x + 3y)$

$2(2x + 3y)^2$

General Binomial

Example:

Simplify $x^2 - 13x - 42 = (x - 6)(x - 7)$.

Example:

Simplify $6x^2 + 39x - 72 = 3(2x^2 + 13x - 24) = 3(2x - 3)(x + 8)$.

Simplifying Fractions That Include Polynomials

To simplify, factor the denominator and the numerator. Then "cancel" terms common to the numerator and the denominator.

Example:

$$\frac{x^2 - 8x + 15}{x^2 - 25} = \frac{(x - 3)\cancel{(x - 5)}}{(x + 5)\cancel{(x - 5)}} = \frac{x - 3}{x + 5}$$

EVALUATING EXPRESSIONS

An expression does not contain an equal sign. To evaluate an expression, substitute the numbers for the variables.

Example:

$3x + 2y - z$. If $z = 8$ and $y = 10$, $x = -4$

$3(-4) + 2(10) - 8 = -12 + 20 - 8 = 0$

SOLVING QUADRATIC EQUATIONS

Quadratic equations can be written in the form $ax^2 + bx + c = 0$. To solve a quadratic equation write the equation in the form $ax^2 + bx + c = 0$. Then factor the equation. Finally set each factor equal to 0, and solve.

Example:

$x^2 + 12 = 7x \Rightarrow$ Write in quadratic form $x^2 - 7x + 12 = 0$

Factor $(x - 3)(x - 4) = 0$

Solve $x - 3 = 0$ and $x - 4 = 0 \Rightarrow x = 3$ and $x = 4$

Example:

$2x^2 - 13x - 20 = 25 \Rightarrow$ Write in quadratic form $2x^2 - 13x - 45 = 0$

Factor $(2x + 5)(x - 9) = 0$

Solve $2x + 5 = 0$ and $x - 9 = 0 \Rightarrow x = -\dfrac{5}{2}$ and $x = 9$

SOLVING INEQUALITIES

When solving an inequality you must switch the sign of the inequality if you multiply or divide by a negative number.

Example:

$-2x + 9 \geq 15 \Rightarrow -2x \geq 6 \Rightarrow x \leq -3.$

ABSOLUTE VALUE

The absolute value of $x, |x|$, is always positive. If $|x| = 3$, then x can be +3 or –3. Therefore, to solve with an absolute value use what is inside the absolute value sign and its negative.

Example:

$$|x - 4| = 6 \Rightarrow \begin{array}{l} x - 4 = 6 \Rightarrow x = 10 \\ \text{or} \\ x - 4 = -6 \Rightarrow x = -2 \end{array}$$

Example:

$|2x + 7| - 6 > 11 \Rightarrow |2x + 7| > 17$

$$\Rightarrow \begin{array}{l} 2x + 7 > 17 \Rightarrow 2x > 10 \Rightarrow x > 5 \\ \text{or} \\ 2x + 7 < -17 \Rightarrow 2x < -24 \Rightarrow x < -12 \end{array}$$

SOLVING SYSTEMS OF EQUATIONS

Systems of equations are sometimes called simultaneous equations.

Example:

$$2x + 4y = 10$$
$$x - 2y = -3$$

Method 1: (Substitution)

Solve for x in the second equation, and substitute for x into the first equation:

$$x - 2y = -3 \implies x = 2y - 3$$

Substitute $(2y - 3)$ for x in the first equation.

$$2(2y - 3) + 4y = 10$$

Solve for y.

$$2(2y - 3) + 4y = 10 \implies 4y - 6 + 4y = 10$$
$$8y - 6 = 10 \implies 8y = 16 \implies y = 2$$

Because $x = (2y - 3)$, and $y = 2$, $x = 2(2) - 3 = 4 - 3 = 1$. The solution to this system of equations is $x = 1$ and $y = 2$. Check the solution. Substitute the values for x and y into either original equation.

Method 2: (Elimination)

Multiply the second equation by 2.

$$2x + 4y = 10$$
$$2(x - 2y) = 2(-3)$$

Add the two equations to eliminate the y.

$$2x + 4y = 10$$
$$2x - 4y = -6$$

Add the two equations to eliminate the y.

$$2x + 4y = 10$$
$$\underline{2x - 4y = -6}$$
$$4x + 0y = 4 \implies 4x = 4 \implies x = 1$$

Substitute the value of x into either of the original equations to find the value of y.

$$2x + 4y = 10 \implies 2(1) + 4y = 10 \implies 2 + 4y = 10$$
$$4y = 8 \implies y = 2$$
$$x - 2y = -3 \implies 1 - 2y = -3$$
$$-2y = -4 \implies y = 2$$

Practice Questions

1. Simplify $(-3x^2 + 7x + 5)(x - 2) + (3x - 4)(x + 8)$.

2. Factor $27x^2 - 72xy + 48y^2$.

3. Factor $50x^2 - 72$.

4. Simplify $\dfrac{x^2 + 9x - 36}{x^2 + 3x - 18}$.

5. If $2x^2 - 2x = -5x + 14$, what are the possible values of x?

6. $3a + 4b = 5$. If $a = 4$, $b = ?$

7. If $|4x - 12| + 15 = 19$, what are the possible values of x?

8. If $|2x + 7| \leq 13$, what are the possible values of x?

9. Solve the system of equations for x and y?

   $-3x - 2y = 8$

   $5x + y = 3$

Practice Answers

1. $-3x^3 + 16x^2 + 11x - 42$

2. $3(3x - 4y)(3x - 4y) = 3(3x - 4y)^2$

3. $2(5x + 6)(5x - 6)$

4. $\dfrac{x + 12}{x + 6}$

5. $(2x + 7)(x - 2) = 0$

$$2x + 7 = 0 \ \Rightarrow\ 2x = -7 \ \Rightarrow\ x = \dfrac{-7}{2} = -3.5$$

$$x - 2 = 0 \ \Rightarrow\ x = 2$$

6. $b = -\dfrac{7}{4} = -1.75$

7. $x = 4$ and $x = 2$

8. $-10 \leq x \leq 3$

9. $x = 2$ and $y = -7$

SOLVED SAT PROBLEMS

---

1. If $x^2 - 16 > 0$, what are the possible values of x?

   A. $x > 4$
   B. $x < 4$
   C. $x > -4$
   D. $-4 < x < 4$
   E. $x < -4$ or $x > 4$

   Answer: **E**

   $x^2 - 16 > 0 \Rightarrow x^2 > 16$. Therefore, $x < -4$ or $x > 4$ when x^2 is greater than 16.

---

2. If $2ab + 6a = 4$ and $a = \dfrac{1}{2}$, $b =$

   A. 1
   B. 2
   C. 3
   D. 4
   E. 5

   Answer: **A**

   Factor out $2a$.

   $2ab + 6a = 4 \quad \Rightarrow \quad 2a(b + 3) = 4$

   Substitute $\dfrac{1}{2}$ for a.

   $2\left(\dfrac{1}{2}\right)(b + 3) = 4$

   Solve for b.

   $b + 3 = 4 \quad \Rightarrow \quad b = 4 - 3 = 1$

BASIC ALGEBRA
PRACTICE SAT QUESTIONS

ANSWER SHEET

Choose the correct answer.

1. Ⓐ Ⓑ Ⓒ Ⓓ Ⓔ	11. Ⓐ Ⓑ Ⓒ Ⓓ Ⓔ	21. Ⓐ Ⓑ Ⓒ Ⓓ Ⓔ
2. Ⓐ Ⓑ Ⓒ Ⓓ Ⓔ	12. Ⓐ Ⓑ Ⓒ Ⓓ Ⓔ	22. Ⓐ Ⓑ Ⓒ Ⓓ Ⓔ
3. Ⓐ Ⓑ Ⓒ Ⓓ Ⓔ	13. Ⓐ Ⓑ Ⓒ Ⓓ Ⓔ	23. Ⓐ Ⓑ Ⓒ Ⓓ Ⓔ
4. Ⓐ Ⓑ Ⓒ Ⓓ Ⓔ	14. Ⓐ Ⓑ Ⓒ Ⓓ Ⓔ	24. Ⓐ Ⓑ Ⓒ Ⓓ Ⓔ
5. Ⓐ Ⓑ Ⓒ Ⓓ Ⓔ	15. Ⓐ Ⓑ Ⓒ Ⓓ Ⓔ	
6. Ⓐ Ⓑ Ⓒ Ⓓ Ⓔ	16. Ⓐ Ⓑ Ⓒ Ⓓ Ⓔ	
7. Ⓐ Ⓑ Ⓒ Ⓓ Ⓔ	17. Ⓐ Ⓑ Ⓒ Ⓓ Ⓔ	
8. Ⓐ Ⓑ Ⓒ Ⓓ Ⓔ	18. Ⓐ Ⓑ Ⓒ Ⓓ Ⓔ	
9. Ⓐ Ⓑ Ⓒ Ⓓ Ⓔ	19. Ⓐ Ⓑ Ⓒ Ⓓ Ⓔ	
10. Ⓐ Ⓑ Ⓒ Ⓓ Ⓔ	20. Ⓐ Ⓑ Ⓒ Ⓓ Ⓔ	

PRACTICE SAT QUESTIONS

1. If $y = 4$ and $x = 3$, then $y^3 - 3x^2 + 3y - 2xy + x =$
   A. 24
   B. 25
   C. 26
   D. 27
   E. 28

2. If $a + b = 5$, then $a^2 + 2ab + b^2 =$
   A. 5
   B. 10
   C. 15
   D. 20
   E. 25

3. $\boxed{x} = x^2 - 5x + 6$, $\boxed{a} = 2$, $a =$
   A. –4
   B. 4
   C. –4 and 4
   D. 1 and 4
   E. 1

4. $x^2 - 3x = 0$, $x =$
   A. 0 and 3
   B. 3
   C. 6
   D. 0 and 6
   E. 3 and 6

5. $(3x - 4)(2x - 5) - (x + 3)(4x - 7) =$
   A. $2x^2 - 28x + 1$
   B. $2x^2 - 28x + 41$
   C. $2x^2 - 14x + 41$
   D. $x^2 - 14x + 1$
   E. $2x^2 - 14x + 1$

6. $5a^2 - 4a - 3 - 3(a^2 + a + 4) = 0$. What is the sum of the possible value of a?
   A. 3
   B. 3.5
   C. 4
   D. 4.5
   E. 5

7. Which of the following statements is true?
   I. $4x^2 - 9y^2 = (2x - 3y)^2$.
   II. $(x - 4)^2 = x^2 - 16$.
   III. $x^2 + 2xy + y^2 = (x + y)^2$.
   A. I
   B. II
   C. III
   D. I and II
   E. I and III

8. $\dfrac{y^2 - x^2}{x^2 - y^2} =$
   A. 1
   B. –1
   C. 0
   D. 2
   E. –2

9. $x^2 - 25 = 12$, $x + 5 = 4$, $x - 5 =$
   A. 2
   B. 3
   C. 4
   D. 6
   E. 12

10. $3(x - 10) = 5(x + 20)$, $x =$
    A. –65
    B. –50
    C. –35
    D. –20
    E. –15

11. $4x = 52$, $x^2 - 5^2 =$
    A. 81
    B. 9
    C. 144
    D. 12
    E. 169

12. $6b^2 - 24b + 24 =$
    A. $6(b - 4)$
    B. $6(b - 4)^2$
    C. $(b - 2)^2$
    D. $6(b - 2)^2$
    E. $6(b - 2)$

13. $(2x^2 + 3x - 5)(x + 2) = ax^3 + bx^2 + cx + d$, $ac - bd =$
    A. 70
    B. 71
    C. 72
    D. 73
    E. 74

14. $(x - 2)(x + 3)(x - 4) = 24$. What is the sum of the possible values of x?
    A. 9
    B. 7
    C. 5
    D. 3
    E. 1

15. $m \# n = m^2 - n^2$, $\dfrac{m \# n}{m - n} =$
    A. $m \# n$
    B. $m - n$
    C. $m \times n$
    D. $m + n$
    E. $\dfrac{m}{n}$

16. $x = \dfrac{ab^2}{3}$, $27x^3 =$
    A. ab^2
    B. a^3b^3
    C. a^3b^6
    D. a^2b^6
    E. a^6b^2

17. $|3x - 15| = 18$. What is the product of all possible values of x?
    A. -11
    B. -10
    C. -9
    D. -8
    E. -7

18. $4x^2 = 9(y^2 + 2)$, $\dfrac{18}{2x - 3y} =$
    A. $x + y$
    B. $2x - 3y$
    C. $2x + 3y$
    D. $x + y$
    E. $x + y$

19. $|x - y| = d$ and $x > y$, which of the following cannot be the value of $y - x$?
    I. d
    II. $-d$
    III. $|y - x|$
    A. I
    B. II
    C. I and II
    D. I and III
    E. II and III

20. $a = \Big|\, |x|^3 - |x - y|^2 - y + x \,\Big|$. If $x = -2$ and $y = 5$, $a =$
    A. 47
    B. 48
    C. 49
    D. 50
    E. 51

21. $-5t - 7 \le 8$. What are all possible values of t?
    A. $t \le 2$
    B. $t \le -2$
    C. $t \ge -3$
    D. $t \le -3$
    E. $t \ge 3$

22. $|3x - 4| > 20$. Which of the following choices is not a possible value for x?
    A. -5.3
    B. 8.2
    C. -5.4
    D. 8.1
    E. -5.5

23. 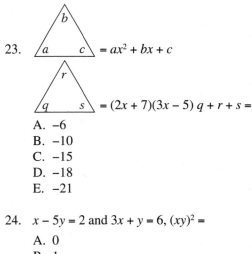 $= ax^2 + bx + c$

    $= (2x + 7)(3x - 5)$ $q + r + s =$
    A. -6
    B. -10
    C. -15
    D. -18
    E. -21

24. $x - 5y = 2$ and $3x + y = 6$, $(xy)^2 =$
    A. 0
    B. 1
    C. 4
    D. 9
    E. 16

■ EXPLAINED ANSWERS

1. *Answer:* **E**

   Substitute and solve.

   $y = 4$ and $x = 3$.

   $y^3 - 3x^2 + 3y - 2xy + x = 4^3 - 3(3)^2 + 3(4) - 2(3)(4) + 3 =$

   $64 - 27 + 12 - 24 + 3 = 25.$

2. *Answer:* **E**

   Factor for the perfect square.

   $a^2 + 2ab + b^2 = (a + b)^2 = 5^2 = 25.$

   Substitute 5 for x. $5^2 = 25.$

   You could also substitute numbers for a and b that have a sum of 5. For example, $2 + 3 = 5$, so let $a = 2$ and $b = 3$. We get: $2^2 + 2(2)(3) + 3^2 = 4 + 12 + 9 = 25.$

3. *Answer:* **D**

   The problem states $\boxed{x} = x^2 - 5x + 6$ and $\boxed{a} = 2$

   So $= a^2 - 5a + 6 = 2.$ $\Rightarrow$ $a^2 - 5a + 4 = 0$

   Factor and solve. $(a - 4)(a - 1) = 0$

   $a - 4 = 0$ and $a - 1 = 0$ $\Rightarrow$ $a = 4$ and $a = 1$

4. *Answer:* **A**

   The problem states $x^2 - 3x = 0.$

   $x^2 - 3x = x(x - 3)$

   Factor and solve. $x(x - 3) = 0$ $\Rightarrow$ $x = 0$ and $x - 3 = 0$ $\Rightarrow$ $x = 0$ and $x = 3$

5. *Answer:* **B**

   Simplify the polynomial

   $(3x - 4)(2x - 5) - (x + 3)(4x - 7)$

   $(6x^2 - 15x - 8x + 20) - (4x^2 - 7x + 12x - 21) =$

   $(6x^2 - 23x + 20) - (4x^2 + 5x - 21)$

   $(6x^2 - 4x^2) + (-23x - 5x) + [20 - (-21)]$

   $2x^2 - 28x + 41$

6. *Answer:* **B**

   Simplify polynomial $5a^2 - 4a - 3 - 3(a^2 + a + 4) = 5a^2 - 4a - 3 - 3a^2 - 3a - 12 = 2a^2 - 7a - 15 = 0$

   Factor quadratic and solve for a. $(2a + 3)(a - 5) = 0$ $\Rightarrow$ $2a + 3 = 0$ and $a - 5 = 0$ $\Rightarrow$ $a = -\dfrac{3}{2}$ and $a = 5$

   Add the solutions. $-\dfrac{3}{2} + 5 = -\dfrac{3}{2} + \dfrac{10}{2} = \dfrac{7}{2} = 3.5$

7. *Answer:* **C**
   I.   False $(2x - 3y)^2 = 4^2 - 12y + 9y^2$
   II. False $(x - 4)^2 = x^2 - 8x + 16$
   III. True $x^2 + 2xy + y^2 = (x + y)^2$

8. *Answer:* **B**

   Choose two numbers and assign them to x and y.

   For example, let $x = 5$ and $y = 3$ $\Rightarrow$
   $$\frac{y^2 - x^2}{x^2 - y^2} = \frac{3^2 - 5^2}{5^2 - 3^2}$$
   $$\frac{9 - 25}{25 - 9} = \frac{-16}{16} = -1.$$

9. *Answer:* **B**

   The problem states $x^2 - 25 = 12$.

   Factor $x^2 - 25 = (x + 5)(x - 5) = 12$.

   Substitute 4 for $(x + 5)$, $4(x - 5) = 12$ $\Rightarrow$ $x - 5 = 3$.

10. *Answer:* **A**

    The problem states $3(x - 10) = 5(x + 20)$.

    Multiply $3x - 30 = 5x + 100$ $\Rightarrow$ $-130 = 2x$ $\Rightarrow$ $-65 = x$.

11. *Answer:* **C**

    The problem states $4x = 52$.

    Solve for x. $x = 13$.

    Substitute 13 for x and solve. $x^2 - 5^2 = 13^2 - 5^2 = 169 - 25 = 144$.

12. *Answer:* **D**

    Factor $6b^2 - 24b + 24 = 6(b^2 - 4b + 4)$.

    $6(b - 2)^2$

13. *Answer:* **C**

    The problem states $(2x^2 + 3x - 5)(x + 2) = ax^3 + bx^2 + cx + d$.

    Simplify. $2x^3 + 4x^2 + 3x^2 + 6x - 5x - 10 = 2x^3 + 7x^2 + x - 10$

    That means, $a = 2$, $b = 7$, $c = 1$, $d = -10$

    So, $ac - bd = (2)(1) - (7)(-10) = 2 - (-70) = 2 + 70 = 72$.

14. *Answer:* **D**

    The problem states $(x - 2)(x + 3)(x - 4) = 24$.

    Simplify $(x - 2)(x + 3)(x - 4) = (x^2 + x - 6)(x - 4) = (x^3 - 4x^2 + x^2 - 4x - 6x + 24) =$
    $x^3 - 3x^2 - 10x + 24 = 24$ $\Rightarrow$ $x^3 - 3x^2 - 10x = 0$

    Factor $x(x^2 - 3x - 10) = x(x - 5)(x + 2) = 0$

    Find solution. $x = 0$, $x = 5$, $x = -2$ $\Rightarrow$ $0 + 5 + (-2) = 3$.

15. *Answer:* **D**

    The problem asks for the value of $\dfrac{m \# n}{m + n}$.

    Divide $\dfrac{m \# n}{m + n} = \dfrac{m^2 + 2mn + n^2}{m + n} = \dfrac{(m + n)^2}{(m + n)} = m + n.$

16. *Answer:* **C**

The problem states $x = \dfrac{ab^2}{3}$

Multiply by 3 as the first step to an equation with $27x^3$. $3x = ab^2$ $\Rightarrow$ $(3x)^3 = (ab^2)^3$
$27x^3 = a^3b^6$.

17. *Answer:* **A**

Solve the absolute value equation for both cases.

$$3x - 15 = 18 \;\Rightarrow\; 3x = 33 \;\Rightarrow\; x = 11$$

$|3x - 15| = 18 \;\Rightarrow\;$ $\qquad\qquad\qquad$ or

$$3x - 15 = -18 \;\Rightarrow\; 3x = -3 \;\Rightarrow\; x = -1$$

Multiply the solutions. $-1 \times 11 = -11$

18. *Answer:* **C**

You want to rewrite $4x^2 = 9(y^2 + 2)$ So $\dfrac{18}{2x - 3y}$ is on one side of the equal sign.

$4x^2 = 9\left(y^2 + 2\right) \;\Rightarrow\; 4x^2 = 9y^2 + 18$

Subtract $9y^2$ to form the difference of two squares. $4x^2 - 9y^2 = 18$ $\Rightarrow$ $(2x + 3y)(2x - 3y) = 18$.

$2x + 3y = \dfrac{18}{2x - 3y}$

19. *Answer:* **D**

We know $x > y$ so $y - x$ is negative.

$|x - y| = d \quad y - x = -d$

That means $(y - x)$ cannot equal these choices.
I. d
III. $|y - x|$

20. *Answer:* **B**

Substitute and solve for a.

$a = \left| |-2|^3 - |-2 - 5|^2 - 5 + (-2) \right| = \left| 2^3 - 7^2 - 5 - 2 \right|$

$\left| 8 - 49 - 5 - 2 \right| = |-48| = 48$

21. *Answer:* **C**

Solve the inequality for t.

$-5t - 7 \le 8 \;\Rightarrow\; -5t \le 15 \;\Rightarrow\; t \ge -3$

22. *Answer:* **A**

Solve the absolute value inequality for both cases.

$|3x - 4| > 20 \;\Rightarrow\;$

$3x - 4 > 20 \;\Rightarrow\; 3x > 24 \;\Rightarrow\; x > 8$

$\qquad\qquad$ or

$3x - 4 < -20 \;\Rightarrow\; 3x < -16 \;\Rightarrow\; x < \dfrac{-16}{3} \;\Rightarrow\; x < -5\dfrac{1}{3}$

That means x cannot be equal to a negative number greater than or equal to $-5\dfrac{1}{3}$.

23. *Answer:* **D**

The problem defines the operation as $ax^2 + bx + c$.

$= (2x + 7)(3x - 5)$

Simplify. $6x^2 - 10x + 21x - 35 = 6x^2 + 11x - 35$

That means $q = 6$, $r = 11$, $s = -35$

Add. $q + r + s = 6 + 11 + (-35) = -18$

24. *Answer:* **A**

Multiply the second equation by 5 to cancel y.

$x - 5y = 2$

$5(3x + y = 6)$

Add the equations and solve for x.

$$\begin{aligned} x - 5y &= 2 \\ 15x + 5y &= 30 \\ \hline 16x + 0y &= 32 \end{aligned} \Rightarrow 16x = 32 \Rightarrow x = 2$$

Substitute x into second original equations to solve for y.

$3(2) + y = 6 \Rightarrow 6 + y = 6 \Rightarrow y = 0$

$(xy)^2 = 0$

CHAPTER 9
COORDINATE GEOMETRY

This section deals primarily with distance, midpoint, and slope on the coordinate plane. You should remember the formulas for each of these geometric ideas. Most of the SAT problems don't ask you directly to solve for distance, midpoint, or slope. You must infer from the way the question is asked which concept is involved. Begin with the mathematics review and then complete and correct the practice problems. There are 2 Solved SAT Problems and 15 Practice SAT Questions with answer explanations.

POINTS

Show points by their coordinates (x, y). Two points on the same line are called co-linear points.

DISTANCE

The distance between two points $A = (x_1, y_1)$ and $B = (x_2, y_2)$ is $\sqrt{(x_2 - x_1)^2 + (y_2 - y_1)^2}$. This equals the length of $\overline{AB}$, the line segment joining points A and B. This length is represented by AB. If the distance between A and B equals the distance between P and Q then $AB = PQ$ or $\overline{AB}$ is congruent to $\overline{PQ}$ ($\overline{AB} \cong \overline{PQ}$).

Example:

What is the distance between $A = (-2,7)$ and $B = (4,6)$?

$$d = \sqrt{(x_2 - x_1)^2 + (y_2 - y_1)^2} = \sqrt{[4 - (-2)]^2 + (6 - 7)^2}$$

$$= \sqrt{(6)^2 + (-1)^2} = \sqrt{36 + 1} = \sqrt{37}.$$

Example:

The distance between $A = (-4,2)$ and $B = (6,t)$ is $2\sqrt{34}$, what is the value of t? Use the distance formula to find the y-coordinate t.

$$d = \sqrt{(x_2 - x_1)^2 + (y_2 - y_1)^2} \Rightarrow 2\sqrt{34} = \sqrt{(6 - [-4])^2 + (t - 2)^2}$$

$$\Rightarrow 2\sqrt{34} = \sqrt{10^2 + (t - 2)^2} \Rightarrow (2\sqrt{34})^2 = (\sqrt{10^2 + (t - 2)^2})^2$$

$$\Rightarrow 4 \times 34 = 10^2 + (t - 2)^2 \Rightarrow 136 = 100 + (t - 2)^2$$

$$\Rightarrow 36 = (t - 2)^2 \Rightarrow \sqrt{36} = \sqrt{(t - 2)^2}$$

$6 = t - 2 \Rightarrow 8 = t.$

MIDPOINT

The Midpoint of $\overline{AB}$ is the point $\left(\dfrac{x_1 + x_2}{2}, \dfrac{y_1 + y_2}{2}\right)$.

Example:

What is the midpoint of $A = (5,13)$ and $B = (-6,-4)$?

$$\left(\dfrac{5 + (-6)}{2}, \dfrac{13 + (-4)}{2}\right) = \left(-\dfrac{1}{2}, \dfrac{9}{2}\right) = (-0.5, 4.5)$$

Example:

If the midpoint of $\overline{AB}$ is $(-1,3)$ and $A = (a, 3)$ and $B = (5, b)$ what are the values of a and b?

$$\left(\dfrac{a + 5}{2}, \dfrac{3 + b}{2}\right) = (-1,3)$$

$$\dfrac{a + 5}{2} = -1 \Rightarrow a + 5 = -2 \Rightarrow a = -7$$

$$\dfrac{3 + b}{2} = 3 \Rightarrow 3 + b = 6 \Rightarrow b = 3$$

SLOPE

The slope (m) of $\overleftrightarrow{AB}$, the line passing through points A and B,

$$m = \dfrac{rise}{run} = \dfrac{change\ in\ y}{change\ in\ x} = \dfrac{\Delta y}{\Delta x} = \dfrac{y_2 - y_1}{x_2 - x_1}.$$

LINES

Parallel lines ($\parallel$) have equal slopes. If m_1 and m_2 are the slopes of two parallel lines, and if $m_1 = \dfrac{a}{b}$, then $m_2 = \dfrac{a}{b}$. Perpendicular lines ($\perp$) have slopes that are opposite reciprocals. That means the product is -1. If m_1 and m_2 are the slopes of two perpendicular lines, and if $m_1 = \dfrac{a}{b}$ then $m_2 = -\dfrac{b}{a}$.

Example:

If $\overleftrightarrow{AB} \parallel \overleftrightarrow{PQ}$ and $A = (5,-3)$ and $B = (7,2)$, what is the slope of $\overleftrightarrow{PQ}$?

$$m_{\overline{AB}} = \dfrac{y_2 - y_1}{x_2 - x_1} = \dfrac{2 - (-3)}{7 - 5} = \dfrac{5}{2}.\ \text{Because}\ \overleftrightarrow{AB} \parallel \overleftrightarrow{PQ}\ m_{\overline{PQ}} = \dfrac{5}{2}.$$

Example:

If $\overleftrightarrow{AB} \perp \overleftrightarrow{PQ}$ and $A = (3,7)$, $B = (-2,2)$, $P = (p,6)$, and $Q = (4,-3)$. What is the value of p?

$$m_{\overline{AB}} = \frac{y_2 - y_1}{x_2 - x_1} = \frac{2 - 7}{-2 - 3} = \frac{-5}{-5} = 1.$$

Because $\overrightarrow{AB} \perp \overrightarrow{PQ}$,

$$m_{\overline{PQ}} = -1 = \frac{-3 - 6}{4 - p} \Rightarrow -1(4 - p) = -9$$

$$-4 + p = -9 \Rightarrow p = -5.$$

Practice Questions

1. What is the distance between $A = (5,-3)$ and $B = (8,3)$?
2. What is the midpoint of $A = (6,2)$ and $B = (-3,-4)$?
3. If the midpoint of $\overline{AB}$ is $(7,2)$, and $A = (a,-5)$ and $B = (-2, b)$, what are the values of a and b?
4. If $\overrightarrow{AB} \perp \overrightarrow{PQ}$, and $A = (13,-5)$ and $B = (3,1)$, what is the slope of $\overrightarrow{PQ}$?

Practice Answers

1. $d = 3\sqrt{5}$
2. $\left(\frac{3}{2}, \frac{-2}{2}\right) = \left(\frac{3}{2}, -1\right)$
3. $a = 16$ and $b = 9$
4. $m = \frac{5}{3}$

SOLVED SAT PROBLEMS

1. $A = (7,-4)$ and $B = (-5,12)$. If point M is the midpoint of $\overline{AB}$ and $\overline{AM} \cong \overline{XY}$, then $XY =$

   A. 10
   B. 11
   C. 12
   D. 13
   E. 14

   Answer: **A**

   $$AB = \sqrt{[12 - (-4)]^2 + (-5 - 7)^2} = \sqrt{16^2 + (-12)^2}$$
   $$\sqrt{256 + 144} = \sqrt{400} = 20.$$

   The length of AB is 20.

   So, $AM = 10$ and $XY = 10$.

2. $A = (3, z)$ and $B = (z, 10)$. If the slope of $\overrightarrow{AB}$ is 6, $z =$

    A. 3
    B. 4
    C. 5
    D. 6
    E. 7

Answer: **B**

Use the slope formula to find z.

$$m = 6 = \frac{10 - z}{z - 3} \Rightarrow 6z - 18 = 10 - z$$

$$7z = 28 \Rightarrow z = 4.$$

COORDINATE GEOMETRY
PRACTICE SAT QUESTIONS

███ **ANSWER SHEET**

Choose the correct answer.
If no choices are given, grid the answers in the section at the bottom of the page.

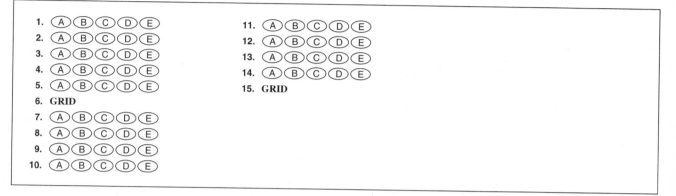

1. Ⓐ Ⓑ Ⓒ Ⓓ Ⓔ   11. Ⓐ Ⓑ Ⓒ Ⓓ Ⓔ
2. Ⓐ Ⓑ Ⓒ Ⓓ Ⓔ   12. Ⓐ Ⓑ Ⓒ Ⓓ Ⓔ
3. Ⓐ Ⓑ Ⓒ Ⓓ Ⓔ   13. Ⓐ Ⓑ Ⓒ Ⓓ Ⓔ
4. Ⓐ Ⓑ Ⓒ Ⓓ Ⓔ   14. Ⓐ Ⓑ Ⓒ Ⓓ Ⓔ
5. Ⓐ Ⓑ Ⓒ Ⓓ Ⓔ   15. **GRID**
6. **GRID**
7. Ⓐ Ⓑ Ⓒ Ⓓ Ⓔ
8. Ⓐ Ⓑ Ⓒ Ⓓ Ⓔ
9. Ⓐ Ⓑ Ⓒ Ⓓ Ⓔ
10. Ⓐ Ⓑ Ⓒ Ⓓ Ⓔ

Use the answer spaces in the grids below if the question requires a grid-in response.

Student-Produced Responses   ONLY ANSWERS ENTERED IN THE CIRCLES IN EACH GRID WILL BE SCORED. YOU WILL
                                    NOT RECEIVE CREDIT FOR ANYTHING WRITTEN IN THE BOXES ABOVE THE CIRCLES.

6.   15.

PRACTICE SAT QUESTIONS

1. Use the graph below. $\overline{OB}$ is twice as long as $\overline{OA}$. What is the length of $\overline{OB}$?

   A. $\sqrt{13}$

   B. $\dfrac{\sqrt{13}}{2}$

   C. $2\sqrt{13}$

   D. $\sqrt{26}$

   E. $2\sqrt{26}$

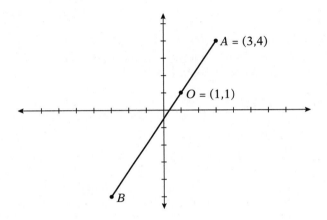

2. Points $R = (6,4)$, $Q = (4,3)$, and $P = (-2,b)$ are co-linear. What is the value of b?

   A. 4
   B. 3
   C. 2
   D. 1
   E. 0

3. Points A, B, and C are co-linear. If $\overline{AC} \cong \overline{BC}$ and $A = (-2,3)$, $B = (2,-4)$, then $C =$

   A. $\left(0, -\dfrac{1}{2}\right)$

   B. $(0,-1)$

   C. $\left(-\dfrac{1}{2}, 0\right)$

   D. $\left(\dfrac{1}{2}, 0\right)$

   E. $\left(0, \dfrac{1}{2}\right)$

4. On the graph below, $\overline{LN}$ is 4 times the length of $\overline{LM}$. How long is $\overline{LM}$?

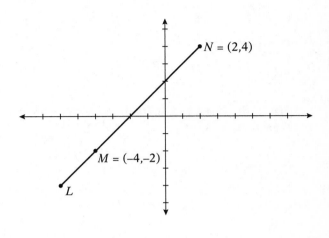

   A. $\sqrt{2}$

   B. $2\sqrt{2}$

   C. $4\sqrt{2}$

   D. $6\sqrt{2}$

   E. $8\sqrt{2}$

5. If $M = (5,2.5)$, is the midpoint of $\overline{XY}$, with $X = (-4,1)$ and $Y = (a,4)$, what is the value of a?

   A. 6
   B. 8
   C. 10
   D. 12
   E. 14

6. Let $M = (x, y)$ be the midpoint of $\overline{AB}$ with $A = (3,7)$ and $B = (-1,3)$. What is the product of x and y?

7. $\overrightarrow{PQ} \parallel \overrightarrow{XY}$. $P = (-3,6)$, $Q = (4,3)$, and $X = (-2,-5)$. Which of the following are the possible coordinates of Y?

   A. $(11,-12)$
   B. $(11,12)$
   C. $(-12,-11)$
   D. $(12,-11)$
   E. $(-12,11)$

8. What is the perimeter of the triangle with vertices $L = (1,5)$, $M = (-3,-3)$, and $N = (3,1)$?

    A. $6\sqrt{10} + 4\sqrt{13}$

    B. $6\sqrt{5} + 2\sqrt{13}$

    C. $4\sqrt{5} + 2\sqrt{18}$

    D. $8\sqrt{18}$

    E. $24\sqrt{2}$

9. $\overrightarrow{AB} \perp \overrightarrow{BC}$, and $A = (2,3)$, $B = (6,-2)$, and $C = (-5,q)$. What is the value of q?

    A. -10
    B. -10.2
    C. -10.4
    D. -10.6
    E. -10.8

10. What is the length of $\overline{AD}$ in the graph below?

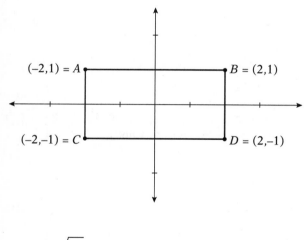

    A. $2\sqrt{10}$

    B. $\sqrt{10}$

    C. $2\sqrt{5}$

    D. $\sqrt{5}$

    E. $\sqrt{15}$

11. A is the midpoint of $\overline{PQ}$ and B is the midpoint of $\overline{XY}$. $P = (2,4)$ $Q = (6,10)$ $X = (-8,2)$, and $Y = (4,-6)$. What is the slope of $\overleftrightarrow{AB}$?

    A. $-\dfrac{2}{3}$

    B. $\dfrac{2}{3}$

    C. $\dfrac{3}{2}$

    D. $\dfrac{4}{7}$

    E. $-\dfrac{7}{4}$

12. $A = (-3,5)$ and $B = (3,-4)$. The absolute value of the slope of $\overline{AB}$ is equal to the slope of $\overline{AC}$. What are the coordinates of point C?

    A. $(8,-1)$
    B. $(-1,8)$
    C. $(-3,2)$
    D. $(2,-3)$
    E. $(-2,3)$

13. Let m_S be the slope of line S and m_T be the slope of line T. If $S \perp T$, which of the following is always true?

    I. $m_S \cdot m_T = -1$
    II. $|m_S| = |m_T|$
    III. $\dfrac{m_S}{m_T} = 1$

    A. I
    B. II
    C. III
    D. I and II
    E. I and III

14. A car travels from Al's house 10 miles south to Brad's house and then 6 miles east. What is the distance from Al's house to Brad's house?

   A. $2\sqrt{34}$
   B. 4
   C. 8
   D. $2\sqrt{17}$
   E. $4\sqrt{17}$

15. In the graph below, M is the midpoint of $\overline{AB}$, X is the midpoint of $\overline{AM}$, and Y is the midpoint of $\overline{BM}$. What is the length of $\overline{XY}$?

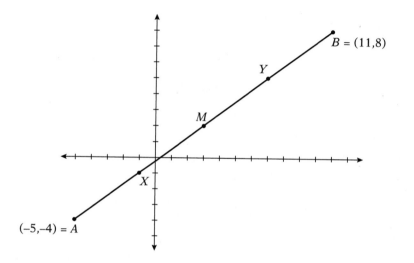

■ **EXPLAINED ANSWERS**

1. *Answer:* **C**

   Find the length of $\overline{OA}$.

   $$OA = \sqrt{(3-1)^2 + (4-1)^2} = \sqrt{(2)^2 + (3)^2} = \sqrt{4+9} = \sqrt{13}.$$

   Multiply OA by 2. $OB = 2\sqrt{13}$.

2. *Answer:* **E**

   First find the slope of $\overrightarrow{RQ}$.

   $$m_{\overline{RQ}} = \frac{3-4}{4-6} = \frac{-1}{-2} = \frac{1}{2}$$

   R, Q, and P are colinear, so the slope of $\overrightarrow{RQ}$ equals the slope of $\overrightarrow{RP}$. That means,

   $$\frac{4-b}{6-(-2)} = \frac{4-b}{8} = \frac{1}{2} \Rightarrow 8 - 2b = 8$$

   $-2b = 0 \Rightarrow b = 0$.

3. *Answer:* **A**

   $\overline{AC} \cong \overline{BC}$, and they are colinear. That means C is the midpoint of $\overline{AB}$.

   $$C = \left(\frac{-2+2}{2}, \frac{3+(-4)}{2}\right) = \left(0, -\frac{1}{2}\right).$$

4. *Answer:* **B**

   Find the length of $\overline{MN}$.

   $$MN = \sqrt{[2-(-4)]^2 + [4-(-2)]^2} = \sqrt{6^2 + 6^2}$$

   $$\sqrt{36+36} = \sqrt{72} = \sqrt{2 \cdot 36} = 6\sqrt{2}.$$

   Because $\overline{LN}$ is 4 times the length of $\overline{LM}$, if $\overline{LN}$ were broken into 4 equal pieces, one piece is $\overline{LM}$, and $\overline{MN}$ makes up the other three pieces. Therefore, $3 \cdot LM = MN$

   $$LM = \frac{MN}{3} = \frac{6\sqrt{2}}{3} = 2\sqrt{2}.$$

5. *Answer:* **E**

   Write an equation for the x coordinate of the midpoint.

   $$\frac{-4+a}{2} = 5$$

   Solve for a. $-4 + a = 10 \Rightarrow a = 14$

6. *Answer:* **5**

   Find the coordinates for the midpoint of M.

   $$M = \left(\frac{3+(-1)}{2}, \frac{7+3}{2}\right) = \left(\frac{2}{2}, \frac{10}{2}\right) = (1,5)$$

   Substitute $x = 1$, $y = 5$. $(x, y) \Rightarrow x = 1, y = 5 \Rightarrow x \cdot y = 5$

7. *Answer:* **D**

The lines are parallel, so the slopes are equal.
Find the slopes.

$$m_{\overline{PQ}} = \frac{3-6}{4-(-3)} = \frac{-3}{7} \text{ and } m_{\overline{XY}} = \frac{-11-(-5)}{12-(-2)} = \frac{-6}{14} = -\frac{3}{7}.$$

Therefore, $Y = (12, -11)$.

8. *Answer:* **B**

Find the lengths of each side of the triangle.

$$LM = \sqrt{(-3-1)^2 + (-3-5)^2} = \sqrt{(-4)^2 + (-8)^2}$$

$$\sqrt{16+64} = \sqrt{80} = \sqrt{16 \cdot 5} = 4\sqrt{5}$$

$$LN = \sqrt{(3-1)^2 + (1-5)^2} = \sqrt{(2)^2 + (-4)^2}$$

$$\sqrt{4+16} = \sqrt{20} = \sqrt{4 \cdot 5} = 2\sqrt{5}$$

$$MN = \sqrt{[3-(-3)]^2 + [1-(-3)]^2} = \sqrt{(6)^2 + (4)^2}$$

$$\sqrt{36+16} = \sqrt{52} = \sqrt{4 \cdot 13} = 2\sqrt{3}$$

The perimeter is $4\sqrt{5} + 2\sqrt{5} + 2\sqrt{13} = 6\sqrt{5} + 2\sqrt{13}$.

9. *Answer:* **E**

Use the slope formulas for $\overline{AB}$ and $\overline{BC}$.

$$m_{\overline{AB}} = \frac{-2-3}{6-2} = \frac{-5}{4}.$$

The segments AB and BC are perpendicular. That means the products of the slopes is -1.

$$m_{\overline{BC}} = \frac{4}{5}$$

$$\frac{q-(-2)}{-5-6} \Rightarrow \frac{4}{5} = \frac{q+2}{-11}$$

$$-44 = 5q + 10 \Rightarrow -54 = 5q \Rightarrow$$

$$q = 10.8$$

10. *Answer:* **C**

Use the distance formula to find the length of $\overline{AD}$.

$$AD = \sqrt{(-1-1)^2 + [2-(-2)]^2} = \sqrt{(-2)^2 + (4)^2}$$

$$\sqrt{4+16} = \sqrt{20} = \sqrt{4 \cdot 5} = 2\sqrt{5}$$

11. **Answer: C**

Find the coordinates of A and B.

$$A = \left(\frac{2+6}{2}, \frac{4+10}{2}\right) = (4,7) \text{ and } B = \left(\frac{-8+4}{2}, \frac{2+(-6)}{2}\right) = (-2,-2)$$

Use the coordinates to find the slope of $\overline{AB}$.

$$m_{\overline{AB}} = \frac{-2-7}{-2-4} = \frac{-9}{-6} = \frac{3}{2}$$

12. **Answer: B**

Use the slope of $\overline{AB}$ to find the slope of AC.

$$\text{Slope } \overline{AB} = \frac{-4-5}{3-(-3)} = \frac{-9}{6} = -\frac{3}{2}$$

$\text{Slope } \overline{AC} = \dfrac{3}{2}$ because the slope of $\overline{AC}$ is the absolute value of the slope of $\overline{AB}$.

Write slope of $\overline{AC}$ equal to the slope formula of $\overline{AC}$

$$\frac{3}{2} = \frac{y-5}{x-(-3)}$$

That means $y - 5 = 3$ and $x + 3 = 2$ and $y = 8$ and $x = -1$.
$C = (-1,8)$.

13. **Answer: A**

I. True. The product of the slopes of perpendicular lines is -1.
II. False. The absolute values of the slopes of perpendicular lines are reciprocals.
III. False. The product of the slopes is negative, so the quotient must be negative.

14. **Answer: A**

Let Al's house $= A = (0,0)$ and Brad's house $= B = (10,-6)$.
Find the length of $\overline{AB}$

$$AB = \sqrt{(10-0)^2 + (-6-0)^2} = \sqrt{10^2 + (-6)^2} = \sqrt{100+36} = \sqrt{136} = \sqrt{4 \cdot 34} = 2\sqrt{34}.$$

15. **Answer: 10**

Notice that XY is half the length of AB. $XY = \dfrac{AB}{2}$.
Find the length of $\overline{AB}$.

$$AB = \sqrt{[11-(-5)]^2 + [8-(-4)]^2} = \sqrt{(16)^2 + (12)^2} = \sqrt{400} = 20.$$

Divide AB by 2. $20 \div 2 = 10$, so $XY = 10$.

CHAPTER 10

FUNCTIONS AND MATHEMATICAL MODELS

Functions are the focus of many SAT questions. Important function topics include the shapes of functions, how to calculate the value of a function, and shifting functions on the coordinate plane. This section reviews all the important function topics. Begin with the mathematics review and then complete and correct the practice problems. There are 2 Solved SAT Problems and 21 Practice SAT Questions with answer explanations.

A **Function,** $y = f(x)$, is a mathematical relation where each element of the <u>Domain</u>, x, produces at least one element of the <u>Range</u>, y, and no two x values produce the same y value. Below you can see the graph of several different functions.

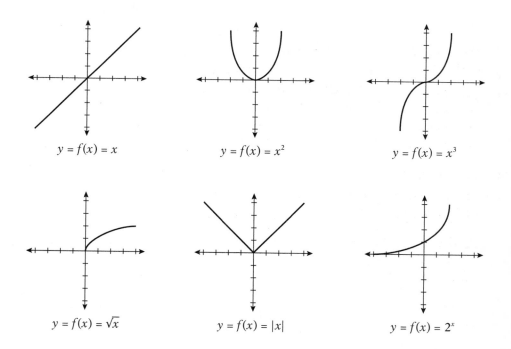

$y = f(x) = x$ $y = f(x) = x^2$ $y = f(x) = x^3$

$y = f(x) = \sqrt{x}$ $y = f(x) = |x|$ $y = f(x) = 2^x$

A **Linear Function** is a special type of function in the form $y = f(x) = mx + b$ whose graph is a straight line on the coordinate plane. The m represents the slope of the line, and the b represents the *y-intercept*, where the graph crosses the *y*-axis.

Example:

Find the linear function $y = f(x)$ given that $f(-2) = 10$ and $f(3) = -5$.
First, find the slope.

$$m = \frac{y_2 - y_1}{x_2 - x_1} = \frac{f(3) - f(-2)}{3 - (-2)} = \frac{-5 - 10}{3 - (-2)} = \frac{-15}{5} = -3$$

Now find the *y-intercept*, **b.** To do this, choose one of the two points and substitute the coordinates for x and y. It does not matter which point you choose.

$$y = f(x) = -3x + b \Rightarrow -5 = -3(3) + b \Rightarrow -5 = -9 + b \Rightarrow 4 = b$$

or

$$y = f(x) = -3x + b \Rightarrow 10 = -3(-2) + b \Rightarrow 10 = 6 + b \Rightarrow 4 = b$$

The equation of this line is $y = f(x) = -3x + 4$.

The graph of a function can be **shifted** in the coordinate plane. Here are the basic rules for shifting graphs.

> $-f(x)$ will flip the graph across the x-axis.
> $f(x + h)$ will shift the original graph to the left h units (x decreases).
> $f(x - h)$ will shift the original graph to the right h units (x increases).
> $f(x) + k$ will shift the original graph up k units (y increases).
> $f(x) - k$ will shift the original graph down k units (y decreases).

Example:

What must be done to the graph of $f(x) = x^3$ to move it so that $f(x)$ will be "placed on top" of the graph of $g(x) = -(x - 2)^3 - 4$?
$f(x)$ must be

- flipped across the x-axis.
- shifted right 2 units.
- shifted down 4 units.

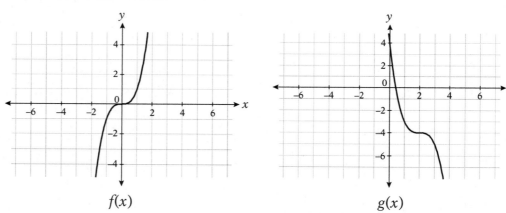

$f(x)$ $g(x)$

Example:

$f(x) = x^2 + 5, f(-2) =$

Substitute and solve.

$$f(-2) = (-2)^2 + 5 = 4 + 5 = 9.$$

Example:

$f(x) = 2^x + 5x, f(3) =$

Substitute and solve.

$$f(3) = 2^3 + 5(3) = 8 + 15 = 23.$$

Example:

$f(x) = x^3 - 4x$ and $g(x) = 2x + 5$, $f[g(2)] =$

Substitute.

$g(2) = 2(2) - 7 = -3 \Rightarrow$

Substitute -3 to $g(2)$ and solve.

$f[g(2)] = f(-3) = (-3)^3 - 4(-3)$

$-27 + 12 = -15.$

Example:

What is the Domain (x value) and Range (y value) of $f(x) = -x^2 + 5$?
Any value of x can be used in this function.

Domain = All real numbers.

The largest possible value of $-x^2$ is 0, therefore the largest value for $-x^2 + 5$ is 5.

Range = All real numbers less than or equal to 5.

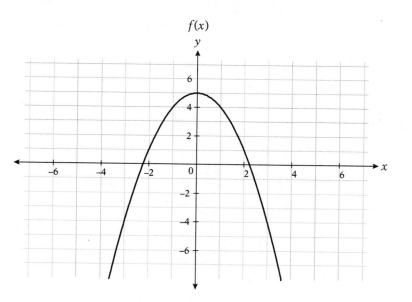

Example:

What is the Domain and Range of $f(x) = \sqrt{x - 3} + 4$?

The square root of a negative number cannot be found on the xy coordinate plane.

$x - 3 \geq 0 \Rightarrow x \geq 3.$

Domain = All real numbers greater than or equal to 3.
Range = All real numbers greater than or equal to 4.

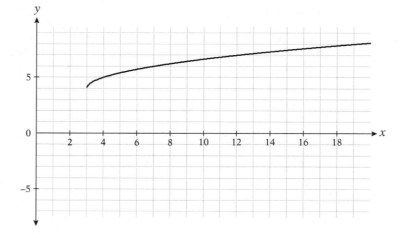

Example:

What is the Domain and Range of $f(x) = \dfrac{1}{x}$?

The denominator of the fraction cannot be 0.

Domain = All real numbers greater except 0.

As x takes on different values it is impossible for $f(x) = 0$.

Range = All real numbers except 0.

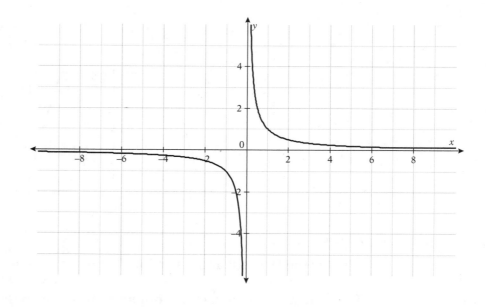

Functions and Graphs of Functions can be used to **model** such real-life situations as economic growth, population growth, crop growth, bacterial growth and decay, decay of radioactive substances, and so forth.

Example:

The original cost of a car was $20,000. The car decreased in value $1,200 every year. Write an equation and draw a graph that models the price of the car, *y*, based on the number of years after it has been purchased, *x*. Subtract $1,200 each year.

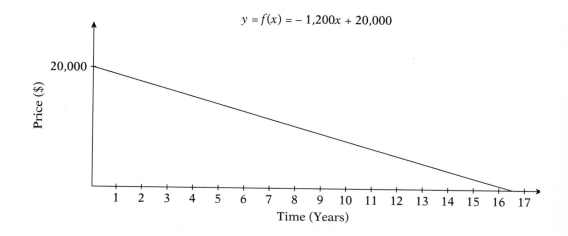

$$y = f(x) = -1,200x + 20,000$$

Example:

In an experiment, there were initially 5 bacteria. The number of bacteria doubles every hour. Write an equation and draw a graph that models the number of bacteria, *y*, based on the number of hours (*x*) that have passed.

Time passed	Number of Bacteria
0 hours	5
1 hour	$5 \cdot 2 = 10$
2 hours	$(5 \cdot 2) \cdot 2 = 5 \cdot 2^2 = 20$
3 hours	$(5 \cdot 2^2) \cdot 2 = 5 \cdot 2^3 = 40$
4 hours	$(5 \cdot 2^3) \cdot 2 = 5 \cdot 2^4 = 80$

After each hour, multiply the previous value by 2 to get the next value, $y = f(x) = 5 \cdot 2^x$.

Essentially the number of bacteria after each hour forms a geometric sequence where 5 is the first number in the sequence, and 2 is the number being multiplied to get from one number in the sequence to the next number in the sequence. {5,10,20,40,80, . . .}

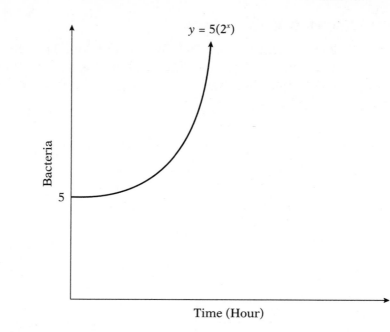

Practice Questions

1. Find the slope of the linear function $f(x)$ given that $f(4) = 8$ and $f(-6) = 2$.
2. What must be done to the graph of $f(x) = \sqrt{x}$ to move it on top of the graph of $h(x) = \sqrt{x + 3} - 7$?
3. $f(x) = 3^x + x^2 - 4x$, $f(2) =$
4. What are the domain and range of $f(x) = -|x + 4| - 3$?
5. The initial population of deer is 50. If the deer increase by 25 each year write an equation that will show the number of deer, y, after x years.

Practice Answers

1. $m = \dfrac{3}{5}$.

2. $f(x) = \sqrt{x}$ must be shifted left 3 units and down 7 units to move it on top of the graph of $h(x) = \sqrt{x + 3} - 7$.
3. $f(2) = 3^2 + (2)^2 - 4(2) = 9 + 4 - 8 = 5$.
4. Domain = All real numbers.
   Range = All real numbers less than or equal to -3.
5. $y = 25x + 50$.

SOLVED SAT PROBLEMS

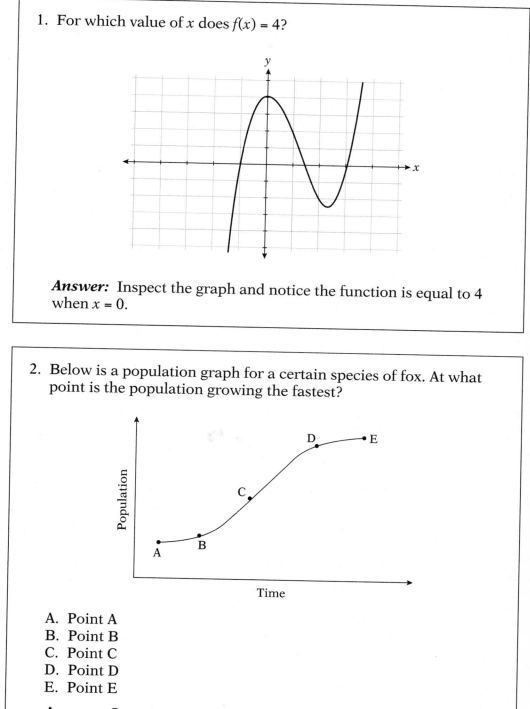

1. For which value of x does $f(x) = 4$?

Answer: Inspect the graph and notice the function is equal to 4 when $x = 0$.

2. Below is a population graph for a certain species of fox. At what point is the population growing the fastest?

A. Point A
B. Point B
C. Point C
D. Point D
E. Point E

Answer: C

The graph is steepest at Point C. Therefore Point C is where the population is growing the fastest.

FUNCTIONS AND MATHEMATICAL MODELS PRACTICE SAT QUESTIONS

ANSWER SHEET

Choose the correct answer.
If no choices are given, grid the answers in the section at the bottom of the page.

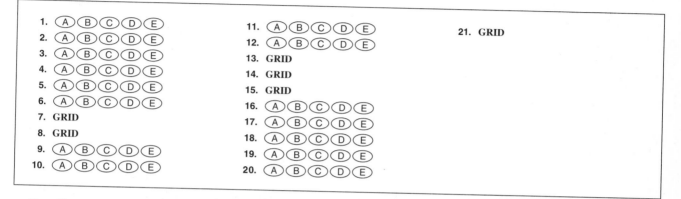

1. Ⓐ Ⓑ Ⓒ Ⓓ Ⓔ
2. Ⓐ Ⓑ Ⓒ Ⓓ Ⓔ
3. Ⓐ Ⓑ Ⓒ Ⓓ Ⓔ
4. Ⓐ Ⓑ Ⓒ Ⓓ Ⓔ
5. Ⓐ Ⓑ Ⓒ Ⓓ Ⓔ
6. Ⓐ Ⓑ Ⓒ Ⓓ Ⓔ
7. GRID
8. GRID
9. Ⓐ Ⓑ Ⓒ Ⓓ Ⓔ
10. Ⓐ Ⓑ Ⓒ Ⓓ Ⓔ

11. Ⓐ Ⓑ Ⓒ Ⓓ Ⓔ
12. Ⓐ Ⓑ Ⓒ Ⓓ Ⓔ
13. GRID
14. GRID
15. GRID
16. Ⓐ Ⓑ Ⓒ Ⓓ Ⓔ
17. Ⓐ Ⓑ Ⓒ Ⓓ Ⓔ
18. Ⓐ Ⓑ Ⓒ Ⓓ Ⓔ
19. Ⓐ Ⓑ Ⓒ Ⓓ Ⓔ
20. Ⓐ Ⓑ Ⓒ Ⓓ Ⓔ

21. GRID

Use the answer spaces in the grids below if the question requires a grid-in response.

Student-Produced Responses — ONLY ANSWERS ENTERED IN THE CIRCLES IN EACH GRID WILL BE SCORED. YOU WILL NOT RECEIVE CREDIT FOR ANYTHING WRITTEN IN THE BOXES ABOVE THE CIRCLES.

7.

8.

13.

14.

15.

21.

PRACTICE SAT QUESTIONS

1. $f(x) = 2x^3 - 3x^2 + 5, f(4) =$
   A. 81
   B. 82
   C. 83
   D. 84
   E. 85

2. If $f(x)$ is a linear function such that $f(2) = 5$ and $f(4) = 13, f(x) =$
   A. $f(x) = 3x - 4$
   B. $f(x) = 4x - 3$
   C. $f(x) = 4x + 3$
   D. $f(x) = \dfrac{1}{4}x + \dfrac{9}{2}$
   E. $f(x) = \dfrac{1}{4}x - \dfrac{9}{2}$

3. A truck rental company charges $20 for a truck rental plus $0.15 for every mile over 100 miles. Which of the following graphs best represents the cost for renting a truck?

A.
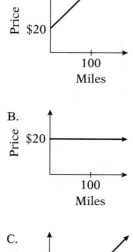

B.

C.
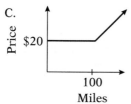

D.
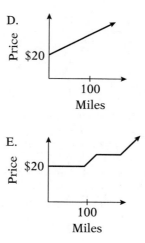

E.

4. The graph of $f(x)$ is seen below. Which of the following choices is the graph of $f(x - 2) + 4$?

Graph of $f(x)$

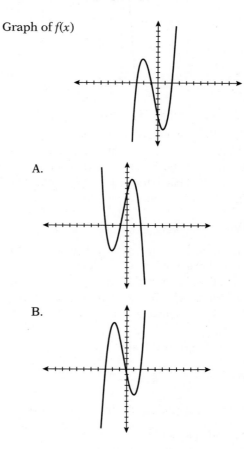

A.

B.

C.

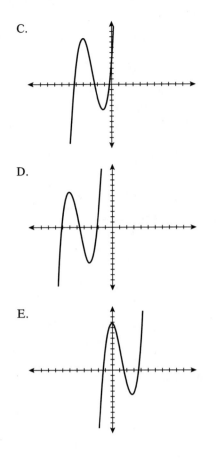

D.

E.

10. The equation of a line is $y = \dfrac{2}{3}x - 6$. What is the equation of a line perpendicular to this line and with the same y-intercept?

A. $y = \dfrac{2}{3}x + 6$

B. $y = \dfrac{2}{3}x - \dfrac{1}{6}$

C. $y = \dfrac{3}{2}x - 6$

D. $y = -\dfrac{2}{3}x + 6$

E. $y = -\dfrac{3}{2}x - 6$

11. The graph of $f(x) = x^3 - 2$ is shown below. Which of the following choice is the graph of $g(x) = (x + 3)^3 - 6$?

Graph of $f(x) = x^3 - 2$

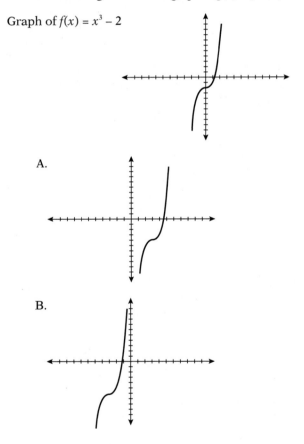

A.

B.

5. What is the range of $f(x) = (x + 2)^2 - 3$?

A. All real numbers greater than or equal to 3
B. All real numbers greater than or equal to 2
C. All real numbers greater than or equal to −3
D. All real numbers greater than or equal to −2
E. All real numbers greater than or equal to −1

6. What is the domain of $f(x) = \sqrt{x + 3} - 7$?

A. All real numbers greater than or equal to 3
B. All real numbers greater than or equal to 2
C. All real numbers greater than or equal to −3
D. All real numbers greater than or equal to −2
E. All real numbers greater than or equal to −1

7. $f(x) = 2x - 4$. If $f(x) = 8$ then $x =$

8. $f(x) = 3x^2 - 7$ and $g(x) = 2x^3 - 4x + 2$. $g[f(2)] =$

9. What is the range of the function $f(x) = \dfrac{2}{x - 2}$?

A. All real numbers greater than 0
B. All real numbers greater than 2
C. All real numbers except 0
D. All real numbers except 2
E. All real numbers less than 0

C.

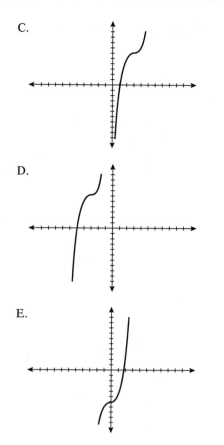

D.

E.

B.

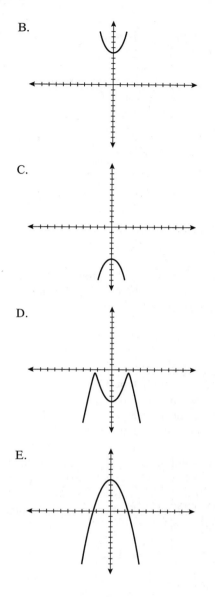

C.

D.

E.

12. The graph of $f(x)$ is shown below. Which of the following choices is the graph of $|f(x)|$?

Graph of $f(x)$

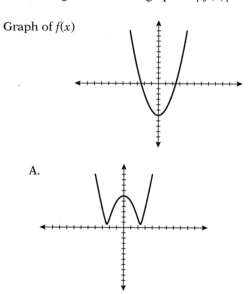

A.

13. Carolyn works at an accounting firm. Her starting salary was $1,000 per week. She received a 7% raise each year. At this raise increase, what will her weekly salary be, rounded to the nearest dollar, after 10 years?

14. The slope of the line below is $\frac{3}{2}$. What is the y-intercept?

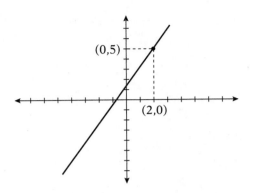

15. The fish population in a lake triples every year for 6 years. If the final population is 3,645, what was the initial fish population?

16. What is the domain of $f(x) = \dfrac{4}{x^2 + x - 6}$?

   A. All real numbers except 4
   B. All real numbers except 0
   C. All real numbers except 6
   D. All real numbers except 4 and 6
   E. All real numbers except −3 and 2

17. The cost of operating a Frisbee company in the first year is $10,000 plus $2 for each Frisbee. Assuming the company sells every Frisbee it makes in the first year for $7, how many Frisbees must the company sell to break even?

   A. 1,000
   B. 1,500
   C. 2,000
   D. 2,500
   E. 3,000

18. The graph of $f(x)$ is shown below, $f(3) =$

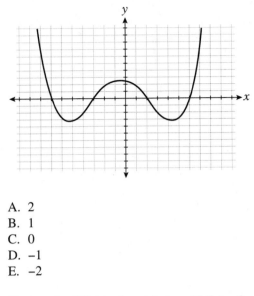

   A. 2
   B. 1
   C. 0
   D. −1
   E. −2

19. The graph of $f(x)$ is shown below. If $f(x) = 0$, $x =$

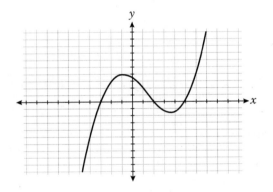

   A. 3
   B. 2
   C. 0
   D. −1
   E. −2

20. The water level in a bay changes with the tides. The tides go through a full cycle every 12 hours, with one low and one high tide. Which of the following graphs shows the water level in the bay during a 24-hour period starting with the high tide?

21. $f(5) = 15$ and $g(x) = f(x + 2) - 5$. $g(3) =$

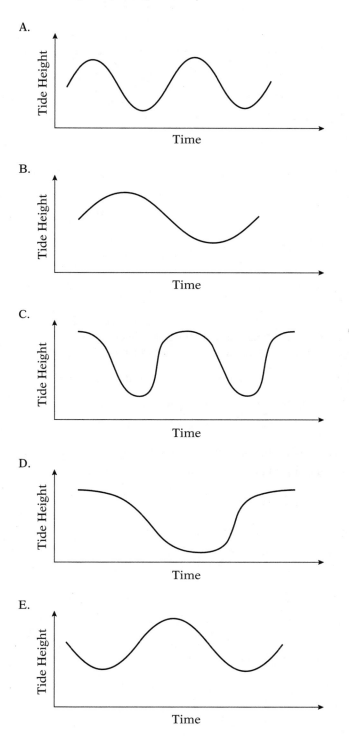

A.

B.

C.

D.

E.

▬ EXPLAINED ANSWERS

1. *Answer:* **E**

   We know $f(x) = 2x^3 - 3x^2 + 5$

   Substitute 4 for x. $f(4) = 2(4)^3 - 3(4)^2 + 5 = 128 - 48 + 5 = 85$.

2. *Answer:* **B**

   – Find the slope.
   – Find the y-intercept.
   – Substitute the slope and the y-intercept in the equation for the line and solve.

   $$m = \frac{13 - 5}{4 - 2} = \frac{8}{2} = 4$$

   $$f(x) = mx + b \Rightarrow f(x) = 4x + b$$

   $$f(2) = 4(2) + b$$

   $$5 = 4(2) + b \Rightarrow 5 = 4(2) + b$$

   $$5 = 8 + b \Rightarrow -3 = b$$

   $$f(x) = 4x - 3$$

3. *Answer:* **C**

   The truck rental costs \$20 for the first 100 miles. Therefore, for the first 100 miles, there will be no change in the cost of renting the truck which is modeled by a horizontal line. After the first 100 miles the charge will be \$0.15 per mile, a constant increase of \$0.15 per mile, which is modeled by a line with a positive slope.

4. *Answer:* **E**

   The graph of $f(x - 2) + 4$ is formed by shifting $f(x)$ to the right 2 units and then up 4 units.

5. *Answer:* **C**

   The smallest y-value of $(x + 2)^2$ is 0. Therefore, the smallest y-value that $f(x) = (x + 2)^2 - 3$ is -3. You can use a graphing calculator, to graph $f(x) = (x + 2)^2 - 3$. As you can see below, the value y never goes below -3.

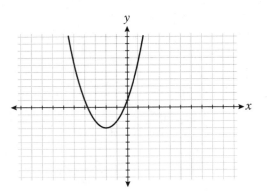

6. ***Answer:*** **C**

   The square root of a negative number cannot be found in the xy coordinate plane. So $x + 3$ must be greater than or equal to zero. That means $x \geq -3$. Use a graphing calculator to graph $f(x) = \sqrt{x + 3} - 7$. As you can see below, the value x is never less than -3.

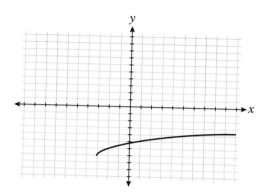

7. ***Answer:*** **6**

   Solve for x.

   $$f(x) = 2x - 4 = 8. \Rightarrow 2x = 12 \Rightarrow x = 6$$

8. ***Answer:*** **232**

   Solve for $f(2)$.

   $$f(x) = 3x^2 - 7 \Rightarrow f(2) = 3(2)^2 - 7 = 12 - 7 = 5$$

   Now find $g[f(2)]$.

   $$g(x) = 2x^3 - 4x + 2.$$

   $$g[f(2)] = g(5) = 2(5)^3 - 4(5) + 2 = 250 - 20 + 2 = 232.$$

9. ***Answer:*** **C**

   The numerator is 2; so y cannot equal 0.

10. ***Answer:*** **E**

    Perpendicular lines have slopes that are opposite reciprocals. Therefore, the slope of the perpendicular line is $-\dfrac{3}{2}$. The y-intercept is also -6 so, $y = -\dfrac{3}{2}x - 6$.

11. ***Answer:*** **B**

    The graph of $f(x) = x^3 - 2$ must be shifted left 3 units and down 4 units to create the graph of $g(x) = (x + 3)^3 - 6$.

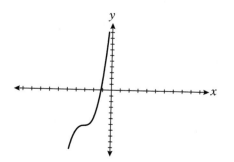

12. ***Answer: A***

    Wherever $f(x)$ is positive, the graphs of $f(x)$ and $|f(x)|$ are the same. Wherever $f(x)$ is negative, the graph $|f(x)|$ is flipped over the x-axis, as shown in choice A.

13. ***Answer: 1,967***

    Every year there is a 7% increase in the previous year's salary. Multiply the previous years' salary by 1.07.

    Write a formula where 10 is the number of years: $S = 1{,}000(1.07)^{10} \approx \$1{,}967$.

14. ***Answer: 2***

    The slope of the line is $\dfrac{3}{2}$, and the point (2,5) is on the graph

    Substitute $m = \dfrac{3}{2}$, $x = 2$, $y = 5$ in the equation for a line. Solve for b.

    $$y = mx + b \Rightarrow 5 = \frac{3}{2}\left(2\right) + b \Rightarrow 5 = 3 + b \Rightarrow 2 = b.$$

15. ***Answer: 5***

    The fish population triples every year. Therefore, to calculate the population after 5 years we must divide the fish population after 6 years by 3. To calculate the fish population after 4 years we must divide the fish population after 5 years by 3. Continue this process to get the initial population, as shown in the table provided below

Years	Population After Number of Years
6	3,645
5	(3,645 ÷ 3) = 1,215
4	(1,215 ÷ 3) = 405
3	(405 ÷ 3) = 135
2	(135 ÷ 3) = 45
1	(45 ÷ 3) = 15
0(Initial)	(15 ÷ 3) = 5

or

You can write an exponential equation.

3^6 (Initial Amount) = 3,645.

729 (Initial Amount) = 3,645

Initial Amount = 5

16. *Answer:* **E**

    The denominator cannot equal 0.

    Write the denominator not equal to 0 to find when that is.

    $$f(x) = \frac{4}{x^2 + x - 6}$$

    so write $x^2 + x - 6 \neq 0$

    $(x + 3)(x - 2) \neq 0 \Rightarrow x \neq -3$ and $x \neq 2$.

17. *Answer:* **C**

    The expression for operating the company in the first year is $2(f) + 10,000$, where f is the number of Frisbees. The expression for the revenue is $7f$.

    The break-even point occurs when revenue equals cost. $7f = 2f + 10,000$

    Solve for f. $5f = 10,000 \Rightarrow f = 2,000$ must be sold to break even.

18. *Answer:* **E**

    It can be seen from the graph that when $x = 3$, $y = f(3) = 0$.

19. *Answer:* **B**

    It can be seen from the graph that $y = f(x) = 0$ when $x = -3$, $x = 2$, and $x = 5$.

    $x = 2$ is the only correct answer given as a choice.

20. *Answer:* **B**

    The graph must start at the highest point, drop down to the lowest point, and then cycle back up to the highest point. This 12-hour cycle repeats to make 24 hours.

21. *Answer:* **10**

    So $g(x) = f(x + 2) - 5$

    Substitute 3 for x. $g(3) = f(3 + 2) - 5$

    Substitute 15 for $f(5)$. $f(5) - 5 = 15 - 5 = 10$.

    That means $g(3) = 10$.

CHAPTER 11

TRIANGLES

You know most of the triangle facts tested on the SAT, but you may still have to relearn many of them. This chapter reviews all of the triangle facts tested on the SAT. Begin with the mathematics review and then complete and correct the practice problems. There are 2 Solved SAT Problems and 26 Practice SAT Questions with answer explanations.

A *triangle* is a three-sided polygon.

Area of triangle: $A = \dfrac{1}{2} \times b \times h$.

Example:

What is the area of the figures below?

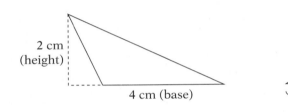

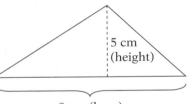

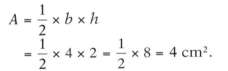

$A = \dfrac{1}{2} \times b \times h$

$\quad = \dfrac{1}{2} \times 4 \times 2 = \dfrac{1}{2} \times 8 = 4 \text{ cm}^2.$

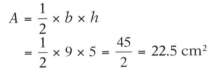

$A = \dfrac{1}{2} \times b \times h$

$\quad = \dfrac{1}{2} \times 9 \times 5 = \dfrac{45}{2} = 22.5 \text{ cm}^2$

Example:

A triangle has a height of 15 in and an area 45 in². What is the length of the base of the triangle?

$A = \dfrac{1}{2} \times b \times h \quad \Rightarrow \quad 45 = \dfrac{1}{2} \times b \times 15 \quad \Rightarrow \quad 90 = b \times 15 \quad \Rightarrow \quad 4 \text{ in} = b$

The *Triangle Inequality Theorem* states that the sum of the length of any two sides of a triangle is greater than the length of the third side.

Example:

What are the possible values of x?

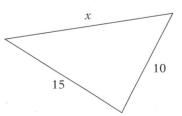

The third side of a triangle has these two characteristics.

– It is less than the sum of the other two sides, $x < 15 + 10$, $x < 25$.
– It is greater than the difference of the other two sides $x > 15 - 10$, $x > 5$.

That means $5 < x < 25$

The largest angle in a triangle is across from the longest side.
The smallest angle in a triangle is across from the shortest side.

Example:

List the angles from smallest to largest.
$m\angle C < m\angle A < m\angle B$

The sum of the interior angles of a triangle is 180°.

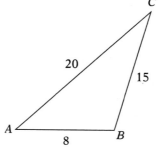

Example:

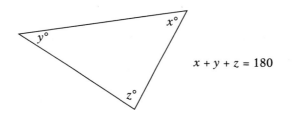

$x + y + z = 180$

What is the value of x?

Sum of the angle measures equals 180.

$x + 2x + 60 = 180$

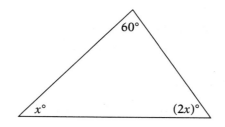

Solve for x. $3x + 60 = 180$

$3x = 120 \implies x = 40$.

The measure of the exterior angle of a triangle is equal to the sum of the two remote interior angles. The remote interior angles are the two angles most distant from the exterior angle.

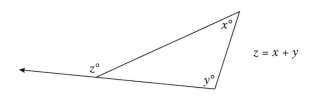

Example:

What is the value of x?

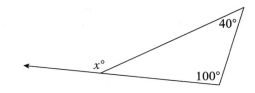

$x = 100 + 40 = 140.$

Example:

What is the value of x?

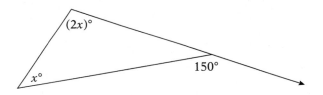

$x + 2x = 150 \quad \Rightarrow \quad 3x = 150 \quad \Rightarrow \quad x = 50.$

SIMILAR TRIANGLES

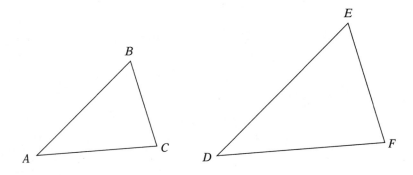

Similar Triangles have the same shape.

Each corresponding pair of angles has the same measure:

$m\angle A = m\angle D \qquad m\angle B = m\angle E \qquad m\angle C = m\angle F$

The ratios of corresponding sides are proportional.

$$\frac{AB}{DE} = \frac{BC}{EF} = \frac{CA}{FD}$$

Example:

In the similar triangle seen on page 124, $AB = 5$, $BC = 3$, $EF = 9$, what is the length of $\overline{DE}$?

$$\frac{AB}{DE} = \frac{BC}{EF} \quad \Rightarrow \quad \frac{5}{DE} = \frac{3}{9}$$

$$3(DE) = 45 \quad \Rightarrow \quad DE = 15$$

Isosceles Triangle—a triangle with at least two congruent sides and two congruent angles, called base angles, which are opposite the congruent sides. The dotted line in both figures is the height. The height of an isosceles triangle bisects both the vertex and the base, and is perpendicular to the base.

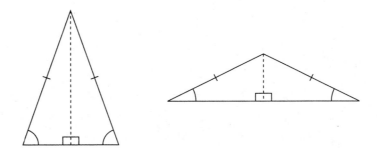

Equilateral Triangle—a triangle with three sides congruent, and all three angles congruent. Each angle measures 60°. The dotted line in the figure is the height. In an equilateral triangle, the height bisects both the vertex and the base and is perpendicular to the base.

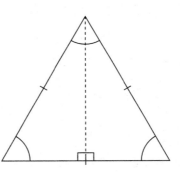

Right Triangle—a triangle with one right angle and two acute angles. The sum of the acute angles is 90°.

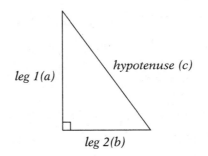

Pythagorean Theorem states that in a right triangle, the sum of the square of the legs is equal to the square of the hypotenuse.

$$\left(\text{leg 1}\right)^2 + \left(\text{leg 2}\right)^2 = \left(\text{hypotenuse}\right)^2$$

$$a^2 \quad + \quad b^2 \quad = \quad c^2$$

Example:

What is the value of x?

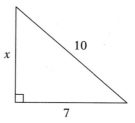

$$x^2 + 7^2 = 10^2 \quad \Rightarrow \quad x^2 + 49 = 100 \quad \Rightarrow \quad x^2 = 51 \quad \Rightarrow \quad x = \sqrt{51}$$

A 3-4-5 Right Triangle is a right triangle where the ratio of leg 1 : leg 2 : hypotenuse = 3 : 4 : 5.

This ratio meets the requirements of the Pythagorean Theorem $3^2 + 4^2 = 9 + 16 = 25 = 5^2$.

Example:

What is the value of x?

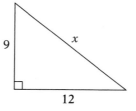

$$3 : 4 : 5 = 9 : 12 : x = \left(3 \cdot 3\right) : \left(3 \cdot 4\right) : x \quad \Rightarrow \quad x = 3 \cdot 5 = 15$$

Or use the Pythagorean Theorem.

$$9^2 + 12^2 = x^2 \quad \Rightarrow \quad 81 + 144 = 225 = x^2 \quad \Rightarrow \quad 15 = x$$

A 5-12-13 Right Triangle is a right triangle where the ratio of leg 1 : leg 2 : hypotenuse = 5 : 12 : 13.

This ratio meets the requirements of the Pythagorean Theorem $5^2 + 12^2 = 25 + 144 = 169 = 13^2$.

Example:

What is the value of x?

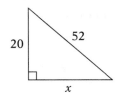

$$5:12:13 = 20:x:52 = (4 \cdot 5):x:(4 \cdot 13) \quad \text{so} \quad x = 4 \cdot 12 = 48$$

Or, use the Pythagorean Theorem.

$$x^2 + 20^2 = 52^2 \quad \Rightarrow \quad x^2 + 400 = 2,704 \quad \Rightarrow \quad x^2 = 2,304 \quad \Rightarrow \quad x = 48$$

A 45°-45°-90° right triangle has a special relationship among the sides. If the sides across from the 45° angles are x, the side across from the 90° angle is $x\sqrt{2}$.

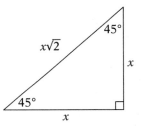

A 30°-60°-90° right triangle also has a special relationship among the sides. If the side across from the 30° angle is x, the side across from the 60° angle is $x\sqrt{3}$ and the side across from the 90° angle is $2x$.

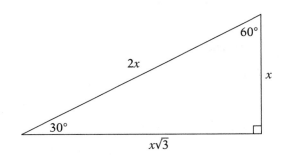

Trigonometry can be used to solve for missing pieces of a triangle. The acronym **SOH CAH TOA** is often used to help remember the rules for each trigonometric function. No problems on the SAT require you to use trigonometry. It is simply another way to solve problems involving 45°-45°-90° and 30°-60°-90° right triangles.

$$\text{Sin}\theta = \frac{\text{Opposite}}{\text{Hypotenuse}} = \frac{O}{H} \quad \text{Cos}\theta = \frac{\text{Adjacent}}{\text{Hypotenuse}} = \frac{A}{H} \quad \text{Tan}\theta = \frac{\text{Opposite}}{\text{Adjacent}} = \frac{O}{A}$$

Certain angles are useful to memorize Sinθ, Cosθ, and Tanθ

	30°	**45°**	**60°**
Sine	$\dfrac{1}{2}$	$\dfrac{1}{\sqrt{2}} = \dfrac{\sqrt{2}}{2}$	$\dfrac{\sqrt{3}}{2}$
Cosine	$\dfrac{\sqrt{3}}{2}$	$\dfrac{1}{\sqrt{2}} = \dfrac{\sqrt{2}}{2}$	$\dfrac{1}{2}$
Tangent	$\dfrac{1}{\sqrt{3}} = \dfrac{\sqrt{3}}{3}$	1	$\sqrt{3}$

Example:

What is the value of x and y?

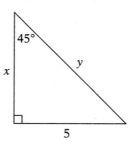

Using 45°-45°-90°, it is clear that $x = 5$, and $y = 5\sqrt{2}$ or

$$\tan(45°) = \frac{5}{x} \quad \Rightarrow \quad x = \frac{5}{\tan(45°)} = 5$$

$$\sin(45°) = \frac{5}{y} \quad \Rightarrow \quad y = \frac{5}{\sin(45°)} = 5\sqrt{2} \approx 7.0711 \text{ (calc approx.)}.$$

Example:

What is the value of x and y?

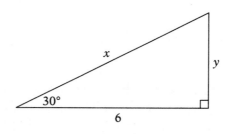

Using 30° -60° -90° $\Rightarrow$ $y\sqrt{3} = 6$ $\Rightarrow$ $y = \dfrac{6}{\sqrt{3}}$

$$y = \frac{6 \times \sqrt{3}}{\sqrt{3} \times \sqrt{3}} = \frac{6\sqrt{3}}{3} = 2\sqrt{3}$$

Because $y = 2\sqrt{3}$ $\Rightarrow$ $x = 2 \cdot (2\sqrt{3}) = 4\sqrt{3}$

or use trigonometry

$$\tan(30°) = \frac{y}{6} \implies \tan(30°) \times 6 = y \implies y = 2\sqrt{3}.$$ (Appears on a calculator as approximately 3.464)

$$\cos(30°) = \frac{6}{x} \implies x = \frac{6}{\cos(30°)} = 4\sqrt{3}.$$ (Appears on a calculator as approximately 6.928)

Practice Questions

1. What is the area of the figure below?

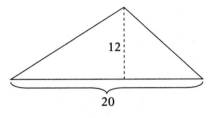

2. A triangle has a base of 12 in and an area 72 in². What is the height of the triangle?

3. What are the possible values of x?

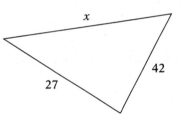

4. List the sides from longest to shortest.

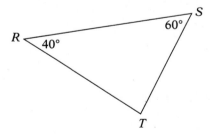

5. What is the value of x?

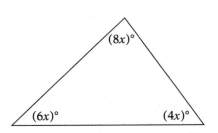

6. What is the value of x?

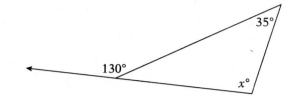

7. What is the value of x?

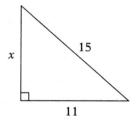

8. What is the value of x?

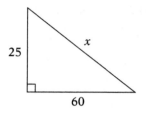

9. What are the values of x and y?

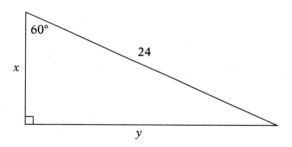

Practice Answers

1. 120
2. 12
3. $15 < x < 69$
4. $RS > RT > ST$
5. $x = 10$
6. $x = 95°$
7. $x = 2\sqrt{26}$
8. $x = 65$
9. $x = 12$ and $y = 12\sqrt{3}$

1. What is the area of the figure below?

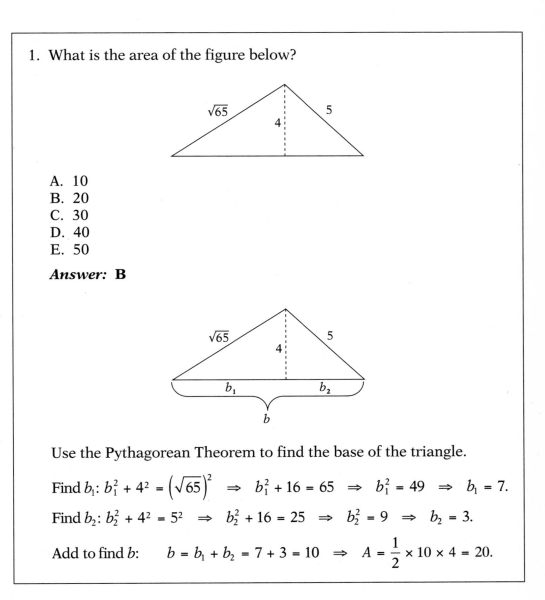

A. 10
B. 20
C. 30
D. 40
E. 50

Answer: **B**

Use the Pythagorean Theorem to find the base of the triangle.

Find b_1: $b_1^2 + 4^2 = \left(\sqrt{65}\right)^2 \Rightarrow b_1^2 + 16 = 65 \Rightarrow b_1^2 = 49 \Rightarrow b_1 = 7.$

Find b_2: $b_2^2 + 4^2 = 5^2 \Rightarrow b_2^2 + 16 = 25 \Rightarrow b_2^2 = 9 \Rightarrow b_2 = 3.$

Add to find b: $b = b_1 + b_2 = 7 + 3 = 10 \Rightarrow A = \dfrac{1}{2} \times 10 \times 4 = 20.$

2. What is the value of $\sqrt{a^2 + b^2}$?

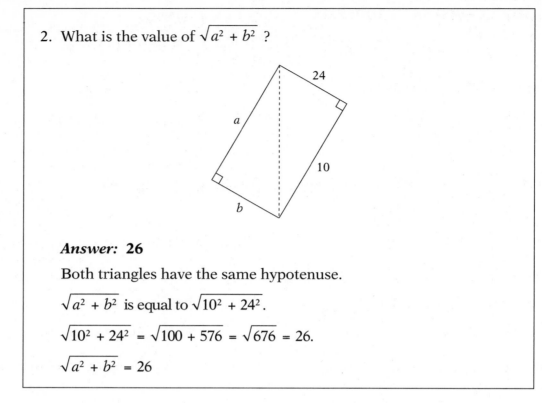

***Answer:* 26**

Both triangles have the same hypotenuse.

$\sqrt{a^2 + b^2}$ is equal to $\sqrt{10^2 + 24^2}$.

$\sqrt{10^2 + 24^2} = \sqrt{100 + 576} = \sqrt{676} = 26.$

$\sqrt{a^2 + b^2} = 26$

TRIANGLES
PRACTICE SAT QUESTIONS

■ ANSWER SHEET

Choose the correct answer.
If no choices are given, grid the answers in the section at the bottom of the page.

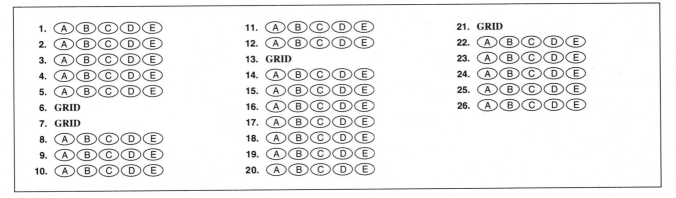

Use the answer spaces in the grids below if the question requires a grid-in response.

Student-Produced Responses

ONLY ANSWERS ENTERED IN THE CIRCLES IN EACH GRID WILL BE SCORED. YOU WILL NOT RECEIVE CREDIT FOR ANYTHING WRITTEN IN THE BOXES ABOVE THE CIRCLES.

PRACTICE SAT QUESTIONS

1. What is the value of *x*?

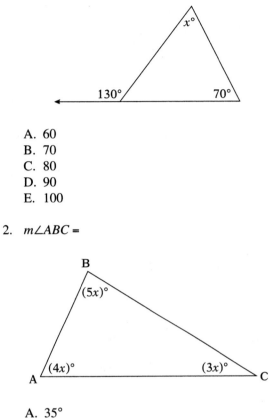

A. 60
B. 70
C. 80
D. 90
E. 100

2. *m∠ABC =*

A. 35°
B. 45°
C. 55°
D. 65°
E. 75°

3. *y − x =*

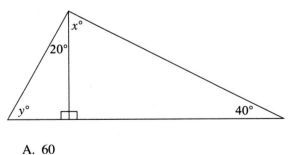

A. 60
B. 50
C. 40
D. 30
E. 20

4. Which of the following statements is correct?

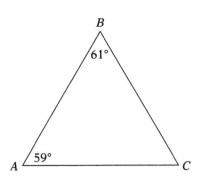

A. *AB < BC < AC*
B. *BC < AB < AC*
C. *AB < AC < BC*
D. *AC < BC < AB*
E. *BC < AC < AB*

5. What is the area of the triangle below?

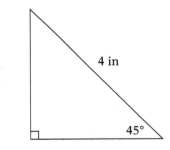

A. 4 in²
B. 5 in²
C. 6 in²
D. 7 in²
E. 8 in²

6. $m\angle BAC = x°$. What is the value of x?

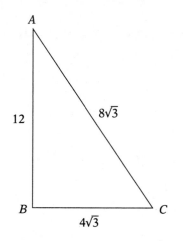

7. The area of the triangle below is 56 cm². What is the height of the triangle?

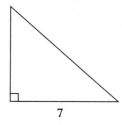

8. Which of the following could be the lengths of the sides of a triangle?
    I. 3,3,6
    II. 3,4,8
    III. 4,5,8

    A. I
    B. II
    C. III
    D. I and II
    E. II and III

9. If the angles of a triangle have a ratio of 1 : 2 : 3 which of the following statements are true?

    I. The triangle is a right triangle.

    II. The ratio of the sides are $1:\sqrt{3}:2$.
    III. The angle measures are 30°, 60°, 90°.

    A. I
    B. II
    C. I and II
    D. II and III
    E. I, II, and III

10. $y - x =$

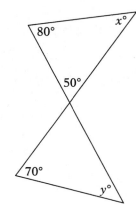

    A. 80
    B. 70
    C. 30
    D. 20
    E. 10

11. $m\angle CBA =$

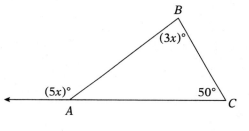

    A. 125
    B. 105
    C. 75
    D. 50
    E. 25

12. What is the perimeter of an equilateral triangle with a height of 6 feet?

    A. $2\sqrt{3}$

    B. $4\sqrt{3}$

    C. $6\sqrt{3}$

    D. $10\sqrt{3}$

    E. $12\sqrt{3}$

13. $x + y =$

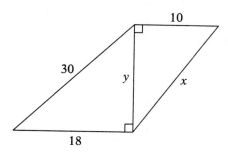

14. Two sides of a triangle are 7 and 16. Which of the following is not the length of the third side?

    A. 22
    B. 17
    C. 12
    D. 10
    E. 9

15. Which of the following is the longest side?

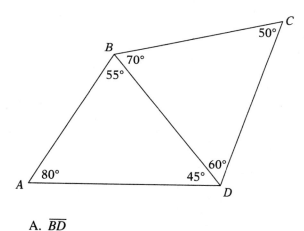

    A. $\overline{BD}$
    B. $\overline{BC}$
    C. $\overline{AB}$
    D. $\overline{DC}$
    E. $\overline{AD}$

16. $a + b + c + x + y =$

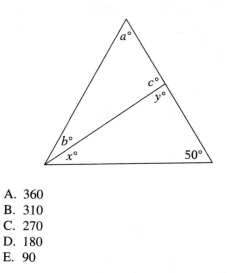

    A. 360
    B. 310
    C. 270
    D. 180
    E. 90

17. The area of an equilateral triangle is $36\sqrt{3}$ cm². What is the height of the triangle?

    A. 6 cm
    B. 12 cm
    C. $6\sqrt{3}$ cm
    D. $12\sqrt{3}$ cm
    E. 36 cm

18. In the figure below, if $BC = 5$ then $AB =$

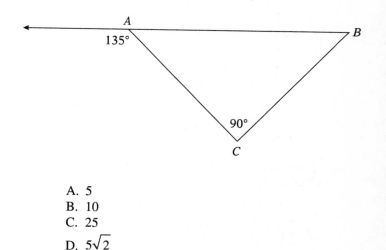

    A. 5
    B. 10
    C. 25
    D. $5\sqrt{2}$
    E. $10\sqrt{2}$

19. $m\angle BCA = 45°$, $m\angle BAC = 60°$
     $m\angle CBA = 75°$, and $m\angle BDC = 90°$. If $DC = 5$
     then $AD =$

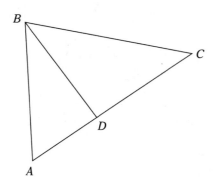

A. $5\sqrt{2}$

B. $5\sqrt{3}$

C. $\dfrac{5\sqrt{3}}{3}$

D. $\dfrac{5\sqrt{2}}{2}$

E. $10\sqrt{2}$

20. What is the value of x?

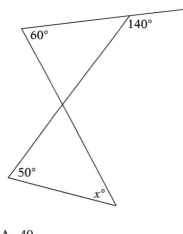

A. 40
B. 50
C. 60
D. 70
E. 80

21. What is the length of the base of the right triangle
     below if the area is 20 in²?

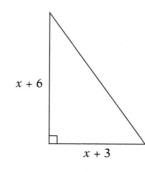

22. What is the value of x?

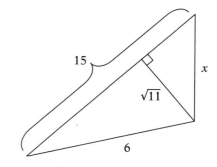

A. $\sqrt{5}$

B. $\sqrt{10}$

C. $\sqrt{11}$

D. $\sqrt{91}$

E. $\sqrt{111}$

23. If $a > b$, which of the following statements is true?

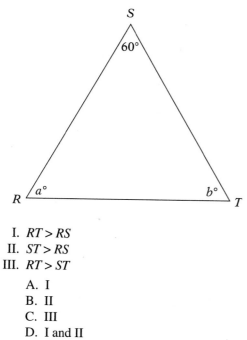

I. $RT > RS$
II. $ST > RS$
III. $RT > ST$

   A. I
   B. II
   C. III
   D. I and II
   E. II and III

24. What is the value of a?

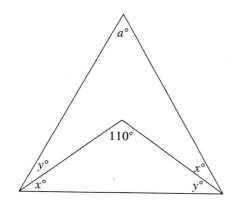

A. 110
B. 70
C. 50
D. 40
E. 30

25. $a + b + c + d =$

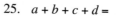

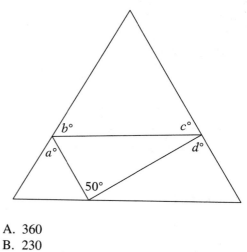

A. 360
B. 230
C. 180
D. 130
E. 90

26. $\triangle ABC$ is an equilateral triangle and $\triangle ADC$ is an isosceles triangle. If $AD = 12$ what is the area of the shaded region?

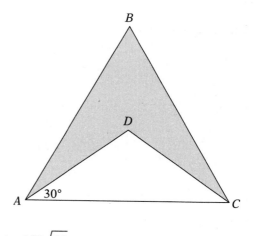

A. $108\sqrt{23}$

B. $72\sqrt{3}$

C. $36\sqrt{3}$

D. 144

E. 72

EXPLAINED ANSWERS

1. *Answer:* **A**

   The measure of the exterior angles is equal to the sum of the remote interior angles.

   $x + 70° = 130° \Rightarrow x = 60°$.

2. *Answer:* **E**

   The sum of the angles is 180°.

   $3x + 4x + 5x = 180 \Rightarrow 12x = 180 \Rightarrow x = 15 \Rightarrow m\angle ABC = 5(15) = 75°$.

3. *Answer:* **E**

   The sum of the acute angles in a right triangle is 90°.

   $y + 20 = 90 \Rightarrow y = 70 \Rightarrow x + 40 = 90 \Rightarrow x = 50 \Rightarrow y - x = 70 - 50 = 20$.

4. *Answer:* **B**

   The sum of the angles is 180°, so $m\angle C = 60°$.

   $m\angle A < m\angle C < m\angle B \Rightarrow BC < AB < AC$.

5. *Answer:* **A**

   The triangle is a 45°-45°-90° right triangle.

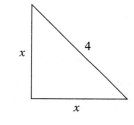

   $$\sqrt{2}x = 4 \Rightarrow x = \frac{4}{\sqrt{2}} \times \frac{\sqrt{2}}{\sqrt{2}} = \frac{4\sqrt{2}}{\sqrt{2}} = 2\sqrt{2}.$$

   The height and base measure $2\sqrt{2}$.

   Find the area.

   $$A = \frac{1}{2} \times \left(2\sqrt{2}\right) \times \left(2\sqrt{2}\right) = \frac{1}{2} \times 4 \times \sqrt{2} \times \sqrt{2}$$

   $$\frac{1}{2} \times 4 \times 2 = 4 \text{ in}^2.$$

6. *Answer:* **30**

   The trick is to recognize the triangle is a 30°-60°-90° triangle.

   $BC : CA : AB = 4\sqrt{3} : 8\sqrt{3} : 12 = 1 : 2 : \sqrt{3}$.

   So $m\angle BAC = 30°$ and $x = 30$.

7. *Answer:* **16**

   Substitute $A = 56$ and $b = 7$ in the area formula.

   $A = \frac{1}{2} \times b \times h \Rightarrow 56 = \frac{1}{2} \times 7 \times h \Rightarrow$ Solve for h $\quad 112 = 7 \times h \Rightarrow 16 \text{ cm} = h$.

8. *Answer:* **C**

   The sum of lengths of the two shortest sides is greater than the length of the longest side.

   I.   3,3,6   NO $3 + 3 \not> 6$
   II. 3,4,8   NO $3 + 4 \not> 8$
   III. 4,5,8   YES $4 + 5 > 8$

9. *Answer:* **E**

   The sum of the angles is 180°.

   Use ratio to write an equation and solve for *x*. The angles are in ratio

   $1 : 2 : 3 \Rightarrow x + 2x + 3x = 180 \Rightarrow 6x = 180 \Rightarrow x = 30.$

   The angle measures are 30, 2(30) = 60 and 3(30) = 90.

   This is a 30°,60°,90° right triangle. In a 30°,60°,90° right triangle the sides have ratio $1 : \sqrt{3} : 2$.

10. *Answer:* **E**

    The sum of the angles is 180°. Write an equation and solve for *x*.

    $x + 80° + 50° = 180° \Rightarrow x + 130° = 180° \Rightarrow x = 50°.$

    Solve for *y*.

    $y + 70° + 50° = 180° \Rightarrow y + 120° = 180° \Rightarrow y = 60°$

    $y - x = 60° - 50° = 10°.$

11. *Answer:* **C**

    The sum of the exterior angles equals the sum of the remote interior angles.

    $3x + 50 = 5x \Rightarrow 50 = 2x \Rightarrow 25 = x \Rightarrow m\angle CBA$

    Substitute 25 for *x*. $3x = 3(25) = 75°.$

12. *Answer:* **E**

    Draw the height on the diagram to form two 30°-60°-90° right triangles.

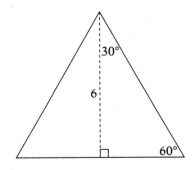

    Use the ratio of the lengths of the sides.

    $\sqrt{3} \cdot x = 6 \Rightarrow x$

    $\dfrac{6}{\sqrt{3}} \times \dfrac{\sqrt{3}}{\sqrt{3}} = \dfrac{6\sqrt{3}}{3} = 2\sqrt{3}.$

    Therefore, the length of one side of the triangle is $4\sqrt{3}$. Because it is an equilateral triangle all three sides are equal, so the perimeter is $3 \times 4\sqrt{3} = 12\sqrt{3}$ feet.

13. *Answer:* **50**

Use the Pythagorean Theorem to find y.

$y^2 + 18^2 = 30^2 \quad \Rightarrow \quad y^2 + 324 = 900 \quad \Rightarrow \quad y^2 = 576 \quad \Rightarrow \quad y = 24.$

Use the Pythagorean Theorem to solve for x.

$x^2 = 24^2 + 10^2 \quad \Rightarrow \quad x^2 = 576 + 100 \quad \Rightarrow \quad x^2 = 676 \quad \Rightarrow \quad x = 26.$

Solve for $x + y$ $\quad x + y = 24 + 26 = 50.$

14. *Answer:* **E**

The third side must be <u>between</u> $16 - 7 = 9$ and $16 + 7 = 23$. That means 9 cannot be the length of the third side.

15. *Answer:* **D**

$\overline{BD}$ is the longest side in $\triangle ABD$, and it is also a side in $\triangle BDC$.

$\overline{DC}$ is the longest side in $\triangle BDC$. $\overline{DC}$ must be longer than $\overline{BC}$. $\overline{DC}$ is the longest side.

16. *Answer:* **B**

The sum of the angles is $180°$.

$x + y + 50 = 180 \quad \Rightarrow \quad x + y = 130 \quad$ and $\quad a + b + c = 180.$

Therefore, $a + b + c + x + y = 180 + 130 = 310.$

17. *Answer:* **C**

Draw the height on the diagram to form two $30°$-$60°$-$90°$ triangles.

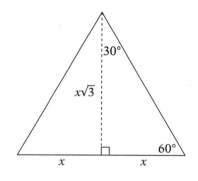

Write the area formula in terms of x and simplify.

$$A = 36\sqrt{3} = \frac{1}{2} \times (2x) \times \left(x\sqrt{3}\right)$$

Solve for x.

$36\sqrt{3} = x^2\sqrt{3} \quad \Rightarrow \quad 36 = x^2 \quad \Rightarrow \quad 6 = x.$

The height is $h = 6\sqrt{3}$.

18. *Answer:* **D**

    The angle measure of $\angle BAC$ is 45° because the sum of a linear pair is 180° (135° + 45° = 180°).

    The measure of $\angle ABC$ is 45° because the sum of the angles in a triangle is 180°.

    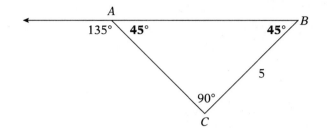

    This is a 45°-45°-90° right triangle $AB = 5\sqrt{2}$.

19. *Answer:* **C**

    You know the circled angle measures from the problem. Use the properties of right triangles to find the other angle measures.

    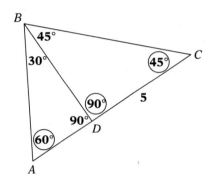

    $DC = 5$ and $\triangle BDC$ is a 45°-45°-90° right triangle, so $BD = 5$.

    $BD = 5$ and $\triangle BDA$ is a 30°-60°-90° right triangle, so $AD\sqrt{3} = 5$
    Find AD.

    $$AD = \frac{5}{\sqrt{3}} \times \frac{\sqrt{3}}{\sqrt{3}} = \frac{5\sqrt{3}}{3}.$$

20. *Answer:* **B**

The sum of the angles is 180°. Use what you know about linear pairs and vertical angles to find the bold angle measures.

$x + 50 + 80 = 180 \implies x + 130 = 180 \implies x = 50.$

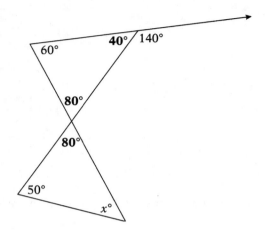

21. *Answer:* **5**

Use the area formula.

$$A = \frac{1}{2} \times (x + 6)(x + 3) = 20 \implies \text{so} \quad (x + 6)(x + 3) = 40.$$

Simplify

$x^2 + 3x + 6x + 12 = 40 \implies x^2 + 9x + 18 = 40$

Subtract 40 from each side.

$x^2 + 9x - 22 = 0.$

Factor the quadrilateral. $(x + 11)(x - 2) = 0$
That means $x + 11 = 0$
Solve $\underline{x = -11}$ and $x - 2 = 0 \implies \underline{x = 2}.$
Substitute for x in $x + 3$
$-11 + 3 = -8$. The base cannot be negative.
$2 + 3 = 5$. The base is 5.

22. ***Answer:*** **E**

    a and *b* have been added to the figure. Use the Pythagorean Theorem to solve for *a*.

    $$a^2 + \left(\sqrt{11}\right)^2 = 6^2 \quad \Rightarrow \quad a^2 + 11 = 36 \quad \Rightarrow \quad a^2 = 25 \quad \Rightarrow \quad a = 5.$$

    The sum of *a* and *b* is 15. *b* = 15 − 5 = 10

    Use the Pythagorean Theorem to solve for *x*.

    $$x^2 = \left(\sqrt{11}\right)^2 + 10^2 \quad \Rightarrow \quad x^2 = 11 + 100 \quad \Rightarrow \quad x^2 = 111 \quad \Rightarrow \quad x = \sqrt{111}.$$

    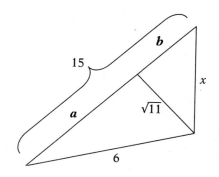

23. ***Answer:*** **D**

    Find the sum of *a* and *b*.

    $$a + b + 60 = 180 \quad \Rightarrow \quad a + b = 120$$

    a > *b* so *a* > 60 and *b* < 60.

    Therefore, *ST* > *RT* > *RS*.

    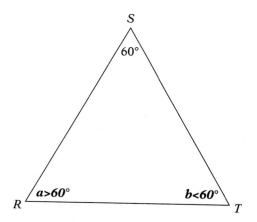

    I.   *RT* > *RS* YES
    II. *ST* > *RS* YES
    III. *RT* > *ST* NO

24. *Answer:* **D**

The sum of the angle measures in a triangle is 180°

That means $x + y + 110 = 180 \Rightarrow x + y = 70$.

Both base angles in the larger triangle are $x + y = 70 \Rightarrow a + 140 = 180$

$a = 40$, because the angle sum is 180°.

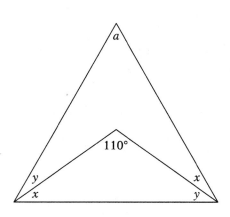

25. *Answer:* **B**

The sum of the angles is 180,

$x + y + 50 = 180 \Rightarrow x + y = 130$.

$a + b + x = 180$ and $c + d + y = 180$ because these angles form a straight line.

$a + b + c + d + x + y = 360$.

Substitute 130 for $x + y$, $a + b + c + d + 130 = 360$

That means $a + b + c + d = 230$.

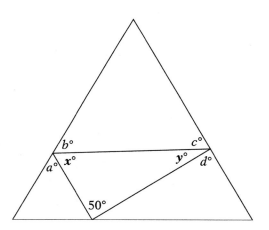

(Angles x and y have been added to the figure.)

26. *Answer:* **B**

- Draw the height of the unshaded triangle to form two 30°-60°-90° right triangles.
- The height is across from the 30° angle, so it is half the length of the hypotenuse or 6.
- The base is across from the 60° angle so the base measures $6\sqrt{3}$.
- That means $AC = \left[2\left(6\sqrt{2}\right)\right] = 12\sqrt{3}$.

Use the area formula.

Area $\triangle ADC = \dfrac{1}{2} \times 12\sqrt{3} \times 6 = 6\sqrt{3} \times 6 = 36\sqrt{3}$.

The area of the shaded region is twice the area of $\triangle ADC$ $2\left(36\sqrt{3}\right) = 72\sqrt{3}$.

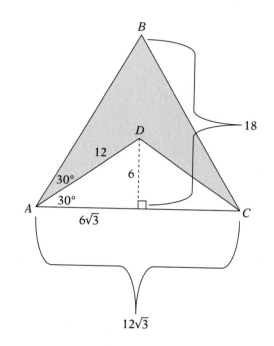

CHAPTER 12

QUADRILATERALS AND OTHER POLYGONS

This section covers several topics dealing with quadrilaterals and other polygons, such as area, perimeter, angle sum, and angle relationships. Begin with the mathematics review and then complete and correct the practice problems. There are 2 Solved SAT Problems and 16 Practice SAT Questions with answer explanations.

Quadrilateral—a four-sided polygon
Parallelogram—a quadrilateral with:

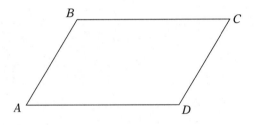

1. Opposite sides parallel. $\overline{AB} \parallel \overline{CD}$ and $\overline{BC} \parallel \overline{AD}$
2. Opposite sides congruent. $\overline{AB} \cong \overline{CD}$ and $\overline{BC} \cong \overline{AD}$
3. Opposite angles congruent. $\angle B \cong \angle D$ and $\angle A \cong \angle C$
4. Consecutive angles supplementary.

$m\angle A + m\angle B = 180°$ and $m\angle B + m\angle C = 180°$.

$m\angle C + m\angle D = 180°$ and $m\angle D + m\angle A = 180°$.

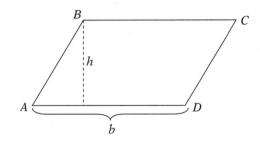

5. $A = b \times h$.

Rectangle—a parallelogram with all right angles.

Square—a rectangle with all sides congruent.

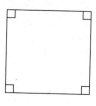

Every polygon can be partitioned into nonoverlapping triangles as shown below.

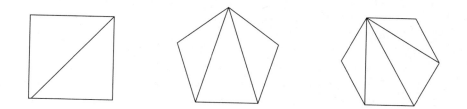

The number of triangles that are formed is two less than the number of sides. The sum of the measures of the angles in a triangle is 180°. Therefore, any polygon having n sides has an angle sum of $(n - 2) \times 180°$.

Regular Polygon—a polygon where all sides are congruent, and all angles are congruent.

A Central Angle of a regular polygon is formed when segments are constructed from the center of the polygon to the vertices of the polygon.

Each Central Angle of a regular polygon is congruent having a measure of $\dfrac{360°}{n}$ where n is the number of angles. The triangles that are formed through this process are also congruent.

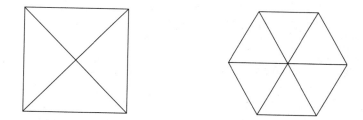

Example:

What is the area of the rectangle seen below?

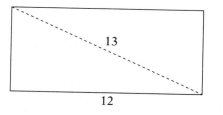

By noticing that a 5-12-13 triangle exists we can see that the height of the triangle is 5. Therefore, $A = 12 \times 5 = 60$.

Example:

The area of the rectangle seen below is 36. What is the value of x?

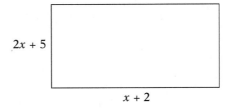

$2x + 5$

$x + 2$

Solve for A = $(2x + 5)(x + 2) = 2x^2 + 9x + 10 = 36$.
Factor $2x^2 + 9x - 26 = 0 \Rightarrow (x - 2)(2x + 13) = 0$

$x - 2 = 0 \Rightarrow x = 2$. : $2x + 13 = 0$, $2x = -13$, $x = -6.5$

$x = 2$ is correct. $x = -6.5$ would create a negative length. That is impossible.

Example:

In the parallelogram seen below, $m\angle ABC =$

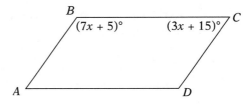

B

$(7x + 5)°$ $(3x + 15)°$ C

A D

$m\angle B + m\angle C = 180°$

$7x + 5 + 3x + 15 = 180° \Rightarrow 10x + 20 = 180°$

$10x = 160° \Rightarrow x = 16$

$m\angle ABC =$ Substitute 16 for x. $7(x) + 5 = 7(16) + 5 = 117°$.

Example:

What is the value of x in the square below?

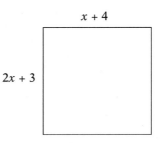

$x + 4$

$2x + 3$

All sides of a square are the same length.
$2x + 3 = x + 4 \Rightarrow x = 1$.

Example:

What is the angle sum of an octagon?
An octagon has eight sides.

$(8 - 2) \times 180° = 6 \times 180° = 1{,}080°$.

Example:

$m\angle A + m\angle B + m\angle C =$

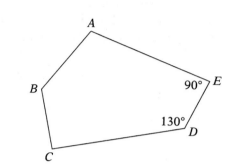

$m\angle A + m\angle B + m\angle C + m\angle D + m\angle E = 3(180°) = 540°$

Substitute $m\angle D = 130°$ $m\angle E = 90°$.

$m\angle A + m\angle B + m\angle C + 130° + 90° = 540°$

$m\angle A + m\angle B + m\angle C + 220° = 540°$

$m\angle A + m\angle B + m\angle C = 320°$

Example:

What is the measure of each central angle in a regular hexagon?
Calculate 360° divided by the number of sides.

$\dfrac{360°}{6} = 60°$

Practice Questions

1. The perimeter of the rectangle below is 50. What is the value of x?

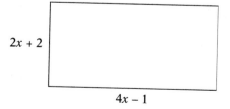

2. In the parallelogram below, $m\angle ABC =$

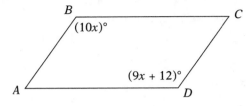

3. The measure of the angles is a quadrilateral are in a ratio of 2:4:5:7. What is the measure of each of the angles?

4. What is the perimeter of the square seen below?

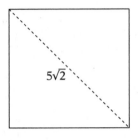

Practice Answers

1. $x = 4$.
2. $m\angle ABC = 120°$.
3. $40°:80°:100°:140°$
4. $P = 20$

SOLVED SAT PROBLEMS

1. The length of each side of the square below is 6. P, Q, R, and S are each midpoints. What is the area of the shaded region (middle region)?

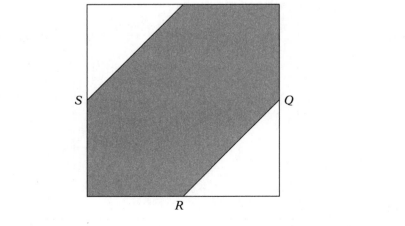

A. 36
B. 27
C. 18
D. 9
E. 4

Answer: **B**

Each side has a length 6.

Each midpoint partitions the sides into segments length 3.

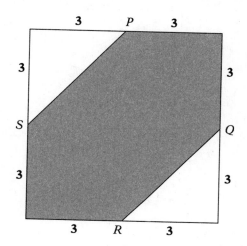

Area of the square is 6 × 6 = 36. The combined area of the two non-shaded triangles is 2($\frac{1}{2}$ × 3 × 3) = 3 × 3 = 9. Therefore, the area of the shaded region is the area of the square minus the area of the nonshaded region. 36 − 9 = 27.

2. All rectangles below are congruent. Which choice lists all those figures with the largest shaded region?

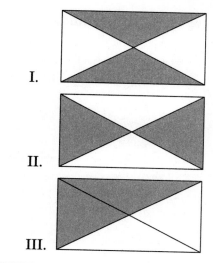

A. I only
B. II only
C. III only
D. I and II
E. I, II, and III

Answer: **E**

Let the length and width of the rectangle be any two values. I will choose **4** and **6.**

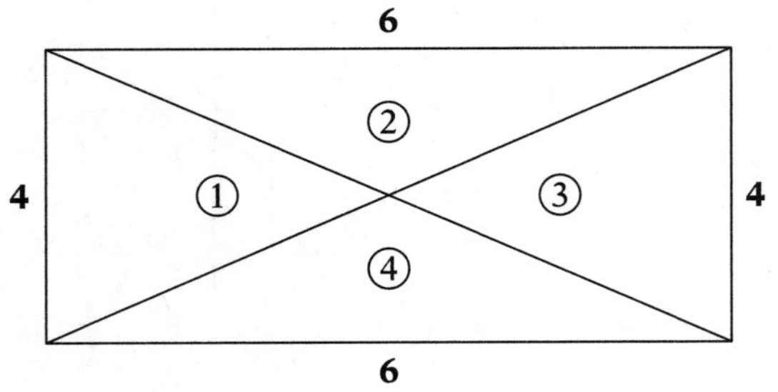

Area of triangles 1 and 3

$b = 4$ and $h = \dfrac{1}{2} \times 6 = 3.$

$A = \dfrac{1}{2} \times 4 \times 3 = 6.$

Area of triangles 2 and 4

$b = 6$ and $h = \dfrac{1}{2} \times 4 = 2.$

$A = \dfrac{1}{2} \times 6 \times 2 = 6.$

All triangles have the same area and all the shaded regions have the same area.

QUADRILATERALS AND OTHER POLYGONS
PRACTICE SAT QUESTIONS

ANSWER SHEET

Choose the correct answer.
If no choices are given, grid the answers in the section at the bottom of the page.

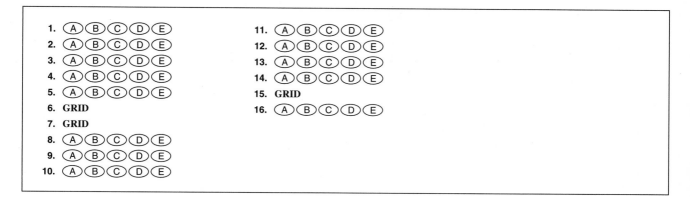

1. (A) (B) (C) (D) (E)
2. (A) (B) (C) (D) (E)
3. (A) (B) (C) (D) (E)
4. (A) (B) (C) (D) (E)
5. (A) (B) (C) (D) (E)
6. GRID
7. GRID
8. (A) (B) (C) (D) (E)
9. (A) (B) (C) (D) (E)
10. (A) (B) (C) (D) (E)

11. (A) (B) (C) (D) (E)
12. (A) (B) (C) (D) (E)
13. (A) (B) (C) (D) (E)
14. (A) (B) (C) (D) (E)
15. GRID
16. (A) (B) (C) (D) (E)

Use the answer spaces in the grids below if the question requires a grid-in response.

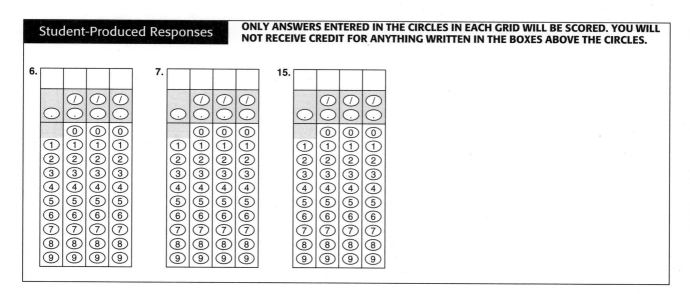

Student-Produced Responses

ONLY ANSWERS ENTERED IN THE CIRCLES IN EACH GRID WILL BE SCORED. YOU WILL NOT RECEIVE CREDIT FOR ANYTHING WRITTEN IN THE BOXES ABOVE THE CIRCLES.

PRACTICE SAT QUESTIONS

1. If the perimeter of the rectangle below is 56, what is the value of the base?

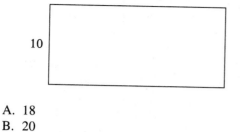

A. 18
B. 20
C. 36
D. 40
E. 56

2. What is the perimeter of a square with area 49?
A. 4
B. 7
C. 14
D. 28
E. 35

3. What is the area of the rectangle below?

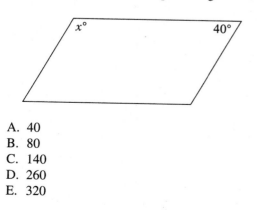

A. $10\sqrt{3}$

B. $20\sqrt{3}$

C. $40\sqrt{3}$

D. $50\sqrt{3}$

E. $100\sqrt{3}$

4. What is the value of x in the parallelogram below?

A. 40
B. 80
C. 140
D. 260
E. 320

5. What is the value of x in the parallelogram below?

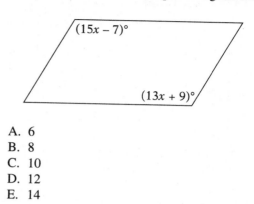

A. 6
B. 8
C. 10
D. 12
E. 14

6. The area of the rectangle below is 40. What is the perimeter?

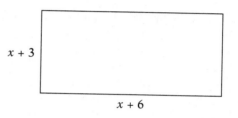

7. What is the area of the square below?

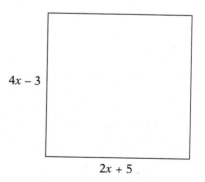

8. If the area of the rectangle is 120, what is the area of triangle *CPD*?

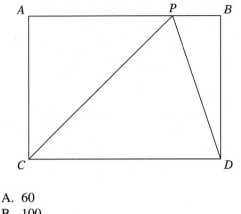

A. 60
B. 100
C. 120
D. 200
E. 240

9. In the parallelogram below, if *x* is 4 times as big as *y*, then *x* − *y* =

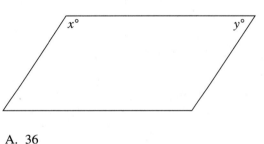

A. 36
B. 108
C. 144
D. 180
E. 220

10. What is the area of the parallelogram below?

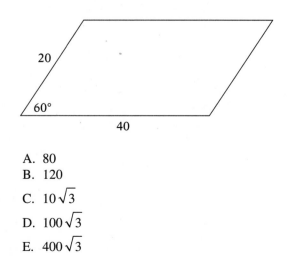

A. 80
B. 120
C. $10\sqrt{3}$
D. $100\sqrt{3}$
E. $400\sqrt{3}$

11. The base of a rectangle is three times as long as the height. If the perimeter is 64, what is the area of the rectangle?
A. 24
B. 64
C. 96
D. 192
E. 216

12. What is the value of *x* in the figure seen below?

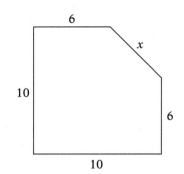

A. 4
B. $4\sqrt{2}$
C. 8
D. $8\sqrt{2}$
E. 16

13. What is the area of a regular hexagon with perimeter 24?

A. $4\sqrt{3}$
B. $8\sqrt{3}$
C. $12\sqrt{3}$
D. $16\sqrt{3}$
E. $24\sqrt{3}$

14. The angles of a pentagon are in ratio 9:10:12:14:15. What is the sum of measures of the smallest and largest angles?
A. 54°
B. 81°
C. 135°
D. 216°
E. 270°

15. What is the area of the figure seen below?

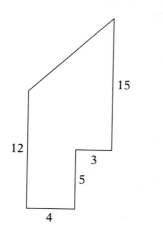

16. Which of the following expressions represents the area of the shaded region below?

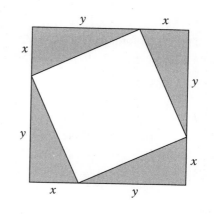

A. $x^2 + y^2$.
B. $2(x^2 + y^2)$.
C. $2xy$
D. $x^2 + 2xy + y^2$.
E. $x + y$.

▄▄ **EXPLAINED ANSWERS**

1. *Answer:* **A**

    Use the perimeter formula. Substitute $P = 56$ and $h = 6$
    $$P = 2h + 2b \Rightarrow 56 = 2(10) + 2b \Rightarrow 56 = 20 + 2b$$

    Solve for b. $36 = 2b \Rightarrow 18 = b$.

2. *Answer:* **D**

    Use the area formula. Substitute $A = 49$ and solve for s.
    $$A = s^2 \Rightarrow 49 = s^2 \Rightarrow 7 = s$$

    Find the perimeter. $P = 4 \times 7 = 28$.

3. *Answer:* **E**

    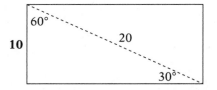

    Notice the triangle is a 30°-60°-90° right triangle. So the height opposite the 30° angle is 10, and the base opposite the 60° angle is $10\sqrt{3}$.
    Find the area.
    $$A = 10 \times 10\sqrt{3} = 100\sqrt{3}.$$

4. *Answer:* **C**

    The sum of x and 40 is 180°.
    That means $x = 180 - 40 = 140$.

5. *Answer:* **B**

    Opposite angles have equal measures.
    $$15x - 7 = 13x + 9 \Rightarrow 2x = 16 \Rightarrow x = 8.$$

6. *Answer:* **26**

    The area equals base times height.
    $$(x + 3)(x + 6) = 40 \Rightarrow x^2 + 9x - 22 = 0 \Rightarrow (x - 2)(x + 11) = 0$$

    Solve for x. $x - 2 = 0 \Rightarrow x = 2$
    $x + 11 = 0 \Rightarrow x = -11$.

    x must equal 2, the length of a side cannot be negative.

    Add to find base and height. $b = x + 6 = 2 + 6 = 8$ and $h = x + 3 = 2 + 3 = 5$
    Find the perimeter. $P = 2(8) + 2(5) = 26$.

7. *Answer:* **169**

   The sides of a square have equal lengths. Write an equation.

   $4x - 3 = 2x + 5 \Rightarrow 2x = 8 \Rightarrow x = 4.$

   Substitute 4 in either equation to find the length of a side.

   $\begin{aligned} s &= 4x - 3 = 4(4) - 3 = 13 \\ s &= 2x + 5 = 2(4) + 5 = 13 \end{aligned} \Rightarrow A = 13^2 = 169$

   Area $= 13^2 = 169$

8. *Answer:* **A**

   The base and height for the triangle and rectangle are equal.
   The area of the rectangle is 120. The area of the triangle is half the area of the rectangle, $\frac{1}{2}(120) = 60.$

9. *Answer:* **B**

   The sum of consecutive angles is 180°

   $x + y = 180$

   Substitute $4y$ for x. $4y + y = 180 \Rightarrow 5y = 180$

   Solve for y. $y = 36$

   Substitute 36 for y. $x = 4(36) = 144.$

   $x - y = 144 - 36 = 108.$

10. *Answer:* **E**

    Draw the height to form a 30°-60°-90° right triangle.

    The height is across from the 60° angle so the height is $10\sqrt{3}$

    Substitute $b = 40$ and $h = 10\sqrt{3}$. $A = b \times h = 40 \times 10\sqrt{3} = 400\sqrt{3}$.

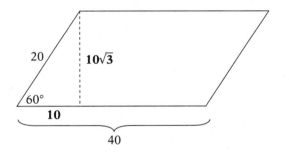

11. *Answer:* **D**

    Draw a picture.

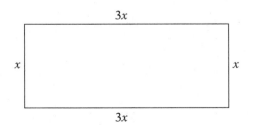

    The perimeter is 64 so $8x = 64 \Rightarrow x = 8$

    So, $h = 8$ and $b = 3(8) = 24.$

    Substitute $h = 8$ and $b = 24$ in the area formula. $A = b \times h = 8 \times 24 = 192.$

12. *Answer:* **B**

Draw on the diagram.

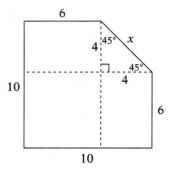

The triangle formed is a 45°-45°-90° right triangle so $x = 4\sqrt{2}$.

13. *Answer:* **E**

In the hexagon below one of the six congruent equilateral triangles that fill in the entire hexagon is shown. Draw the height to form two 30°-60°-90° right triangles. The height is $2\sqrt{3}$ because it is across from the 60° angle.

Substitute $b = 4$ and $h = 2\sqrt{3}$ in the triangle area formula. $A = \dfrac{1}{2} \times b \times h = \dfrac{1}{2} \times 4 \times 2\sqrt{3} = 4\sqrt{3}$.

Therefore, the area of the entire hexagon is $= 6 \times 4\sqrt{3} = 24\sqrt{3}$.

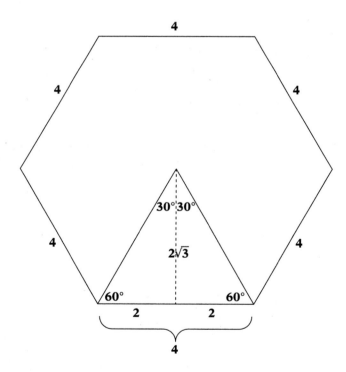

14. **Answer: D**

The angle sum of the angles in a pentagon

$(5 - 2) \times 180° = 3 \times 180° = 540°$.

Use the ratio from the problem to write an equation. Solve for x.

$9x + 10x + 12x + 14x + 15x = 540° \Rightarrow 60x = 540° \Rightarrow x = 9$.

The smallest angle is $9(9) = 81°$ and the largest angle is $15(9) = 135°$.
Therefore, the sum of the smallest angle and the largest angle is $81° + 135° = 216°$.

15. **Answer: 97**

Split the figure in to regions. Find the area of each region.

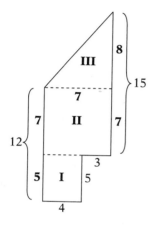

$A_I = 4 \times 5 = 20 \quad A_{II} = 7 \times 7 = 49 \quad A_{III} = \dfrac{1}{2} \times 7 \times 8 = 28$.

Total Area $= 20 + 49 + 28 = 97$.

16. **Answer: C**

The base of each of the shaded triangles is x, and the height of each is y. The area of each of the shaded triangles is

$A_T = \dfrac{1}{2}xy$. That means the area of the entire shaded region is $A_S = 4\left(\dfrac{1}{2}xy\right) = 2xy$.

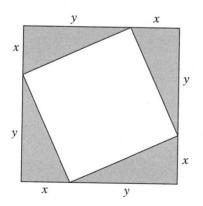

CHAPTER 13

CIRCLES

On the SAT you will calculate both the area and circumference of circles, as well as the area and arc length of part of a circle. You will also solve problems about lines tangent to circles. Begin with the mathematics review and then complete and correct the practice problems. There are 2 Solved SAT Problems and 15 Practice SAT Questions with answer explanations.

Circle—a set of points equidistant from a given point, the center.
Radius—the distance from the center of a circle to its perimeter.

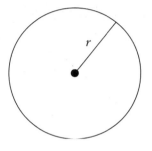

Diameter—the maximum distance from one point on the circle to another point on the circle.
The diameter is twice the length of the radius. $d = 2r$

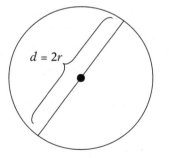

Circumference—the perimeter of the circle, $C = 2\pi r = \pi d$.

Example:

What is the radius of a circle with circumference of 30π?
Substitute $C = 30\pi$ in the circumference formula.

$C = 2\pi r \Rightarrow 30\pi = 2\pi r \Rightarrow 15 = r$.

Area of a circle is $A = \pi r^2$.

Example:

What is the area of a circle with diameter 20?
Find the radius.

$d = 2r \Rightarrow 20 = 2r \Rightarrow 10 = r$.

Substitute 10 for r in the area formula.

$A = \pi r^2 \Rightarrow A = \pi \times 10^2 \Rightarrow A = 100\pi$.

Central Angle—the angle with endpoints located on a circle's circumference and vertex located at the circle's center. $\angle AOC$ below is a central angle.

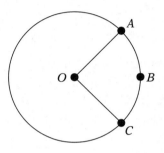

Arc—a piece of the circumference.

$$\frac{\text{Arc length}}{\text{Circumference}} = \frac{\text{Measure of central angle}}{360°}$$

Example:

What is the measure of Arc *ABC* in circle O seen below?

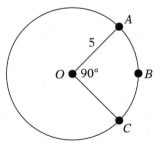

$\dfrac{90°}{360°} = \dfrac{1}{4}$ So the arc length is $\dfrac{1}{4}\left(10 \times \pi\right) = \dfrac{5\pi}{2}$

Sector—a piece of the area.

$$\frac{\text{Area of sector}}{\text{Area of circle}} = \frac{\text{Measure of central angle}}{360°}$$

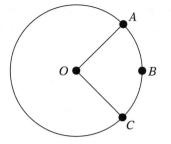

Example:

The area of a sector in a circle with radius 3 is 3π. What is the measure of the central angle?

Use 3π for the sector area and $\pi(3)^2 = 9\pi$ for the circle area $\dfrac{3\pi}{9\pi} = \dfrac{1}{3}$

There are 360° in a circle so $\dfrac{1}{3}(360°) = 120°$, the measure of the central angle.

Tangent—a line that touches the circle at one point. In the figure below $\overrightarrow{AB}$ is tangent to circle O.

When a line is tangent to a circle, the line is perpendicular to the radius at the point of tangency. Therefore, in the figure below $m\angle OAB = 90°$.

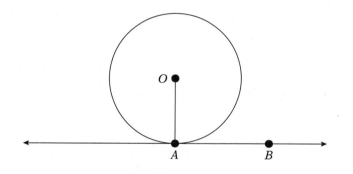

Example:

$\overrightarrow{AB}$ is tangent to circle O at point A. $OB = 13$, and $AB = 12$. What is the radius of the circle?

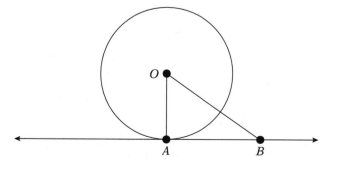

Use the Pythagorean Theorem. $(OA)^2 + (AB)^2 = (OB)^2$
Substitute $AB = 12$ and $OB = 13$. $(OA)^2 + 12^2 = 13^2$.
Solve for OA. $(OA)^2 + 144 = 169 \Rightarrow (OA)^2 = 25 \Rightarrow OA = 5$.

Therefore, the radius is 5. You could also notice the triangle is a 5-12-13 right triangle. This observation would allow you to find the length of the radius much more quickly.

Practice Questions

1. What is the circumference of a circle with diameter 20?
2. What is the diameter of a circle with an area 121π?
3. The length of an arc in a circle with circumference 14π is 7π. What is the measure of the central angle?
4. What is the area of the shaded sector in circle O seen below?

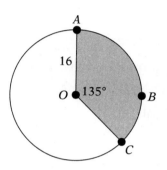

5. $\overrightarrow{AB}$ is tangent to circle O at point A. The area of $\triangle OAB$ is 224. What is the value of AB?

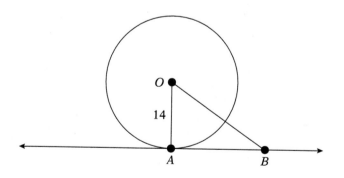

Practice Answers

1. 20π
2. 22
3. 180°
4. 96π
5. 32

SOLVED SAT PROBLEMS

1. $\overrightarrow{AB}$ is tangent to circle O at point A. The circumference of circle O is 18π. If the area of $\triangle OAB$ is 72, then $AB =$

   A. 8
   B. 9
   C. 16
   D. 18
   E. 20

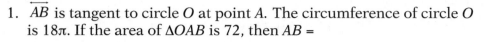

   Answer: C

   Substitute $C = 18\pi$ in the circumference formula.

   $C = 18\pi = 2\pi r$

   Solve for r. $r = 9$

   So $OA = 9$.

   Substitute $A = 72$ and $h = 9$ in the triangle area formula. $\frac{1}{2} \times hb$

   $72 = \frac{1}{2}\ 9b$.

   Solve for b. $144 = 9 \times b \Rightarrow 16 = b$.

2. The length of each arc of the congruent sectors in circle O is 2π. What is the area of the shaded region rounded to the nearest whole number?

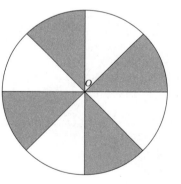

   Answer: $32\pi \approx 101$

   The length of each arc is 2π, so the circumference is $C = 8 \times 2\pi = 16\pi$

   Substitute 16π for C in the circumference formula, $16\pi = 2\pi r$

   Solve for r. $8 = r$

   Substitute 8 for r in the area formula. $A = \pi r^2 = \pi(8)^2 = 64\pi$.

   The shaded region is exactly half the entire circle, therefore, the area of the shaded region is 32π.

CIRCLES
PRACTICE SAT QUESTIONS

▬▬ **ANSWER SHEET**

Choose the correct answer.
If no choices are given, grid the answers in the section at the bottom of the page.

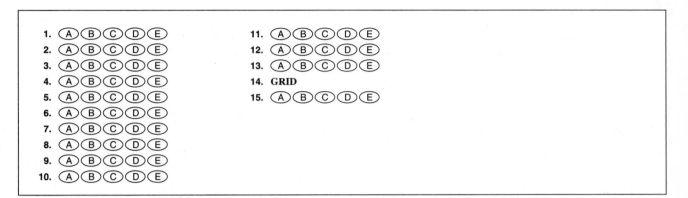

1. Ⓐ Ⓑ Ⓒ Ⓓ Ⓔ
2. Ⓐ Ⓑ Ⓒ Ⓓ Ⓔ
3. Ⓐ Ⓑ Ⓒ Ⓓ Ⓔ
4. Ⓐ Ⓑ Ⓒ Ⓓ Ⓔ
5. Ⓐ Ⓑ Ⓒ Ⓓ Ⓔ
6. Ⓐ Ⓑ Ⓒ Ⓓ Ⓔ
7. Ⓐ Ⓑ Ⓒ Ⓓ Ⓔ
8. Ⓐ Ⓑ Ⓒ Ⓓ Ⓔ
9. Ⓐ Ⓑ Ⓒ Ⓓ Ⓔ
10. Ⓐ Ⓑ Ⓒ Ⓓ Ⓔ

11. Ⓐ Ⓑ Ⓒ Ⓓ Ⓔ
12. Ⓐ Ⓑ Ⓒ Ⓓ Ⓔ
13. Ⓐ Ⓑ Ⓒ Ⓓ Ⓔ
14. **GRID**
15. Ⓐ Ⓑ Ⓒ Ⓓ Ⓔ

Use the answer spaces in the grids below if the question requires a grid-in response.

Student-Produced Responses — ONLY ANSWERS ENTERED IN THE CIRCLES IN EACH GRID WILL BE SCORED. YOU WILL NOT RECEIVE CREDIT FOR ANYTHING WRITTEN IN THE BOXES ABOVE THE CIRCLES.

14.

PRACTICE SAT QUESTIONS

1. What is the area of a circle whose circumference is 12π?

    A. 9π
    B. 12π
    C. 16π
    D. 25π
    E. 36π

2. What is the diameter of a circle whose area is 4?

    A. $\dfrac{2}{\sqrt{\pi}}$

    B. $\dfrac{4}{\sqrt{\pi}}$

    C. $4\sqrt{\pi}$
    D. 2π
    E. 4π

3. What is the area of the shaded region?

    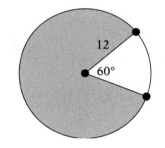

    A. 24π
    B. 60π
    C. 90π
    D. 120π
    E. 144π

4. The inner circle is tangent to the outer circle at point P. Point O is the center of the outer circle and $\overline{PO}$ is the diameter of the inner circle. What is the ratio of the area of the outer circle to the area of the inner circle?

    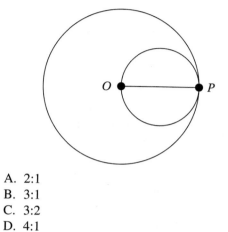

    A. 2:1
    B. 3:1
    C. 3:2
    D. 4:1
    E. 5:2

5. If the ratio of the area of a sector to the area of the circle is 3:5, what is the ratio of the length of the arc in the sector to the circumference of the circle?

    A. $\dfrac{3}{5}$

    B. $\dfrac{1}{2}$

    C. $\dfrac{9}{25}$

    D. $\dfrac{1}{4}$

    E. $\dfrac{1}{3}$

6. What is the area of the circle O if the length of ArcPQR is 8π?

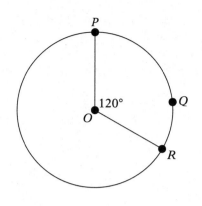

 A. 24π
 B. 60π
 C. 90π
 D. 120π
 E. 144π

7. The area of the circle O below is 81π. What is the length of $\overline{BA}$?

 A. 4.5
 B. 5
 C. 5.5
 D. 6
 E. 6.5

8. The area of the $\triangle ABC$ is 18, what is the area of the shaded region?

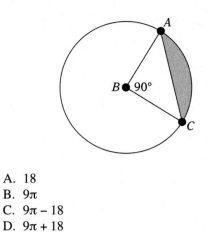

 A. 18
 B. 9π
 C. $9\pi - 18$
 D. $9\pi + 18$
 E. 27π

9. Point O is the center of both circles seen below. What is the area of the shaded regions?

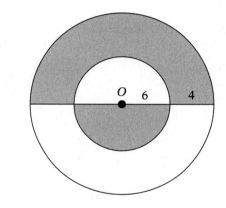

 A. 100π
 B. 50π
 C. 36π
 D. 16π
 E. 4π

10. The area of circle P is 64π. $\overline{QR}$ is tangent to circle P at point Q. If $QR = 12$, then $PR =$

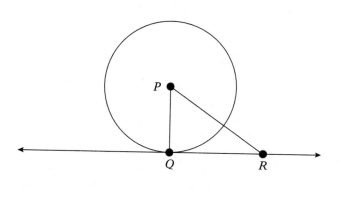

A. $16\sqrt{13}$

B. $4\sqrt{13}$

C. $2\sqrt{13}$

D. 16

E. 14

11. The area of a circle is doubled. What is the ratio of the circle's new radius to the circle's original radius?

A. $\dfrac{\sqrt{2}}{1}$

B. $\dfrac{\sqrt{3}}{1}$

C. $\dfrac{4}{1}$

D. $\dfrac{1}{2}$

E. $\dfrac{1}{4}$

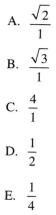

12. What is the value of x in circle O seen below?

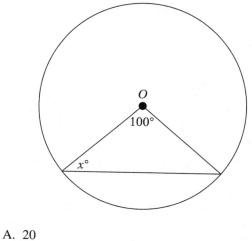

A. 20

B. 30

C. 40

D. 50

E. 60

13. The diameter of the large circle is 12. The center of each of the three congruent smaller circles lies on the diameter of the larger circle. What is the area of the shaded region?

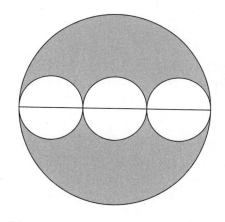

A. 36π

B. 24π

C. 18π

D. 12π

E. 6π

14. The area of the outer square is 256. What is the area of the inner square?

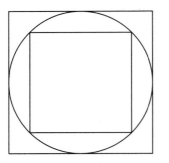

15. All the circles below are congruent. The total area of the nine congruent circles is 324π. The square passes through the center of eight circles as shown. What is the area of the shaded region?

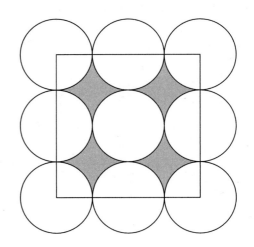

A. 1,296 – 144π
B. 576 – 144π
C. 324 – 144π
D. 576 – 72π
E. 324 – 72π

■ EXPLAINED ANSWERS

1. *Answer:* **E**

   Substitute $C = 12\pi$ in the circumference formula. $C = 12\pi = 2\pi r$

   Solve for r. $6 = r$

   Substitute $r = 6$ and solve for A. $A = \pi r^2 = \pi(6)^2 = 36\pi$.

2. *Answer:* **B**

   Substitute $A = 4$ in the area formula and solve for r.

   $$A = 4 = \pi r^2 \Rightarrow \frac{4}{\pi} = r^2 \Rightarrow \sqrt{\frac{4}{\pi}} = r \Rightarrow \frac{2}{\sqrt{\pi}} = r$$

   The diameter is twice the radius. $d = 2\dfrac{2}{\sqrt{\pi}} = \dfrac{4}{\sqrt{\pi}}$

3. *Answer:* **D**

   The circle is 360° and the shaded region is 300°. Write a fraction.

   $\dfrac{\text{Area of Shaded Region}}{\text{Area of Circle}} = \dfrac{300}{360} = \dfrac{5}{6}$. The shaded region is $\dfrac{5}{6}$ of the circle.

   Area of the circle $= \pi r^2 = \pi(12)^2 = 144\pi$

   $144\pi \times \dfrac{5}{6} = 120\pi$

4. *Answer:* **D**

   Let d be the diameter of the inner circle. That means the <u>radius</u> of the outer circle is d, and the radius of the inner

   circle is $\dfrac{d}{2}$. The area of the outer circle is πd^2,

   The area of the inner circle is $= \pi\left(\dfrac{d}{2}\right)^2 = \dfrac{\pi d^2}{4}$

   The ratio of the outer circle to the inner circle is $\dfrac{\pi d^2}{\dfrac{\pi d^2}{4}} = 4 : 1$

5. *Answer:* **A**

   The ratio of sector area to circle area is proportional to the ratio of sector arc length to circumference.

   The answer is $\dfrac{3}{5}$.

6. *Answer:* **E**

   The central angle is 120°. Find the circumference.

   Circumference $= \dfrac{360°}{120°}(8\pi) = 24\pi$

   Circumference also equals $\pi d = \pi(2r) = 24\pi$, so $r = 12$

   Find the area $\pi r^2 = \pi(12)^2 = 144\pi$

7. *Answer:* **A**

Substitute 81π for A. $A = 81\pi = \pi r^2$

Solve for r. $81 = r^2 \Rightarrow 9 = r$

That means $OC = 9$ and $OA = 9$.

$OB = 4.5$ and $OA = 9$ so $BA = 9 - 4.5 = 4.5$

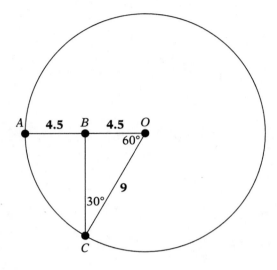

8. *Answer:* **C**

Area of $\triangle ABC = 18 = \dfrac{1}{2} \times b \times h$. The base and the height of the triangle are both radii.

Substitute r for b and h in the area formula.

Area of $\triangle ABC = 18 = \dfrac{1}{2} \times r^2$

Solve for r. $36 = r^2 \Rightarrow 6 = r$.

Area of circle is $\pi(6)^2 = 36\pi$

The central angle is $90°$ and area of the circle is 36π.

Area of sector $= \dfrac{90°}{360°}(36\pi) = \dfrac{1}{4}(36\pi) = 9\pi$

The area of the shaded region is area of sector – area of triangle $= 9\pi - 18$.

9. *Answer:* **B**

Combining the shaded regions is equal to half of the larger circle. Therefore, the area of the shaded regions is

$A = \dfrac{\pi r^2}{2} = \dfrac{\pi \times 10^2}{2} = 50\pi.$

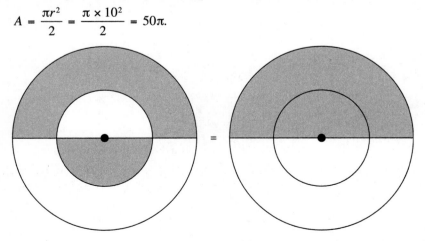

10. **Answer: B**

The area of the circle is $A = 64\pi = \pi r^2$ and $r^2 = 64$

That means $r = 8$ and $PQ = 8$.

$\overline{QR}$ is tangent to circle P at point Q so ΔPQR is a right triangle.

Use the Pythagorean Theorem. $PA = 8$, $QR = 12$.

$$(PR)^2 = (PQ)^2 + (QR)^2 \Rightarrow (PR)^2 = 8^2 + 12^2$$

$$(PR)^2 = 64 + 144 = 208.$$

$$PR = \sqrt{208} = \sqrt{16 \times 13} = 4\sqrt{13}.$$

11. **Answer: A**

πr^2 is the area of the original circle, and $2(\pi r^2)$ is the doubled area.

Rewrite $2\pi r^2 = \pi(2r^2) = \pi(\sqrt{2}\,r)^2$

That means the radius for the doubled area is $\sqrt{2}\,r$.

The ratio of the new radius to the old radius is $\dfrac{\sqrt{2}r}{r} = \dfrac{\sqrt{2}}{1}$.

12. **Answer: C**

The triangle has two radii as sides. The angles across from these sides must be equal.

The sum of the angles in a triangle is $180°$, so $2x + 100 = 180$

Solve for x. $2x = 80 \Rightarrow x = 40$.

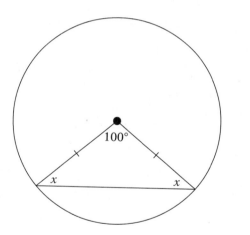

13. **Answer: B**

The diameter of the large circle is 12, so the radius is 6.

The area of the large circle is $\pi \cdot 6^2 = 36\pi$.

The radius of each small circle is $\dfrac{6}{3} = 2$. The area of each small circle is $\pi \cdot 2^2 = 4\pi$.

The area of the shaded region is $36\pi - 3(4\pi) = 36\pi - 12\pi = 24\pi$.

14. **Answer: 128**

The area of the outer square is 256. The length of each side of the outer square is $s^2 = 256 \Rightarrow s = 16$.

The length of each side of the outer square is equal to the diameter of the circle. That means the radius of the circle is $16 \div 2 = 8$. Two radii and the side of the inner square form a $45°$-$45°$-$90°$ right triangle. The side of the inner square is the hypotenuse of the triangle. That means the length of the side of the inner square is $8\sqrt{2}$. The length of each side of the inner square is $8\sqrt{2}$.

So, the area of the inner square is $(8\sqrt{2})^2 = 64 \times 2 = 128$.

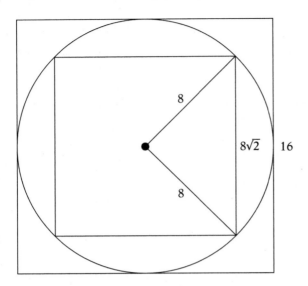

15. *Answer:* **B**

We know from the problem that the area of all nine circles is 324π.

The area of each circle is $A_C = \dfrac{324\pi}{9} = 36\pi$.

Area $= \pi r^2 = \pi \cdot 36 = \pi(6)(6)$, $r = 6$.

Each side of the square is made up of one diameter and two radii. Each side of the square is $12 + 6 + 6 = 24$. The area of the square is $A = 24^2 = 576$.

There is one full circle in the square along with four half circles, and four quarter circles. Together this makes a total of four full circles with a total area of $4 \times 36\pi = 144\pi$. Subtract to find the area of the shaded region: $576 - 144\pi$.

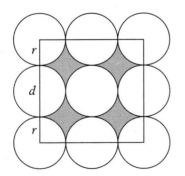

CHAPTER 14
INTERSECTING LINES

When lines intersect, a variety of angle types are formed. These angles often have a sum of 90° or a sum of 180°. Many may have the same angle measure. It is important to know which rules apply to which angles. Begin with the mathematics review and then complete and correct the practice problems. There are 2 Solved SAT Problems and 15 Practice SAT Questions with answer explanations.

The diagram below shows two lines, *l* and *m*, intersected by a transversal, *t*.

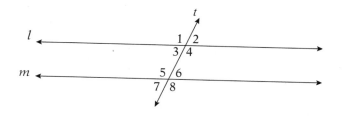

Vertical Angles are congruent because their measures are equal.

∠1 and ∠4, ∠2 and ∠3, ∠5 and ∠8, ∠6 and ∠7 are vertical angles.

$\angle 1 \cong \angle 4 \Rightarrow m\angle 1 = m\angle 4$ and $\angle 2 \cong \angle 3 \Rightarrow m\angle 2 = m\angle 3$.

Linear Pairs are supplementary because the sum of their measures is 180°.

∠1 and ∠2, ∠2 and ∠4, ∠4 and ∠3, ∠3 and ∠1, ∠5 and ∠6, ∠6 and ∠8, ∠8 and ∠7, ∠7 and ∠5 are linear pairs.

$m\angle 1 + m\angle 2 = 180°$ and $m\angle 2 + m\angle 4 = 180°$ and $m\angle 4 + m\angle 3 = 180°$ and $m\angle 3 + m\angle 1 = 180°$.

$m\angle 5 + m\angle 6 = 180°$ and $m\angle 6 + m\angle 8 = 180°$ and $m\angle 8 + m\angle 7 = 180°$ and $m\angle 7 + m\angle 5 = 180°$.

Alternate Interior Angles are congruent if *l* is parallel to *m*, *l* ∥ *m*.

∠3 and ∠6, ∠4 and ∠5 are alternate interior angles.

Alternate Exterior Angles are congruent if *l* is parallel to *m*, *l* ∥ *m*.

∠2 and ∠7, ∠1 and ∠8

Corresponding Angles are congruent if *l* is parallel to *m*, *l* ∥ *m*.

∠1 and ∠5, ∠2 and ∠6, ∠3 and ∠7, ∠4 and ∠8

Same Side Interior Angles are supplementary if *l* is parallel to *m*, *l* ∥ *m*.

∠3 and ∠5, ∠4 and ∠6.

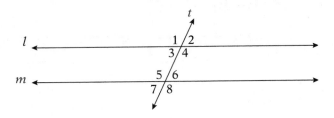

Example:

In the diagram above, $m\angle 2 = 30°$ and $l \parallel m$ find the measure of all the other angles.

$m\angle 1 = m\angle 4 = m\angle 5 = m\angle 8 = 150°$.

$m\angle 2 = m\angle 3 = m\angle 6 = m\angle 7 = 30°$.

Example:

In the diagram above, $l \parallel m$.

$m\angle 1 = (7x - 3)$ and $m\angle 6 = (3x + 13)$.

$m\angle 1 = ?$ and $m\angle 6 = ?$

$m\angle 1 + m\angle 6 = 180°$.

Substitute $m\angle 1 = 7x - 3$ and $m\angle 6 = 3x + 13$. $7x - 3 + 3x + 13 = 180$

Solve for x. $10x + 10 = 180 \Rightarrow 10x = 170 \Rightarrow x = 17$.

Substitute $x = 17$ for $m\angle 1$ and $m\angle 6$.

$m\angle 1 = 7(17) - 3 = 116°$ and $m\angle 6 = 3(17) + 13 = 64°$.

In the diagram below, line r is Perpendicular to line s r, written $\perp s$. Perpendicular lines form right angles $m\angle AOB = m\angle BOD = m\angle DOC = m\angle COA = 90°$.

$\angle 1$ and $\angle 2$ are referred to as Complimentary Angles because $m\angle 1 + m\angle 2 = 90°$.

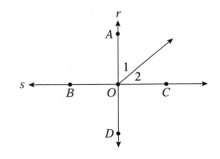

Example:

In the diagram above, $r \perp s$, $m\angle 1 = (4x - 9)°$, $m\angle 2 = (2x + 3)°$. $m\angle 1 = ?$ and $m\angle 2 = ?$

Find the measure of angle 1 and angle 2.

$m\angle 1 + m\angle 2 = 90° \Rightarrow 4x - 9 + 2x + 3 = 90$

Solve for x. $6x - 6 = 90$, $6x = 96 \Rightarrow x = 16$.

Substitute $x = 16$ for both $m\angle 1$ and $m\angle 2$.

$m\angle 1 = 4(16) - 9 = 55°$ and $m\angle 2 = 2(16) + 3 = 35°$.

Practice Questions

1. $m\angle 5 = (4x + 6)°$ and $m\angle 8 = (7x - 15)$

   $m\angle 5 =$ and $m\angle 8 =$

2.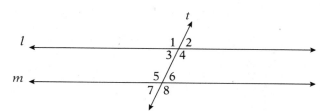

   $l \parallel m$, $m\angle 4 = (3x + 5)°$ and $m\angle 6 = (4x - 7)°$

   $m\angle 4 =$ and $m\angle 6 =$

3.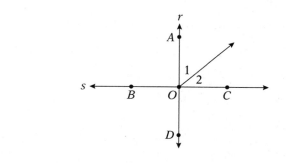

   $r \perp s$, $m\angle AOB = (8x - 20)°$ $x =$

Practice Answers

1. $m\angle 5 = 34°$ and $m\angle 8 = 34°$.

2. $m\angle 4 = 83°$ and $m\angle 6 = 97°$.

3. $x = 13.75$.

SOLVED SAT PROBLEMS

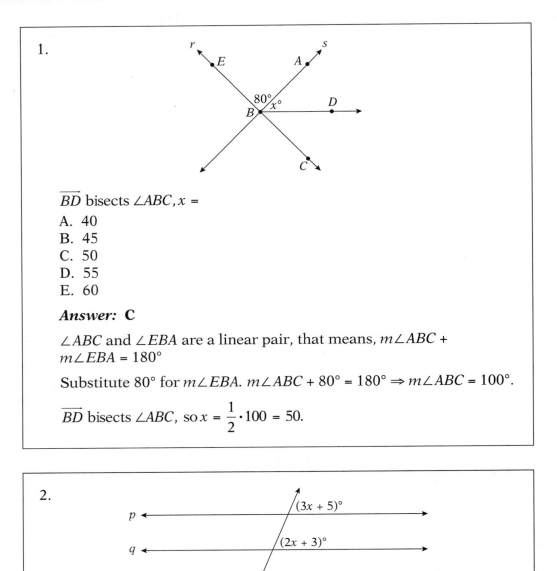

1.

$\overrightarrow{BD}$ bisects $\angle ABC$, $x =$

A. 40
B. 45
C. 50
D. 55
E. 60

Answer: **C**

$\angle ABC$ and $\angle EBA$ are a linear pair, that means, $m\angle ABC + m\angle EBA = 180°$

Substitute 80° for $m\angle EBA$. $m\angle ABC + 80° = 180° \Rightarrow m\angle ABC = 100°$.

$\overrightarrow{BD}$ bisects $\angle ABC$, so $x = \dfrac{1}{2}\cdot 100 = 50$.

2.

Using the above diagram with $p \parallel q$, what is the value of x?

A. −2
B. −3
C. −4
D. −5
E. −6

Answer: **A**

The two angles represented by $3x + 5$ and $2x + 3$ are corresponding angles, and $p \parallel q$;

That means, $3x + 5 = 2x + 3$ Now, solve for x. $x = -2$.

INTERSECTING LINES
PRACTICE SAT QUESTIONS

ANSWER SHEET

Choose the correct answer.
If no choices are given, grid the answers in the section at the bottom of the page.

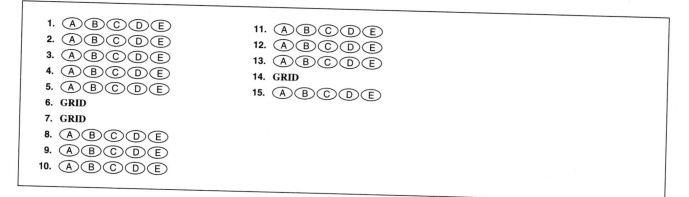

Use the answer spaces in the grids below if the question requires a grid-in response.

Student-Produced Responses   ONLY ANSWERS ENTERED IN THE CIRCLES IN EACH GRID WILL BE SCORED. YOU WILL NOT RECEIVE CREDIT FOR ANYTHING WRITTEN IN THE BOXES ABOVE THE CIRCLES.

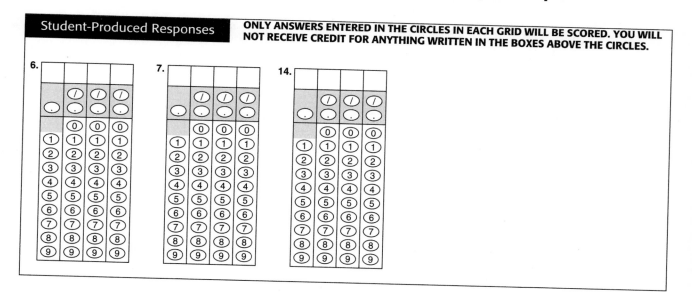

PRACTICE SAT QUESTIONS

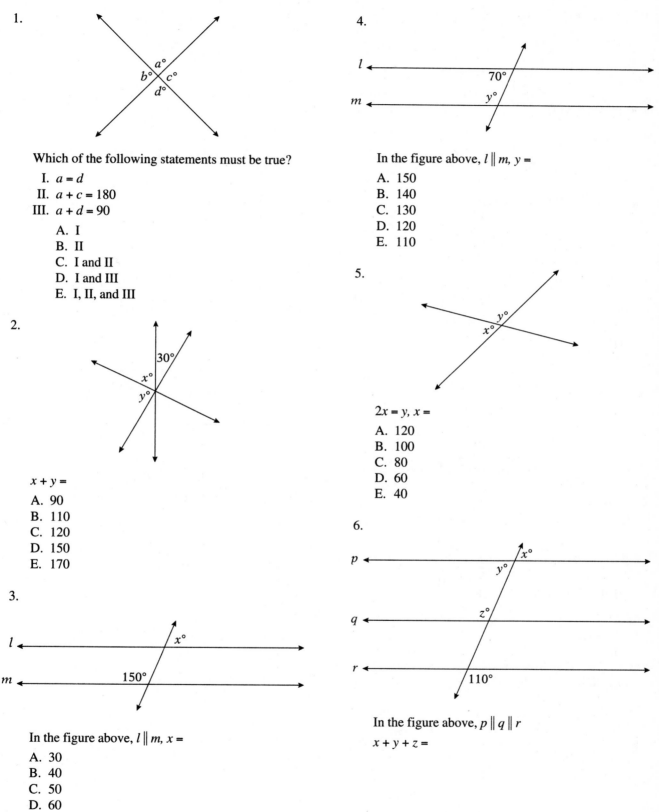

1.

Which of the following statements must be true?

I. $a = d$
II. $a + c = 180$
III. $a + d = 90$

A. I
B. II
C. I and II
D. I and III
E. I, II, and III

2.

$x + y =$

A. 90
B. 110
C. 120
D. 150
E. 170

3.

In the figure above, $l \parallel m$, $x =$

A. 30
B. 40
C. 50
D. 60
E. 70

4.

In the figure above, $l \parallel m$, $y =$

A. 150
B. 140
C. 130
D. 120
E. 110

5.

$2x = y$, $x =$

A. 120
B. 100
C. 80
D. 60
E. 40

6.

In the figure above, $p \parallel q \parallel r$

$x + y + z =$

7. $x + y =$

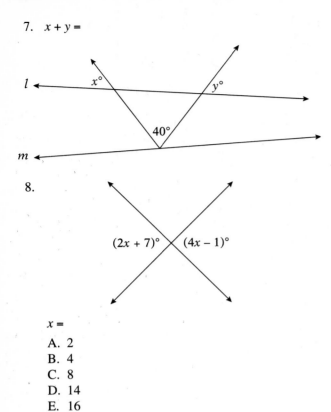

8.

$x =$
A. 2
B. 4
C. 8
D. 14
E. 16

9.

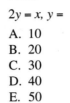

In the figure above, $l \parallel m$ and $p \parallel q$

$y =$
A. 45
B. 75
C. 90
D. 105
E. 135

10.

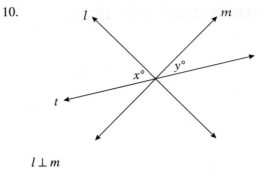

$l \perp m$

$2y = x, y =$
A. 10
B. 20
C. 30
D. 40
E. 50

11.

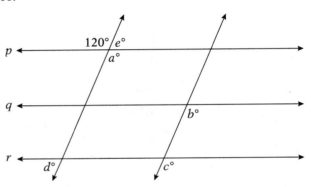

In the figure above, $p \parallel q \parallel r$.

Which of the following statements is not true?

A. $a + e = 180.$
B. $a = b.$
C. $b + c = 180.$
D. $c + d = 180.$
E. $d = e.$

12.

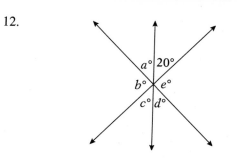

$360° - (a + b + d + e) =$

A. 10
B. 20
C. 30
D. 40
E. 50

13.

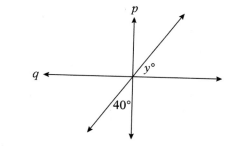

$p \perp q,$

$y =$

A. 40
B. 45
C. 50
D. 55
E. 60

14.

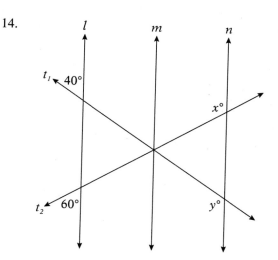

In the above figure, $l \parallel m \parallel n$

$x + y =$

15.

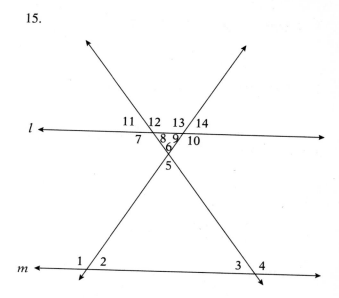

In the figure above, $l \parallel m$

Which of the following pairs of angles are supplementary?

  I. 1 and 9
 II. 6 and 8
III. 13 and 14

    A. I
    B. II
    C. I and II
    D. II and III
    E. I and III

▓▓▓ **EXPLAINED ANSWERS**

1. *Answer:* **C**

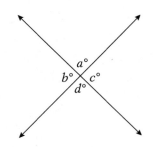

>   I.   Vertical angles are congruent, so $a = d$.
>   II. Linear pairs are supplementary, so $a + c = 180°$.

2. *Answer:* **D**

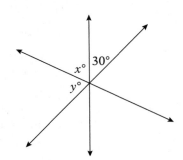

$x + y + 30$ "forms" a straight line, so $x + y + 30 = 180$

so $x + y = 150$.

3. *Answer:* **A**

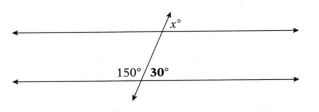

Corresponding angles are congruent, so $x = 30$.

4. *Answer:* **E**

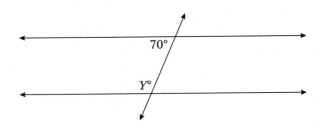

Same side interior angles are supplementary, so,

$y + 70 = 180 \Rightarrow y = 110$.

5. *Answer:* **D**

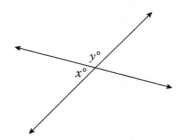

A linear pair is supplementary, so $x + y = 180$.

Substitute $2x$ for y. $x + 2x = 180$.

Solve for x. $3x = 180 \Rightarrow x = 60$.

6. *Answer:* **250**

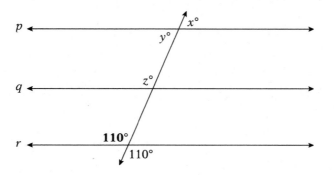

Corresponding angles are congruent, so $z = 110$.

$y + z = 180$.

Same side interior angles are supplementary, so $y + 110 = 180$.

$y = 70$.

Vertical angles are congruent. $x = y \Rightarrow x = 70$.

That means, $x + y + z = 70 + 70 + 110 = 250$.

7. *Answer:* **140**

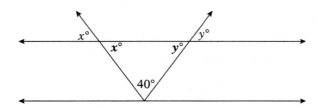

The sum of the angles in a triangle is 180°.

$x + y + 40 = 180 \Rightarrow x + y = 140$.

8. *Answer:* **B**

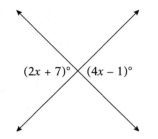

Vertical angles are congruent, so $2x + 7 = 4x - 1$.

Solve for x. $2x + 7 = 4x - 1 \Rightarrow 8 = 2x \Rightarrow 4 = x$.

9. *Answer:* **E**

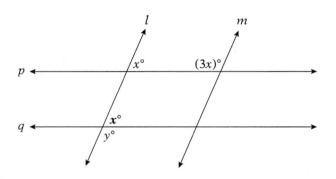

Notice that there are two sets of intersecting parallel lines.

$3x + x = 180$. (Same side interior angles are supplementary.)

Solve for x. $4x = 180 \Rightarrow x = 45$.

$x + y = 180$ because x and y form a linear pair.

Substitute 45 for x and solve. $y = 180 - 45 = 135$.

10. *Answer:* **C**

l is perpendicular to m, so these lines form a 90° angle.

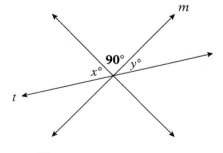

The sum of x, y, and 90 is 180, so $x + y = 90$

Substitute $x = 2y$. $2y + y = 90$, $3y = 90$ so $y = 30$.

CHAPTER 14 / INTERSECTING LINES

11. *Answer:* **C**

    Use the rules of parallel lines cut by a transversal to find the angle measures.

    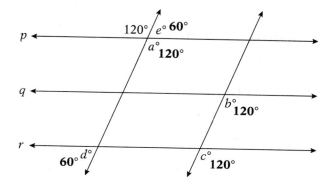

12. *Answer:* **D**

    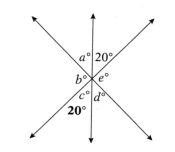

    The sum of the angles around the point is 360°. Vertical angles are congruent, so $c = 20$, $2 \times (20) = 40$. That leaves 320° for angles a, b, d, and e.

    $360 - (a + b + d + e) = 360 - 320 = 40$.

13. *Answer:* **C**

    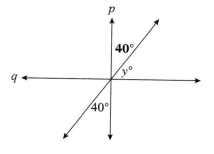

    We know $p \perp q$ so $y + 40 = 90$.

    That means $y = 50$.

14. *Answer:* **260**

Use the rules for parallel lines cut by a transversal to find the angle measures.

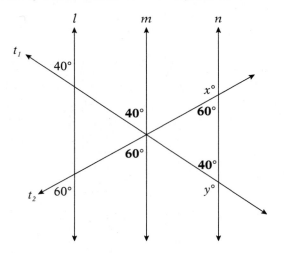

A linear pair is supplementary, so:

$x + 60 = 180$ and $x = 120$.

$y + 40 = 180$ and $y = 140$.

That means, $x + y = 120 + 140 = 260$.

15. *Answer:* **E**

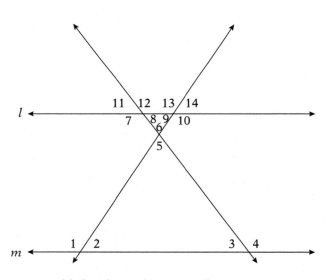

I.   YES $\angle 1$ and $\angle 9$ because same side interior angles are supplementary.

II. NO $\angle 6$ and $\angle 8$ are two angles in a triangle. That means the sum of the measures of these angles is less than 180°. They cannot be supplementary.

III. YES $\angle 13$ and $\angle 14$ because a linear pair is supplementary.

CHAPTER 15
SOLIDS

Solids occupy three-dimensional space. SAT questions about solids often ask you to find the volume or surface area of a solid or of a part of a solid. As you will see, a solid can contain several different figures such as line segments, triangles, circles, rectangles, and other polygons. You will receive plenty of practice solving the types of problems dealing with solids. Work through the review, answer the practice questions, look over the 2 Solved SAT Problems and complete the 15 Practice SAT Questions.

Right Prism—a solid with two congruent parallel polygons, called the bases, with all the remaining sides rectangles, called the faces.

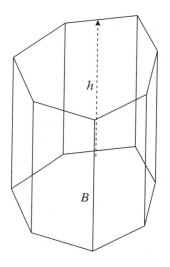

Right Prism

Surface Area

The surface area of a right prism is the sum of the area of the faces and the area of the bases (B).
The volume of a right prism is the product of the area of the base (B) and the height (h).

Regular Prism—a prism in which the bases are regular polygons.

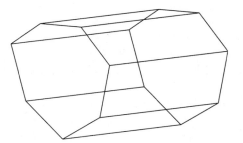

Rectangular Prism—a regular prism with six faces in which two faces have the area *lh,* two faces have the area *lw,* and two faces have the area *hw.*

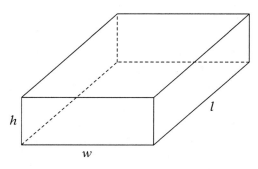

Surface Area = $SA = 2\,lh + 2\,lw + 2\,hw = 2(lh + lw + hw)$.

Volume = $V = Bh = lwh$.

Example:

What is the surface area of a rectangular prism if $V = 200$ in³, $l = 10$ in, and $h = 5$ in?

> Substitute these values in the volume formula $V = lwh \Rightarrow 200 = 10 \cdot w \cdot 5$
> $\Rightarrow 200 = 50 \cdot w \Rightarrow 4$ in $= w$, $w = 4$ in.
> Now substitute $l = 10$, $h = 5$, and $w = 4$. $SA = 2(lh + lw + hw) = 2(10 \cdot 5 + 10 \cdot 4 + 5 \cdot 4) = 2(110) = 220$ in².

Cube—a rectangular prism whose six faces are congruent squares.

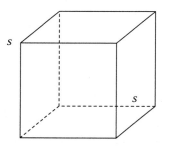

Surface Area = $SA = 6\,s^2$.
Volume = $V = Bs = s^2 s = s^3$.

Example:

What is the volume of a cube if surface area is 1,014 cm²?

> Substitute $S.A. = 1014$ $SA = 6s^2 = 1{,}014$
> Solve for s. $s^2 = 169 \Rightarrow s = 13$ cm.
> Substitute $s = 13$. $V = s^3 = 13^3 = 2{,}197$ cm³.

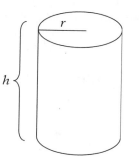

Cylinder—two congruent, parallel, circular bases with radius r connected by a rectangular face with height h.

When the cylinder is rolled out, we can see that the width of the rectangular face is equal to the circumference of one of the circular bases.

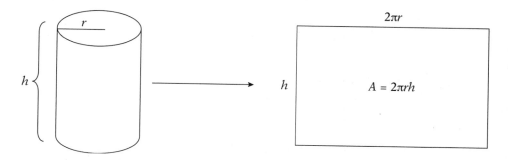

Surface Area = Area of rectangle + 2(Area of base) = $2\pi rh + 2\pi r^2$.
Volume = $Bh = \pi r^2 h$.

Example:

What is the volume of a cylinder with height 10 ft and whose rectangular face has an area of 120π ft².

Substitute 120π for the Area of the face. Area of face = $2\pi rh = 120\pi$
Substitute 10 for h. $2\pi r \cdot 10 = 120\,\pi$.
Solve for r. $20\pi r = 120\pi \Rightarrow r = 6$ ft.
Substitute $r = 6$. $V = \pi r^2 h = \pi(6)^2 \cdot 12 = 432\pi$ *ft³*.

Cone—a circular base with radius (r) and a single vertex a fixed height (h) from the center of the base.

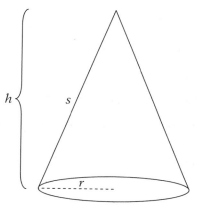

Volume = $\dfrac{1}{3} Bh = \dfrac{1}{3} \pi r^2 h.$

Example:

What is the radius of a cone with $V = 144\pi$ m³ and $h = 9$ m?

Substitute 144π for V. $V = \frac{1}{3}\pi r^2 h$

Substitute $h = 9$. $144\pi = \frac{1}{3}\pi r^2 \cdot 9$

Solve for r. $144\pi = 3\pi r^2$.

$48 = r^2 \Rightarrow 48 = r^2 \Rightarrow \sqrt{48} = r \Rightarrow \sqrt{16 \cdot 3} = r \Rightarrow 4\sqrt{3}\text{m} = r$.

Triangular Pyramid (Tetrahedran)—a pyramid made up of four congruent equilateral triangles.

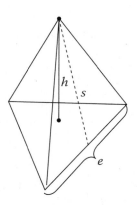

Square Pyramid—a pyramid made up of a square base four congruent triangular faces.

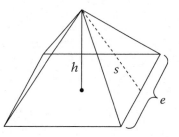

The area of each triangular face in a triangular pyramid and a square pyramid is $A = \frac{1}{2}e \times s$.

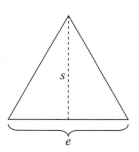

Surface Area (SA)—the sum of the areas of the triangular faces and the area of the base, B.

Volume (V) = $\frac{1}{3}$ Bh.

Example:

What is the surface area of the square pyramid seen below?

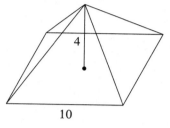

Use the Pythagorean Theorem to find s, the height of one of the four congruent triangles. Then find the area of one of the triangles.

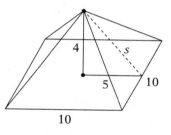

$$s^2 = 4^2 + 5^2 = 16 + 25 = 41 \Rightarrow s = \sqrt{41}$$

Find the area of the triangular face. $A_T = \frac{1}{2} \times 10 \times \sqrt{41} = 5\sqrt{41}$.

The surface area is the sum of the area of the base and the four triangles.

$$SA = 10^2 + 4 \times 5\sqrt{41} = 100 + 20\sqrt{41}.$$

Example:

The length of each edge of a tetrahedran is 8. What is the surface area of the tetrahedran?

A tetrahedran has 4 triangular faces. The edges have the same length, so the faces are congruent equilateral triangles.

Draw the height in one triangle to form two 30°-60°-90° right triangles. Find the area of one face and multiply it by 4.

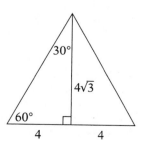

Substitute $b = 8$ and $h = 4\sqrt{3}$ in the triangle area formula.

$$A_T = \frac{1}{2} \times 8 \times 4\sqrt{3} = 4 \times 4\sqrt{3} = 16\sqrt{3}$$

The Surface Area is $4 \times (16\sqrt{3}) = 64\sqrt{3}$.

Sphere—a set of points equidistant from a given point.

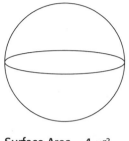

Surface Area = $4\pi r^2$.

Volume = $\frac{4}{3}\pi r^3$.

Example:

What is the volume of a sphere that has a surface area of $1{,}156\pi$ cm².

Substitute $1{,}156\pi$ for Surface Area. $4\pi r^2 = 1{,}156\pi$
Solve for r. $r^2 = 289 \Rightarrow r = 17$ cm.

Substitute $r = 17$. $V = \frac{4}{3}\pi r^3 = \frac{4}{3}\pi(17)^3 = \frac{4}{3} \times 4{,}913\pi = \frac{19{,}652\pi}{3}$.

Practice Questions

1. What is the surface area of a rectangular prism if $V = 440$ m³, $l = 11$ m, and $w = 5$ m?
2. What is the surface area of a cube if volume is 729 cm³?
3. What is the radius of a cylinder with height 12 in and $V = 2{,}352\pi$ in³?
4. What is the volume of a cone with $r = 15$ m and $h = 9$ m?
5. What is the volume of a square pyramid with base area 64 ft² and height twice the length of a base edge?
6. The length of each edge of a tetrahedran is 12 cm. What is the surface area of the tetrahedran?
7. What is the surface area of a sphere that has a volume of $2{,}304\pi$ cm³.

Practice Answers

1. $SA = 366$ m²
2. $SA = 486$ cm³
3. $r = 14$ in
4. $V = 675\pi$ m³
5. $V = \frac{1{,}024}{3}$ ft³
6. $SA = 144\sqrt{3}$ cm²
7. $SA = 576\pi$ cm²

▬▬ SOLVED SAT PROBLEMS

1. What is the surface area of the prism seen below if the bases are isosceles triangles?

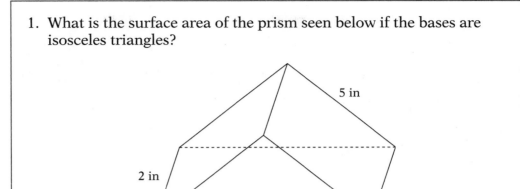

Answer: 56

Draw the height of the triangle. Notice the height creates two 3-4-5 right triangles.

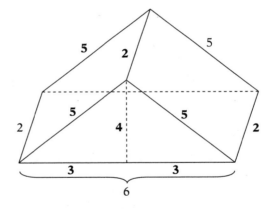

SA = 2(Area of triangular base) + 2(Area of slanted rectangles) + (Area of flat rectangle).

Substitute $SA = 2(\frac{1}{2} \times 6 \times 4) + 2(2 \times 5) + 6 \times 2 = 56$ in².

2. The base area of a square pyramid is 144 cm², and the height is 8 cm. What is the surface area of the square pyramid?

Answer: **384 cm²**

Draw the figure. Find the area of the base and the sum of the area of the faces. We know that the area of the base is 144 cm², we must now find the area of one of the triangles. To find the area of a triangular face we must know the height of the triangle, *s*, and the base of the triangle, *e*. Because the area of the base is 144 cm² $\Rightarrow e = 12$ cm, we must now find *s*. A right triangle can be formed with hypotenuse *s*, one leg $h = 8$, and the other leg half of $e = \frac{1}{2}(12) = 6$.

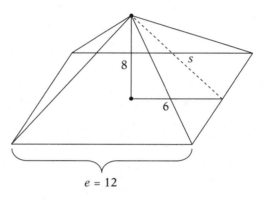

$e = 12$

The triangle formed in the figure is a 3-4-5 right triangle. So $s = 2(5) = 10$. The area of the triangular face of the pyramid is $\frac{1}{2}(e)(s)$. Substitute $e = 12$ and $s = 10$ and the area of the triangular face is $\frac{1}{2}(12 \cdot 10) = \frac{1}{2} \cdot 120 = 60$. So the surface area of the pyramid is $SA = 144 + 4(60) = 144 + 240 = 384$.

SOLIDS
PRACTICE SAT QUESTIONS

ANSWER SHEET

Choose the correct answer.
If no choices are given, grid the answers in the section at the bottom of the page.

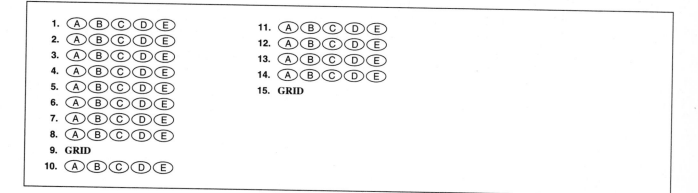

1. Ⓐ Ⓑ Ⓒ Ⓓ Ⓔ
2. Ⓐ Ⓑ Ⓒ Ⓓ Ⓔ
3. Ⓐ Ⓑ Ⓒ Ⓓ Ⓔ
4. Ⓐ Ⓑ Ⓒ Ⓓ Ⓔ
5. Ⓐ Ⓑ Ⓒ Ⓓ Ⓔ
6. Ⓐ Ⓑ Ⓒ Ⓓ Ⓔ
7. Ⓐ Ⓑ Ⓒ Ⓓ Ⓔ
8. Ⓐ Ⓑ Ⓒ Ⓓ Ⓔ
9. GRID
10. Ⓐ Ⓑ Ⓒ Ⓓ Ⓔ

11. Ⓐ Ⓑ Ⓒ Ⓓ Ⓔ
12. Ⓐ Ⓑ Ⓒ Ⓓ Ⓔ
13. Ⓐ Ⓑ Ⓒ Ⓓ Ⓔ
14. Ⓐ Ⓑ Ⓒ Ⓓ Ⓔ
15. GRID

Use the answer spaces in the grids below if the question requires a grid-in response.

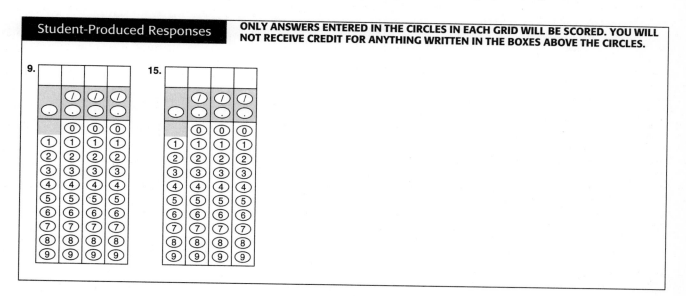

Student-Produced Responses

ONLY ANSWERS ENTERED IN THE CIRCLES IN EACH GRID WILL BE SCORED. YOU WILL NOT RECEIVE CREDIT FOR ANYTHING WRITTEN IN THE BOXES ABOVE THE CIRCLES.

9.

15.

▌ PRACTICE SAT QUESTIONS

1. What is the height of a right cylinder with radius 5 in and volume $150\,\pi$ in³?

   A. 5 in
   B. 6 in
   C. 7 in
   D. 8 in
   E. 9 in

2. What is the radius of a right cone with height 15 cm and volume $90\,\pi$ cm³?

   A. $3\sqrt{2}$ cm
   B. $2\sqrt{3}$ cm
   C. 6 cm
   D. 9 cm
   E. 18 cm

3. A cube and a rectangular prism have the same surface area. If the dimensions of the rectangular prism are $h = 9$ ft, $w = 18$ ft, and $l = 10$ ft, how long is each side of the cube?

   A. $\sqrt{12}$ ft
   B. $2\sqrt{2}$ ft
   C. $6\sqrt{2}$ ft
   D. 72 ft
   E. 12 ft

4. What is the surface area of a cube with a volume of 5,832 ft³?

   A. 2,916 ft²
   B. 2,430 ft²
   C. 1,944 ft²
   D. 1,458 ft²
   E. 972 ft²

5. A sphere is created with half the radius of the original sphere. What is the ratio of the volume of the original sphere to the volume of the new sphere?

   A. 1:8
   B. 8:1
   C. 2:1
   D. 1:2
   E. 4:1

6. In the rectangular pyramid below, the area of one triangular face is 21 ft². What is the height of the pyramid?

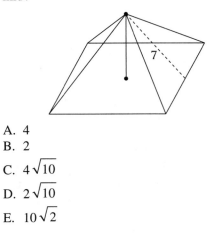

   A. 4
   B. 2
   C. $4\sqrt{10}$
   D. $2\sqrt{10}$
   E. $10\sqrt{2}$

7. The area of the base of a cylinder is $100\,\pi$ m². The volume of the cylinder is $900\,\pi$ m³. What is the height of the cylinder?

   A. 9 m
   B. 10 m
   C. 11 m
   D. 12 m
   E. 13 m

8. Each side of the cube below has a length of 5 in.

   $AF =$

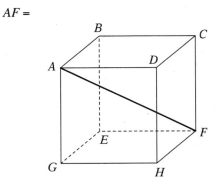

   A. $5\sqrt{2}$
   B. $5\sqrt{3}$
   C. 10
   D. $10\sqrt{2}$
   E. $10\sqrt{3}$

9. What is the value of *PD* in the square pyramid below?

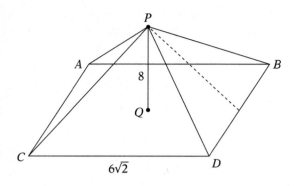

10. A cone has a radius twice the height. The height of the cone is equal to the radius of a sphere. Which of the statements is true about the ratio between the volume of the cone and the volume of the sphere?

    A. 2:1
    B. 1:2
    C. 4:1
    D. 1:4
    E. 1:1

11. A rectangular prism has dimensions $h = 2$ ft, $w = 7$ ft, and $l = 4$ ft. The prism is cut into two separate rectangular prisms by a plane parallel to one of the faces. What is the maximum increase in the surface area between the original prism and the two separate prisms?

    A. 8 ft
    B. 14 ft
    C. 16 ft
    D. 28 ft
    E. 56 ft

12. The volume of a rectangular prism is 1,080 cm³. The ratio $l:w:h = 2:4:5$. What is the surface area of the prism?

    A. 2,052 ft²
    B. 1,368 ft²
    C. 1,080 ft²
    D. 684 ft²
    E. 342 ft²

13. What is the volume of a regular hexagonal prism with height 13 ft and base-edge length of 10 ft?

    A. $1,950\sqrt{3}$
    B. $750\sqrt{3}$
    C. $150\sqrt{3}$
    D. $25\sqrt{3}$
    E. $5\sqrt{3}$

14. The conical tank below is filled with liquid. How much liquid has poured from the tip of the cone if the water level is 9 feet from the tip?

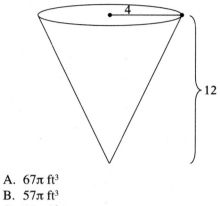

    A. 67π ft³
    B. 57π ft³
    C. 47π ft³
    D. 37π ft³
    E. 27π ft³

15. The base area of a cylinder is 16π m². A plane cuts the cylinder in half forming the rectangle below. If the volume of the cylinder is 240π m³ what is the area of the rectangle?

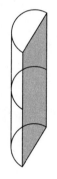

EXPLAINED ANSWERS

1. ***Answer:*** **B**

    Substitute $V = 150\pi$ and $r = 5$.

    $$V = \pi r^2 h = 150\pi \Rightarrow \pi(5)^2 h = 150\pi$$

    Solve for h. $25\pi h = 150\pi \Rightarrow h = 6$ in

2. ***Answer:*** **A**

    Substitute $V = 90\pi$ and $h = 15$.

    $$V = \frac{1}{3}\pi r^2 h \Rightarrow \frac{1}{3}\pi r^2 (15) = 90\pi \Rightarrow 5\pi r^2 = 90\pi$$

    Solve for r. $r^2 = 18 \Rightarrow r = \sqrt{18} \Rightarrow r = \sqrt{9 \cdot 2} = 3\sqrt{2}$

3. ***Answer:*** **E**

    Use the Surface Area formula for a rectangular prism.

    SA of rectangular prism $= 2(lh + lw + hw) = 2(10 \cdot 9 + 10 \cdot 18 + 9 \cdot 18) = 2(432) = 864$.

    Use the surface area formula for a cube.

    SA of cube $= 6\,s^2 = 864$

    Solve for s. $s^2 = 144 \Rightarrow s = \sqrt{144} = 12$.

4. ***Answer:*** **C**

    Substitute $V = 5832$. $V = s^3 = 5,832$

    Solve for s. $s = 18$

    Substitute $s = 18$. $SA = 6\,s^2 = 6(18)^2 = 1,944$ ft².

5. ***Answer:*** **B**

    The volume of the original sphere is $\frac{4}{3}\pi r^3$.

    The volume of the new sphere is $= \frac{4}{3}\pi \left(\frac{r}{2}\right)^3 = \frac{4}{3}\pi \frac{r^3}{8}$.

    $$\frac{\text{volume of original sphere}}{\text{volume of new sphere}} = \frac{\frac{4}{3}\pi r^3}{\frac{4}{3}\pi \frac{r^3}{8}} = \frac{1}{\frac{1}{8}} = \frac{8}{1} = 8:1.$$

6. *Answer:* **D**

   The length of the base (b) of the triangular face is also a side of the square base of the pyramid.

   Use the formula for the area of a triangle. Substitute $A = 21$ and $h = 7$

   $$A = \frac{1}{2}bh \Rightarrow 21 = \frac{1}{2}(b)(7) \text{ Solve for } b. \ 42 = b(7) \Rightarrow b = 6$$

   Construct a right triangle shown below inside the pyramid. Notice the length of the base of the triangle(s) is half the length of the square. The hypotenuse of the triangle (7) is the slant height of the pyramid.

   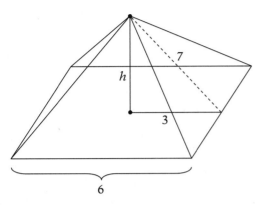

   Use the Pythagorean Theorem to solve for h.

   $$h^2 + 3^3 = 7^2 \Rightarrow h^2 + 9 = 49 \Rightarrow h^2 = 40. \ h = \sqrt{40} = \sqrt{4 \cdot 10} = 2\sqrt{10}$$

7. *Answer:* **A**

   Find the area of the base.

   $$A = \pi r^2 = 100\pi$$

   Substitute $\pi r^2 = 100\,\pi$ and $V = 900\,\pi$.

   $$V = \pi r^2 h \Rightarrow 900\pi = 100\pi h \Rightarrow 9\,\text{m} = h$$

8. *Answer:* **B**

   A right triangle can be formed with legs $\overline{AG}$ and $\overline{GF}$ and hypotenuse $\overline{AF}$

   $\overline{AG}$ is one of the sides of the cube, so, $AG = 5$.

   $\overline{GF}$ is the hypotenuse of a 45°-45°-90° right triangle whose legs are the sides of the cube, so $GF = 5\sqrt{2}$.

   Now, use the Pythagorean Theorem, to solve for AF. Substitute $AG = 5$ and $GF = 5\sqrt{2}$.

   $$\left(AF\right)^2 = \left(AG\right)^2 + \left(GF\right)^2 = \left(5\right)^2 + \left(5\sqrt{2}\right)^2 = 25 + 50 = 75$$

   $$\left(AF\right)^2 = 75 \Rightarrow AF = \sqrt{75} \Rightarrow AF = \sqrt{25 \cdot 3} = 5\sqrt{3}.$$

   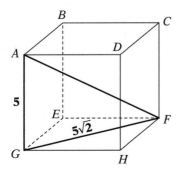

9. *Answer:* **10**

A right triangle can be formed with legs $PQ = 8$ and $\overline{QD}$ and hypotenuse $\overline{PD}$

$\overline{QD}$ is one leg of a 45°-45°-90° right triangle whose hypotenuse is $CD = 6\sqrt{2}$. That means $QD = 6$. Using the Pythagorean Theorem, we can solve for PD.

PD is the hypotenuse of a 3-4-5 right triangle. So, $PD = 2(5) = 10$.

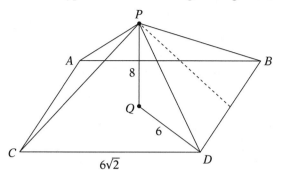

10. *Answer:* **E**

–Volume of a cone is $\frac{1}{3}\pi r^2 h$.

Substitute $r = 2h$.

$V = \frac{1}{3}\pi(4h^2)h = \frac{4}{3}\pi h^3$.

–Volume of a sphere is $\frac{4}{3}\pi r^3$.

The radius of the sphere and the height of the cone are equal.

The ratio is 1:1.

11. *Answer:* **E**

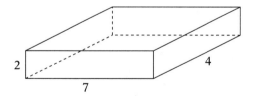

There are three possible ways to cut the prism by a plane parallel to a face.

First:

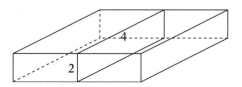

Therefore, through the creation of the two new prisms there would be two faces added each having a surface area of $2 \times 4 = 8$ increasing the total surface area by 16 ft².

Second:

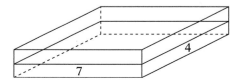

Therefore, through the creation of the two new prisms there would be two faces added each having a surface area of $7 \times 4 = 28$ increasing the total surface area by 56 ft².

Third:

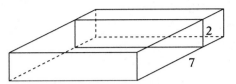

Therefore, through the creation of the two new prisms, there would be two faces added each having a surface area of $7 \times 2 = 14$ increasing the total surface area by 28 ft².

Therefore, the maximum increase in surface area would be 56 ft².

12. ***Answer: D***

Use the volume formula for a rectangular prism.

Substitute $V = 1,080$, $l = 2x$, $w = 4x$, $h = 5x$.

$$(2x)(4x)(5x) = 1,080 \Rightarrow 40x^3 = 1,080$$

$x^3 = 27 \Rightarrow x = 3$.

Solve for x. $l = 2(3) = 6$, $w = 4(3) = 12$, $h = 5(3) = 15$.

Use the surface area formula. Substitute $l = 6$, $w = 12$, and $h = 15$.

$$SA = 2(lh + lw + hw) = 2\left[(6 \cdot 15) + (6 \cdot 12) + (15 \cdot 12)\right] = 2(90 + 72 + 180) = 684 \text{ ft}^2.$$

The surface area is 684 square feet.

13. ***Answer: A***

First find the area of the hexagonal base. We know the length of each side of the hexagon is 10. We can find the area of one of the central equilateral triangles and multiply that area by 6. Use the rules of a 30°-60°-90°

right triangle, to find the height of the triangle is $5\sqrt{3}$.

The area of the triangle is

$$A = \frac{1}{2} \times 10 \times 5\sqrt{3} = 25\sqrt{3}$$

Area of hexagon is $6(25\sqrt{3}) = 150\sqrt{3}$ ft².

Substitute $B = 150\sqrt{3}$ and $h = 3$. The volume of the prism is $V = Bh = (150\sqrt{3}) \times 13 = 1,950\sqrt{3}$ ft³.

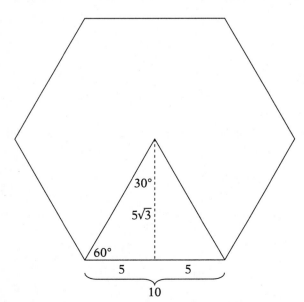

14. **Answer: D**

Use the cone volume formula to find the original amount of liquid in the cone. Substitute $r = 4$ and $h = 12$ to solve for V.

$$V = \frac{1}{3}\pi r^2 h = \frac{1}{3}\pi(4)^2 12 = \frac{192\pi}{3} = 64\pi \text{ ft}^3.$$

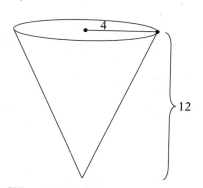

When the liquid level decreases to 9 feet, the remaining liquid forms a new cone whose height is 9. We must now find the radius of this new cone. The ratio of radius to height stays constant.

Substitute $h = 9$. $\dfrac{r}{h} = \dfrac{4}{12} \dfrac{r}{9} = \dfrac{1}{3} \Rightarrow 3r = 9 \Rightarrow r = 3.$

Substitute $r = 3$ and $h = 9$.

Solve for r. The new amount of liquid is

$$V = \frac{1}{3}\pi(3)^2 9 = \frac{81\pi}{3} = 27\pi \text{ ft}^3.$$

So the amount of liquid that has poured out is the difference between the two volumes. $64\pi \text{ ft}^3 - 27\pi \text{ ft}^3 = 37\pi \text{ ft}^3$.

15. **Answer: 120**

The base area of the cylinder is a circle. $B = \pi r^2$

Substitute $16\pi = B$ and solve for r. $16\pi \Rightarrow r = 4.$

The volume of the cylinder is $V = 240\,\pi = Bh$. Substitute $B = 16\pi$ and solve for h. $240\,\pi = 16\,\pi \times h \Rightarrow 15 = h.$

The plane cuts the cylinder in half, so the width of the rectangle is the diameter of the circular base $w = 8$ and the height of the rectangle is $h = 15$. Therefore, the area of the rectangle is $A = wh = 8 \cdot 15 = 120 \text{ m}^2$.

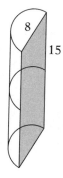

CHAPTER 16

COUNTING, PROBABILITY, AND LOGIC PROBLEMS

This chapter reviews the ideas and strategies required to solve the SAT counting, probability, and logic problems. The solutions are grounded in sound logic. Begin with the mathematics review and then complete and correct the practice problems. There are 2 Solved SAT Problems and 21 Practice SAT Questions with answer explanations.

Probability—the likelihood that an event will occur. If an event is impossible, the probability is 0. If an event will always occur, the probability is 1. All other probabilities fall between 0 and 1.

$$\text{The probability of an event} = P(E) = \frac{\text{number of ways the event can occur}}{\text{total number of possible outcomes}}$$

Example:

There are 60 red marbles, 40 green marbles, and 50 blue marbles in a jar. A marble is picked at random. What is the probability that the marble is red?

$$P(\text{red}) = \frac{60}{150} = \frac{6}{15} = \frac{2}{5} = 0.4.$$

Example:

There are 7 red marbles, 5 green marbles, and 6 blue marbles in a jar. What is the minimum number of marbles to choose, without replacement, to guarantee that there is one of each color marble?

It is possible to get all 7 red marbles, then all 6 blue marbles, and then a green marble. You must choose a minimum of 7 + 6 + 1 = 14 marbles to guarantee that you have one of each color marble.

Example:

A four-digit PIN number is needed to access a bank account. How many different four-digit PIN numbers are there?

There are four positions for each 10 digits.
So there are $\underline{10} \times \underline{10} \times \underline{10} \times \underline{10} = 10{,}000$ different PIN numbers.

Example:

A four-digit PIN number is needed to access a bank account. How many different four-digit PIN numbers are possible if no number can be used twice?

There are four digits, 10 digits in the first position, 9 in the second, 8 in the third, and 7 in the fourth.

$\underline{10} \times \underline{9} \times \underline{8} \times \underline{7} = 5{,}040$ different PIN numbers

Example:

A four-digit PIN number is needed to access a bank account. How many different four-digit PIN numbers are possible if the first and third digits must be odd?

$\underline{5} \times \underline{10} \times \underline{5} \times \underline{10} = 2{,}500$ different PIN numbers

Example:

A four-digit pin number is needed to access a bank account. How many different four-digit PIN numbers are possible if no number can be used twice, and the first and third digits must be odd, and the second and fourth digits must be even?

$\underline{5} \times \underline{5} \times \underline{4} \times \underline{4} = 400$ different PIN numbers

Example:

The figure is made up of one circle inside another. What is the probability that a point picked at random will be in the shaded region?

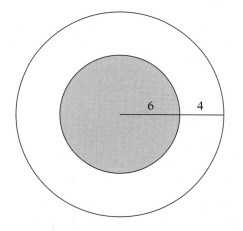

The area of the entire circle is $100\,\pi$ and the area of the shaded circle is $36\,\pi$.

$P\text{ (point in shaded region)} = \dfrac{36\,\pi}{100\,\pi} = \dfrac{36}{100} = 0.36$

Practice Questions

1. Twenty-five people were asked to name their favorite baseball team. Eight answered New York Yankees, seven answered Atlanta Braves, five answered Chicago Cubs, and five answered San Francisco Giants. What is the probability that a person chosen at random has the Atlanta Braves or San Francisco Giants as their favorite team?
2. How many computer passwords can be created with three digits followed by three letters if the first number cannot be 0 and no number or letter can be repeated?

3. What is the probability that a point picked at random in the figure below will be in the shaded region?

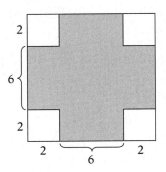

4. Thirty students are asked if they play soccer or basketball. Every student plays at least one of the two sports. Twenty students said they play soccer and 15 said they play basketball. How many students play both sports?

Practice Answers

1. $\frac{12}{25} = 0.48$.

2. $\underline{9} \times \underline{9} \times \underline{8} \times \underline{26} \times \underline{25} \times \underline{24} = 10{,}108{,}800$.

3. $P(\text{shaded}) = \frac{100 - 16}{100} = \frac{84}{100} = 0.84$.

4.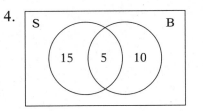

Five students play both sports.

SOLVED SAT PROBLEMS

1. Jerry knows how to play six chords on a guitar: A, C, D, E, F, and G. He makes up exactly one song for every three chords he knows how to play. For example, the chords A, E, and F are only used in one song together. How many songs did Jerry make up?

   A. 5
   B. 10
   C. 15
   D. 20
   E. 25

   Answer: **D**

   Here is a list of the chords.

   ACD, ACE, ACF, ACG, ADE, ADF, ADG, AEF, AEG, AFG, CDE, CDF, CDG, CEF, CEG, CFG, DEF, DEG, DFG, EFG

2. A password is made up of two letters followed by two single-digit numbers. If a person is assigned a password at random, what is the probability, rounded to the nearest hundredth, that the password uses only even digits for the numbers?

   Answer: **0.25**

   There are a total of $\underline{26} \times \underline{26} \times \underline{10} \times \underline{10} = 67{,}600$ possible passwords, of which $\underline{26} \times \underline{26} \times \underline{5} \times \underline{5} = 16{,}900$ use only even digits.

   $$P(\text{even digits}) = \frac{16{,}900}{67{,}000} \approx 0.25.$$

COUNTING, PROBABILITY, AND LOGIC PROBLEMS
PRACTICE SAT QUESTIONS

ANSWER SHEET

Choose the correct answer.
If no choices are given, grid the answers in the section at the bottom of the page.

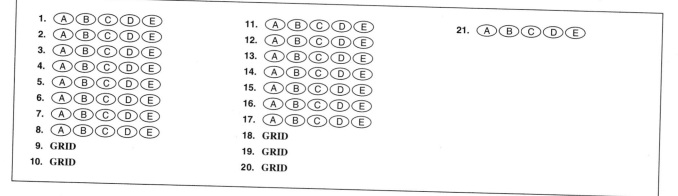

Use the answer spaces in the grids below if the question requires a grid-in response.

Student-Produced Responses   ONLY ANSWERS ENTERED IN THE CIRCLES IN EACH GRID WILL BE SCORED. YOU WILL NOT RECEIVE CREDIT FOR ANYTHING WRITTEN IN THE BOXES ABOVE THE CIRCLES.

PRACTICE SAT QUESTIONS

1. 60 blue marbles and 40 red marbles are in a jar. How many red marbles must be removed from the jar so that the probability of choosing a blue marble from the jar is $\frac{3}{4}$?

   A. 5
   B. 10
   C. 15
   D. 20
   E. 25

2. How many positive 4-digit numbers are there with an even digit in the hundreds position and an odd digit in the tens position?

   A. 10,000
   B. 5,040
   C. 2,500
   D. 2,250
   E. 2,150

3. John buys a cake at a bakery and a hammer at a hardware store. If there are five hardware stores and three bakeries, in how many different combinations of stores can he purchase the cake and the hammer?

   A. 20
   B. 15
   C. 8
   D. 5
   E. 3

4. The figure below consists of two congruent semicircles on either end of a square. What is the probability, rounded to the nearest hundredth, that a point in the region chosen at random is not in the shaded area?

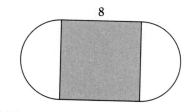

8

   A. 0.56
   B. 0.52
   C. 0.48
   D. 0.46
   E. 0.44

5. Three coins are tossed at the same time. What is the probability that exactly two heads are face up?

   A. $\frac{1}{8}$

   B. $\frac{1}{4}$

   C. $\frac{3}{8}$

   D. $\frac{1}{2}$

   E. $\frac{5}{8}$

6. There are 15 students on the Prom Committee and 20 students on the Yearbook Committee. If 10 students are on both committees, how many students are on only one committee?

   A. 5
   B. 10
   C. 15
   D. 20
   E. 25

7. Five people want to rent the last two copies of a movie. How many ways can these five people rent the two movies?

   A. 10
   B. 9
   C. 8
   D. 7
   E. 6

8. There are 10 orange sodas, 15 cream sodas, and 7 cherry sodas in an ice chest. How many sodas must be removed from the ice chest to guarantee that one of each type of soda has been chosen?

   A. 16
   B. 18
   C. 23
   D. 25
   E. 26

9. How many 5-digit numerals have 9 as the first digit, 3 or 6 as the third digit, and no digit repeated?

10. Someone writes a five digit numeral that reads the same from left to right as right to left (a palindrome). How many 5-digit palindromes are there?

11. A jar contains 10 blue, 8 green, and 6 red marbles. Every time a marble is removed from the jar, it is not replaced. What is the probability, to the nearest hundredth, that the second marble chosen is green if the first marble chosen is green?

    A. 0.28
    B. 0.29
    C. 0.30
    D. 0.31
    E. 0.32

12. Five people, all different ages, are arranged in a row so that the oldest person is in the middle and the two youngest people are on the ends. How many different arrangements of this type exist?

    A. 32
    B. 16
    C. 8
    D. 4
    E. 2

13. A teacher gives stickers to students as a reward for good work. The stickers are on a long strip and repeat in a regular order: Balloon, Happy Face, Clown Face, and Spaceship. What are the 63rd and 65th stickers handed out by the teacher?

    A. Balloon and Happy Face
    B. Clown face and Balloon
    C. Spaceship and Clown Face
    D. Clown Face and Happy Face
    E. Balloon and Spaceship

14. Seventy people are seated at a dinner party. Each table at the party can seat eight people. What is the minimum number of tables needed for the party?

    A. 12
    B. 11
    C. 10
    D. 9
    E. 8

15. Frank scored 26 points in a basketball game. All of his points came from either a two-point or three-point basket. If Frank scored at least one three-point basket, what is the maximum number of two-point baskets that Frank could have scored?

    A. 11
    B. 10
    C. 9
    D. 8
    E. 7

16. Fifty people went to see two different movies. Forty saw Movie A and twenty saw both Movie A and Movie B. How many people saw Movie B?

    A. 10
    B. 20
    C. 30
    D. 40
    E. 50

17. Blaire, Chad, Erin, and Jordan randomly arranged in four seats at the front row of the classroom. What is the probability that Chad and Blaire are sitting next to each other?

    A. 0.15
    B. 0.25
    C. 0.35
    D. 0.4
    E. 0.5

18. Using the diagram below, how many different ways can you get from point A to point C and then back to point A?

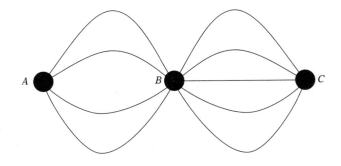

19. A dart is thrown randomly at the target below. The radius of the innermost circle is 2, and the radius of each circle doubles as the circles get bigger. What is the probability the dart will hit the shaded region, to the nearest hundredth of a percentage?

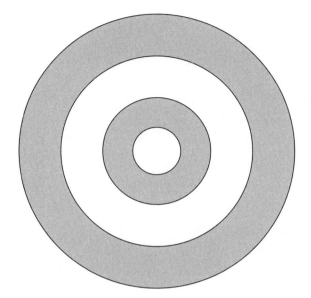

20. A certain communication system is made up of 40 symbols. A maximum of two symbols placed together, order not mattering, make up a word. What is the maximum number of words in this communication system?

21. $X = \{-4,-2,1,3\}$ $Y = \{-1,4,5\}$. If x is a number from set X, and y is a number from set Y. The probability that $x + y$ is positive is closest to

A. 0.5
B. 0.6
C. 0.7
D. 0.8
E. 0.9

EXPLAINED ANSWERS

1. ***Answer:* D**
    If 20 red marbles are removed, there are 60 blue marbles and 20 red marbles remaining. $P(\text{Blue}) = \dfrac{60}{80} = \dfrac{6}{8} = \dfrac{3}{4}$.

2. ***Answer:* D**
    The first digit can be any digit but 0.

    The second position must be even {0,2,4,6,8}.

    The third position must be odd. {1,3,5,7,9}.

    The fourth position can be any digit/
    $\underline{9} \times \underline{5} \times \underline{5} \times \underline{10} = 2,250$

3. ***Answer:* B**
    There are $\underline{5} \times \underline{3} = 15$.

4. ***Answer:* E**
    The two semicircles, which make up a single circle, have the same diameter as one side of the square, $d = 8$ and $r = 4$. That means the area of the entire figure is $8^2 + \pi(4)^2 = 64 + 16\,\pi$.

    The area of the nonshaded region, which is the two semicircles, is $\pi(4)^2 = 16\,\pi$.

    The probability of choosing a point not in the shaded region is the probability of not choosing a point in the shaded region. $\dfrac{16\,\pi}{64 + 16\,\pi} \approx 0.44$

5. ***Answer:* C**
    First, list all the possible outcomes when three coins are tossed in the air. When a coin is tossed, there are two outcomes, Heads or Tails. When three coins are tossed, there are $\underline{2} \times \underline{2} \times \underline{2} = 8$ possible outcomes
    {*HHH, HHT, HTH, THH, HTT, THT, TTH, TTT*}.

    Three of these outcomes have exactly two heads.

    Therefore, $P(\text{exactly two heads}) = \dfrac{3}{8}$.

6. ***Answer:* C**
    The best approach is to create a Venn diagram. First fill in the part common to both and then fill in the rest.

    P = Prom Committee Y = Yearbook Committee

    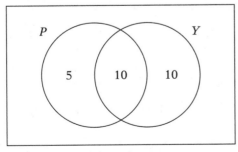

    We can see that 5 students are on the Prom Committee only and 10 students are on the Yearbook Committee only. A total of $5 + 10 = 15$ students are on only one committee.

7. *Answer:* **A**

   Let A, B, C, D, and E represent the five people who want to rent the two movies. List the different pairs of people to find there are 10 pairs {AB, AC, AD, AE, BC, BD, BE, CD, CE, DE}.

8. *Answer:* **E**

   It is possible to first choose all 15 cream sodas, then 10 orange sodas, and finally a cherry soda. That means we must choose 15 + 10 + 1 = 26 sodas to guarantee that at least one of each type of soda is chosen.

9. *Answer:* **672**

   There is one way to choose 9 as the first digit. There are two ways to choose 3 or 6 as the third digit. No number can be used twice, so this leaves us with 8 choices for the second digit, 7 choices for the fourth digit, and 6 choices for the fifth digit.

   $\underline{1} \times \underline{8} \times \underline{2} \times \underline{7} \times \underline{6}$ = 672 possible numbers

10. *Answer:* **900**

    The middle digit can be any digit, giving us 10 choices for the third digit. The first digit cannot be zero. There are nine choices for the first digit. The fifth digit is the same as the first digit—one choice. The second digit can be any digit, so there are 10 choices. The fourth digit is the same as the second digit—one choice. There are $\underline{9} \times \underline{10} \times \underline{10} \times \underline{1} \times \underline{1}$ = 900 five-digit palindromes.

11. *Answer:* **C**

    Because the first marble drawn is green that means there are a total of 23 marbles remaining. Seven of these are green.

    $P(\text{second green}) = \dfrac{7}{23} \approx 0.30$.

12. *Answer:* **D**

    The middle person is the oldest person, so there is only one choice for the middle position. The first position will be one of the two youngest people, so there are two choices for the first position. The fifth position will be the other youngest, so there is one choice. The second position will be one of the two people remaining, so there are two choices. The fourth position will be the last person left, so there is one choice. There are $\underline{2} \times \underline{2} \times \underline{1} \times \underline{1} \times \underline{1}$ = 4 ways to arrange the people.

13. *Answer:* **B**

    There are four stickers. When the position is divided by 4, the remainder identifies the sticker.

    Balloon-Remainder 1   Clown Face-Remainder 3

    Happy Face-Remainder 2   Spaceship-Remainder 0

    4 divides into 63 fifteen times with a remainder of 3, therefore the 3rd sticker will be the 63rd sticker, which is the Clown Face.

    4 divides into 65 sixteen times with a remainder of 1, therefore the 1st sticker will be the 65th sticker, which is the Balloon.

    63rd sticker = Clown Face and the 65th sticker = Balloon.

14. *Answer:* **D**

    A party planner needs a table for everyone. 70 divided by 8 is 8 with 6 remaining. Therefore, the minimum number of tables needed for the party is 9.

15. *Answer:* **B**

   If Frank scored only one 3-pointer that means there are 23 points left to be scored by 2-pointers, which is impossible because 2 does not divide 23 evenly.

   If Frank scored two 3-pointers that means there are 20 points left to be scored by 2-pointers, which is possible because 2 divides 20 ten times.

   The maximum number of 2-pointers that Frank can score is **10.**

16. *Answer:* **C**

   The best way to answer the question is to create a Venn diagram. First fill in the part common to both movies and then fill in the rest.

   A = Saw Movie A B = Saw Movie B

   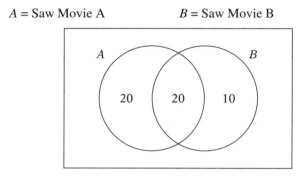

   Using the Venn diagram, we can see that 30 people saw Movie B.

17. *Answer:* **E**

   There are a total of $\underline{4} \times \underline{3} \times \underline{2} \times \underline{1} = 24$ ways to arrange four people.

   Let B = Blaire, C = Chad, E = Erin, and J = Jordan. The different arrangements where Chad is next to Blaire are: BCEJ, BCJE, CBEJ, CBJE, JBCE, EBCJ, JCBE, ECBJ, EJBC, JEBC, EJCB, and JECB. There are 12 ways for Chad to be seated next to Blaire.

   $P(\text{Chad next to Blaire}) = \dfrac{12}{24} = \dfrac{1}{2} = 0.5$

18. *Answer:* **240**

   There are 4 paths from A to B, 5 paths from B to C. No path can be used again so there are four paths from C back to B, and 3 paths from B back to A. There are a total of $\underline{4} \times \underline{5} \times \underline{4} \times \underline{3} = 240$ different ways from A to C and back without using any path twice.

19. *Answer:* **0.80**

    The outer shaded region has an area of $\pi(16)^2 - \pi(8)^2 = 256\pi - 64\pi = 192\pi$.

    The inner shaded region has an area of $\pi(4)^2 - \pi(2)^2 = 16\pi - 4\pi = 12\pi$.

    The total shaded area is $192\pi + 12\pi = 204\pi$.

    The area of the entire region is $\pi(16)^2 = 256\pi$.

    $P(\text{shaded area}) = \dfrac{204\,\pi}{256\,\pi} = 0.80$.

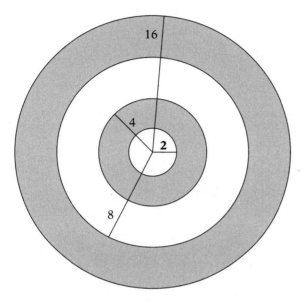

20. *Answer:* **840**

    There are $40 \times 40 = 1{,}600$ ways to place two symbols together. Because the order does not matter. There are half as many words. There are $\dfrac{1600}{2} = 800$ words made up of two symbols. There are 40 words made up of one symbol.

    There are a total of $800 + 40 = 840$ words in this system.

21. *Answer:* **C**

    Split the problem into four cases, one for each possible value of x. Then add each possible value of y $(-1, 4, 5)$.

$x = -4$	$x = -2$
$x + y = -4 + -1 = -5$	$x + y = -2 + -1 = -3$
$x + y = -4 + 4 = 0$	$x + y = -2 + 4 = 2$
$x + y = -4 + 5 = 1$	$x + y = -2 + 5 = 3$
$x = 1$	$x = 3$
$x + y = 1 + -1 = 0$	$x + y = 3 + -1 = 2$
$x + y = 1 + 4 = 5$	$x + y = 3 + 4 = 7$
$x + y = 1 + 5 = 6$	$x + y = 3 + 5 = 8$

    There are 12 answers to $(x + y)$. Eight of these are greater than 0.

    The probability that the sums of x and y are positive (greater than zero) is $\dfrac{8}{12} = 0.66\ldots$, which is closest to 0.7.

CHAPTER 17

DATA INTERPRETATION

Data interpretation often requires you to gather information from graphs and tables. You will use these data to calculate such values as mean, median, mode, and percentile. SAT problems frequently ask you to add, multiply, and compare these values. Begin with the mathematics review and then complete and correct the practice problems. There are 2 Solved SAT Problems and 24 Practice SAT Questions with answer explanations.

Bar Graph—data represented by rectangles. Bar graphs can be used to compare two different datasets.

Example:

The bar graphs below show the land area, in square miles, for six different states. Which of these states has the largest land area?

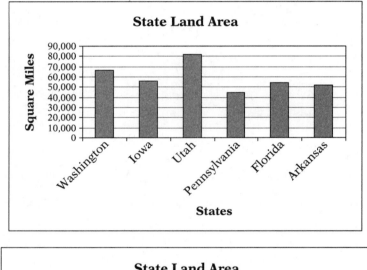

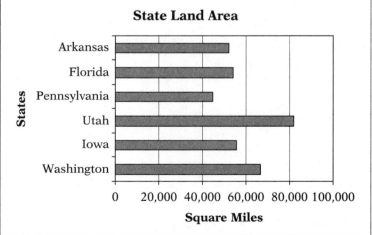

Both bar graphs show the same information. Utah has the longest graph, so it has the largest land area.

Example:

The side-by-side bar graphs below show the population in six different states. Which state has greatest increase in population from 1990 to 2000?

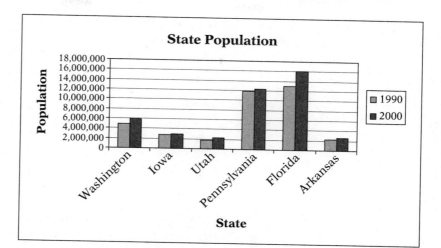

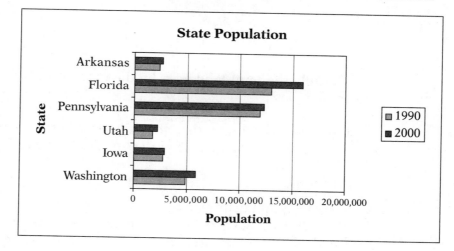

Notice that both graphs display the same information.

Inspection of the graph reveals that Florida has the greatest increase in population.

Pie Chart—a partitioned circle that displays the size of related pieces of information. Pie charts are used to display the relative size of parts.

Example:

The pie chart below shows the percentage of land in Rhode Island split up among the different counties. If Rhode Island has a total of 1,045 square miles of land, how many square miles does Kent County have?

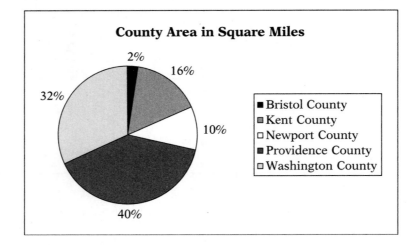

Multiply the total land area by the percent in Kent County. $1,045 \times 0.16 = 167.2$ miles^2.

Line Graph—a graph that shows how data vary depending on one another. The numbers along a side of the line graph are called the scale.

Example:

The line graph below shows the number of home runs for Barry Bonds from 1993–2003. What was his percent decrease in home runs from 2001 to 2002? Divide the decrease in home runs by the number of home runs in 2001.

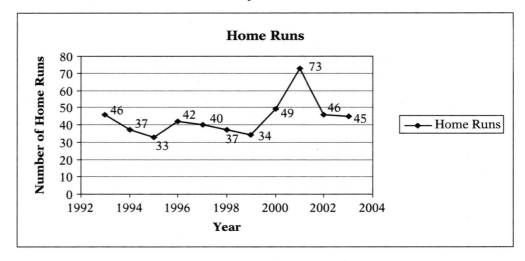

Percent Decrease $= \dfrac{73 - 46}{73} = \dfrac{27}{73} \approx 0.37 = 37\%$

Scatter Plot—shows the relationship between two numeric variables. If the data have a general move up and to the right, then the data have a positive correlation—direct Variation. If the data move down and to the right then, the data have a negative correlation—Inverse Variation.

Example:

The scatterplot below displays the height against weight of several different males. Do the data show a negative correlation, positive correlation, or neither?

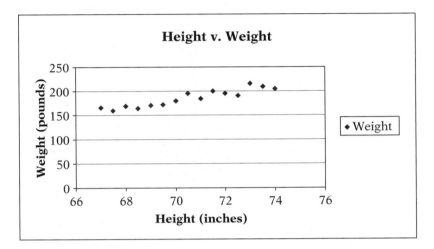

The graph moves slightly up and to the right, showing a slight positive correlation.

Table—displays data in numerical form.

Example:

The data in the table below shows the population of a certain county based on age. What percent of the population comes from the 25 to 34 age group?

Age	Population
Under 5 years	3,960
5 to 9 years	4,334
10 to 14 years	3,877
15 to 19 years	4,393
20 to 24 years	4,314
25 to 34 years	7,912
35 to 44 years	10,855
45 to 54 years	10,519
55 to 59 years	3,625
60 to 64 years	3,242
65 to 74 years	4,848
75 to 84 years	2,899
85 years and over	1,005
Total Population	65,783

Divide the population of the 25 to 34 age group by the total population.

$$\frac{7,912}{65,783} \approx 0.12 = 12\%$$

Pictograph—uses pictures to represent quantities of an item.

Example:

Using the graph below, how many more houses were built in 1999 than in 2001?

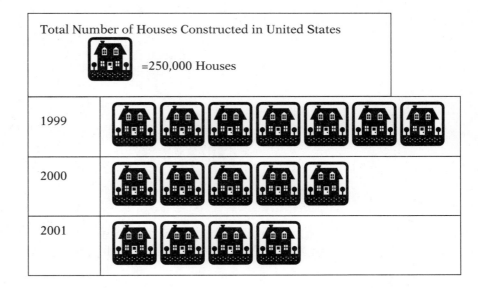

Total Number of Houses Constructed in United States

=250,000 Houses

1999	
2000	
2001	

There are 7 pictures for 1999 and 4 pictures for 2001, a difference of 3.

There are 3 × 250,000 = 750,000 more homes built in 1999 than in 2001.

Practice Questions

1. The bar graph below shows the land area, in square miles, for six different states. Which of these states has land area greater than 60,000 square miles?

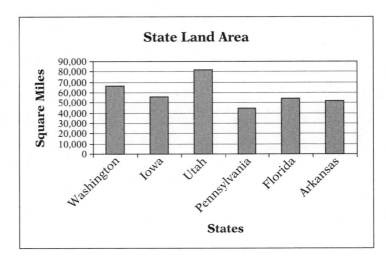

2. The pie chart below shows the percent of land in Rhode Island in the different counties. If Rhode Island has a total of 1,045 square miles of land, how many square miles are in Bristol County and Newport County combined?

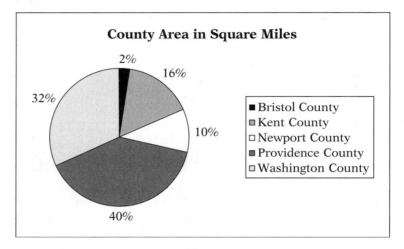

County Area in Square Miles

■ Bristol County
▤ Kent County
☐ Newport County
■ Providence County
☐ Washington County

3. The line graph below shows the number of home runs Barry Bonds hit from 1993–2003. In what year(s) did Barry Bonds hit 46 home runs?

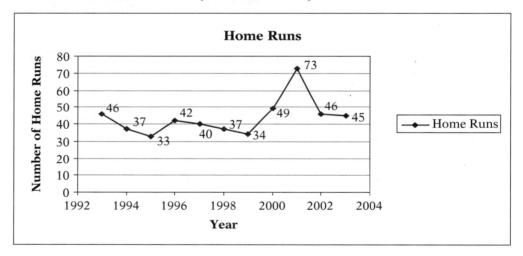

4. The data below show the population of a certain county according to age. What percent of the population comes from the 45 to 54 age group?

Age	Population
Under 5 years	3,960
5 to 9 years	4,334
10 to 14 years	3,877
15 to 19 years	4,393
20 to 24 years	4,314
25 to 34 years	7,912
35 to 44 years	10,855
45 to 54 years	10,519
55 to 59 years	3,625
60 to 64 years	3,242
65 to 74 years	4,848
75 to 84 years	2,899
85 years and over	1,005
Total Population	65,783

Practice Answers

1. Washington and Utah
2. 125.4 square miles
3. 1993 and 2002
4. 16%

SOLVED SAT PROBLEMS

1. In what percent of the months does Portland, Oregon, have fewer rainy days than Portland, Maine?

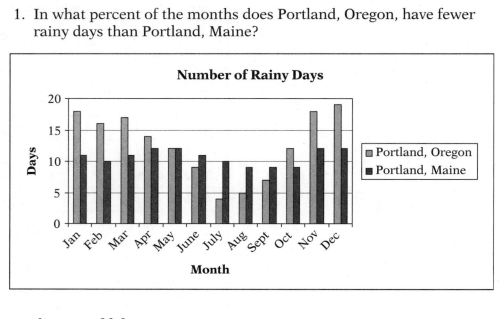

Answer: 33.3

Portland, Oregon, has fewer rainy days in June, July, August, and September. The percent of the months Portland, Oregon, has fewer rainy days than Portland, Maine, is

$$\frac{4}{12} = \frac{1}{3} = 33.3.$$

The exact answer is $33\frac{1}{3}$, but you can't grid this in because $33\frac{1}{3} =$ 33,333.... Use 33.3.

2. Which of the following choices is the best estimator for the slope of the line that best fits the data?

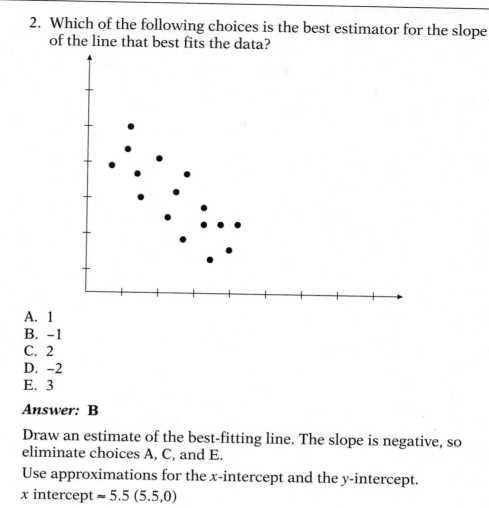

A. 1
B. –1
C. 2
D. –2
E. 3

***Answer:* B**

Draw an estimate of the best-fitting line. The slope is negative, so eliminate choices A, C, and E.

Use approximations for the x-intercept and the y-intercept.

x intercept ≈ 5.5 (5.5,0)

y intercept ≈ 5.5 (0,5.5)

$$m = \frac{5.5 - 0}{0 - 5.5} = \frac{5.5}{5.5} = -1$$

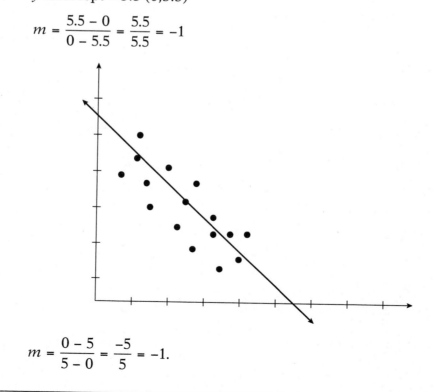

$$m = \frac{0 - 5}{5 - 0} = \frac{-5}{5} = -1.$$

DATA INTERPRETATION
PRACTICE SAT QUESTIONS

ANSWER SHEET

Choose the correct answer.
If no choices are given, grid the answers in the section at the bottom of the page.

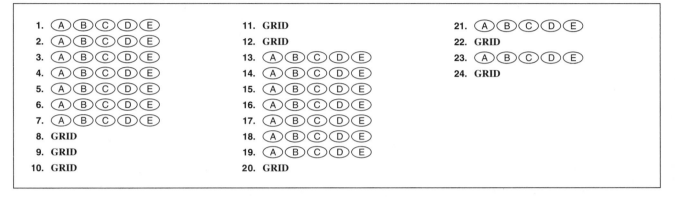

1. (A) (B) (C) (D) (E)   11. GRID   21. (A) (B) (C) (D) (E)
2. (A) (B) (C) (D) (E)   12. GRID   22. GRID
3. (A) (B) (C) (D) (E)   13. (A) (B) (C) (D) (E)   23. (A) (B) (C) (D) (E)
4. (A) (B) (C) (D) (E)   14. (A) (B) (C) (D) (E)   24. GRID
5. (A) (B) (C) (D) (E)   15. (A) (B) (C) (D) (E)
6. (A) (B) (C) (D) (E)   16. (A) (B) (C) (D) (E)
7. (A) (B) (C) (D) (E)   17. (A) (B) (C) (D) (E)
8. GRID   18. (A) (B) (C) (D) (E)
9. GRID   19. (A) (B) (C) (D) (E)
10. GRID   20. GRID

Use the answer spaces in the grids below if the question requires a grid-in response.

| Student-Produced Responses | ONLY ANSWERS ENTERED IN THE CIRCLES IN EACH GRID WILL BE SCORED. YOU WILL NOT RECEIVE CREDIT FOR ANYTHING WRITTEN IN THE BOXES ABOVE THE CIRCLES. |

PRACTICE SAT QUESTIONS

Questions 1 and 2.

The table below shows the prices of the six different cell phones that a store carries.

Phone	Price
SJ-119	$ 49.99
SJ-220	$ 69.99
RV-375	$ 79.99
RV-400	$ 99.99
RKV-5000	$139.99
RKV-9000	$159.99

1. What is the average price of the cell phones?
    A. $69.99
    B. $79.99
    C. $89.99
    D. $99.99
    E. $109.99

2. What is the median price of the cell phones?
    A. $69.99
    B. $79.99
    C. $89.99
    D. $99.99
    E. $109.99

3. The graph below represents the average points per game of a certain basketball player from 1995–2000. What is the percent increase over the 6-year period to the nearest hundredth of a percent?

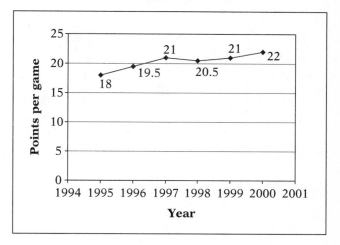

    A. 18%
    B. 18.18%
    C. 20%
    D. 22%
    E. 22.22%

4. Five hundred families were surveyed about the number of computers in their home. The circle graph seen below shows the results. How many families had no computer?

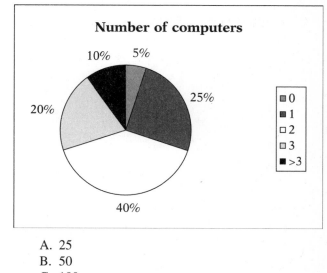

    A. 25
    B. 50
    C. 100
    D. 125
    E. 200

Questions 5 and 6

The bar graph below displays the data gathered when individuals were polled about their favorite type of movie. Each person polled chose one movie type.

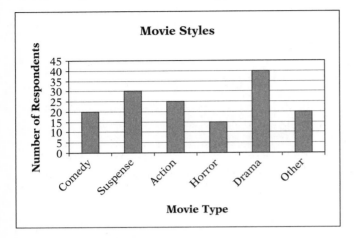

5. What percent of the respondents chose Action or Horror?

   A. $36\frac{2}{3}\%$

   B. $33\frac{1}{3}\%$

   C. $26\frac{2}{3}\%$

   D. $23\frac{1}{3}\%$

   E. $16\frac{2}{3}\%$

6. What is the ratio of Drama to Suspense?

   A. 3:4
   B. 4:3
   C. 3:5
   D. 5:3
   E. 2:3

7. The pie chart below shows the percent sales of the top five selling fruits in a supermarket. The total sales for one day was 1,000 pounds of these fruits. What is the difference between Peach sales and Plum sales?

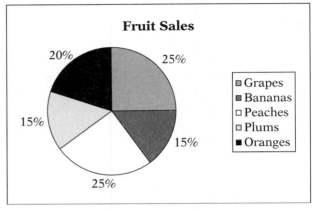

   A. 50 pounds
   B. 100 pounds
   C. 150 pounds
   D. 200 pounds
   E. 250 pounds

8. A total of 250 students participate in five different school-sponsored clubs. The bar graph below shows the number of students who participate in each club. 40% of the members of Club A are in Club B. How many of the members in Club A are not in Club B?

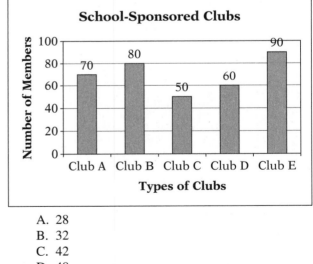

   A. 28
   B. 32
   C. 42
   D. 48
   E. 52

Questions 9–12

The table below displays people's opinion, by age, about a school referendum.

	18–25	26–40	41–60	61 and over	Total
For	56	85	64	x	258
Against	47	85	70	24	226
Undecided	77	50	36	63	226
Total	**180**	**220**	**170**	**140**	**710**

9. What is the value of x?

10. What percent of the people, rounded to the nearest whole number, are for the referendum?

11. What percent of the 18–25 age group, rounded to the nearest whole number, are undecided?

12. What percent of those against the referendum, rounded to the nearest whole number, are in the 41–60 age group?

Questions 13 and 14

The scatterplot below shows a student's grade on a test against the numbers of hours that student spend studying each night.

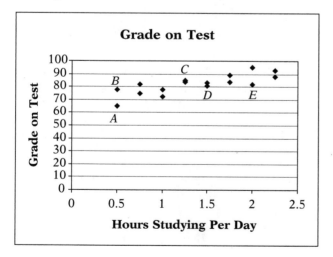

13. Which of the labeled points above represents the highest grade on the test?
    A. *A*
    B. *B*
    C. *C*
    D. *D*
    E. *E*

14. Based on the correlation of the data, which would most likely be the test grade of a student who studies 3 hours a day?
    A. 50
    B. 60
    C. 70
    D. 80
    E. 90

Questions 15 and 16

The table below displays the expected ticket sales for a concert.

Price per Ticket	Expected Number of Tickets Sold
$15	8,500
$20	8,000
$25	7,000
$30	5,000
$35	4,500

15. Which ticket price produces the most revenue?
    A. $15
    B. $20
    C. $25
    D. $30
    E. $35

16. How much more money would be made for tickets priced $35 than for tickets price $30?
    A. $5,000
    B. $7,500
    C. $10,000
    D. $12,500
    E. $15,000

Questions 17 and 18

The bar graph below compares the average monthly temperatures for Charlotte, NC, and Los Angeles, CA.

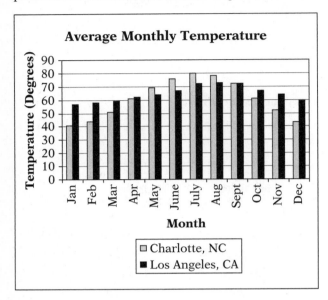

17. In how many months is Charlotte's average temperature greater than Los Angeles's average temperature?
   A. 3
   B. 4
   C. 5
   D. 6
   E. 7

18. In how many months are both cities' average temperature above 60 degrees?
   A. 5
   B. 6
   C. 7
   D. 8
   E. 9

Questions 19 and 20

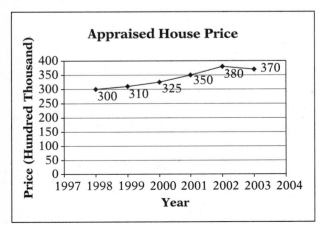

The appraised price of a house is shown in the line graph below.

19. What is the average increase in the price of the house per year?
   A. $5,000
   B. $10,000
   C. $14,000
   D. $35,000
   E. $70,000

20. What is the percent decrease in the price of the house from 2002 to 2003 to the nearest hundredth of a percent?

Question 21

The circle graphs below show the production numbers for certain Ford Mustangs in 1965 and 1971.

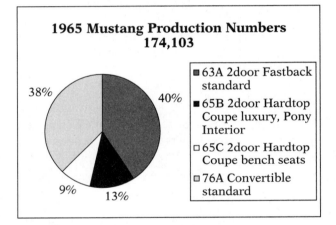

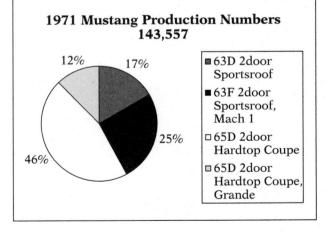

21. Approximately how many more two-door hardtop coupes were made in 1971 than in 1965?
   A. 36,000
   B. 38,303
   C. 44,960
   D. 74,303
   E. 83,263

CHAPTER 17 / DATA INTERPRETATION

Questions 22 and 23

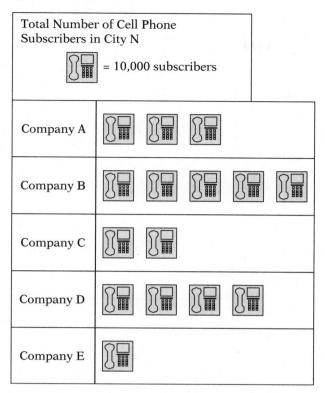

22. Of the total number of subscribers in City N, what percent more subscribers does Company A have than Company C?

23. What two companies account for 60% of all cell phone subscribers in this city?

    A. Company B and Company C
    B. Company B and Company D
    C. Company A and Company B
    D. Company A and Company E
    E. Company D and Company E

24. Below is a scatter plot showing the number of acres of land a house is on compared to the price of the house. What percentage of the houses on more than 4 acres cost less than $400,000?

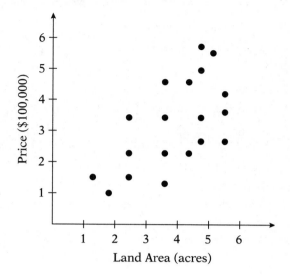

▬▬ EXPLAINED ANSWERS

1. *Answer:* **D**

   Add the prices and divide by 6.

   $$\frac{\$49.99 + \$69.99 + \$79.99 + \$99.99 + \$139.99 + \$159.99}{6} = \$99.9$$

2. *Answer:* **C**

   There are six numbers, so take the average of the middle 2 to find the mode.

   $$\frac{\$79.99 + \$99.99}{2} = \$89.99$$

3. *Answer:* **E**

   Divide the change in average points by the average points in 1995.

   $$\text{Percent increase} = \frac{22 - 18}{18} = \frac{4}{18} \approx 22.22\%$$

4. *Answer:* **A**

   Calculate 5% of 500.

   Number with no computer = $0.05 \times 500 = 25$

5. *Answer:* **C**

   First find the total number of people surveyed.

   Comedy = 20   Suspense = 30   Action = 25

   Horror = 15   Drama = 40   Other = 20

   $20 + 30 + 25 + 15 + 40 + 20 = 150$ were surveyed

   Now find the number of people who chose Action or chose Horror.

   $25 + 15 = 40$ were either Action or Horror

   Write a fraction and calculate percent.

   $$\text{Percent of Action or Horror} = \frac{40}{150} = 26\frac{2}{3}\%$$

6. *Answer:* **B**

   Find the number of people who chose Suspense and who chose Drama.

   Suspense = 30 and Drama = 40

   Write a ratio. Drama:Suspense = 40:30 = 4:3

7. *Answer:* **B**

   Find the number of pounds of peaches = $(0.25) \times 1{,}000 = 250$

   Find the number of pounds of plums = $(0.15) \times 1000 = 150$.

   Pounds of Peaches – Pounds of Plums = $250 - 150 = 100$.

8. *Answer:* **C**

   40% of the students in Club A are in Club B. That means 60% of the students in Club A are not in Club B. Find 60% of 70. $0.60 \times 70 = 42$ students in Club A are not in Club B.

9. *Answer:* **53**

   Add the values in the "For" row and solve for x.

   $56 + 85 + 64 + x = 258 \Rightarrow 205 + x = 258 \Rightarrow x = 53$

   Add the values in the 61 and over column and solve for x.

   $x + 24 + 63 = 140 \Rightarrow x + 87 = 140 \Rightarrow x = 53$

10. *Answer:* **36**

    There are a total of 710 surveyed of which 258 are for the referendum.

    Find the percent. $\dfrac{258}{710} \approx 0.36 \approx 36\%$

11. *Answer:* **43**

    There are a total of 180 in the 18–25 age group of which 77 are undecided.

    Find the percent. $\dfrac{77}{180} \approx 0.43 \approx 43\%$

12. *Answer:* **31**

    There are a total of 226 against the referendum of which 70 are in the 41–60 age group.

    Find the percent. $\dfrac{70}{226} \approx 0.31 \approx 31\%$

13. *Answer:* **C**

    Test grades are along the vertical axis. That means the higher the point, the better the test grade. Of the indicated points, point C is the highest.

14. *Answer:* **E**

    This scatterplot indicates a positive correlation between study time and grade. Every student who studied more than two hours scored 80 or better on the test; several of these in the 90 range. Therefore, of the choices given, a student who studies 3 hours a day would be expected to earn a 90.

15. *Answer:* **C**

    Calculate the estimated revenue for each ticket price.
    A. $\$15 \times 8{,}500 = \$127{,}500$
    B. $\$20 \times 8{,}000 = \$160{,}000$
    C. $(\$25 \times 7{,}000 = \$175{,}000)$ $25 is the price that maximizes revenue
    D. $\$30 \times 5{,}000 = \$150{,}000$
    E. $\$35 \times 4{,}500 = \$157{,}500$

16. *Answer:* **B**

    Subtract the revenue for the $30 ticket price from the revenue for the $35 ticket price.

    $\$157{,}500 - \$150{,}000 = \$7{,}500.$

17. *Answer:* **B**

    Charlotte shows a longer bar than Los Angeles in three pairs of bars.

18. *Answer:* **C**

    Both bars are above 60 degrees in 7 months.

19. *Answer:* **C**

    The house price increased from $300,000 in 1998 to $370,000 by 2003. Divide the total increase in price, $70,000, by the 5 years over which the increase took place.

    The average yearly increase is:

    $$\frac{370,000 - 300,000}{2003 - 1998} = \frac{\$70,000}{5} = \$14,000$$

20. *Answer:* **2.63**

    Find the change in house price and divide by the original house price.

    $$\text{Percent decrease} = \frac{380,000 - 370,000}{380,000} \approx 0.0263 = 2.63\%$$

21. *Answer:* **C**

    In 1971, 46% + 12% = 58% of the cars listed were two-door hardtop coupes. Therefore, there were approximately $0.58 \times 143,557 \approx 83,263$ two-door hardtop coupes produced.

    In 1965, 13% + 9% = 22% of the cars listed were two-door hardtop coupes. That means, there were approximately $0.22 \times 174,103 \approx 38,303$ two-door hardtop coupes produced.

    There were approximately 83,263 – 38,303 = 44,960 more coupes produced in 1971 then in 1965.

22. *Answer:* **6.67**

    Company A has $3 \times 10,000 = 30,000$ subscribers. Company C has $2 \times 10,000 = 20,000$ subscribers. Company A has 10,000 more subscribers than Company B. There are a total of $15 \times 10,000 = 150,000$ subscribers in all.

    Divide to find the percent. $\frac{10,000}{150,000} = 0.0\overline{666} = 6\frac{2}{3}\%$ Company A has 6.67% more subscribers than Company B.

23. *Answer:* **B**

    Find 60% of 150,000.

    $0.60 \times 150,000 = 90,000.$

    That means the companies represented by nine phones on the chart; that only happens for Company B and Company D.

24. *Answer:* **50**

    There are 10 houses that have more than four acres. Five of these houses cost less than $400,000. Therefore, 50% of the houses with more than 4 acres of land cost less than $400,000.

CHAPTER 18

SAT WORD PROBLEMS

Most SAT mathematics problems are word problems. This chapter describes an approach to solving word problems and gives you a chance to solve word problem types not covered in other chapters. All the skills needed to solve the problems have been previously reviewed. Begin with the mathematics review and then complete and correct the practice problems. There are 2 Solved SAT Problems and 20 Practice SAT Questions with answer explanations.

When solving word problems it is helpful to follow the following steps.

1. Decide what is being asked of you to solve.
2. Identify the given information.
3. Decide what information is needed to solve the problem.
4. Formulate a technique to solve problem.
5. Work out the answer.
6. Double check the solution to be certain you have answered the question that is asked.

Example:

Alice is three more than twice Tom's age. If Tom is 15 years old, how old is Alice?

Write an equation to describe the relationship.
A = Alice's age; T = Tom's age: $A = 3 + 2T$
Substitute 15 for T and solve for A. $3 + 2(15) = 3 + 30 = 33$

Example:

Janet purchased three skirts and two blouses at the store. Janet spent a total of $65 dollars and the skirts were $10 each, how much did she spend on the blouses?

Write an equation to describe the relationship.
S = Skirt price; B = Blouse price: $3S + 2B = 65$
Substitute 10 for S and solve for B. $3(10) + 2B = 65 \Rightarrow 30 + 2B = 65$
$2B = 35$. Therefore, Janet spent $35 on the blouses.

Example:

A store is having a sale on all items for 20% off the original price. If x represents the original price of an item, what expression represents the sale price of the item?

A 20% discount means an item costs 80% of its original price.

$0.80x$

Example:

At the end of the school year, Anthony was 66 inches tall. When he came back from summer break for school this year he was 6 feet tall. What percentage has Anthony's height increased since the end of last school year?

First convert 6 feet into 72 inches. Therefore, Anthony went from 66 inches to 72 inches.

Divide the height difference by the original height.

$$\text{Percent increase} = \frac{72 - 66}{66} = \frac{6}{66} \approx 9.09\%$$

Practice Questions

1. Jack earns twice as much as Phil. Don earns 3 times as much as Phil. If J is Jack's salary, what is Don's salary with respect to J?
2. Car A travels 300 miles in 5 hours. Car B traveled the same distance in 7 hours. If R_A is the rate of Car A, and R_B is the rate of Car B, what is the rate of Car B with respect to the rate of Car A?
3. The average score for 10 students on a math test is 85. If the average of 8 of the students is 88, what is the average of the other two students?

Practice Answers

1. $\dfrac{3}{2}J$
2. $\dfrac{5}{7}R_A$
3. 73

SOLVED SAT PROBLEMS

1. $\dfrac{3}{4}$ of the senior class went to the prom, of which $\dfrac{1}{3}$ brought a date from a different high school. If 38 people at the prom were not from the high school, how many students are there in the senior class?

Answer:

Let x be the total number of students in the senior class.

$\dfrac{3}{4}$ x is the number of seniors from the school who attended the prom.

$\dfrac{1}{3}$ of those attending brought a date from a different high school.

$\frac{1}{3}\left(\frac{3}{4}x\right) = \frac{1}{4}x$ are the number of students who brought a date from another school.

We know 38 seniors brought a date from a different high school. $\frac{1}{4}x = 38 \Rightarrow x = 152$ seniors.

---

2. In a game, scoring with a blue ball earns a team 2 points, and scoring with a red ball earns a team 3 points. Team 1 scored a total of 32 points, and Team 2 scored a total of 28 points. If both teams scored the same number of red balls, how many more blue balls did Team 1 score than Team 2?

   A. 1
   B. 2
   C. 3
   D. 4
   E. 5

Answer: **B**

Define the variables.

R = Number of red balls scored by each team

B_1 = Number of blue balls for Team 1

B_2 = Number of blue balls for Team 2

Write simultaneous equations to describe the relationship.

$2B_1 + 3R = 32$

$2B_2 + 3R = 28$

Subtract the equations.

$2B_1 + 3R = 32$

$-2B_2 + 3R = 28$

$\overline{2B_1 - 2B_2 = 4}$

Solve for $B_1 - B_2 \Rightarrow 2B_1 - 2B_2 = 4 \Rightarrow 2(B_1 - B_2) = 4$

$B_1 - B_2 = 2$.

Team 1 scored two more blue balls than Team 2.

SAT WORD PROBLEMS
PRACTICE SAT QUESTIONS

ANSWER SHEET

Choose the correct answer.
If no choices are given, grid the answers in the section at the bottom of the page.

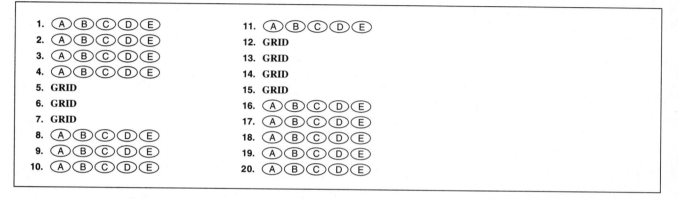

1. Ⓐ Ⓑ Ⓒ Ⓓ Ⓔ
2. Ⓐ Ⓑ Ⓒ Ⓓ Ⓔ
3. Ⓐ Ⓑ Ⓒ Ⓓ Ⓔ
4. Ⓐ Ⓑ Ⓒ Ⓓ Ⓔ
5. GRID
6. GRID
7. GRID
8. Ⓐ Ⓑ Ⓒ Ⓓ Ⓔ
9. Ⓐ Ⓑ Ⓒ Ⓓ Ⓔ
10. Ⓐ Ⓑ Ⓒ Ⓓ Ⓔ

11. Ⓐ Ⓑ Ⓒ Ⓓ Ⓔ
12. GRID
13. GRID
14. GRID
15. GRID
16. Ⓐ Ⓑ Ⓒ Ⓓ Ⓔ
17. Ⓐ Ⓑ Ⓒ Ⓓ Ⓔ
18. Ⓐ Ⓑ Ⓒ Ⓓ Ⓔ
19. Ⓐ Ⓑ Ⓒ Ⓓ Ⓔ
20. Ⓐ Ⓑ Ⓒ Ⓓ Ⓔ

Use the answer spaces in the grids below if the question requires a grid-in response.

Student-Produced Responses | ONLY ANSWERS ENTERED IN THE CIRCLES IN EACH GRID WILL BE SCORED. YOU WILL NOT RECEIVE CREDIT FOR ANYTHING WRITTEN IN THE BOXES ABOVE THE CIRCLES.

5. 6. 7. 12. 13.

14. 15.

PRACTICE SAT QUESTIONS

1. On Tuesday Ray rode his bike 10 miles. On Wednesday he increased Tuesday's distance by 5 miles. On Thursday he decreased Wednesday's distance by 7 miles. On Friday he increased Thursday's distance by 12 miles. How many total miles did Ray ride over the 4-day period?

   A. 50
   B. 51
   C. 52
   D. 53
   E. 54

2. 4 times x is equal to x increased by 6.

   $x =$

   A. 1
   B. 2
   C. 3
   D. 4
   E. 5

3. 2 times x plus 6 is equal to 5 times x less 3.

   $x =$

   A. 1
   B. 2
   C. 3
   D. 4
   E. 5

4. The sum of x and y is twice x.

   $y =$

   A. x
   B. $2x$
   C. x^2
   D. $\dfrac{x}{2}$
   E. $x - 2$

5. The product of a and 4 is twice the sum of 3 and 5.

   $a =$

6. The product of x and x increased by 5 is equal to -6. What is the product of the possible values of x?

7. Every day before work Matt buys a cup of coffee at the local coffee shop. If Matt has spent $27 on his last 20 cups of coffee, each cup the same price, how much is each cup of coffee?

8. It takes a copy machine 6 minutes to complete a certain copy job. How many minutes until the copy machine is finished with the job after $\dfrac{2}{3}$ of the job has been completed?

   A. 4 minutes
   B. 3.5 minutes
   C. 3 minutes
   D. 2.5 minutes
   E. 2 minutes

9. Julie worked 3 less than twice as many hours as Bruce. Which of the following choices represents the number of hours that Julie, J, worked based on the number of hours that Bruce, B, worked?

   A. $J = 2B - 3$
   B. $J = 2 - 3B$
   C. $J = 2B + 3$
   D. $J = 3 - 2B$
   E. $J = -2B - 3$

10. 40% of the students in a class are female. If there are 10 females in the class, how many males are there in the class?

    A. 5
    B. 10
    C. 15
    D. 20
    E. 25

11. Lindsey earns $15 hour for the first 40 hours she works in a week and 50% more for every hour over 40. How many hours did Lindsey work in a week, when she was paid $937.50 before taxes?

    A. 15 hours
    B. 30 hours
    C. 40 hours
    D. 45 hours
    E. 55 hours

12. Bob invested in a stock that increased in value by 17% to 25.74. What was the actual increase in the stock's value?

13. Zach earns $1,400 plus 15% commission of his sales every month. What was Zach's total sales for a month when he earned $2,000 in that month?

14. Sarah ran 1 mile in 8 minutes, at a constant rate. There are 5,280 feet in a mile. How many feet did Sarah run in 120 seconds?

15. Gary's winning time in a 100-yard race is 11 seconds. Frank is 3 yards behind Gary when Gary finishes the race. What is Frank's average speed in feet per second when Gary crosses the finish line, to the nearest tenth?

16. During a 4-week proper eating and exercise program, Bill lost 9 pounds. If the amount he lost in the second 2-week period is half the amount he lost in the first 2-week period, how many pounds did Bill lose in the second 2-week period?

    A. 3 pounds
    B. 4 pounds
    C. 5 pounds
    D. 6 pounds
    E. 7 pounds

17. On a varsity baseball team $\frac{1}{2}$ of the players are seniors, $\frac{1}{4}$ of the players are juniors, and the remaining 5 players are sophomores. How many players are on the team?

    A. 16
    B. 17
    C. 18
    D. 19
    E. 20

18. A theater charges $5 for children and $7 for adults to attend a children's play. A total of 1,600 tickets were sold for a total of $9,200. How many childrens' tickets were sold?

    A. 600
    B. 700
    C. 800
    D. 900
    E. 1,000

19. Tim earns $2,000 more a year than Pete. If Pete gets a 5% raise, their earnings would be equal. How much money does Pete earn a year?

    A. $30,000
    B. $35,000
    C. $40,000
    D. $45,000
    E. $50,000

20. During a baseball season Andrew got a hit in 35% of his at-bats, 12.5% of which were doubles. If Andrew hit 21 doubles in the season, how many at-bats did he have?

    A. 168
    B. 240
    C. 360
    D. 480
    E. 540

EXPLAINED ANSWERS

1. *Answer:* **D**

Day	Miles
Tuesday	10
Wednesday	10 + 5 = 15
Thursday	15 − 7 = 8
Friday	8 + 12 = 20
Total	10 + 15 + 8 + 20 = 53

2. *Answer:* **B**

   Write an equation that describes the relationship.
   $4x = x + 6$

   Solve for x. $3x = 6 \Rightarrow x = 2$

3. *Answer:* **C**

   Write an equation that describes the relationship.
   $2x + 6 = 5x - 3$

   Solve for x. $9 = 3x \Rightarrow 3 = x$

4. *Answer:* **A**

   Write an equation that describes the relationship.
   $x + y = 2x$

   Solve for $y = 2x - x$, $y = x$

5. *Answer:* **4**

   Write an equation that describes the relationship.
   $4a = 2(3 + 5)$

   Solve for a. $4a = 2(8) \Rightarrow 4a = 16 \Rightarrow a = 4$

6. *Answer:* **6**

   Write an equation that describes the relationship.
   $x(x + 5) = -6$

   $x^2 + 5x = -6 \Rightarrow x^2 + 5x + 6 = 0$

   Factor $(x + 2)(x + 3) = 0 \Rightarrow x = -2$ and $x = -3$
   Multiply the solutions. $(-2)(-3) = 6$

7. *Answer:* **1.35**

   Divide the amount by the number of cups.
   $\dfrac{\$27}{20} = \$1.35$ per cup

8. *Answer:* **E**

   Because $\dfrac{2}{3}$ of the job is completed, there is $\dfrac{1}{3}$ of the job remaining.

So, it will take $\dfrac{1}{3} \times 6 = 2$ minutes to finish the job.

9. *Answer:* **A**

   Scan the solutions to find which choice describes the relationship.
   $J = 2B - 3$

10. *Answer:* **C**

    Let x = total number of students in class.

    Find the total number of students. $0.4x = 10 \Rightarrow x = 25$

    10 of the students are females, $25 - 10 = 15$ of the students are males.

11. *Answer:* **E**

    If Lindsey worked 40 hours, she would earn $40 \times \$15 = \$600$.

    So, $\$937.50 - \$600 = \$337.50$ of her pay was from overtime, when she earned $\$15 \times 1.5 = \$22.5$ per hour.

    That means she worked $\dfrac{\$337.50}{\$22.5} = 15$ hours of overtime.

    She worked a total of $40 + 15 = 55$ hours.

12. *Answer:* **3.74**

    Let x = original stock price.

    The stock increased in value by 17%. The stock is worth 117% of the original price.

    Calculate the original price of the stock.
    $1.17x = 25.74 \Rightarrow x = \$22$.

    The actual increase is $\$25.74 - \$22 = \$3.74$.

13. *Answer:* **4,000**

    Let x = total sales.

    Write an equation that describes the relationship.
    $1,400 + 0.15x = 2,000$

    Solve for x. $0.15x = 600 \Rightarrow x = \$4,000$ total sales.

14. *Answer:* **1,320 feet**

    Convert 8 minutes to seconds.

    8 minutes = $8 \times 60 = 480$ seconds. Sarah ran 5,280 feet in 480 seconds, or $\dfrac{1}{4}$ mile in 120 seconds.

    $\dfrac{1}{4} \times 5,280 = 1,320$. Sarah ran 1,320 feet in 120 seconds.

15. *Answer:* **26.5**

    Gary ran 100 yards in 11 seconds, and Frank was 3 yards behind Gary. That means Frank ran 97 yards in 11 seconds. The problem asks for the rate in feet per second, so convert from yards to feet. Frank ran $97 \times 3 = 291$ feet in 11 seconds.

    Frank is running at a rate of $\dfrac{291}{11} \approx 26.5$ feet per second.

16. *Answer:* **A**

    Find two numbers where the sum is 9, and one number is half the other number. Those numbers are 6 and 3.

    The amount lost in the second 2-week period will be the smaller of the two numbers.

    He lost 3 pounds in the second 2-week period.

17. *Answer:* **E**

    We know that $\dfrac{1}{2} = \dfrac{2}{4}$ of the players are seniors and $\dfrac{1}{4}$ of the players are juniors. That means that $\dfrac{1}{4}$ of the players are sophomores.

    That means $\dfrac{1}{4} x = 5$ and $x = 20$.

    There are a total of 20 players on the team.

18. *Answer:* **E**

    Let c = number of children tickets.
    Let a = number of adult tickets.

    To answer this question we will set up simultaneous equations, eliminate the a and solve for c.

$$a + c = 1{,}600 \quad \text{multiply top equation by 7}$$
$$7a + 5c = 9{,}200$$

$$\Rightarrow \begin{array}{l} 7a + 7c = 11{,}200 \\ 7a + 5c = 9{,}200 \end{array}$$

Subtract the bottom equation from the top equation

$$\begin{array}{r} 7a + 7c = 11{,}200 \\ -7a + 5c = 9{,}200 \\ \hline 0a + 2c = 2{,}000 \end{array} \Rightarrow 2c = 2{,}000 \Rightarrow$$
$$c = 1{,}000 \text{ children.}$$

19. *Answer:* **C**

    Let t = Amount Tim earned.
    Let p = Amount Pete earned.

    Write two equations to represent the relationships described in the problem.

    $t = p + 2{,}000$ and $t = 1.05\, p$.

    Substitute $1.05p$ for t in the first equation.

    $1.05p = p + 2{,}000 \Rightarrow 0.05p = 2{,}000 \Rightarrow p = \$40{,}000$.

20. *Answer:* **D**

    Let x = total number of at-bats.

    $0.35x$ is equal to the number of hits Andrew got.

    12.5% of the hits were doubles so, $0.125(0.35x)$ is equal to the number of doubles.

    Andrew hit 21 doubles. $0.125(0.35x) = 21$

    Solve for x. $0.35x = 168 \Rightarrow x = 480$ at-bats

Directions for Multiple-Choice Questions

In this section, solve each problem, using any available space on the page for scratchwork. Then decide which is the best of the choices given and fill in the corresponding oval on your answer sheet.

- You may use a calculator on any problem. All numbers used are real numbers.
- Figures are drawn as accurately as possible EXCEPT when it is stated that the figure is not drawn to scale.
- All figures lie in a plane unless otherwise indicated.

Directions for Student-Produced Response Questions

Student Response questions are always numbered 9–18. Complete the grids at the bottom of the answer sheet for the test where the student response questions appear.

- If your answer is 2/3 or .666 . . . , you must enter **the most accurate value the grid can accommodate,** but you may do this in 1 of 4 ways:

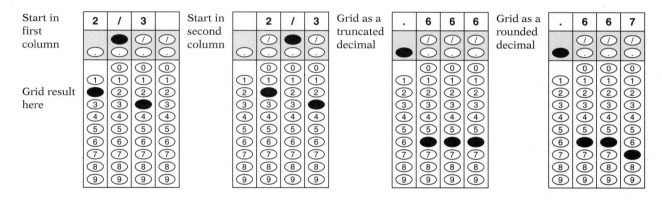

- In the example above, gridding a response of 0.67 or 0.66 is **incorrect** because it is less accurate than those above.
- The scoring machine cannot read what is written in the top row of boxes. You **MUST** fill in the numerical grid accurately to get credit for answering any question correctly. You should write your answer in the top row of boxes only to aid your gridding.

Reference Information

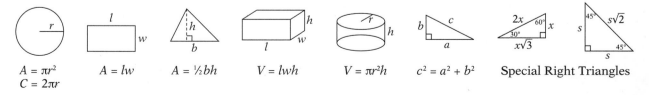

$A = \pi r^2$ $A = lw$ $A = \frac{1}{2}bh$ $V = lwh$ $V = \pi r^2 h$ $c^2 = a^2 + b^2$ Special Right Triangles
$C = 2\pi r$

The arc of a circle measures 360°.
Every straight angle measures 180°.
The sum of the measures of the angles in a triangle is 180°.

Start with number 1 for each new section. If a section has fewer questions than answer spaces, leave the extra answer spaces blank. Be sure to erase any errors or stray marks completely.

25 Minutes

SECTION 2

1. (A) (B) (C) (D) (E) 6. (A) (B) (C) (D) (E) 11. (A) (B) (C) (D) (E) 16. (A) (B) (C) (D) (E)
2. (A) (B) (C) (D) (E) 7. (A) (B) (C) (D) (E) 12. (A) (B) (C) (D) (E) 17. (A) (B) (C) (D) (E)
3. (A) (B) (C) (D) (E) 8. (A) (B) (C) (D) (E) 13. (A) (B) (C) (D) (E) 18. (A) (B) (C) (D) (E)
4. (A) (B) (C) (D) (E) 9. (A) (B) (C) (D) (E) 14. (A) (B) (C) (D) (E) 19. (A) (B) (C) (D) (E)
5. (A) (B) (C) (D) (E) 10. (A) (B) (C) (D) (E) 15. (A) (B) (C) (D) (E) 20. (A) (B) (C) (D) (E)

25 Minutes

SECTION 5

1. (A) (B) (C) (D) (E) 3. (A) (B) (C) (D) (E) 5. (A) (B) (C) (D) (E) 7. (A) (B) (C) (D) (E)
2. (A) (B) (C) (D) (E) 4. (A) (B) (C) (D) (E) 6. (A) (B) (C) (D) (E) 8. (A) (B) (C) (D) (E)

Student-Produced Responses   ONLY ANSWERS ENTERED IN THE CIRCLES IN EACH GRID WILL BE SCORED. YOU WILL NOT RECEIVE CREDIT FOR ANYTHING WRITTEN IN THE BOXES ABOVE THE CIRCLES.

9, 10, 11, 12, 13, 14, 15, 16, 17, 18 — grid-in response boxes with digits 0–9, decimal points, and fraction slashes.

20 Minutes

SECTION 8

1. (A) (B) (C) (D) (E) 5. (A) (B) (C) (D) (E) 9. (A) (B) (C) (D) (E) 13. (A) (B) (C) (D) (E)
2. (A) (B) (C) (D) (E) 6. (A) (B) (C) (D) (E) 10. (A) (B) (C) (D) (E) 14. (A) (B) (C) (D) (E)
3. (A) (B) (C) (D) (E) 7. (A) (B) (C) (D) (E) 11. (A) (B) (C) (D) (E) 15. (A) (B) (C) (D) (E)
4. (A) (B) (C) (D) (E) 8. (A) (B) (C) (D) (E) 12. (A) (B) (C) (D) (E) 16. (A) (B) (C) (D) (E)

TEST 1 QUESTIONS
SECTION 2

1. If $2x + 6 = 4x - 1$, what is the value of x?
   A. 2.5
   B. 3
   C. 3.5
   D. 4
   E. 4.5

2. What is the next term in the sequence: 4,9,6,11,8, 13, . . . ?
   A. 18
   B. 16
   C. 10
   D. 9
   E. 8

3. A bicycle company makes five styles of bikes in seven different colors. How many different bicycles can the company make when considering both style and color?
   A. 35
   B. 12
   C. 7
   D. 5
   E. 2

4. Which of the following statements is NOT true for the function $f(x) = 2(x - 3)^2$?
   A. The domain is all real numbers.
   B. The range is all real numbers greater than or equal to zero.
   C. The graph of the function touches the x-axis when $x = -3$.
   D. The graph of the function never goes below the x-axis.
   E. $f(2) = f(4)$.

5. The amount of pancake mix required to make pancakes is proportional to the number of pancakes that are being made. The table below shows the required amount of pancake mix and water to make 6 pancakes. How many cups of water are needed to make 15 pancakes?

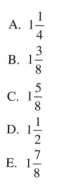

Pancakes	Amount of Mix	Amount of Water
6	1 cup	$\frac{3}{4}$ cup

   A. $1\frac{1}{4}$
   B. $1\frac{3}{8}$
   C. $1\frac{5}{8}$
   D. $1\frac{1}{2}$
   E. $1\frac{7}{8}$

6. In the diagram below $\overline{AB} \cong \overline{BC}$. Which of the following statements must be true?

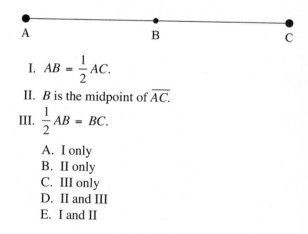

   I. $AB = \frac{1}{2} AC$.
   II. B is the midpoint of $\overline{AC}$.
   III. $\frac{1}{2} AB = BC$.

   A. I only
   B. II only
   C. III only
   D. II and III
   E. I and II

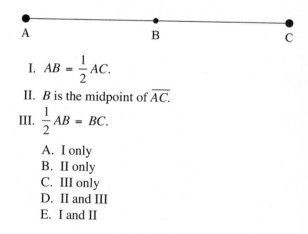 GO ON TO THE NEXT PAGE

7. A company has two manufacturing plants, Plant A and Plant B. Three times Plant A's production is equal to one half of the total produced by the company. If T represents the total produced by the company, which of the following is equal to the amount produced by Plant B?

    A. $\dfrac{5}{6}T$

    B. $\dfrac{2}{3}T$

    C. $\dfrac{1}{2}T$

    D. $\dfrac{1}{3}T$

    E. $\dfrac{1}{6}T$

8. There are a total of s seats in a movie theater. During a certain week there were a total of v viewings at the theater with an average of t unsold tickets for each viewing. Which of the following equations represents the total number of tickets that were not sold during that week?

    A. t

    B. v

    C. $\dfrac{t}{v}$

    D. tv

    E. $\dfrac{v}{t}$

9. In the figure below, $a \parallel b$. What is the value of z?

    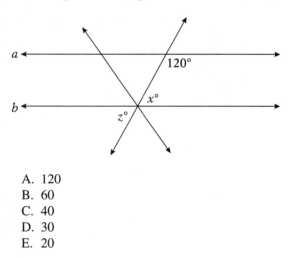

    A. 120
    B. 60
    C. 40
    D. 30
    E. 20

10. For which points on the number line below is the statement $x^3 > x^2$ true?

    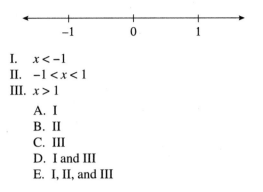

    I. $x < -1$
    II. $-1 < x < 1$
    III. $x > 1$

    A. I
    B. II
    C. III
    D. I and III
    E. I, II, and III

11. The area of the base of Cylinder A is 4 times the area of the base of Cylinder B. What is the radius of Cylinder A (r_A) in terms of the radius of Cylinder B (r_B)?

    A. $r_A = r_B$.
    B. $r_A = 4r_B$.
    C. $r_A = 2r_B$.
    D. $r_A = \dfrac{r_B}{4}$.
    E. $r_A = \dfrac{r_B}{2}$.

12. A jar contains blue, red, and green marbles. The ratio of blue:red:green = 3:5:4. What is the probability that a marble chosen at random is NOT red?

    A. $\dfrac{1}{4}$

    B. $\dfrac{5}{12}$

    C. $\dfrac{3}{4}$

    D. $\dfrac{7}{12}$

    E. $\dfrac{2}{4}$

13. Jim is a car salesman who gets a base monthly salary and a commission for each car he sells. Jim's monthly earnings are given by the function $f(x) = c(4 + x)$, where x represents the number of cars he sold for the month. If Jim sells 6 cars in a month he earns \$2,000. How much is Jim's base salary?

    A. \$500
    B. \$600
    C. \$700
    D. \$800
    E. \$900

GO ON TO THE NEXT PAGE

14. Which of the following statements must be true about the x and y coordinates that satisfy the equation $ay + ax = 0$, $a \neq 0$, $x \neq 0$, $y \neq 0$?

    A. $x > y$

    B. $x = y$

    C. $x = -y$

    D. $x < y$

    E. $x = \dfrac{1}{y}$

15. What is the area of the triangle below?

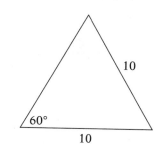

    A. $25\sqrt{3}$

    B. $50\sqrt{3}$

    C. $100\sqrt{3}$

    D. 25

    E. 50

16. If $x^2 + 2xy + y^2 = 81$, $x + y =$

    A. 7

    B. 8

    C. 9

    D. 10

    E. 11

17. In the xy-plane, line q and line r are parallel. Line q passes through the point $(3,7)$, and line r passes through the point $(3,2)$. If the y-intercept for line r is -2, what is the equation of a line perpendicular to line q, which intersects line q on the y-axis?

    A. $y = \dfrac{4}{3}x + 3.$

    B. $y = -\dfrac{3}{4}x + 3.$

    C. $y = -\dfrac{4}{3}x + 11.$

    D. $y = \dfrac{4}{3}x + 11.$

    E. $y = -\dfrac{3}{4}x + 11.$

18. If c is equal to the sum of a and twice b, which of the following is the average (arithmetic mean) of a and c?

    A. c

    B. $a + b$

    C. a

    D. b

    E. $a + c$

19. The rectangle in the figure below is inscribed in a circle with a radius $5\sqrt{5}$. If the height of the rectangle is twice its base, what is the area of the rectangle?

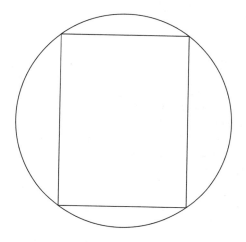

    A. 500

    B. 400

    C. 300

    D. 200

    E. 100

20. When 17 is divided by k, where k is a positive integer less than 17, the remainder is 3. What is the remainder when the sum of the possible values of k is divided by 17?

    A. 2

    B. 3

    C. 4

    D. 5

    E. 6

GO ON TO THE NEXT PAGE

SECTION 5

1. If $x + y = 4$, then $2(x + y) =$

   A. 2
   B. 4
   C. 6
   D. 8
   E. 10

2. In the rectangular prism below $EF = 8$ and $FG = 6$. What is the value of EG?

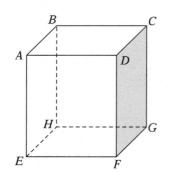

   A. 10
   B. 12
   C. 14
   D. 16
   E. 18

3. The table below shows the number of students in a high school who play varsity sports. Which of the following circle graphs displays the information shown in the table?

Grade	Frequency
Freshmen	10
Sophomores	20
Juniors	40
Seniors	80

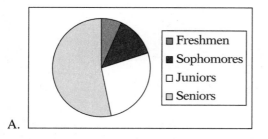

A.

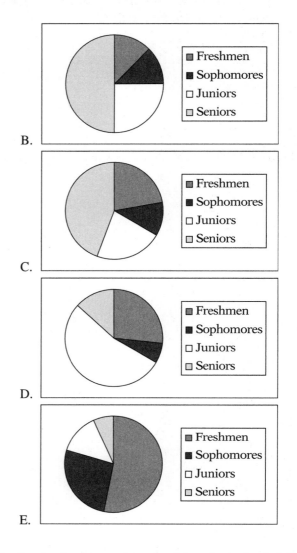

B.

C.

D.

E.

4. In a hardware store the ratio of shovels to rakes is 3:5. If there are 10 more rakes than shovels, how many rakes are there in the hardware store?

   A. 10
   B. 15
   C. 20
   D. 25
   E. 30

GO ON TO THE NEXT PAGE

5. In the rectangle $ABCD$ below, M is the midpoint of $\overline{CD}$. If the length of rectangle $ABDC$ is 3 times the width, and the area of triangle AMB is 18, what is the length of $\overline{CM}$?

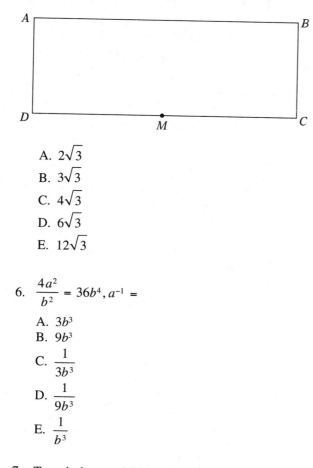

A. $2\sqrt{3}$

B. $3\sqrt{3}$

C. $4\sqrt{3}$

D. $6\sqrt{3}$

E. $12\sqrt{3}$

6. $\dfrac{4a^2}{b^2} = 36b^4, a^{-1} =$

A. $3b^3$

B. $9b^3$

C. $\dfrac{1}{3b^3}$

D. $\dfrac{1}{9b^3}$

E. $\dfrac{1}{b^3}$

7. Two airplanes at 25,000 feet above the ground are flying toward the same airport. Airplane A is flying due south toward the airport at 200 miles per hour, and Airplane B is flying due west toward the airport at 250 miles per hour. At 10:00 AM Airplane A is 700 miles from the airport, and Airplane B is 925 miles from the airport. How far are the two airplanes from each other at 10:30 AM?

A. 1,000 miles

B. 1,160 miles

C. 1,400 miles

D. 1,625 miles

E. 1,800 miles

8. The function graphed below is a cubic function. $f(a) = -f(2)$. Which of the following could be the value of a?

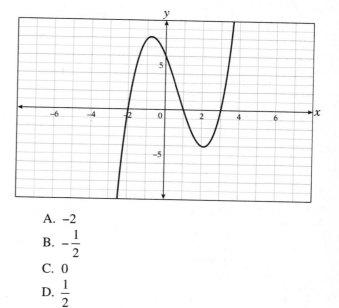

A. -2

B. $-\dfrac{1}{2}$

C. 0

D. $\dfrac{1}{2}$

E. 2

9. Three couples host a dinner party. Each couple invites 4 guests, none of whom are the same. The tables for the party seat 5 people. If everyone attends the party, what is the minimum number of tables needed to seat everyone?

10. $|2x - 3| \leq 7$ and $|x - 2| \leq 4$. If x is an integer, what value of x is a solution for one inequality but not the other?

GO ON TO THE NEXT PAGE

11. $x =$

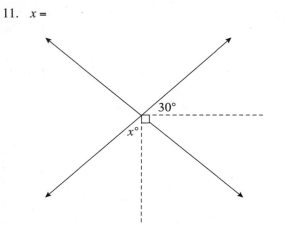

12. The sum of 10 consecutive integers is 105. What is the median of these 10 integers?

13. $f(x) = 2x + 3$, $f(c + 2) = 15$, $f(c) =$

14. In triangle ABC, shown below, $\overline{AB} \cong \overline{BC}$. What is the value of x?

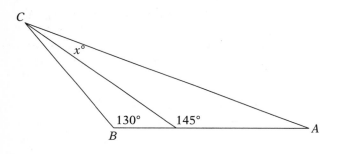

15. A jar contains green, red, and blue marbles. The probability of choosing a blue marble is $\frac{1}{3}$, the probability of choosing a red marble is $\frac{1}{2}$, the probability of choosing a green marble is $\frac{1}{6}$. If there are 12 marbles in the jar, and then three green marbles are added, what is the new probability of choosing a red marble from the jar?

16. Increasing x by 19% is equal to decreasing y by 15%. $\frac{y}{x} =$

17. The volume of a cylinder is 32π. The height of the cylinder is equal to the square root of the radius. What is the radius of the cylinder?

18. The distance between two points $(3, x)$ and $(13, -12)$ is 26. What is the value of x?

GO ON TO THE NEXT PAGE

SECTION 8

1. Which of the following is the element of the set containing all the even numbers and the set containing all the prime numbers?

   A. 1
   B. 2
   C. 3
   D. 4
   E. 5

2. $\sqrt{x-5} + 6 = 11, \quad x =$

   A. 5
   B. 10
   C. 20
   D. 25
   E. 30

3. The table below shows the number of men and women polled and the percent who were in favor of a certain law. How many were not in favor of the law?

	Number Polled	Percent in Favor
Men	250	24%
Women	350	22%

   A. 83
   B. 137
   C. 190
   D. 273
   E. 463

4. $x + y =$

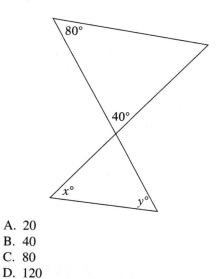

   A. 20
   B. 40
   C. 80
   D. 120
   E. 140

5. The bar graph below shows the price of houses in two different years. Which house price increases by the greatest percent?

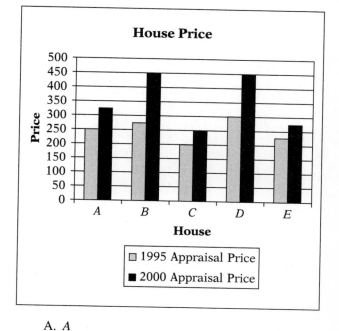

   A. A
   B. B
   C. C
   D. D
   E. E

GO ON TO THE NEXT PAGE

6. Part of the graph of the function $f(x)$ is below. If $f(x) = f(-x)$, $f(1.5) =$

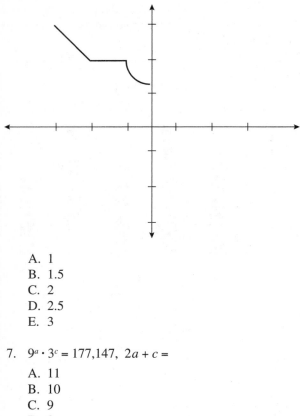

A. 1
B. 1.5
C. 2
D. 2.5
E. 3

7. $9^a \cdot 3^c = 177,147$, $2a + c =$

A. 11
B. 10
C. 9
D. 8
E. 7

8. The center of a circle is $(2,1)$ and the point $(-3,13)$ is on the circle. What is the area of the circle?

A. 25π
B. 144π
C. 169π
D. 196π
E. 225π

9. Which of the following inequalities create the graph below?

A. $|x - 8| < 4$.
B. $|-x - 3| < 8$.
C. $|x - 4| < 8$.
D. $|-x - 4| > 8$.
E. $|x - 8| > 4$.

```
  ←——○———————————+————○——————→
     -12                0    4
```

10. Cylinder A has a volume of 256π and a height of 4. Cylinder B has the same volume as Cylinder A and a height equal to the radius of Cylinder A. What is the radius of Cylinder B?

A. 8
B. $8\sqrt{2}$
C. 4
D. $4\sqrt{2}$
E. 2

11. $\boxed{k} = \left(-k, \dfrac{k}{2}\right)$ where k is an integer. What is the

equation of the line passing through $\boxed{k}$?

A. $y = 2x + 2$.
B. $y = 2x$.
C. $y = -2x$.
D. $y = \dfrac{1}{2}x - 2$.
E. $y = -\dfrac{1}{2}x$.

12. Population of Town A is 75% of the population of Town B. Population of Town C is 20% of the population of Town B. The population of Town A is what percent of the population of Town C?

A. 375%
B. 300%
C. 175%
D. 100%
E. 75%

13. x, y, and z are positive integers. Which of the following lists all the possible ways for $x + y + z$ to be an odd number?

I. One of the numbers is odd.
II. Two of the numbers are odd.
III. Three of the numbers are odd.

A. I
B. I and II
C. I and III
D. II and III
E. I, II, and III

GO ON TO THE NEXT PAGE

14. $-1 < x < 0$. Which of the following choices includes all the true statements from the list below?

    I. $x^3 > x$.

    II. $x > x^2$.

    III. $x^3 > x^2$.

        A. I only

        B. III only

        C. II and III

        D. I and III

        E. I, II, and III

15. The scatterplot below shows the number of hours students spent studying for a history test and the grade the students received. Which of the following is the equation of the best fitting line to the scatter plot below?

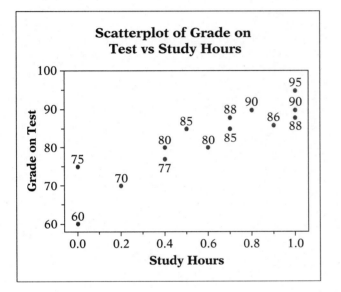

    A. $y = 68x + 24$

    B. $y = -24x + 68$

    C. $y = 24x + 68$

    D. $y = 24x + 24$

    E. $y = -24x + 24$

16. What is the area of the figure shown below if the length of each side of the four congruent regular hexagons is 10?

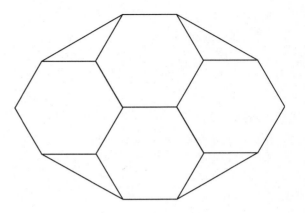

    A. $25\sqrt{3}$

    B. $150\sqrt{3}$

    C. $175\sqrt{3}$

    D. $700\sqrt{3}$

    E. $900\sqrt{3}$

ANSWERS AND EXPLANATIONS
SECTION 2

1. *Answer:* **C**

    Solve the equation.

    $2x + 6 = 4x - 1$

    $7 = 2x \Rightarrow 3.5 = x$

2. *Answer:* **C**

    See the pattern below. The sequence 4,9,6,11,8,13, . . . is formed by adding 5 and then subtracting 3. We can see that the next term in the sequence will be 10.

+5		−3		+5		−3		+5		−3
4		9		6		11		8		13		[10]

3. *Answer:* **A**

    Multiply the number of styles, 5, by the number of colors, 7, to get the number of bicycles that can be made by the company, $5 \cdot 7 = 35$. Therefore, there are a total of 35 different types of bicycles that can be made by the company.

4. *Answer:* **C**

    Look at the graph of the function $f(x) = 2(x - 3)^2$. Notice that the graph does not touch the x-axis when $x = -3$ but when $x = 3$.

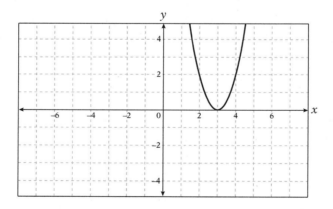

5. *Answer:* **E**

    Solve the proportion.

    $$\frac{\frac{3}{4}}{6} = \frac{x}{15}$$

    $$\frac{3}{4} \cdot \frac{1}{6} = \frac{x}{15} \Rightarrow \frac{1}{8} = \frac{x}{15}$$

    $$8x = 15 \Rightarrow x = \frac{15}{8} = 1\frac{7}{8} \text{ cups.}$$

6. *Answer:* **E**

Because $\overline{AB} \cong \overline{BC}$ then $AB = BC$. Therefore, B is the midpoint of $\overline{AC}$, so statement I is true.

Because B is the midpoint of $\overline{AC}$, $AB = \frac{1}{2}AC$, and statement II is true. As stated above, $AB = BC$; therefore,

$\frac{1}{2}AB \neq BC$, so statement III is false. Statements I and II are true. That's choice E.

7. *Answer:* **A**

A = the amount produced by Plant A.

B = the amount produced by Plant B.

T = the total amount produced by the company.

Three times the Plant A production is one-half the total.

$$3A = \frac{1}{2}T \Rightarrow A = \frac{1}{6}T.$$

Because Plant A and Plant B are the only two production plants and Plant A production is $\frac{1}{6}$ of total production,

$$A = \frac{1}{6}T \text{ so } B = \frac{5}{6}T.$$

8. *Answer:* **D**

Multiply the average number of unsold tickets by the number of viewings per week. Total number of unsold tickets $= tv$.

9. *Answer:* **B**

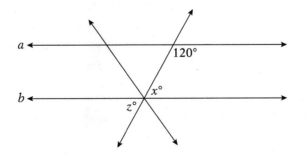

- $x + 120 = 180$ because a ∥ b, and because same-side interior angles are supplementary. That means $x = 60$
- Since z and x are vertical angles and vertical angles are congruent, $z = 60$.

10. *Answer:* **C**

    For any number less than −1, $x^3 < x^2$

    $(-2)^3 = -8 < 4 = (-2)^2$.

    For any number between −1 and 1 $x^3 < x^2$

    $$\left(-\frac{1}{2}\right)^3 = -\frac{1}{8} < \frac{1}{4} = \left(-\frac{1}{2}\right)^2.$$
    $$\left(\frac{1}{2}\right)^3 = \frac{1}{8} < \frac{1}{4} = \left(\frac{1}{2}\right)^2.$$

    However for any number greater than 1 $x^3 > x^2$

    $(2)^3 = 8 > 4 = (2)^2$.

11. *Answer:* **C**

    The question mentions that the base area of Cylinder A is four times the base area of Cylinder B. The base of a cylinder is a circle. Let r_A be radius of Cylinder A and r_B be the radius of Cylinder B.

    $$\pi\left(r_A\right)^2 = 4\pi\left(r_B\right)^2 \Rightarrow \left(r_A\right)^2 = 4\left(r_B\right)^2$$
    $$\sqrt{\left(r_A\right)^2} = \sqrt{4\left(r_B\right)^2} \Rightarrow r_A = 2r_B.$$

12. *Answer:* **D**

    The ratio of nonred marbles to total number of marbles is $7{:}12 = \dfrac{7}{12}$.

13. *Answer:* **D**

Write an equation for Jim's monthly earnings.	$c(4 + x) = \$2{,}000$
Jim sold six cars. Substitute 6 for x.	$c(4 + 6) = \$2{,}000$
Solve for c.	$10c = \$2{,}000$ so $c = \$200$
Substitute \$200 for c and find $f(x)$ to be sure.	$f(x) = \$200\,(4 + x) = \$800 + \$200x$

    The expression tells us that Jim earned a base salary of \$800 and a commission of \$200 per car.

14. *Answer:* **C**

    If $ay + ax = 0$, that means $a(x + y) = 0$, which means $x + y = 0$. Therefore, x and y must be opposites. In other words $x = -y$.

15. *Answer:* **A**

We know that if the sides are equal, the angles across from the sides have equal measure. We also know that the sum of the measures of the angles of a triangle is 180°. Therefore, the given triangle must be an equilateral triangle. Because it is equilateral, we can break the triangle up to find the height of the triangle.

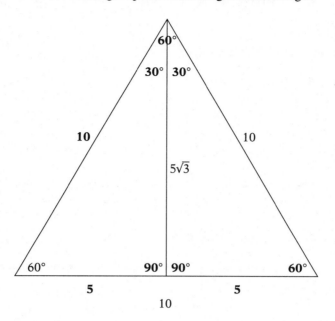

The diagram shows how the equilateral triangle can be partitioned into two 30°-60°-90° right triangles.

The length of each side of the new triangles across from the 30° angle is 5, half of 10.

That means the side across from the 60° angle is $5\sqrt{3}$.

That means that the base of the original triangle is 10, and the height is $5\sqrt{3}$.

Now find the area.

$$A = \frac{1}{2}bh = \frac{1}{2} \cdot 10 \cdot 5\sqrt{3} = 25\sqrt{3}.$$

16. *Answer:* **C**

$$x^2 + 2xy + y^2 = 81$$

Factor the quadratic equation.

$$\left(x + y\right)^2 = 81$$

Notice that it is a perfect square.

$$\Rightarrow x + y = 9.$$

17. *Answer:* **B**

Find the slope of line r.

Line r passes through the points (3,2) and (0,–2) [y-intercept of –2]. The slope of line r is $\dfrac{2 - (-2)}{3 - 0} = \dfrac{4}{3}$.

Find the equation of line q.

Line r and line q are parallel, so the slope line q is also $\dfrac{4}{3}$.

Line q passes through the point (3, 7).

$$y = mx + b \Rightarrow y = \frac{4}{3}x + b \Rightarrow 7 = \frac{4}{3}(3) + b \Rightarrow 7 = 4 + b \Rightarrow 3 = b$$

The equation of line q is $y = \dfrac{4}{3}x + 3$.

$y = -\dfrac{3}{4}x + 3$ is the equation of the line with the same y-intercept as line q and perpendicular to line q.

18. *Answer:* **B**

Find the sum of A and C to find the average of A and C.

Because $c = a + 2b$ then $a + c = a + (a + 2b) = 2a + 2b$. Therefore, the average of a and c is $\dfrac{2a + 2b}{2} = a + b$.

19. *Answer:* **D**

Draw a figure to show the height ($2x$) is twice the base (x).

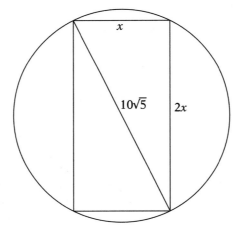

Use the Pythagorean Theorem to solve for x in the right triangle.

$$x^2 + (2x)^2 = \left(10\sqrt{5}\right)^2$$

That means $x^2 + 4x^2 = 500$

$5x^2 = 500$, so $x^2 = 100 \Rightarrow x = 10$.

Therefore, the base of the rectangle is 10, and the height of the rectangle is 20, so the area of the rectangle is $A = b \cdot h = 10 \cdot 20 = 200$.

20. *Answer:* **C**

Think of the positive integers less than 17.

The only two positive integers less than 17 that divide into 17 with a remainder of 3 are 7 and 14. Therefore, the sum of the possible value of k is 21. When 21 is divided by 17, the remainder is 4.

SECTION 5

1. **Answer: D**

   $x + y = 4$, then $2(x + y) = 2(4) = 8$.

2. **Answer: A**

   Draw dimensions on the diagram.

   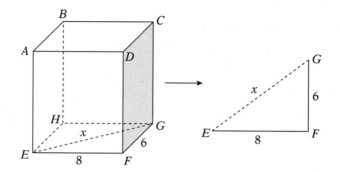

   Use the Pythagorean Theorem to find EG.

   $x^2 = 6^2 + 8^2 \Rightarrow x^2 = 36 + 64 = 100$

   $x = 10$. Therefore, $EG = 10$. You might have noticed that $EG = 10$ because $\triangle EFG$ is a 3-4-5 right triangle.

3. **Answer: A**

Grade	Frequency
Freshmen	10
Sophomores	20
Juniors	40
Seniors	80

   The table shows that the number of students in a grade playing a varsity sport is twice the previous grade. That means the sophomore wedge should be twice the size as the freshmen wedge, the junior wedge should be twice the size as the sophomore wedge, and the senior wedge should twice the size as the junior wedge.

   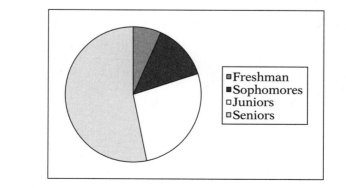

4. *Answer:* **D**

   Let s = number of shovels. Therefore, $10 + s$ = number of rakes. Write and solve a proportion to find the number of shovels.

   $$\frac{3}{5} = \frac{s}{10 + s} \Rightarrow 30 + 3s = 5s \Rightarrow 30 = 2s \Rightarrow 15 = s.$$

   There are 15 shovels, which means that there are 25 rakes.

5. *Answer:* **B**

   Write the dimensions and draw dotted segments as shown below.

   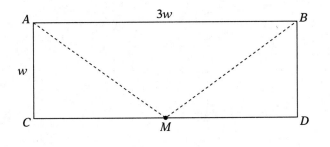

   Use formula for the area of triangle AMB to find the width of the rectangle ($h = w$, $b = 3w$).

   $$\text{Area of triangle } AMB = \frac{1}{2} \cdot w \cdot 3w = 18 \Rightarrow 3w^2 = 36$$

   $w^2 = 12 \Rightarrow w = \sqrt{12} = \sqrt{4 \cdot 3} = 2\sqrt{3}$. The base of the rectangle is three times the width, shown as $3(2\sqrt{3}) = 6\sqrt{3}$. The length of $\overline{CM}$ is half the length of the base of the rectangle because M is the midpoint of the base $\overline{CD}$. Therefore, the length of $\overline{CM}$ is $\dfrac{6\sqrt{3}}{2} = 3\sqrt{3}$.

6. *Answer:* **C**

   Solve for a.

   $$\frac{4a^2}{b^2} = 36b^4 \Rightarrow 4a^2 = 36b^4 \cdot b^2$$

   $$4a^2 = 36b^6 \Rightarrow a^2 = 9b^6.$$

   $$a = \sqrt{9b^6} \Rightarrow a = 3b^3$$

   Find the inverse of a. $a^{-1} = \dfrac{1}{3b^3}$.

7. *Answer:* **A**

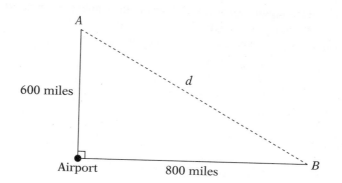

Airplane A is flying at 200 miles per hour. So, from 10:00 AM to 10:30 AM, it will travel 100 miles. Airplane A is now 700 − 100 = 600 miles from the airport.

Airplane B is flying at 250 miles per hour. So, from 10:00 AM to 10:30 AM, it will travel 125 miles. Airplane A is now 925 − 125 = 800 miles from the airport.

The diagram shows the position of the two airplanes at 10:30 AM. The dotted line represents the distance the two airplanes are from each other.

Use the Pythagorean Theorem. $d^2 = 600^2 + 800^2 \Rightarrow d^2 = 360,000 + 640,000 \Rightarrow d^2 = 1,000,000 \Rightarrow d = 1,000$. The two airplanes are 1,000 miles apart.

You could have also used the fact that this is a 3-4-5 right triangle.

8. *Answer:* **D**

Based on the graph we can see that $f(2) = -4$. So we are looking for a value of a where $f(a) = 4$. Inspect answer choices.

Notice that only $a = \dfrac{1}{2}$ means $f(a) = 4$.

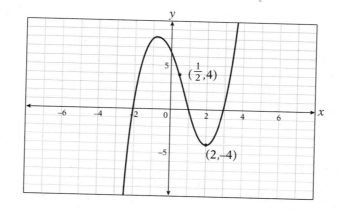

9. *Answer:* **4**

   Each of the three couples invites four guests, none of whom are the same; there are $3 \cdot 4 = 12$ guests. Then, we must consider the three couples who will attend the party, giving us 6 more people. There are a total of 18 people at the party. Each table can seat five people. Three tables seat a maximum of 15 people, so it will take a minimum of four tables to seat 18 people.

10. *Answer:* **6**

    Solve the absolute value inequality.

    $$2x - 3 \leq 7 \Rightarrow 2x \leq 10 \Rightarrow x \leq 5.$$
    $$|2x - 3| \leq 7$$
    $$2x - 3 \geq -7 \Rightarrow 2x \geq -4 \Rightarrow x \geq -2.$$

    $$x - 2 \leq 4 \Rightarrow x \leq 6.$$
    $$|x - 2| \leq 4$$
    $$x - 2 \geq -4 \Rightarrow x \geq -2.$$

    Notice that 6 is a solution to the second inequality but not to the first inequality.

11. *Answer:* **60**

    Use the diagram. Write 90 degrees for the right angle.

    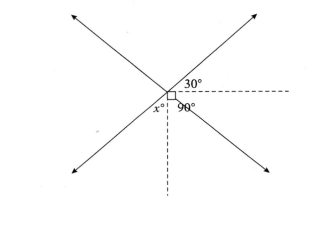

    $$x + 90 + 30 = 180$$
    $$x + 120 = 180$$
    $$x = 60$$

12. *Answer:* **10.5**

    You can use your calculator to guess and check to find that the ten consecutive integers are 6,7,8,9,10,11,12,13,14, and 15. These are ten numbers, the median is the average of the middle two numbers: 10 and 11. Therefore the median of the two numbers is 10.5. The mean and median of consecutive integers are always equal.

13. *Answer:* **11**

$$f(x) = 2x + 3$$

Substitute $(c + 2)$ for x.

$$f(c + 2) = 2(c + 2) + 3 = 15.$$

Solve for c.

$$2c + 4 + 3 = 15 \Rightarrow 2c + 7 = 15 \Rightarrow 2c = 8 \Rightarrow c = 4.$$

Find $f(c)$.

$$f(c) = f(4) = 2(4) + 3 = 8 + 3 = 11.$$

14. *Answer:* **10**

Because $\overline{AB} \cong \overline{BC}$ $\triangle ABC$ is an isosceles triangle. That means the measure of $\angle A$ and the measure of $\angle C$ are equal. A triangle has 180°, therefore, $\angle A$ and $\angle C$ each have a measure 25°. Therefore, $x + 15 = 25 \Rightarrow x = 10$.

15. *Answer:* $\dfrac{2}{5}$ **or 0.4**

Original number of red marbles in jar	$\dfrac{1}{2} \cdot 12 = 6$
Number of red marbles in jar after adding three green	6
Probability of choosing a red marble after three green have been added, making a total of 15 marbles	$\dfrac{6}{15} = \dfrac{2}{5}$

16. *Answer:* **1.4 or** $\dfrac{7}{5}$

Write the equation $x + .19x = y - .15y$

Divide to find $\dfrac{y}{x}$, $1.19x = 0.85y \Rightarrow \dfrac{1.19}{0.85} = \dfrac{y}{x} \Rightarrow 1.4 = \dfrac{y}{x}$.

17. *Answer:* **4**

Write square root of r in exponent form.

$$\sqrt{r} = r^{\frac{1}{2}}, h = r^{\frac{1}{2}}.$$

Use the formula for volume of a cylinder.

$$V = \pi r^2 h$$

Substitute $r^{\frac{1}{2}}$ for h.

$$\pi r^2 \, r^{\frac{1}{2}} = \pi r^{\frac{4}{2}} \, r^{\frac{1}{2}} = \pi r^{\frac{5}{2}}.$$

$$32\pi = \pi r^{\frac{5}{2}} \Rightarrow 32 = r^{\frac{5}{2}} \Rightarrow (32)^{\frac{2}{5}} = \left(r^{\frac{5}{2}} \right)^{\frac{2}{5}} \Rightarrow 4 = r.$$

18. *Answer:* **12**

Use distance formula: $d = \sqrt{\left(x_2 - x_1\right)^2 + \left(y_2 - y_1\right)^2}$

$$26 = \sqrt{(3 - 13)^2 + \left[x - (-12)\right]^2}$$

Square both sides.

$$(26)^2 = \left(\sqrt{(3 - 13)^2 + (x + 12)^2} \right)^2.$$

Simplify.

$$676 = \left(-10\right)^2 + \left(x + 12\right)^2$$

$$676 = 100 + \left(x + 12\right)^2. \Rightarrow 576 = \left(x + 12\right)^2$$

Take square root of each side.

$$\sqrt{576} = \sqrt{(x + 12)^2}$$

$$24 = x + 12 \Rightarrow 12 = x.$$

SECTION 8

1. ***Answer:* B**

   The only number that is both even and prime is 2. Therefore, the intersection of the set containing all the even numbers and the set containing all the prime numbers is {2}.

2. ***Answer:* E**

   Solve the equation.

   $$\sqrt{x-5} + 6 = 11 \Rightarrow \sqrt{x-5} = 5$$

   Square both sides.

   $$\left(\sqrt{x-5}\right)^2 = 5^2 \Rightarrow x - 5 = 25$$

   Solve for x.

   $$x = 30$$

3. ***Answer:* E**

	Number Polled	Percentage Not in Favor	Number Not in Favor
Men	250	76%	$0.76 \cdot 250 = 190$
Women	350	78%	$0.78 \cdot 350 = 273$

   Therefore, there were a total of $190 + 273 = 463$ Not in Favor of the law.

4. ***Answer:* E**

   Use the diagram.

   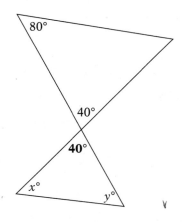

   We know the top angle in the bottom triangle is 40° because vertical angles are congruent.

   The sum of the angles in a triangle is 180°.

   $180 - 40 = 140$. That means $x + y = 140$.

5. *Answer:* **B**

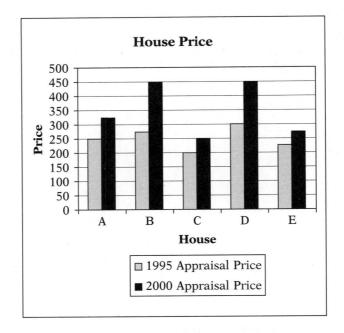

Inspect to eliminate choices A, C, and E, which are all less than 50%.

The 2000 price for houses *B* and *D* is the same, while the 1995 price is less for house *B*. That means there is a greater percent change for house *B*.

> **House *B*:**
>
> $$\frac{450 - 275}{275} = \frac{175}{275} = 63.\overline{63}\%$$

House *D*:

$$\frac{450 - 300}{300} = \frac{150}{300} = 50\%$$

6. *Answer:* **C**

Because $f(x) = f(-x)$, the graph of $f(x)$ is symmetric with respect to the *y*-axis, as shown below. Inspect the graph to see that $f(1.5) = 2$.

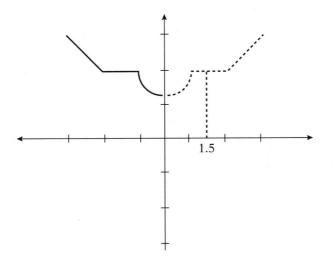

7. *Answer:* **A**

The key is to rewrite 9 as 3^2. $9^a \cdot 3^c = (3^2)^a \cdot 3^c = 3^{2a} \cdot 3^c = 3^{2a+c} = 177{,}147$.

Use the guess and check method to find the power of 3 that will result is 177,147.

$3^{11} = 177{,}147$. $3^{2a+c} = 177{,}147$ so $2a + c = 11$.

8. *Answer:* **C**

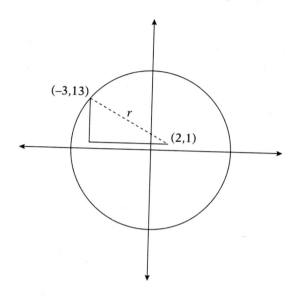

The distance between the center and a point on the circle is equal to the radius of the circle.

$$r = \sqrt{[2 - (-3)]^2 + (1 - 13)^2} = \sqrt{5^2 + (-12)^2} = \sqrt{25 + 144} = \sqrt{169} = 13.$$

The radius of the circle is 13. The area of the circle is $A = \pi r^2 = \pi(13)^2 = 169\pi$.

9. *Answer:* **D**

The arrows are pointing out. Choose a greater than inequality. The midpoint of -12 and 4 is -4. This is only true for Choice D. Check your solution.

$$-x - 4 > 8 \Rightarrow -x > 12 \Rightarrow x < -12.$$

$|-x - 4| > 8$

$$-x - 4 < -8 \Rightarrow -x < -4 \Rightarrow x > 4.$$

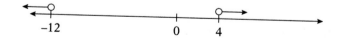

10. *Answer:* **D**

Cylinder A:

Use the volume formula to find the radius of Cylinder A.

$h = 4$.

$V = \pi r^2 h = 256\pi \Rightarrow \pi r^2 (4) = 256\pi$

$r^2 = 64 \Rightarrow r = 8$.

Cylinder B:

The radius of Cylinder A is 8, so

$h = 8$.

Use the volume formula to find the radius of Cylinder B.

$V = \pi r^2 h = 256\pi \Rightarrow \pi r^2 (8) = 256\pi$

$r^2 = 32 \Rightarrow r = \sqrt{32} = 4\sqrt{2}$.

11. *Answer:* **E**

Choose two values of k to find two points.

$\boxed{2} = (-2, 1)$ and $\boxed{4} = (-4, 2)$.

Use these points to find the slope of the line.

$$m = \frac{2 - 1}{-4 - (-2)} = \frac{1}{-2}$$

Find the y-intercept of the line using the point $(-2, 1)$.

$$y = mx + b \Rightarrow y = -\frac{1}{2}x + b \Rightarrow 1 = -\frac{1}{2}(-2) + b \Rightarrow 1 = 1 + b \Rightarrow 0 = b.$$

Therefore, the equation of the line is $y = -\dfrac{1}{2}x$.

12. *Answer:* **A**

A, B, and C represent the populations of the towns.

$A = 0.75B$

$C = 0.20B$

Divide A by C. $\dfrac{A}{C} = \dfrac{0.75B}{0.20B} = 3.75$

The population of Town A is 375%. The population of Town C.

13. *Answer:* **C**

> I. One of the numbers is odd
>
> Let x be odd.
>
> Let y and z be even.
>
> $y + z$ is even. An even plus an odd is odd, so $x + y + z$ is odd.

II. Two of the numbers are odd.

Let x be even.

Let y and z be odd.

$y + z$ is even $\Rightarrow x + y + z$ is even.

> III. Three of the numbers are odd.
>
> Let x, y, and z be odd.
>
> $x + y$ is even $\Rightarrow x + y + z$ is odd.

14. *Answer:* **A**

By choosing one value of x to test all three statements we can see that only statement I is true. Let $x = -0.5$. Remember you are multiplying negative numbers.

I. $(-0.5)^3 > -(0.5)$ True: $(-0.5)^3 = -0.125$, which is greater than (-0.5).

II. $-0.5 > (-0.5)^2$ False: $(-0.5)^2$ is positive.

III. $(-0.5)^3 > (-0.5)^2$ False: $(-0.5)^2$ is positive; $(-0.5)^3$ is negative.

15. *Answer:* **C**

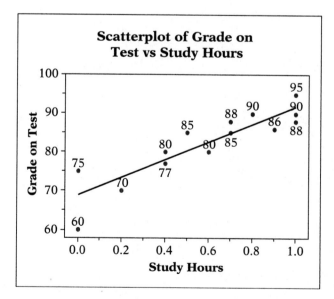

Begin by sketching what appears to be the best fitting line. Notice that the y-intercept is between 65 and 70. In the equation of a line, $y = mx + b$, b represents the y-intercept. Since the y-intercept for choices A, B, and E is 24, these can be eliminated. The line has a positive slope. In the equation of a line $y = mx + b$, m represents the slope. For choice B, the slope is -24 and for choice C the slope is 24. Choice B can be eliminated leaving, leaving us with choice C as the correct answer.

16. *Answer:* **D**

There are four congruent hexagons and four congruent isosceles triangles. Find the area of one isosceles triangle and one hexagon, add them together, and then multiply by 4.

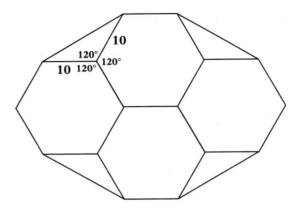

There are four isosceles triangles in the original figure. Find the area of one of them. Partition the triangle into two 30°-60°-90° triangles. Use the properties of 30°-60°-90° triangles to complete the diagram.

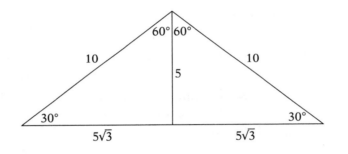

Use the formula to find the area.

$$A = \frac{1}{2}bh = \frac{1}{2} \cdot 10\sqrt{3} \cdot 5 = 25\sqrt{3}.$$

Hexagon:

Find the area of one of the central equilateral triangles and multiply that area by 6. We already know that the base of the triangle is 10. Use the rules of a 30°-60°-90° right triangle. Find the height of the triangle to be $5\sqrt{3}$. The area of the triangle is $A = \dfrac{1}{2} \times 10 \times 5\sqrt{3} = 25\sqrt{3} \Rightarrow$ Area of hexagon is $6\left(25\sqrt{3}\right) = 150\sqrt{3}$.

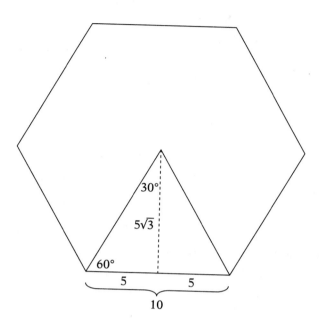

Therefore, the sum of these two areas is $25\sqrt{3} + 150\sqrt{3} = 175\sqrt{3}$, so the area of the region is $4 \cdot 175\sqrt{3} = 700\sqrt{3}$.

SCORE ESTIMATOR

Use this sheet to estimate your SAT Mathematics scale score. These scores are <u>estimates</u>, and your performance on the actual SAT could easily fall outside your scale score range for this test. One primary reason for the difference is that you did not take this test in a completely realistic test setting.

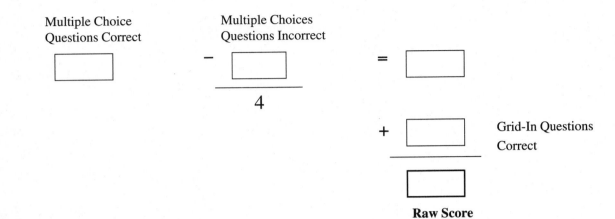

Raw Score	Scale Score Range	Raw Score	Scale Score Range
54	800	27	470–550
53	740–800	26	470–540
52	710–800	25	460–540
51	690–790	24	450–530
50	680–760	23	440–520
49	670–750	22	430–510
48	650–740	21	430–500
47	640–730	20	420–490
46	630–720	19	420–480
45	620–710	18	410–470
44	610–700	17	400–460
43	600–680	16	390–450
42	600–670	15	390–450
41	590–660	14	380–440
40	570–650	13	370–430
39	560–640	12	360–430
38	550–630	11	350–430
37	540–620	10	340–430
36	540–610	9	330–430
35	530–600	8	320–420
34	530–600	7	310–410
33	520–590	6	300–400
32	510–580	5	290–390
31	500–570	4	280–380
30	490–560	3	270–370
29	490–560	2	240–340
28	480–550	1, 0, or less	200–320

CHAPTER 20

SAT MATH PRACTICE TEST 2

Directions for Multiple-Choice Questions

In this section, solve each problem, using any available space on the page for scratchwork. Then decide which is the best of the choices given and fill in the corresponding oval on your answer sheet.

- You may use a calculator on any problem. All numbers used are real numbers.
- Figures are drawn as accurately as possible EXCEPT when it is stated that the figure is not drawn to scale.
- All figures lie in a plane unless otherwise indicated.

Directions for Student-Produced Response Questions

Student Response questions are always numbered 9–18. Complete the grids at the bottom of the answer sheet for the test where the student response questions appear.

- If your answer is 2/3 or .666 . . . , you must enter **the most accurate value the grid can accommodate,** but you may do this in 1 of 4 ways:

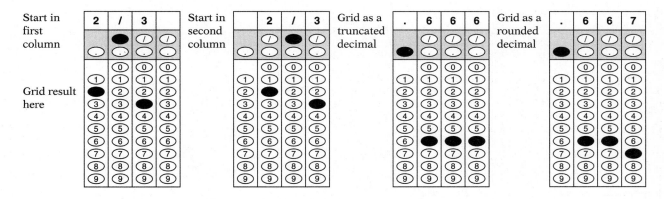

- In the example above, gridding a response of 0.67 or 0.66 is **incorrect** because it is less accurate than those above.

- The scoring machine cannot read what is written in the top row of boxes. You **MUST** fill in the numerical grid accurately to get credit for answering any question correctly. You should write your answer in the top row of boxes only to aid your gridding.

Reference Information

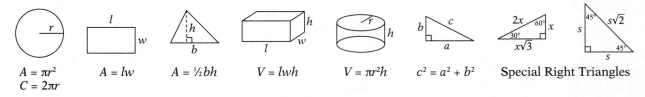

$A = \pi r^2$ $A = lw$ $A = \frac{1}{2}bh$ $V = lwh$ $V = \pi r^2 h$ $c^2 = a^2 + b^2$ Special Right Triangles
$C = 2\pi r$

The arc of a circle measures 360°.
Every straight angle measures 180°.
The sum of the measures of the angles in a triangle is 180°.

Start with number 1 for each new section. If a section has fewer questions than answer spaces, leave the extra answer spaces blank. Be sure to erase any errors or stray marks completely.

25 Minutes

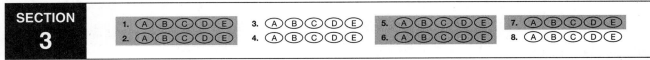

SECTION 3

1. Ⓐ Ⓑ Ⓒ Ⓓ Ⓔ   3. Ⓐ Ⓑ Ⓒ Ⓓ Ⓔ   5. Ⓐ Ⓑ Ⓒ Ⓓ Ⓔ   7. Ⓐ Ⓑ Ⓒ Ⓓ Ⓔ
2. Ⓐ Ⓑ Ⓒ Ⓓ Ⓔ   4. Ⓐ Ⓑ Ⓒ Ⓓ Ⓔ   6. Ⓐ Ⓑ Ⓒ Ⓓ Ⓔ   8. Ⓐ Ⓑ Ⓒ Ⓓ Ⓔ

Student-Produced Responses ONLY ANSWERS ENTERED IN THE CIRCLES IN EACH GRID WILL BE SCORED. YOU WILL NOT RECEIVE CREDIT FOR ANYTHING WRITTEN IN THE BOXES ABOVE THE CIRCLES.

Grids 9, 10, 11, 12, 13 (top row) and 14, 15, 16, 17, 18 (bottom row), each with fraction bar and decimal point options and digits 0–9.

25 Minutes

SECTION 4

1. Ⓐ Ⓑ Ⓒ Ⓓ Ⓔ   6. Ⓐ Ⓑ Ⓒ Ⓓ Ⓔ   11. Ⓐ Ⓑ Ⓒ Ⓓ Ⓔ   16. Ⓐ Ⓑ Ⓒ Ⓓ Ⓔ
2. Ⓐ Ⓑ Ⓒ Ⓓ Ⓔ   7. Ⓐ Ⓑ Ⓒ Ⓓ Ⓔ   12. Ⓐ Ⓑ Ⓒ Ⓓ Ⓔ   17. Ⓐ Ⓑ Ⓒ Ⓓ Ⓔ
3. Ⓐ Ⓑ Ⓒ Ⓓ Ⓔ   8. Ⓐ Ⓑ Ⓒ Ⓓ Ⓔ   13. Ⓐ Ⓑ Ⓒ Ⓓ Ⓔ   18. Ⓐ Ⓑ Ⓒ Ⓓ Ⓔ
4. Ⓐ Ⓑ Ⓒ Ⓓ Ⓔ   9. Ⓐ Ⓑ Ⓒ Ⓓ Ⓔ   14. Ⓐ Ⓑ Ⓒ Ⓓ Ⓔ   19. Ⓐ Ⓑ Ⓒ Ⓓ Ⓔ
5. Ⓐ Ⓑ Ⓒ Ⓓ Ⓔ   10. Ⓐ Ⓑ Ⓒ Ⓓ Ⓔ   15. Ⓐ Ⓑ Ⓒ Ⓓ Ⓔ   20. Ⓐ Ⓑ Ⓒ Ⓓ Ⓔ

20 Minutes

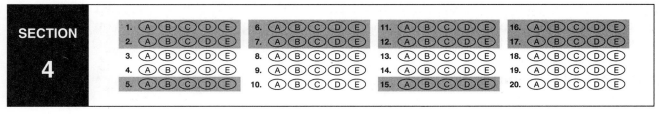

SECTION 9

1. Ⓐ Ⓑ Ⓒ Ⓓ Ⓔ   5. Ⓐ Ⓑ Ⓒ Ⓓ Ⓔ   9. Ⓐ Ⓑ Ⓒ Ⓓ Ⓔ   13. Ⓐ Ⓑ Ⓒ Ⓓ Ⓔ
2. Ⓐ Ⓑ Ⓒ Ⓓ Ⓔ   6. Ⓐ Ⓑ Ⓒ Ⓓ Ⓔ   10. Ⓐ Ⓑ Ⓒ Ⓓ Ⓔ   14. Ⓐ Ⓑ Ⓒ Ⓓ Ⓔ
3. Ⓐ Ⓑ Ⓒ Ⓓ Ⓔ   7. Ⓐ Ⓑ Ⓒ Ⓓ Ⓔ   11. Ⓐ Ⓑ Ⓒ Ⓓ Ⓔ   15. Ⓐ Ⓑ Ⓒ Ⓓ Ⓔ
4. Ⓐ Ⓑ Ⓒ Ⓓ Ⓔ   8. Ⓐ Ⓑ Ⓒ Ⓓ Ⓔ   12. Ⓐ Ⓑ Ⓒ Ⓓ Ⓔ   16. Ⓐ Ⓑ Ⓒ Ⓓ Ⓔ

TEST 2 QUESTIONS
SECTION 3

1. At a wallpaper store 30 square feet of wallpaper costs $18. At this price, how much does 90 square feet of wallpaper cost?

   A. $24
   B. $36
   C. $48
   D. $54
   E. $72

2. $\frac{x}{y} = 5$, $\quad 2 \cdot \frac{x^2}{y^2} =$

   A. 10
   B. 25
   C. 50
   D. 100
   E. 125

3. If $x + y > 8$, which of the following statements is true?

   A. $x^2 + 2xy + y^2 = 64$.
   B. $x^2 + 2xy + y^2 > 64$.
   C. $x^2 + 2xy + y^2 < 64$.
   D. $x^2 + 2xy + y^2 > 16$.
   E. $x^2 + 2xy + y^2 < 16$.

4. What is the perimeter of a triangle in the xy-coordinate plane whose vertices are the points (5,8), (5,2), and (9,8)?

   A. 6
   B. 10
   C. $2\sqrt{13}$
   D. $2 + 2\sqrt{13}$
   E. $10 + 2\sqrt{13}$

5. 4, 12, 36, 108, and 324 are the first five terms of a sequence. Each term in the sequence is formed by multiplying the preceding term by 3. $4(3)^{10}$ is what term in this sequence?

   A. 12
   B. 11
   C. 10
   D. 9
   E. 8

6. In the figure below $\overleftrightarrow{BE}$ bisects $\angle FOD$. What is the measure of $\angle FOA$?

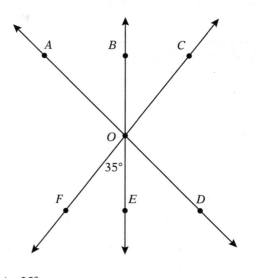

   A. 35°
   B. 55°
   C. 70°
   D. 110°
   E. 145°

7. The sum of two numbers is 10, and the difference of the two numbers is 4. Which is the smaller of the two numbers?

   A. 3
   B. 4
   C. 6
   D. 7
   E. 8

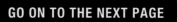

GO ON TO THE NEXT PAGE

8. Below are the strikeout totals for two pitchers, Tom and Frank, during three games. How many strikeouts must Frank have on his next game so that Frank's strikeout average for 4 games is equal to Tom's strikeout average for 3 games?

Game #	Tom's Strikeout Total	Frank's Strikeout Total
1	7	8
2	12	13
3	8	5

A. 8
B. 9
C. 10
D. 11
E. 12

9. $\dfrac{x-3}{4} = 3, \dfrac{x}{5} =$

10. When half a number is increased by 13, the result is 74. What is the number?

11. A survey of college freshmen asked them if they have decided on a major. Part of the information that was gathered is shown in the table below. What percent of the women surveyed said that they have chosen a major?

	Men	Women	Total
Yes	1,000		
No		500	
Total	3,000		5,000

12. The rectangle below in the xy-coordinate plane has two points on the x-axis and two points on the graph of the function $f(x) = -x^2 + 11$. What is the area of the rectangle?

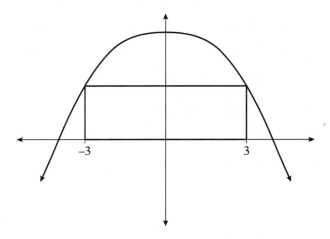

13. $2xy + \sqrt{z} = x^2$. If $x = -3$ and $y = 2$ then $z =$

14. In the figure below line a and line b are not parallel. If line t bisects the acute angle PQR, this means y cannot equal what number?

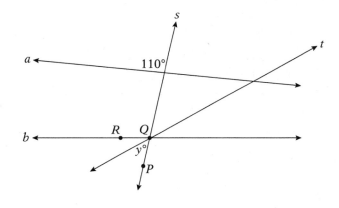

15. At Jim's Italian Restaurant, the early bird special includes one main course and two side items, no two of which are the same. There are four main courses to choose from and four side items to choose from. How many different specials can be ordered?

GO ON TO THE NEXT PAGE

16. The radius of the outer circle is twice the radius of the inner circle. What is the probability that a point chosen at random inside the outer circle will be inside the inner shaded region?

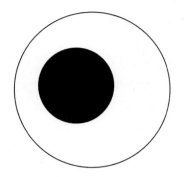

17. Let $n = c \cdot p$, where p is a prime number, and c is a composite number less than p. The number c has three unique prime factors. How many unique prime factors does n^2 have?

18. A parabola whose equation is in the form $y = 2x^2 + bx + c$ passes through the points $(3,16)$ and $(1,-12)$. What is the value of y when $x = 4$?

GO ON TO THE NEXT PAGE

SECTION 4

1. $\frac{a}{3} = b$ where b is a positive integer. What is the smallest possible value of a?

    A. 1
    B. 3
    C. 5
    D. 7
    E. 9

2. Which of the following graphs is symmetric with respect to the y-axis?

    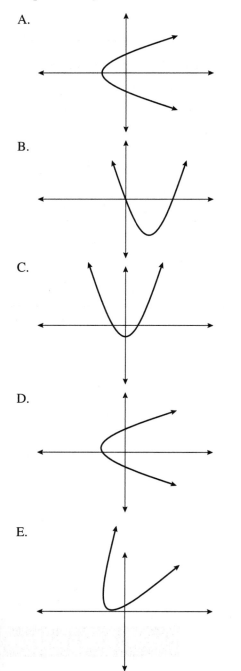

    A.

    B.

    C.

    D.

    E.

3. A salesperson earns $1,000 per month plus 8% of sales. Which of the following represents the salesperson's monthly salary if his total sales for the month is (s)?

    A. $1,000 + 8s$
    B. $1,000 + 0.8s$
    C. $1,000 + 0.08s$
    D. $800 + 0.8s$
    E. $80 + 0.08s$

4. Two movie theaters, Theater A and Theater B, sell tickets at two different prices. Theater A sells tickets at $6 per ticket, and Theater B sells tickets at $8 per ticket. Theater A sold 15,000 tickets. How many tickets does Theater B need to sell to earn the same amount of money?

    A. 90,000
    B. 45,000
    C. 15,000
    D. 11,250
    E. 7,500

5. Snow accumulation for five cities in 2000 and 2001 are shown below. Which city had the greatest decrease in snowfall accumulation from 2000 to 2001?

    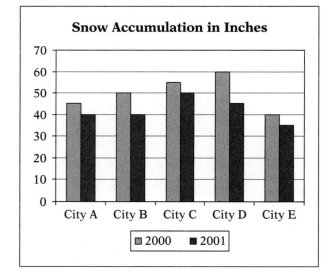

    A. A
    B. B
    C. C
    D. D
    E. E

GO ON TO THE NEXT PAGE

6. The average (arithmetic mean) of five numbers is 10. The sum of three of the numbers is 30. What is the sum of the other two numbers?

    A. 5
    B. 10
    C. 20
    D. 30
    E. 40

7. In the figure seen below, $\overline{AB} \perp \overline{BC}$, $x =$

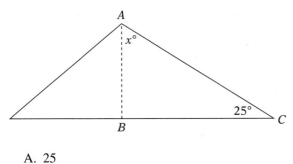

    A. 25
    B. 65
    C. 90
    D. 115
    E. 155

8. During a basketball game, Marla scored all of her points either from a two-point basket or a three-point basket. If she scored 15 points, which of the following could be the number of three-point baskets that Marla scored?

    A. 8
    B. 6
    C. 4
    D. 3
    E. 2

9. An experiment requires that all heights are listed in feet. When gathering the data, heights were measured in both feet (F) and inches (I). Which of the following equation will convert all measurements to feet?

    A. $F + \dfrac{I}{12}$
    B. $F + 12I$
    C. $12F + I$
    D. $12(F + I)$
    E. $\dfrac{(F + I)}{12}$

10. $x^2 + 9x + 20 = 0$, which of the following lists all possible values of x?

    A. -4
    B. 5
    C. -4 and -5
    D. -4 and 5
    E. 4 and -5

11. $\dfrac{x^4}{16} = y^8 z^{12}$, therefore, $x =$

    A. $8y^2 z^3$
    B. $2y^4 z^3$
    C. $8y^4 z^3$
    D. $16y^2 z^3$
    E. $2y^2 z^3$

12. The function of $f(x)$ is graphed below. At which of the following points would a line with a slope $-\dfrac{1}{2}$ be perpendicular to $f(x)$?

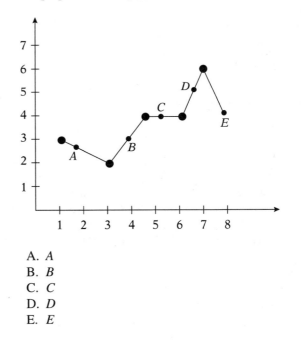

    A. A
    B. B
    C. C
    D. D
    E. E

GO ON TO THE NEXT PAGE

13. A four-digit (0–9) password must meet the following restrictions:

    - The first digit must be prime.
    - The second digit must be odd.
    - The third digit must be divisible by 5.
    - The fourth digit must be a nonprime odd number.

    How many possible passwords of this type exist?

    A. 40
    B. 45
    C. 80
    D. 90
    E. 120

14. $x^2 + 14x + 49 = 49 - x^2$, $x =$

    A. 0
    B. 7
    C. −7 and 7
    D. 0 and 7
    E. 0 and −7

15. Which of the following could be the lengths of the sides of a right triangle?

    A. 3,4,6
    B. 4,7,10
    C. 6,8,10
    D. $\sqrt{5}, 5\sqrt{2}, 10$
    E. 5,12,15

16. An airplane traveled from City A to City B and then from City B to City C. From City A, the airplane traveled east 700 miles and then north 800 miles to get to City B. From City B, the airplane traveled west 1,200 miles and then north 400 miles to get to City C. How many miles is City C from City A?

    A. 500
    B. 1,200
    C. 1,300
    D. 2,400
    E. 2,600

17. The perimeter of a rectangle is 72. The length of the rectangle is three times the width. What is the area of the rectangle?

    A. 3
    B. 9
    C. 27
    D. 81
    E. 243

18. The average (arithmetic mean) of five positive integers is 56. The difference between the largest and smallest integer is 4. What is the median of the numbers?

    A. 55
    B. 55.5
    C. 56
    D. 56.5
    E. 57

19. $x^{\frac{1}{2}} = k^{\frac{3}{2}}$ and $k^{\frac{5}{2}} = y^{\frac{5}{6}}$, what is the value of x in terms of y?

    A. $\dfrac{y}{2}$
    B. y
    C. $2y$
    D. $\dfrac{y}{4}$
    E. $4y$

GO ON TO THE NEXT PAGE

20. The graphs of $f(x)$ and $g(x)$ are given below. If $g(x) = f(x + h) + k$, what is the value of h?

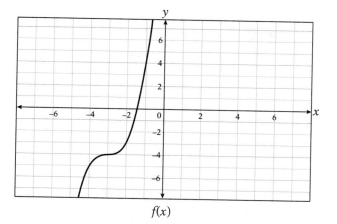

$f(x)$

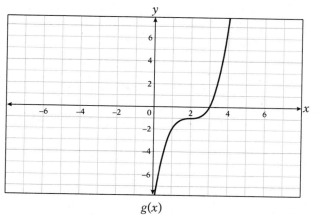

$g(x)$

A. −5
B. 5
C. −3
D. 3
E. −2

GO ON TO THE NEXT PAGE

SECTION 9

1. A jar contains 4 blue marbles, 2 red marbles, and 6 green marbles. What is the probability that a marble chosen at random is red?

    A. $\dfrac{1}{2}$

    B. $\dfrac{1}{3}$

    C. $\dfrac{1}{4}$

    D. $\dfrac{1}{5}$

    E. $\dfrac{1}{6}$

2. In the triangle seen below, $\overline{BD} \perp \overline{AC}$, $\overline{AB} \cong \overline{CB}$, and the measure of angle ABC is 60°, which of the following statements are true?

    I.   Triangle ABC is an equilateral triangle.
    II. The length of $\overline{AB}$ is twice the length of $\overline{AD}$.
    III. The length of $\overline{AD}$ is equal to the length of $\overline{CD}$.

    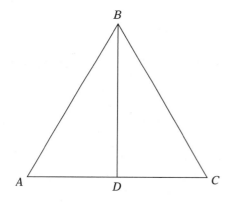

    A. I only
    B. II only
    C. I and III
    D. II and III
    E. I, II, and III

3. 20 is 40% of x. x is 25% of what number?

    A. 200
    B. 50
    C. 20
    D. 8
    E. 2

4. If n is an odd number, which of the following is not odd?

    I. $n + 2$.
    II. $2n$.
    III. $n + 1$.

    A. I only
    B. II only
    C. I and III
    D. II and III
    E. I, II, and III

5. The ratio of Dan's height to Phil's height is proportional to the ratio of Jim's height to Mike's height. If Dan is 76 inches tall, Phil is 80 inches tall, and Mike is 74 inches tall, how tall is Jim?

    A. 70.3 in.
    B. 77.9 in.
    C. 79.3 in.
    D. 82.2 in.
    E. 84.5 in.

6. The legend in a certain pictograph uses 🖥 to represent a certain number of computers. The pictograph below represents 1,750 computers. Therefore,

    🖥 represents how many computers?

    🖥 🖥 🖥 🖥

    A. 250
    B. 500
    C. 750
    D. 1,000
    E. 1,250

7. $a^2 + b^2 + 7^2 = 74 - 2ab$, $a + b =$

    A. 7
    B. 5
    C. 3
    D. 1
    E. 0

GO ON TO THE NEXT PAGE

8. The distance between adjacent marks on the number line is one unit. Use the number line below to determine which of the following points is not equal to $|x - y|$.

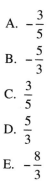

A. $|a - b|$
B. $e - d$
C. c
D. x
E. $|x|$

9. When x is increased by 5, the result is 60% of increasing x by 15. What is the value of x?

A. 6
B. 8
C. 10
D. 12
E. 14

10. On a map $\frac{1}{4}$ of an inch represents 15 miles. If John is taking a 700-mile trip, which of the following equations represents the distance left on the trip if he has traveled x inches on the map?

A. $700 - 15x$
B. $700 - 30x$
C. $700 - 45x$
D. $700 - 60x$
E. $700 - 75x$

11. In the xy-coordinate plane, line k is a reflection of the line l about the line $y = x$. If the slope of line l is $-\frac{3}{5}$, which of the following is the slope of line k?

A. $-\frac{3}{5}$
B. $-\frac{5}{3}$
C. $\frac{3}{5}$
D. $\frac{5}{3}$
E. $-\frac{8}{3}$

12. $x + 2y = 1$ and $5x - 4y = -23$. $x - y =$

A. 2
B. -3
C. -5
D. 5
E. 3

13. What is the value of $x + y$?

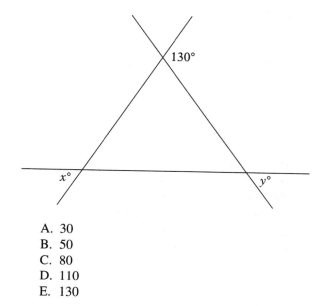

A. 30
B. 50
C. 80
D. 110
E. 130

14. The graph of $f(x)$ below $-f(a) = 2$; which of the following is the value of a?

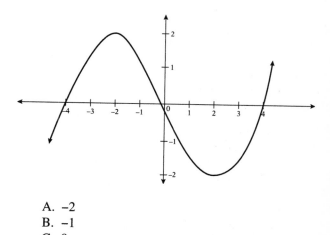

A. -2
B. -1
C. 0
D. 1
E. 2

GO ON TO THE NEXT PAGE

15. The cube shown below has edges of length 4. Points A, B, and C are midpoints of three different edges. What is the area of triangle ABC?

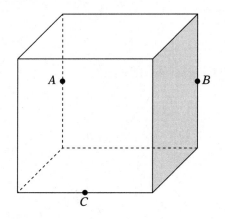

   A. $2\sqrt{3}$

   B. $4\sqrt{3}$

   C. $8\sqrt{3}$

   D. $16\sqrt{3}$

   E. $32\sqrt{3}$

16. $\boxed{X} = x^2 + 7x + 5$. If $\boxed{2a} = \boxed{3a}$, then what is a possible value of a?

   A. 1.4

   B. 1.2

   C. 0.7

   D. 0.6

   E. 0

ANSWERS AND EXPLANATIONS
SECTION 3

1. ***Answer:*** **D**

    Ninety feet of wallpaper costs three times the cost of thirty feet.

    $3 \times \$18 = \$54$

2. ***Answer:*** **C**

    $$\frac{x}{y} = 5$$

    Square each side to find $\dfrac{x^2}{y^2}$.

    $$\frac{x^2}{y^2} = 5^2 = 25$$

    $$2 \cdot \frac{x^2}{y^2} = 2 \cdot 25 = 50.$$

3. ***Answer:*** **B**

    $x^2 + 2xy + y^2$ is a perfect square, $(x + y)^2$

    You know $(x + y)$, so $(x + y)^2 > 8^2$ or 64

    That means $(x^2 + 2xy + y^2) > 64$

4. ***Answer:*** **E**

    To find the perimeter, find the length of each side and add.

    - $(5,8)$ and $(5,2)$

      Because there is no change in the x-values, the distance between the two points will be equal to the change in the y-values. Therefore, the distance between the two points is $8 - 2 = 6$.

    - $(5,8)$ and $(9,8)$

      Because there is no change in the y-values, the distance between the two points will be equal to the change in the x-values. Therefore, the distance between the two points is $9 - 5 = 4$.

    - $(5,2)$ and $(9,8)$

      Because there is a change in both the x and y values, we must use the distance formula: $d = \sqrt{(9 - 5)^2 + (8 - 2)^2} = \sqrt{4^2 + 6^2} = \sqrt{16 + 36} = \sqrt{52} = 2\sqrt{13}$.

    Therefore, the perimeter of the triangle is $6 + 4 + 2\sqrt{13} = 10 + 2\sqrt{13}$.

5. ***Answer:*** **B**

    Because 4 is the first term in the sequence, and $4 = 4(3)^0$. A numbers position in the sequence is one more than the exponent value. The term represented by $4(3)^{10}$ must be the $10 + 1 = 11$th term in the sequence.

6. *Answer:* **D**

   Because $\overleftrightarrow{BE}$ bisects $\angle FOD$, then the measures of $\angle FOE$ and $\angle EOD$ must be equal; therefore, both have a measure of 35°. The diagram shows the sum of the measures of $\angle FOE$, $\angle EOD$, and $\angle FOA$ is 180°. Because $\angle FOE$ and $\angle EOD$ each have a measure of 35°, the sum is 70°. That means, the measure of $\angle FOA$ is 180° − 70° = 110°.

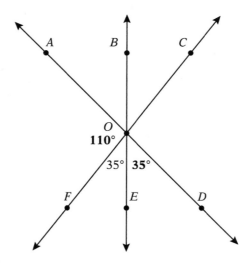

7. *Answer:* **A**

   Choices C (6), D (7), and E (8) cannot be the smallest number in a pair of numbers with a sum of 10.

   Choice B (4) cannot be correct because 4 + 6 = 10 but 6 − 4 is not 4.

   That leaves choice A (3). $\begin{array}{l} 3 + 7 = 10 \\ 7 - 3 = 4 \end{array}$.

8. *Answer:* **C**

   Tom's average

   $$\frac{7 + 12 + 8}{3} = \frac{27}{3} = 9$$

   Frank's average

   Frank's average must equal Tom's average of 9 strikeouts.

   That means he needs 36 strikeouts in four games.

   He has 26 strikeouts in three games.

   That means he needs 10 strikeouts in the fourth game.

9. *Answer:* **3**

   Solve for x.

   $$\frac{x - 3}{4} = 3 \Rightarrow x - 3 = 12 \Rightarrow x = 15$$

   Substitute 15 for x.

   $$\frac{x}{5} = \frac{15}{5} = 3.$$

10. *Answer:* **122**

    Subtract 13 from 74 to find half the number $74 - 13 = 61$

    Multiply 61 by 2 to find the number $2 \times 61 = 122$

11. *Answer:* **75**

    Complete the table

	Men	Women	Total
YES	1,000	1,500	2,500
NO	2,000	500	2,500
Total	3,000	2,000	5,000

    The percent of women who have chosen a major is $\dfrac{1,500}{2,000} = 75\%$.

12. *Answer:* **12**

    The rectangle's base goes from $x = -3$ to $x = 3$. The base of the rectangle is 6. The height of the rectangle is the value of the function either at $x = -3$ or $x = 3$. Find either $f(-3)$ or $f(3)$. The height of the rectangle is $f(3) = -(3)^2 + 11 = -9 + 11 = 2$. The area of the rectangle is $A = 6 \cdot 2 = 12$.

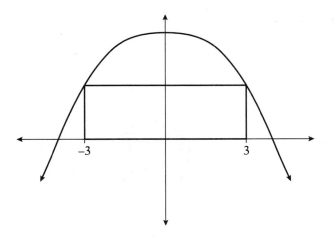

13. *Answer:* **441**

    Substitute $x = -3$, $y = 2$ in the equation.

    $$2xy + \sqrt{z} = x^2 \Rightarrow 2(-3)(2) + \sqrt{z} = (-3)^2$$

    Solve for z.

    $$-12 + \sqrt{z} = 9 \Rightarrow \sqrt{z} = 21 \Rightarrow z = 441.$$

14. *Answer:* **35**

The secret to solving this problem is to notice how non-parallel lines create different angle measures than parallel lines. If a and b were parallel, then m$\angle RQP$ *would* be 70°. But a and b are not parallel, so the measure of $\angle RQP$ cannot be 70°. That means t bisects $\angle RQP$ and y cannot be 35.

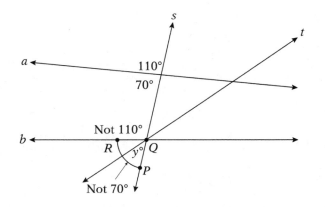

15. *Answer:* **24**

There are four main courses.

There are 4 side items: A, B, C, and D.

There are six ways to choose two side items:

AB AC AD BC BD CD

Therefore, there are a total of 4 × 6 = 24 specials that can be ordered.

16. *Answer:* $\dfrac{1}{4}$ **or 0.25**

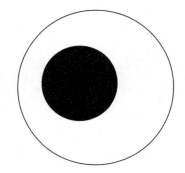

Let πr^2 represent the area of the inner circle.

The radius of the outer circle is twice the radius of the inner circle.

Let $\pi(2r)^2$ represent the area of the outer circle

Divide to find the probability $\dfrac{\pi r^2}{\pi(2r)^2} = \dfrac{\cancel{\pi r^2}}{4\cancel{\pi r^2}} = \dfrac{1}{4}$.

17. *Answer:* **4**

We know that $n = c \times p$, where p is a prime number. The number c has three unique prime factors, and all of these prime factors are less than p.

The number n has a total of 4 unique prime factors, p and the three unique prime number that form c. Squaring n is the same as squaring each of these 4 unique prime factors. What results is a list of numbers that are not prime, and no more prime numbers are formed.

18. **Answer: 36**

This is a multiple-step problem. Start by finding simultaneous equations.

Step 1. Substitute the known values of x and y in the equation. The result will be equations with just the unknowns b and c.

$$\underline{(3,16) : y = 2x^2 + bx + c}$$
$$16 = 2(3)^2 + b(3) + c$$
$$16 = 18 + 3b + c \Rightarrow -2 = 3b + c$$

$$\underline{(1,-12) : y = 2x^2 + bx + c}$$
$$-12 = 2(1)^2 + b(1) + c$$
$$-12 = 2 + b + c \Rightarrow -14 = b + c$$

We created two simultaneous equations.

Step 2. Subtract the equations to solve for b.

$$\begin{array}{r} (-2) = 3b + c \\ -(-14) = b + c \\ \hline 12 = 2b \quad \Rightarrow 6 = b \end{array}$$

Step 3. Substitute 6 for b in either equation. Solve for c.

$$-2 = 3b + c \Rightarrow -2 = 3(6) + c \qquad -14 = b + c$$
$$\text{or}$$
$$-2 = 18 + c \Rightarrow -20 = c \qquad -14 = 6 + c \Rightarrow -20 = c$$

Step 4. Substitute in the parabola equation: $b = 6$, $c = 20$.

$y = 2x^2 + bx + c$ is $y = 2x^2 + 6x - 20$

Step 5. Substitute: $x = 4$.

Solve for y.

$$y = 2(4)^2 + 6(4) - 20 = 2(16) + 24 - 20 = 36$$

When $x = 4$, $y = 36$.

Section 4

1. *Answer:* **B**

   The smallest positive integer is 1, so the smallest possible value of *b* is 1. That means the smallest possible value for *a* is 3. $\dfrac{a}{3} = b \Rightarrow \dfrac{3}{3} = 1$.

2. *Answer:* **C**

   When a graph is symmetric with respect to the *y*-axis, the graph will match itself when folded across the *y*-axis.

   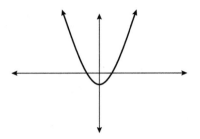

3. *Answer:* **C**

   Since 8% is 0.08, the correct answer is $1,000 + 0.08\,s$.

4. *Answer:* **D**

   Theater A:

   Theater A earned $\$6 \cdot 15,000 = \$90,000$

   Theater B:

   Divide \$90,000 by the \$8 ticket price for Theater B. $\$90,000 \div \$8 = 11,250$

   Theater B must sell 11,250 tickets to earn the same amount as Theater A.

5. *Answer:* **D**

   We can see from the bar graph that City D had the greatest decrease in snow accumulation.

   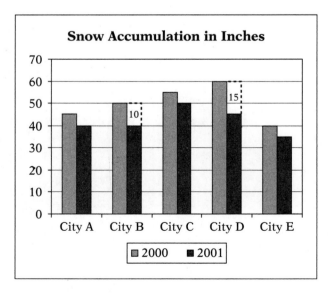

6. ***Answer:* C**

   The arithmetic mean of the five numbers is 10. That means the sum of the numbers is 50. The sum of three numbers is 30, so the sum of the remaining two numbers is $50 - 30 = 20$.

7. ***Answer:* B**

   Segments $\overline{AB}$ and $\overline{BC}$ are perpendicular, so the measure of $\angle ABC$ is 90°.

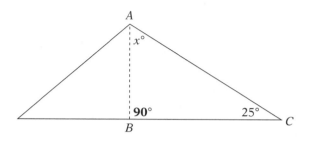

   The sum of the angles in a triangle is 180°. We know the sum of two angle measures is 115°. So $180 - 115 = x$, $x = 65$.

8. ***Answer:* D**

   A. NO $8 \cdot 3 = 24$. She only scored 15 points, so she could not have made eight three-pointers.

   B. NO $6 \cdot 3 = 18$. She only scored 15 points, so she could not have made six three-pointers.

   C. NO $4 \cdot 3 = 12$. Because she scored 15 points, she could not have scored the other three points from 2-point baskets.

   D. YES $3 \cdot 3 = 9$. She scored 9 points from three-point baskets. She could have scored the other six points from two-point baskets for a total of 15 points.

   E. NO $2 \cdot 3 = 6$. She scored 15 points, so she could not have scored the other nine points from 2-point baskets.

9. ***Answer:* A**

   There are 12 inches in a foot. Divide I by 12 to convert inches to feet.

   $F + \dfrac{I}{12}$ represents the number of feet.

10. ***Answer:* C**

    Factor the quadratic equation.

    $x^2 + 9x + 20 = 0 \Rightarrow (x + 5)(x + 4)$

    Find the values of x.

    $x + 5 = 0 \Rightarrow x = -5$

    $x + 4 = 0 \Rightarrow x = -4$

11. ***Answer:* E**

    Isolate x^4.

    $\dfrac{x^4}{16} = y^8 z^{12} \Rightarrow x^4 = 16y^8 z^{12}$

    Raise both sides of the equation to the $\dfrac{1}{4}$ power and solve for x.

    $\left(x^4\right)^{\frac{1}{4}} = \left(16y^8 z^{12}\right)^{\frac{1}{4}} \Rightarrow x = 2y^2 z^3$

12. **Answer: D**

The slope of $f(x)$ must equal 2 for $f(x)$ to be perpendicular to a line whose slope is a line $-\dfrac{1}{2}$. Eliminate choices A, C, and E because their slopes are not positive.

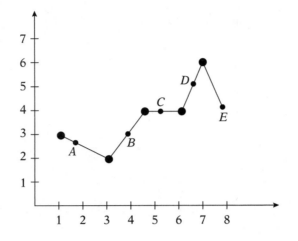

The slope at point B is $\dfrac{2-4}{3-5} = \dfrac{-2}{-2} = 1$.

The slope at point D is $\dfrac{4-6}{6-7} = \dfrac{-2}{-1} = 2$.

13. **Answer: C**
    - First digit must be prime {2,3,5,7}. (4 digits)
    - Second digit must be odd {1,3,5,7,9}. (5 digits)
    - Third digit must be divisible by 5 {0,5}. (2 digits)
    - Fourth digit must be a nonprime odd number {1,9}. (2 digits)

Multiply $\underline{4} \cdot \underline{5} \cdot \underline{2} \cdot \underline{2}$ = 80 different passwords.

14. **Answer: E**

Combine like terms.

$x^2 + 14x + 49 = 49 - x^2 \Rightarrow 2x^2 + 14x = 0$

Factor.

$2x(x + 7) = 0.$

Solve for x.

$2x = 0 \Rightarrow x = 0.$

$x + 7 = 0 \Rightarrow x = -7.$

15. **Answer: C**

This is a right triangle. That means the sides satisfy the Pythagorean Theorem $a^2 + b^2 = c^2$. That's choice C(6,8,10) because $6^2 + 8^2 = 10^2$.

16. *Answer:* **C**

Draw a diagram.

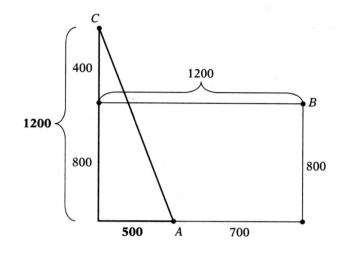

The distance from A to C is the hypotenuse of a right triangle.

Subtract to find the base of the right triangle. $1,200 - 700 - 500$.

Add to find the height. $800 + 400 + 1,200$. Use the Pythagorean Theorem.

$$(AC)^2 = 500^2 + 1,200^2 \Rightarrow (AC)^2 = 250,000 + 1,440,000.$$

$$AC = \sqrt{1,690,000} = 1,300 \text{ miles.}$$

17. *Answer:* **E**

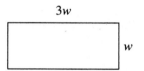

Use the perimeter to find the width.

$$2(w) + 2(3w) = 72 \Rightarrow 2w + 6w = 72 \Rightarrow 8w = 72 \Rightarrow w = 9.$$

The width of the rectangle is 9, and the length of the rectangle is 27. Multiply to find the area.

$$A = 9 \cdot 27 = 243.$$

18. *Answer:* **C**

The difference between the largest and smallest of the five integers is 4. That means the five integers must be consecutive integers. In turn, that means the mean and median are equal. They are each 56.

19. *Answer:* **B**

Solve for x.

$$x^{\frac{1}{2}} = k^{\frac{3}{2}} \Rightarrow \left(x^{\frac{1}{2}}\right)^2 = \left(k^{\frac{3}{2}}\right)^2 \Rightarrow x = k^3.$$

Solve for y.

$$\left(k^{\frac{5}{2}}\right)^{\frac{6}{5}} = \left(y^{\frac{5}{6}}\right)^{\frac{6}{5}} \Rightarrow k^3 = y.$$

Both x and y equal k^3. Therefore, $x = y$.

20. *Answer:* **A**

The graphs of $f(x)$ and $g(x)$ are shown below.

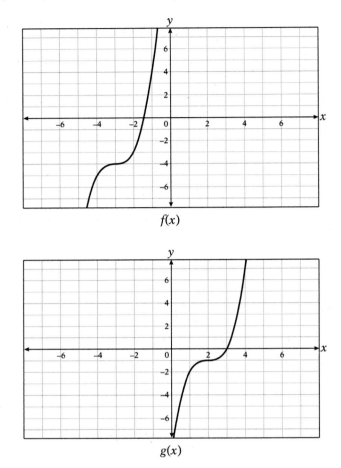

$f(x)$

$g(x)$

The graph of $f(x)$ is shifted 5 units to the right and 3 units up to become the graph of $g(x)$. The variable h shows the horizontal shift. Subtract to show a shift to the right: $h = -5$.

Symbolically, $g(x) = f(x + h) + k = f(x - 5) + 3 \Rightarrow h = -5$.

SECTION 9

1. **Answer: E**

   Write a fraction.

   $$\frac{\text{number of red marbles}}{\text{total number of marbles}} = \frac{2}{12} = \frac{1}{6}.$$

2. **Answer: E**

   Consider each case. We present the cases out of order (I–III–II) to make things easier to explain.

   I.

   $\overline{AB} \cong \overline{CB}$, so the measure of $\angle A$ is equal to the measure of $\angle C$.

   The measure of angle $\angle ABC$ 60°, so the sum of the measures of $\angle A$ and $\angle C$ is 120°.

   Therefore $\angle A$ and $\angle C$ each have a measure of 60°. That means all angles of triangle ABC have a measure of 60° and triangle ABC is an equilateral triangle.

   III.

   $\overline{BD} \perp \overline{AC}$ and triangle ABC is an equilateral triangle so $\overline{BD}$ bisects $\overline{AC}$ and the length of $\overline{AD}$ is equal to the length of $\overline{CD}$

   II.

   Triangle ABC is an equilateral triangle so the length of $\overline{AB}$ is equal to the length of $\overline{AC}$. The length of $\overline{AC}$ is twice the length of $\overline{AD}$ because $\overline{BD}$ bisects $\overline{AC}$. That means the length of $\overline{AB}$ is twice the length of $\overline{AD}$.

   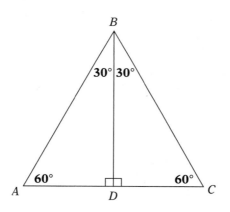

3. **Answer: A**

   Solve for x. $20 = .4x \Rightarrow x = 50$.

   50 is 25% of 200.

   So, x is 25% of 200.

4. **Answer: D**

   Choose any odd value for n. Say $n = 5$.

   I. $n + 2 \Rightarrow 5 + 2 = 7$. This value is still odd.

   II. $2n \Rightarrow 2(5) = 10$. This value is even.

III. $n + 1 \Rightarrow 5 + 1 = 6$. This value is even.

Choices II and III are not odd.

5. ***Answer:* A**

   D = Dan's height.

   P = Phil's height.

   M = Mike's height.

   J = Jim's height.

   Write a proportion

   $$\frac{D}{P} = \frac{J}{M} \Rightarrow \frac{76}{80} = \frac{J}{74}$$

   Solve for J. $80J = 5{,}624 \Rightarrow J = 70.3$ inches.

6. ***Answer:* B**

   3.5 symbols represent 1,750 computers.

   $1{,}750 \div 3.5 = 500$

   Each  represents 500 computers.

7. ***Answer:* B**

   Add $2ab$ to each side

   $$a^2 + b^2 + 7^2 = 74 - 2ab \Rightarrow a^2 + 2ab + b^2 + 49 = 74$$

   Subtract 49 from each side.

   $$a^2 + 2ab + b^2 = 25.$$

   Factor the perfect square.

   $$(a + b)^2 = 25$$

   Solve for $a + b$.

   $$a + b = 5.$$

8. ***Answer:* D**

   $$a \quad y \quad b \quad x \quad 0 \quad c \quad d \quad e$$

   Absolute value represents distance. The distance from x to y is 2.

   $$|x - y| = 2$$

   Find the value of each choice.

   A. $|a - b| = 2.$
   B. $e - d = 2.$
   C. $c = 2.$
   D. $x = -2.$
   E. $|x| = 2.$

   Only Choice D is not equal to 2.

9. **Answer: C**

   Write an equation and solve for x.

   $x + 5 = 0.6(x + 15) \Rightarrow x + 5 = 0.6x + 0.6 \cdot 15$

   $x + 5 = 0.6x + 9 \Rightarrow 0.4x = 4 \Rightarrow x = 10.$

10. **Answer: D**

    Every $\dfrac{1}{4}$ of an inch on the map represents 15 miles. Every inch represents 60 miles. With a total of 700 miles to travel, the distance left on the trip is $700 - 60x$.

11. **Answer: B**

    When line l is reflected about the line $y = x$, the x and y coordinates of each point switch. That means if the slope of line l is $-\dfrac{3}{5}$, then the slope of line k is $-\dfrac{5}{3}$.

12. **Answer: C**

    Solve simultaneous equations for x.

    $$\begin{array}{ccc} x + 2y = 1 & 2(x + 2y = 1) & 2x + 4y = 2 \\ 5x - 4y = -23 & 5x - 4y = -23 & \underline{5x - 4y = -23} \\ & & 7x = -21 \Rightarrow \quad x = -3. \end{array}$$

    Substitute -3 for x in either of the original equations to solve for y.

    $x + 2y = 1 \Rightarrow -3 + 2y = 1 \Rightarrow 2y = 4 \Rightarrow y = 2.$

    $5x - 4y = -23 \Rightarrow 5(-3) - 4y = -23 \Rightarrow -15 - 4y = -23 \Rightarrow -4y = -8 \Rightarrow y = 2.$

    Subtract to find $x - y = -3 - 2 = -5.$

13. **Answer: E**

    Draw on the diagram.

    The two base angles have measures of $x°$ and $y°$ *(bold)* because vertical angles are congruent.

    The sum of x and y is 130 because the sum of the two remote interior angles is equal to the measure of the exterior angle.

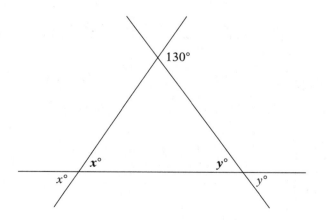

14. ***Answer:*** **E**

Solve for $f(a)$.

We know $-f(a) = 2$

$f(a) = -2$. That means the y value is -2.

Find the matching x value.

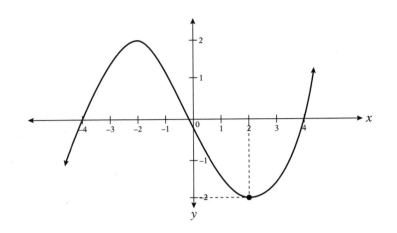

15. ***Answer:*** **B**

Draw the line segments on the diagram. The length of $\overline{AB}$ is 4 because each edge length is 4. Find the height of triangle ABC. Point D has been added to the picture, and $\overline{CD}$ represents the height of triangle ABC. $\overline{CD}$ is the hypotenuse of the right triangle formed in the middle of the figure. The legs of this right triangle are lengths 2 and 4.

Use the Pythagorean Theorem to solve for CD.

$$(CD)^2 = 4^2 + 2^2 \Rightarrow (CD)^2 = 16 + 4 \Rightarrow \sqrt{(CD)^2} = \sqrt{20} \Rightarrow CD = \sqrt{20} = 2\sqrt{5}.$$

Therefore, $CD = 2\sqrt{5}$. The area of triangle ABC is

$$A = \frac{1}{2}bh = \frac{1}{2} \cdot 4 \cdot 2\sqrt{5} = 4\sqrt{5}.$$

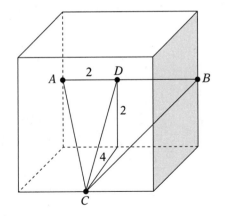

16. *Answer:* **E**

$\boxed{X} = x^2 + 7x + 5.$

$\boxed{2a} = \boxed{3a}$

Substitute $2a$ for $\boxed{X}$ $(2a)^2 + 7(2a) + 5$

Substitute $3a$ for $\boxed{X}$. $(3a)^2 + 7(3a) + 5$

Write as equal expressions.

$(2a)^2 + 7(2a) + 5 = (3a)^2 + 7(3a) + 5.$

Simplify.

$4a^2 + 14a + 5 = 9a^2 + 21a + 5$

Combine like terms and solve for a.

$0 = 5a^2 + 7a.$

$0 = a(5a + 7)$

$a = 0$ or $5a + 7 = 0 \Rightarrow 5a = -7 \Rightarrow a = -1.4$

$a = 0$ is the only answer choice given.

SCORE ESTIMATOR

Use this sheet to estimate your SAT Mathematics scale score. These scores are <u>estimates</u>, and your performance on the actual SAT could easily fall outside your scale score range for this test. One primary reason for the difference is that you did not take this test in a completely realistic test setting.

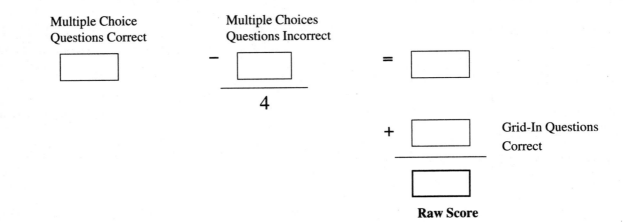

Raw Score	Scale Score Range	Raw Score	Scale Score Range
54	800	27	470–550
53	740–800	26	470–540
52	710–800	25	460–540
51	690–790	24	450–530
50	680–760	23	440–520
49	670–750	22	430–510
48	650–740	21	430–500
47	640–730	20	420–490
46	630–720	19	420–480
45	620–710	18	410–470
44	610–700	17	400–460
43	600–680	16	390–450
42	600–670	15	390–450
41	590–660	14	380–440
40	570–650	13	370–430
39	560–640	12	360–430
38	550–630	11	350–430
37	540–620	10	340–430
36	540–610	9	330–430
35	530–600	8	320–420
34	530–600	7	310–410
33	520–590	6	300–400
32	510–580	5	290–390
31	500–570	4	280–380
30	490–560	3	270–370
29	490–560	2	240–340
28	480–550	1, 0, or less	200–320

CHAPTER 21

SAT MATH PRACTICE TEST 3

Directions for Multiple-Choice Questions

In this section, solve each problem, using any available space on the page for scratchwork. Then decide which is the best of the choices given and fill in the corresponding oval on your answer sheet.

- You may use a calculator on any problem. All numbers used are real numbers.
- Figures are drawn as accurately as possible EXCEPT when it is stated that the figure is not drawn to scale.
- All figures lie in a plane unless otherwise indicated.

Directions for Student-Produced Response Questions

Student Response questions are always numbered 9–18. Complete the grids at the bottom of the answer sheet for the test where the student response questions appear.

- If your answer is 2/3 or .666 . . . , you must enter **the most accurate value the grid can accommodate,** but you may do this in 1 of 4 ways:

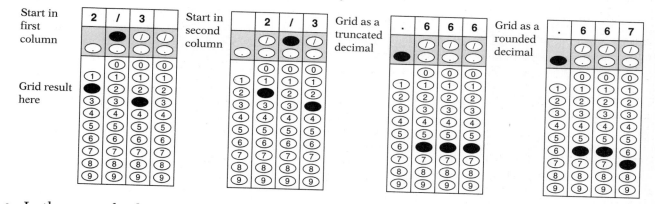

- In the example above, gridding a response of 0.67 or 0.66 is **incorrect** because it is less accurate than those above.

- The scoring machine cannot read what is written in the top row of boxes. You **MUST** fill in the numerical grid accurately to get credit for answering any question correctly. You should write your answer in the top row of boxes only to aid your gridding.

Reference Information

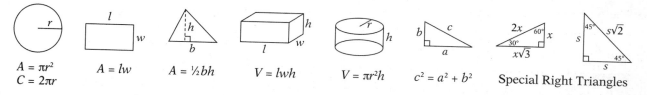

$A = \pi r^2$
$C = 2\pi r$

$A = lw$

$A = \frac{1}{2}bh$

$V = lwh$

$V = \pi r^2 h$

$c^2 = a^2 + b^2$

Special Right Triangles

The arc of a circle measures 360°.
Every straight angle measures 180°.
The sum of the measures of the angles in a triangle is 180°.

Start with number 1 for each new section. If a section has fewer questions than answer spaces, leave the extra answer spaces blank. Be sure to erase any errors or stray marks completely.

25 Minutes

SECTION 3

1. Ⓐ Ⓑ Ⓒ Ⓓ Ⓔ
2. Ⓐ Ⓑ Ⓒ Ⓓ Ⓔ
3. Ⓐ Ⓑ Ⓒ Ⓓ Ⓔ
4. Ⓐ Ⓑ Ⓒ Ⓓ Ⓔ
5. Ⓐ Ⓑ Ⓒ Ⓓ Ⓔ
6. Ⓐ Ⓑ Ⓒ Ⓓ Ⓔ
7. Ⓐ Ⓑ Ⓒ Ⓓ Ⓔ
8. Ⓐ Ⓑ Ⓒ Ⓓ Ⓔ

Student-Produced Responses — ONLY ANSWERS ENTERED IN THE CIRCLES IN EACH GRID WILL BE SCORED. YOU WILL NOT RECEIVE CREDIT FOR ANYTHING WRITTEN IN THE BOXES ABOVE THE CIRCLES.

9 10 11 12 13
14 15 16 17 18

25 Minutes

SECTION 6

1–20. Ⓐ Ⓑ Ⓒ Ⓓ Ⓔ

20 Minutes

SECTION 9

1–16. Ⓐ Ⓑ Ⓒ Ⓓ Ⓔ

TEST 3 QUESTIONS
SECTION 3

1. Which number below is between 0.15 and 0.20?

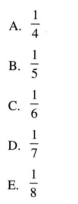

  A. $\dfrac{1}{4}$

  B. $\dfrac{1}{5}$

  C. $\dfrac{1}{6}$

  D. $\dfrac{1}{7}$

  E. $\dfrac{1}{8}$

2. Which segment in the figure below is the longest?

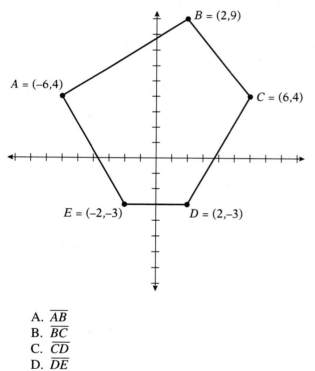

  A. $\overline{AB}$
  B. $\overline{BC}$
  C. $\overline{CD}$
  D. $\overline{DE}$
  E. $\overline{EA}$

3. In the figure shown below $l \perp m$. What is the value of x?

  A. 30
  B. 45
  C. 60
  D. 90
  E. 120

4. If $y - 5 = 4(x - 2)$, what is the value of x if $y = 13$?

  A. 0
  B. 2
  C. 4
  D. 8
  E. 16

5. If $\dfrac{x^8}{x^k} = x^{15}$ and $(x^7)^z = x^{21}$, what is the product of k and z?

  A. −23
  B. −21
  C. −11
  D. −7
  E. −3

GO ON TO THE NEXT PAGE

6. The cost of a pen decreases as the number of pens purchased increases. Which of the following could be the segment that best fits the scatterplot representing the number of pens purchased against the cost per pen?

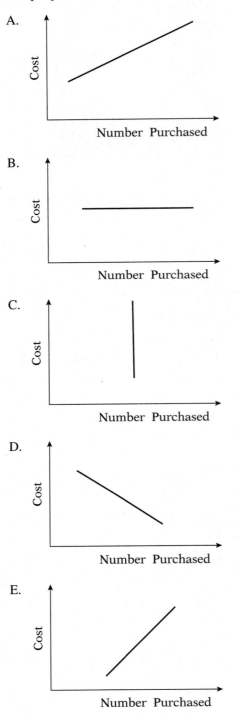

A.

B.

C.

D.

E.

7. In the figure below $\overline{AB} \perp \overline{CB}$, $\overline{BD} \perp \overline{AC}$, $AD = 5$, and the measure of angle BAC is 60°. What is the length of $\overline{BC}$?

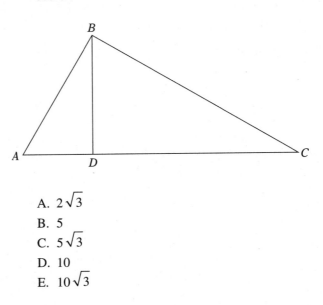

A. $2\sqrt{3}$
B. 5
C. $5\sqrt{3}$
D. 10
E. $10\sqrt{3}$

8. A car travels 70 miles on x gallons of gasoline. Each gallon of gasoline costs y dollars. In terms of x and y, how much does it cost for the car to travel 1 mile?

A. $\dfrac{yx}{70}$.

B. $\dfrac{70}{xy}$.

C. $\dfrac{70y}{x}$.

D. $\dfrac{70x}{y}$.

E. $70xy$.

9. $4:7 = a:28$, $a =$

10. What is the sixth term of the geometric sequence whose first three terms are 120, 60, and 30?

11. The length of $\overline{AB}$ is 24. Point C is the midpoint of $\overline{AB}$. Let D be a point equidistant from points A and B such that $DC = 9$. What is the length of $\overline{AD}$?

GO ON TO THE NEXT PAGE

12. The average of six consecutive positive integers is 14.5. What is the value of the smallest positive integer?

13. Jill bought a bracelet for $83.74. The price includes the 6% sales tax. What was the sticker price of the bracelet?

14. A circle has a radius 8. A cone is formed by cutting out a 60° wedge and placing together the two ends of the remaining part of the circle (diagram below). What is the surface area of the cone rounded to the nearest whole number, excluding the circular base?

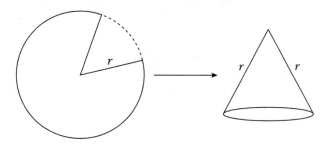

15. $x - y = 3$, what is the value of $x^2 - 2xy + y^2$?

16. The shaded part of the rectangular figure below has a constant width. What is the area of the shaded part?

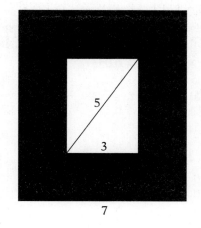

17. k divided by 4 has a remainder of 3. What is the remainder when $k + 3$ is divided by 4?

18. The total price of two items at a department store is $140. If the price of one item is increased by 20%, and the price of the other item is decreased by 25%, the average price of the two items is $70.50. What is the original price of the more expensive item minus the original price of the less expensive item?

GO ON TO THE NEXT PAGE

Section 6

1. Phil has x quarters, y dimes, and z nickels and nothing else. Which of the following expressions represents the amount of money that Phil has, in dollars?

   A. $0.25x + 0.10y + 0.05z$.
   B. $2.5x + 1.0y + 0.5z$.
   C. $25x + 10y + 5z$.
   D. $0.25x + 0.10y + 0.5z$.
   E. $25x + 10y + 50z$.

2. If $x - 4 = 10$, then $3x - 12 =$

   A. 10
   B. 20
   C. 30
   D. 40
   E. 50

3. In the expression a^n, n is an even power. Which of the following expressions does not have even power?

   A. a^{n+1}
   B. a^{2n}
   C. a^{n+2}
   D. a^{3n}
   E. a^{n+4}

4. The height of triangle ABC is twice the height of parallelogram $ADEC$. If the area of triangle ABC is 14, what is the area of parallelogram $ADEC$?

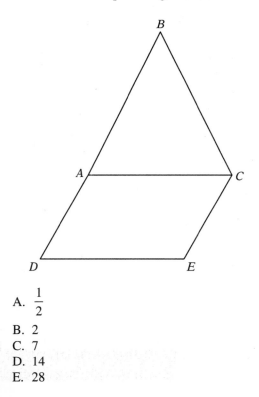

   A. $\frac{1}{2}$
   B. 2
   C. 7
   D. 14
   E. 28

5. The circle graph below shows the percent of an exercise routine that is spent on each body part. If approximately 37 minutes is spent on shoulders and back, which of the following choices best approximates the amount of time spent on arms and legs?

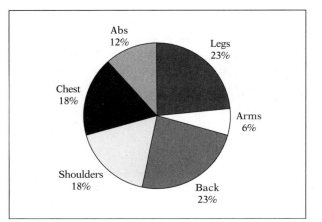

   A. 25 minutes
   B. 26 minutes
   C. 27 minutes
   D. 28 minutes
   E. 29 minutes

6. If there are no gaps between tiles used for a kitchen floor, how many 8-square-inch tiles are needed to cover a kitchen floor that is 10 feet wide and 14 feet long?

   A. 120
   B. 168
   C. 210
   D. 2,520
   E. 20,160

7. Jim's and Al's ages total 30. Doubling Jim's age and adding it to Ed's age equals 46. Subtracting Al's age from Ed's age equals 3. How old is Jim?

   A. 13
   B. 20
   C. 33
   D. 46
   E. 59

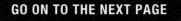
GO ON TO THE NEXT PAGE

8. The picture of a building is shown in a college architecture book. In the book, every half-inch represents 25 feet. How tall is the building in the book if the actual building is 350 feet tall?

    A. 175 inches
    B. 125 inches
    C. 25 inches
    D. 7 inches
    E. 5 inches

9. What is the product of the x-coordinates for the intersection points of the graphs for functions $f(x) = x^2 - 5$ and $g(x) = -2x + 3$?

    A. −8
    B. −4
    C. −2
    D. 2
    E. 8

10. Shawn can swim two laps every 100 seconds. Brian can swim four laps every 4 minutes. If both Shawn and Brian start swimming at the same time, Shawn will swim how many more laps than Brian in 5 minutes?

    A. 1
    B. 2
    C. 3
    D. 4
    E. 5

11. The table below gives values of a function which describes the path of an object that has been dropped from a height of 16 feet. Which of the following equations is equal to $f(x)$?

x	0	1	2	3	4
$f(x)$	16	15	12	7	0

    A. $f(x) = x^2 - 16$.
    B. $f(x) = -x^2 + 16$.
    C. $f(x) = x^2 + 8x + 16$.
    D. $f(x) = -x^2 - 16$.
    E. $f(x) = x^2 + 4x + 16$.

12. The scatter plot below shows the relationship between the weight of a car and average miles per gallon of the car. Which of the following accurately describes the relationship?

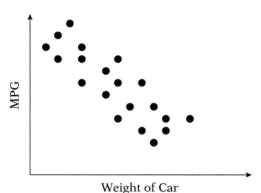

Weight of Car

    A. As the weight of the car increases the miles per gallon increase.
    B. As the weight of the car increases the miles per gallon decrease.
    C. As the weight of the car increases the miles per gallon does not change.
    D. As the weight of the car decreases the miles per gallon decrease.
    E. As the weight of the car decreases the miles per gallon does not change.

13. A password is formed with two letters followed by three one-digit numbers (0–9). If no letter and no number can be repeated, how many passwords of this type can be formed?

    A. 676,000
    B. 650,000
    C. 585,000
    D. 520,000
    E. 468,000

GO ON TO THE NEXT PAGE

14. The graph of $f(x)$ is shown below. Which of the following is the graph of $|f(x)|$?

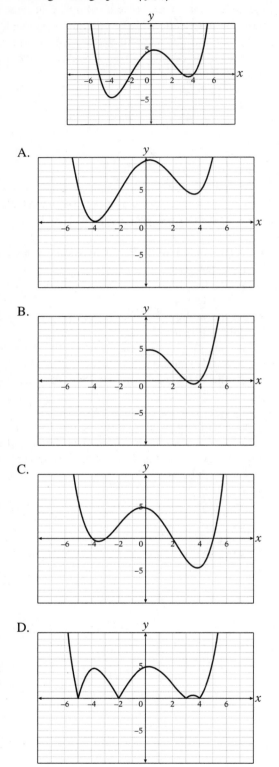

A.

B.

C.

D.

E.

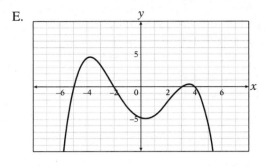

15. The perimeter of the regular hexagon below is 12. What is the length of $\overline{AB}$, if A is equidistant from each vertex?

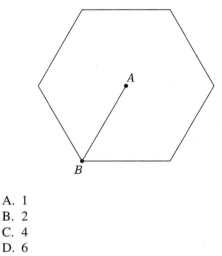

A. 1
B. 2
C. 4
D. 6
E. 8

16. There is an inverse relationship between the squirrel (s) and the fox (f) population in a certain wooded area. The point (s, f) represents the number of squirrels and foxes. If the point (200,100) correctly represents these two populations at a certain time of the year, which of the following points could also properly represent these populations?

A. (200,150)
B. (250,200)
C. (150,150)
D. (175,75)
E. (225,125)

GO ON TO THE NEXT PAGE

17. Every year Jack's investment of $700 increases by 5%. In which year will his investment first exceed $1,000?

    A. 6
    B. 7
    C. 8
    D. 9
    E. 10

18. Four blocks are placed side-by-side.

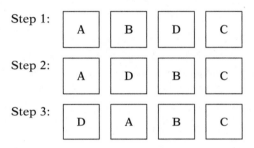

STARTING POSITION

A full cycle is completed when the block in the furthest most right position is moved to the furthest most left position. But the full cycle must be completed using the specific steps below.

Step 1:

Step 2:

Step 3:

Begin at the Starting Position. Using this process, how many steps are needed to return the blocks to the Starting Position position?

    A. 3
    B. 6
    C. 9
    D. 12
    E. 15

19. The *standard deviation* of a set of numbers is the average distance the set of numbers is from the mean of the set of numbers. If the *standard deviation* of a set of numbers is 6, which of the following would be the *standard deviation* of the new set of numbers formed by adding three to each number in the original set of numbers?

    A. 3
    B. 6
    C. 9
    D. 12
    E. 15

20. The figure below is the side view of a pool that is 10 feet wide. What is the volume of the water in the pool when it is filled to 2 feet below the top?

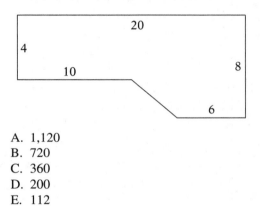

    A. 1,120
    B. 720
    C. 360
    D. 200
    E. 112

GO ON TO THE NEXT PAGE

SECTION 9

1. If $2x + 5 \geq 3$, which of the following is not a possible value of x?
    A. −2
    B. −1
    C. 0
    D. 1
    E. 2

2. $x - k = x$, what is the value of k?
    A. −2
    B. −1
    C. 0
    D. 1
    E. 2

3. $a \parallel b$, $x =$

    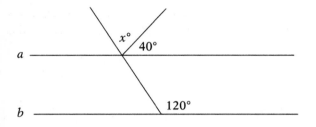

    A. 20
    B. 40
    C. 60
    D. 80
    E. 120

4. A box contains metal and plastic paper clips. There are 16 fewer metal paper clips than plastic paper clips. If there are 100 paper clips in the box, how many plastic paper clips are there?
    A. 84
    B. 58
    C. 42
    D. 29
    E. 21

5. A statistics class has 10 sophomores, 5 juniors, and 15 seniors. What is the probability that a student chosen at random form the class is not a sophomore?
    A. $\dfrac{1}{3}$
    B. $\dfrac{2}{3}$
    C. $\dfrac{1}{2}$
    D. $\dfrac{5}{6}$
    E. $\dfrac{1}{6}$

6. The quantity of beans used in a stew is proportional to the number of servings. If three cups of beans are used for 8 servings, how many cups of beans will be used for 12 servings?
    A. 36
    B. 12
    C. 9
    D. 5.5
    E. 4.5

7. In the figure below, which of the following choices is the median of 100 and y?

    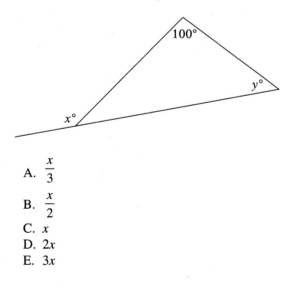

    A. $\dfrac{x}{3}$
    B. $\dfrac{x}{2}$
    C. x
    D. $2x$
    E. $3x$

8. $a = x^3$ and $b = x^2$, for which of the following values of x is $b > a$?

A. 0
B. 0.5
C. 1
D. 2
E. 3

9. $k =$

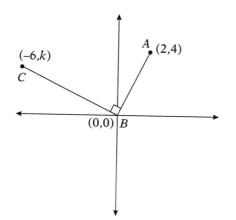

A. 5
B. 4
C. 3
D. 2
E. 1

10. $\| t| + s - 3| = 5$, what is the largest possible value of s?

A. −2
B. 3
C. 5
D. 8
E. 10

11. A company produces a total of T clocks each year at several different plants. The total production is three times the amount produced in Plant A. Plant B produces half the amount Plant A produces. Which of the following represents the proportion of the total production produced in Plant B?

A. $\frac{5}{6}T$

B. $\frac{2}{3}T$

C. $\frac{2}{5}T$

D. $\frac{2}{7}T$

E. $\frac{1}{6}T$

12. In the figure below $\overline{BC} \parallel \overline{DE}$ and point B is the midpoint of $\overline{AD}$. If the area of triangle ABC is 12, what is the area of triangle ADE?

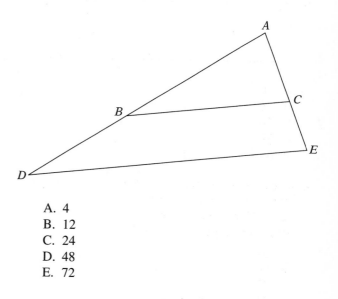

A. 4
B. 12
C. 24
D. 48
E. 72

GO ON TO THE NEXT PAGE

13. $g(f(2)) =$

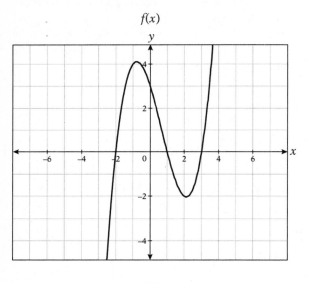

f(x)

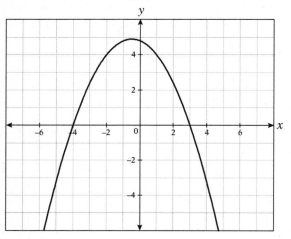

g(x)

A. −2.5
B. −2
C. −1.5
D. 2
E. 4

14. The graph of $h(x)$ is shown below. Which of the following is the graph of $h(x + 2) + 4$?

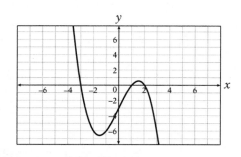

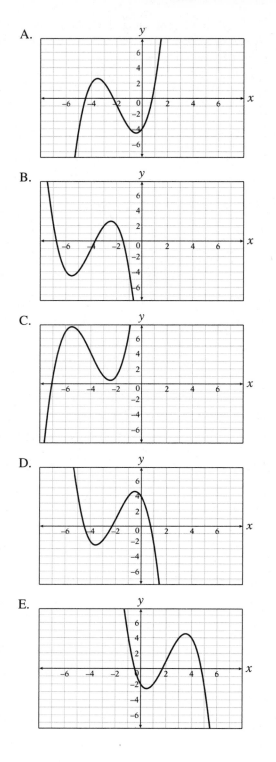

A.

B.

C.

D.

E.

GO ON TO THE NEXT PAGE

15. Tom purchased a bicycle for $402.50. This was 15% more than Rich spent on a bike. Alex purchased a bicycle that was 20% less than the amount Rich spent. How much did Alex's bicycle cost?

   A. $503.13
   B. $473.53
   C. $350
   D. $280
   E. $70

16. The area of the circle below is 64π. The measure of arc ABC is $\dfrac{4\pi}{3}$. What is the area of the shaded region?

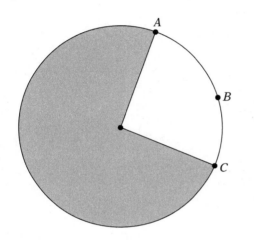

   A. $\dfrac{176\pi}{3}$

   B. $\dfrac{58\pi}{3}$

   C. $\dfrac{16\pi}{3}$

   D. $\dfrac{8\pi}{3}$

   E. $\dfrac{4\pi}{3}$

ANSWERS AND EXPLANATIONS
SECTION 3

1. ***Answer:*** **C**

    Use a calculator to represent a fraction as a decimal.

    $$\frac{1}{6} = 0.16\overline{6}.$$

    $0.16\overline{6}$ is between 0.15 and 0.20.

2. ***Answer:*** **A**

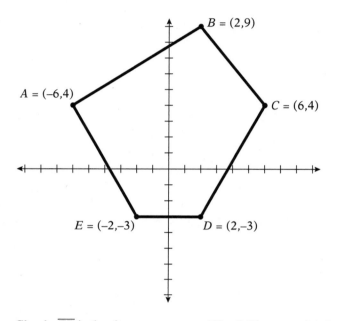

    Clearly $\overline{ED}$ is the shortest segment. $AE = DC$ because the change in the x-value for both is 4, and the change in the y-value for both is 9. Therefore, neither segment can be the longest because they are equal. $AB > CB$ because the change in the y-value for both is the same but the change in the x-value for segment $\overline{AB}$ is greater than the change in the x-value for segment $\overline{CB}$. Therefore, $\overline{AB}$ must be the longest segment.

3. ***Answer:*** **B**

    Because $l \perp m$, l and m meet to form a right angle. That means $2x = 90$ and $x = 45$.

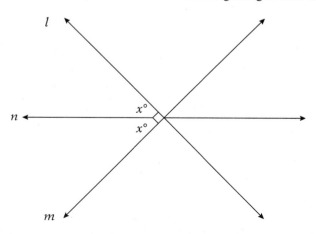

4. **Answer: C**

   Substitute 13 for y.

   $y - 5 = 4(x - 2) \Rightarrow 13 - 5 = 4(x - 2)$

   Solve for x.

   $8 = 4(x - 2) \Rightarrow 2 = x - 2 \Rightarrow 4 = x$.

5. **Answer: B**

   Use the rules of exponents to find the value of k.

   $\dfrac{x^8}{x^k} = x^{15} \Rightarrow x^8 = x^{15} \cdot x^k$

   $\dfrac{x^8}{x^{15}} = x^k \Rightarrow x^{-7} = x^k \Rightarrow k = -7$.

   Use the rules of exponents to find the value of z.

   $(x^7)^z = x^{21}$, so $x^{7z} = x^{21}$

   $7z = 21 \Rightarrow z = 3$

   Multiply k and z.

   $kz = -7 \cdot 3 = -21$.

6. **Answer: D**

   As the number of pens increase, cost decreases. Therefore there must be a negative slope.

   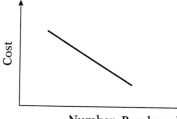

7. **Answer: E**

   With the given information and using the sum of the angles in a triangle is 180°, we know the following information about the figure.

   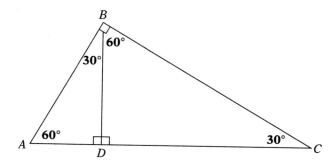

   Triangle ABD is a 30°-60°-90° right triangle. That means $AD = 5$ so $BD = 5\sqrt{3}$.

   Triangle CBD is a 30°-60°-90° right triangle. That means $BD = 5\sqrt{3}$ so $BC = 2 \cdot 5\sqrt{3} = 10\sqrt{3}$.

8. *Answer:* **A**

    The car travels 70 miles on x gallons.

    That means the car travels 1 mile on $\dfrac{x}{70}$ gallons.

    One gallon costs y dollars, so $\dfrac{x}{70}$ gallons costs $(\dfrac{x}{70})(y)$ dollars.

    $\dfrac{x}{70} \cdot y = \dfrac{xy}{70}$ dollars. That's what it costs to travel 1 mile.

9. *Answer:* **16**

    Write a proportion.

    $4{:}7 = a{:}28 \Rightarrow \dfrac{4}{7} = \dfrac{a}{28}$

    Cross-multiply to solve for a.

    $7a = 112 \Rightarrow a = 16$.

10. *Answer:* **3.75 or $\dfrac{15}{4}$**

    The problem states the sequence is a geometric sequence and that the first three terms are 120, 60, and 30. Notice that you divide by 2 to find the next term.

    4th term: $\dfrac{30}{2} = 15$.

    5th term: $\dfrac{15}{2} = 7.5$.

    6th term: $\dfrac{7.5}{2} = 3.75$.

11. *Answer:* **15**

    The best way to solve this problem is to draw a diagram. The only way for point D to be equidistant from points A and B is if D is on a perpendicular bisector of $\overline{AB}$.

    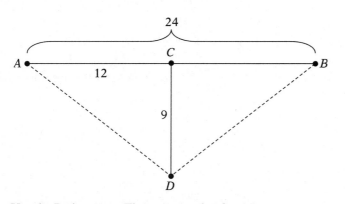

    Use the Pythagorean Theorem to solve for AD.

    $(AD)^2 = 12^2 + 9^2 \Rightarrow (AD)^2 = 144 + 81$

    $(AD)^2 = 225 \Rightarrow AD = \sqrt{225} = 15$

12. *Answer:* **12**

    The average of the six consecutive positive integers is 14.5. Three integers will be immediately below 14.5 and the 3 integers will be immediately above 14.5. The six consecutive positive integers whose average is 14.5 are 12, 13, 14, 15, 16, and 17. The smallest of these integers is 12.

13. *Answer:* **79**

Write an equation in which x is the price and .06 is the tax.

$x + 0.06x = \$83.74 \Rightarrow$

Solve for x.

$1.06x = \$83.74 \Rightarrow x = 79$.

14. *Answer:* **168**

The surface area of the cone is equal to the area of the portion of the circle that remains.

The area of the circle is 64π. Sixty degrees, $\frac{1}{6}$ of a 360° circle, is removed. That means $\frac{5}{6}$ is left. $\frac{5}{6} \times 64\pi = \frac{320}{6}\pi$ ≈ 167.55. The surface area to the nearest whole number is 168.

15. *Answer:* **9**

Factor the perfect square.

$x^2 - 2xy + y^2 = (x - y)^2$

Substitute 3 for $(x - y)$ and solve, $3^2 = 9$

16. *Answer:* **44**

First, find the length of the inner rectangle.

The triangle formed in the inner rectangle is a right triangle.

One leg is 3, the hypotenuse is 5. That tells us this is a 3-4-5 right triangle. The length of the inner rectangle is 4.

The base of the outer rectangle is 7, and the base in the inner rectangle is 3. The border must be 2 on each side. The length of the inner rectangle is 4, and the border is 2 on each side, the length of the outer rectangle is $4 + 2 + 2 = 8$.

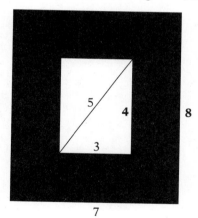

The area of the shaded region is

Area of Outer Rectangle – Area of Inner Rectangle.

$7 \cdot 8 - 3 \cdot 4 = 56 - 12 = 44$.

17. *Answer:* **2**

Do an example.

Choose $k = 7$

Add $3 \Rightarrow 7 + 3 = 10$

$10 \div 4 = 2$ R2

The remainder of $(k + 3) \div 4$ is 2.

18. *Answer:* **20**

Let x and y represent the original prices. Two equations can be created. Use the equations to solve for x and y.

Write an equation for the sum of the original prices.

$x + y = 140$

Solve for y.

$y = 140 - x$.

Write an equation for the average of the new prices.

$$\frac{1.20x + 0.75y}{2} = 70.50$$

$1.20x + 0.75y = 141$.

$y = 140 - x$ from the first equation. Substitute $140 - x$ for y in the second equation.

Solve for x.

$1.20x + 0.75(140 - x) = 141$.

$1.2x + 105 - .75x = 141$.

$.45x + 105 = 141$.

$.45x = 36 \Rightarrow x = 80$.

Solve for y.

$y = 140 - x \Rightarrow y = 140 - 80 = 60$.

More expensive – less expensive = $\$80 - \$60 = \$20$

SECTION 6

1. *Answer:* **A**

   Multiply the value of each coin by the number of coins and add.

   $0.25x + 0.10y + 0.05z$.

2. *Answer:* **C**

   Factor $3x - 12 = 3(x - 4)$

   Substitute 10 for $x - 4$.

   $3(10) = 30$.

3. *Answer:* **A**

   Because n is an even power, $n + 1$ is an odd power. That means a^{n+1} has an odd power. The powers in the other choices are even.

4. *Answer:* **D**

   The bases of this particular parallelogram and this particular triangle are equal.

   If a parallelogram and a triangle have the same base and height, the area of the parallelogram is twice the area of the triangle.

   Area of a triangle is $\frac{1}{2} bh$. Area of a parallelogram is bh.

   The height of this parallelogram is half this height of the triangle.

   That means the area of each figure is the same. The area of the parallelogram is 14.

5. *Answer:* **B**

   First find the total exercise time.

   Let x = minutes spent exercising.

   41% of the workout is spent on shoulders and back, therefore

   $0.41x \approx 37 \Rightarrow x \approx 90.24$ minutes.

   Find the time spent on arms and legs.

   29% of the workout is spent on arms and legs.

   $0.29(90.24) \approx 26.17$ minutes.

   The best approximation is 26 minutes.

6. *Answer:* **D**

   Convert the size of the kitchen floor from feet to inches. The kitchen floor is $10 \cdot 12 = 120$ inches wide and $14 \cdot 12 = 168$ inches long. The kitchen has an area of $120 \cdot 168 = 20,160$ square inches. The total number of 8-square inch tiles needed to cover the kitchen floor is $\frac{20,160}{8} = 2,520$.

7. *Answer:* **A**

   Let J = Jim's age.   Let A = Al's age.   Let E = Ed's age.

   Use the given information to form three equations.

   (1) $J + A = 30$.   (2) $2J + E = 46$.   (3) $E - A = 3$.

   Then add the first and third equations to eliminate A.

   $$\begin{array}{r} J + A = 30 \\ \underline{E - A = 3} \\ J + E = 33 \end{array}$$

Now subtract this new equation from the second equation to solve for *J*, Jim's age.

$$2J + E = 46$$
$$\underline{J + E = 33}$$
$$J = 13$$

8. ***Answer:*** **D**

    A half-inch equals 25 feet means an inch equals 50 feet.

    $350 \div 50 = 7$

    That means the picture of the building is 7 inches tall.

9. ***Answer:*** **A**

    $f(x) = x^2 - 5$ and $g(x) = -2x + 3$.

    Set the equations equal to find the common points.

    $x^2 - 5 = -2x + 3 \Rightarrow x^2 + 2x - 8 = 0$

    Factor:

    $(x + 4)(x - 2) = 0$

    Solve for *x*.

    $x + 4 = 0 \Rightarrow x = -4$
    $x - 2 = 0 \Rightarrow x = 2$

    The graphs intersect at two points, when $x = -4$ and $x = 2$. $-4 \times 2 = -8$.

10. ***Answer:*** **A**

    Find how many seconds it takes each swimmer to swim one lap.

    Shawn can swim one lap in $\dfrac{100}{2} = 50$ seconds.

    Brian can swim one lap in $\dfrac{4 \cdot 60}{4} = 60$ seconds.

    In 5 minutes, 300 seconds:

    Shawn swims $\dfrac{300}{50} = 6$ laps, and Brian swims $\dfrac{300}{60} = 5$ laps.

    Therefore, Shawn will swim <u>one</u> more lap than Brian in 5 minutes.

11. ***Answer:*** **B**

    We can see that every point in the table makes the function $f(x) = -x^2 + 16$ true.

x	0	1	2	3	4
f(x)	16	15	12	7	0

$f(0) = -(0)^2 + 16 = 0 + 16 = 16.$
$f(1) = -(1)^2 + 16 = -1 + 16 = 15.$
$f(2) = -(2)^2 + 16 = -4 + 16 = 12.$
$f(3) = -(3)^2 + 16 = -9 + 16 = 7.$
$f(4) = -(4)^2 + 16 = -16 + 16 = 0.$

You might also notice that $f(x)$ decreases, which eliminates choices A, C, and E. Then use the table and notice that $f(0) = 16$, which eliminates choice D. That leaves choice B.

12. *Answer:* **B**

You can see from the graph in the problem that as the weight of the car increases, the miles per gallon decreases.

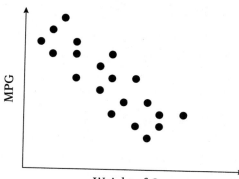

13. *Answer:* **E**

There are 26 letters and 10 digits, none of which can be repeated

$26 \cdot 25 \cdot 10 \cdot 9 \cdot 8 = 468{,}000.$

14. *Answer:* **D**

In the graph of $|f(x)|$ any part of the graph of $f(x)$ below the x axis is reflected above the x axis.

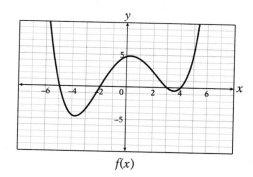

$f(x)$

D.

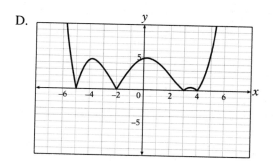

15. *Answer:* **B**

A regular hexagon consists of six equilateral triangles. The perimeter is 12, so the length of each side of the regular

hexagon is $\left(\dfrac{12}{6}\right)$ = 2. That means the length of each side of the triangle shown is 2, and AB = 2.

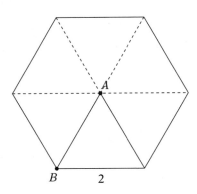

16. *Answer:* **C**

There is an inverse relationship between the squirrel population and fox population. If one population increases, the other population must decrease; (200,100) was the given point.

A. (200,150) One stays the same and the other decreases.
B. (250,200) Both increase.

C. (150,150) One increases and the other decreases.

D. (175,75) Both decrease.
E. (225,125) Both increase.

17. *Answer:* **C**

The amount of money that Jack has in the investment is equal to

$A = 700(1.05)^t$, where t represent years. The best way to solve this is to use your calculator to find the smallest value of t that will produce more than $1,000.

$A = 700(1.05)^7 \approx \$984.97.$

$A = 700(1.05)^8 \approx \$1,034.22.$

After 7 years, there is $984.97 in the investment.

After 8 years, there is $1,034.22 in the investment.

The investment first exceeds $1,000 in the 8th year.

18. *Answer:* **D**

Each cycle has three steps. There are four blocks so that is 3 × 4 = 12 steps. Here is the complete list.

Start:	A	B	C	D
Step 1:	A	B	D	C
Step 2:	A	D	B	C
Step 3:	D	A	B	C
Step 4:	D	A	C	B
Step 5:	D	C	A	B
Step 6:	C	D	A	B
Step 7:	C	D	B	A
Step 8:	C	B	D	A
Step 9:	B	C	D	A
Step 10:	B	C	A	D
Step 11:	B	A	C	D
Step 12:	A	B	C	D

A total of 12 steps are needed to return blocks to original position.

19. *Answer:* **B**

The *standard deviation* is not affected when a value is added to every number in a set of numbers.

Example: Let $\{-9,0,9\}$ be the set of numbers. The mean of these numbers is $\dfrac{-9+0+9}{3} = 0$. -9 is a distance of 9 from the mean, 0 is a distance of 0 from the mean, and 9 is a distance of 9 from the mean. Therefore, the standard deviation is $\dfrac{9+0+9}{3} = \dfrac{18}{3} = 6$.

Now add three to each of the numbers. The new number set is $\{-6,3,12\}$.

The mean of these numbers is $\dfrac{-6+3+12}{3} = 3$. -6 is a distance of 9 from the mean, 3 is a distance of 0 from the mean, and 12 is a distance of 9 from the mean. Therefore, the standard deviation for the new set of numbers is $\dfrac{9+0+9}{3} = \dfrac{18}{3} = 6$.

20. *Answer:* **B**

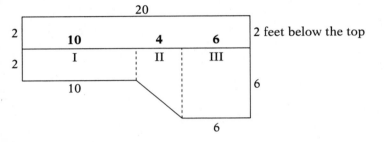

Partition the diagram into regions.

Region I (Rectangle)—$A_I = bh = 2 \cdot 10 = 20$

Region II (Trapezoid)—$A_{II} = \dfrac{1}{2} \cdot h(b_1 + b_2) = \dfrac{1}{2} \cdot 4(2 + 6) = \dfrac{1}{2} \cdot 4 \cdot 8 = 16$

Region III (Square)—$A_{III} = bh = 6 \cdot 6 = 36$

The area of the figure is $20 + 16 + 36 = 72$.

The volume is width times area: $10 \cdot 72 = 720$.

SECTION 9

1. **Answer: A**

   Solve the inequality for x.

   $2x + 5 \geq 3$

   $2x \geq -2 \Rightarrow x \geq -1$.

2. **Answer: C**

   This equation is only true when $k = 0$.

   $x - k = x \Rightarrow x - 0 = x$.

3. **Answer: D**

   The sum of x and 40 is 120 because corresponding angles are congruent.

   $x + 40 = 120 \Rightarrow x = 80$.

   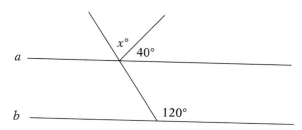

4. **Answer: B**

   x = number of plastic paper clips.

   $x - 16$ = number of metal paper clips.

   Add the quantities and solve the equation.

   $x + (x - 16) = 100 \Rightarrow 2x - 16 = 100 \Rightarrow 2x \Rightarrow 116 \quad x = 58$

5. **Answer: B**

   There are a total of $10 + 5 + 15 = 30$ students in the class, of which $5 + 15 = 20$ are not sophomores. The probability that a student chosen at random from the class is <u>not</u> a sophomore is $\dfrac{20}{30} = \dfrac{2}{3}$.

6. **Answer: E**

   Set up a proportion and solve.

   $\dfrac{3}{8} = \dfrac{b}{12} \Rightarrow 8b = 36 \Rightarrow b = 4.5$ cups.

7. **Answer: B**

   The sum of the two remote interior angles equals the exterior angle. That means $100 + y = x$. The median of 100 and y is $\dfrac{100 + y}{2}$. That's the same as $\dfrac{x}{2}$.

8. *Answer:* **B**

    You can substitute values from the answer choices.

    $a = x^3$ and $b = x^2$.

    A. 0 $a = 0^3 = 0$ and $b = 0^2 = 0$.

B. 0.5	$a = (0.5)^3 = 0.125$ and $b = (0.5)^2 = 0.25$.

    C. 1 $a = 1^3 = 1$ and $b = 1^2 = 1$.

    D. 2 $a = 2^3 = 8$ and $b = 2^2 = 4$.

    E. 3 $a = 3^3 = 27$ and $b = 3^2 = 9$.

    You might also know that the square of any number between 0 and 1 is greater than the cube of that number.

9. *Answer:* **C**

    Use the diagram.

    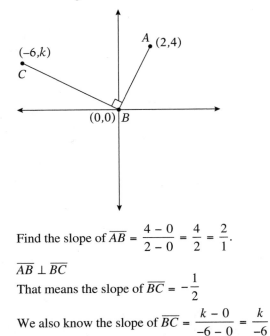

    Find the slope of $\overline{AB} = \dfrac{4-0}{2-0} = \dfrac{4}{2} = \dfrac{2}{1}$.

    $\overline{AB} \perp \overline{BC}$

    That means the slope of $\overline{BC} = -\dfrac{1}{2}$

    We also know the slope of $\overline{BC} = \dfrac{k-0}{-6-0} = \dfrac{k}{-6}$

    Write a proportion and solve.

    $\dfrac{-1}{2} = \dfrac{k}{-6} \Rightarrow$ cross multiply $2k = 6$

    Solve the equation

    $2k = 6 \Rightarrow k = 3$

10. *Answer:* **D**

    Write the two equations for the absolute value. Solve for $|t|$.

    $\big||t| + s - 3\big| = 5$

    $|t| + s - 3 = 5 \Rightarrow |t| + s = 8$

    $|t| = 8 - s$.

    $|t| + s - 3 = -5 \Rightarrow |t| + s = -2$

    $|t| = -2 - s$.

    Review the equations to find the largest possible value of s.

    $|t|$ must be greater than or equal to zero. In the equation $|t| = 8 - s$, s could be as large as 8 because $8 - 8 = 0$. In the equation $|t| = -t - s$, s could be as large as -2 because $-2 - (-2) = -2 + 2 = 0$. The means the largest value for s is 8.

11. **Answer: E**

T = total amount produced.

A = amount produced at plant A.

B = amount produced at plant B.

Write the following equations.

$(1)\, 3A = T \qquad (2)\, B = \dfrac{1}{2}A \Rightarrow 2B = A.$

Substitute $2B$ from Equation (2) in for A in Equation (1).

$3(2B) = T \Rightarrow 6B = T$

$B = \dfrac{1}{6}T.$

12. **Answer: D**

Notice $\triangle ABC$ and $\triangle ADE$ are similar triangles.

We know from the question that B is the midpoint of $\overline{AD}$.

That means $\overline{AD}$ is twice the length of $\overline{AB}$.

It follows that there is a 2 to 1 ratio between the lengths at corresponding parts of $\triangle ADE$ and $\triangle ABC$.

$2^2 = 4$, so the area of $\triangle ADE$ is four times the area of $\triangle ABC$.

Area of $\triangle ABC = 12$; Area of $\triangle ADE$ is $4 \times 12 = 48$.

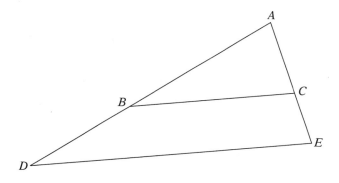

13. *Answer:* **E**

First find $f(2)$.

$f(2) = -2$

Now find $g\left[f(2)\right] = g(-2) = 4$.

$f(x)$

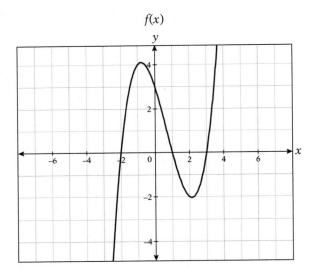

$g(x)$

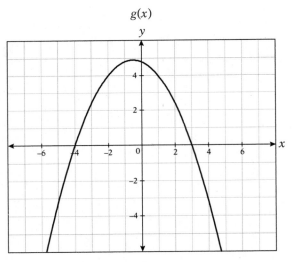

14. *Answer:* **D**

Adding 2 to x shifts the graph two units left.

Adding 4 to y shifts the graph four units up.

$h(x + 2) + 4$

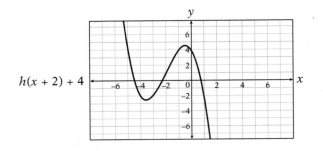

15. **Answer: D**

   T = Amount Tom spent on his bike.

   R = Amount Rich spent on his bike.

   A = Amount Alex spent on his bike.

   From the given information we know $T = \$402.50$.

   Write and solve an equation to find how much Rich spent.

   $1.15R = \$402.50$

   $R = \dfrac{402.50}{1.15} = \$350.$

   Write and solve an equation for the amount Alex spent.

   $0.80R = A \Rightarrow 0.80(\$350)$

   $A \Rightarrow \$280 = A.$

   Alex spent $280 on his bicycle.

16. **Answer: A**

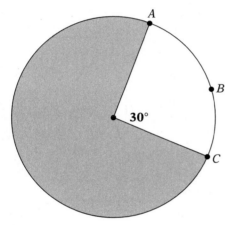

   Step 1. Find the radius and circumference.

   The area of the circle is 64π.

   The area formula is πr^2.

   Solve for r:

   $\pi r^2 = 64\pi \Rightarrow r = 8$

   Find the circumference: $2\pi r = 2 \cdot 8 \cdot \pi = 16\pi$

   Step 2. Find the area of the nonshaded sector.

   The ratio of arc length to circumference is proportional to the ratio of sector area to circle area

   Arc length = $\dfrac{4\pi}{3}$ $C = 16\pi$ Circle area = 64π Sector area = x

   $\dfrac{\frac{4\pi}{3}}{16\pi} = \dfrac{x}{64\pi} \Rightarrow$ Cross-multiply $16\pi x = \dfrac{256\pi^2}{3}$

   Solve for x: $48\pi x = 256\pi^2 \Rightarrow 48x = 256\pi$

   $x = \dfrac{16\pi}{3}$

   Step 3. Find the area of the shaded sector.

   $64\pi - \dfrac{16\pi}{3} = \dfrac{192}{3}\pi - \dfrac{16}{3}\pi = \dfrac{176}{3}\pi$

SCORE ESTIMATOR

Use this sheet to estimate your SAT Mathematics scale score. These scores are <u>estimates</u>, and your performance on the actual SAT could easily fall outside your scale score range for this test. One primary reason for the difference is that you did not take this test in a completely realistic test setting.

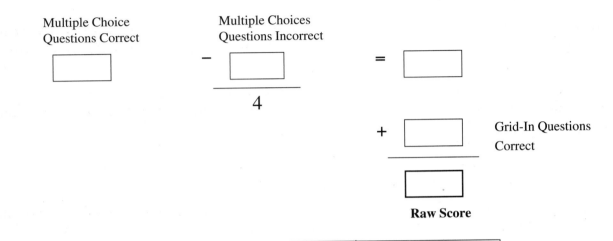

Raw Score	Scale Score Range	Raw Score	Scale Score Range
54	800	27	470–550
53	740–800	26	470–540
52	710–800	25	460–540
51	690–790	24	450–530
50	680–760	23	440–520
49	670–750	22	430–510
48	650–740	21	430–500
47	640–730	20	420–490
46	630–720	19	420–480
45	620–710	18	410–470
44	610–700	17	400–460
43	600–680	16	390–450
42	600–670	15	390–450
41	590–660	14	380–440
40	570–650	13	370–430
39	560–640	12	360–430
38	550–630	11	350–430
37	540–620	10	340–430
36	540–610	9	330–430
35	530–600	8	320–420
34	530–600	7	310–410
33	520–590	6	300–400
32	510–580	5	290–390
31	500–570	4	280–380
30	490–560	3	270–370
29	490–560	2	240–340
28	480–550	1, 0, or less	200–320

CHAPTER 22

SAT MATH PRACTICE TEST 4

Directions for Multiple-Choice Questions

In this section, solve each problem, using any available space on the page for scratchwork. Then decide which is the best of the choices given and fill in the corresponding oval on your answer sheet.

- You may use a calculator on any problem. All numbers used are real numbers.
- Figures are drawn as accurately as possible EXCEPT when it is stated that the figure is not drawn to scale.
- All figures lie in a plane unless otherwise indicated.

Directions for Student-Produced Response Questions

Student Response questions are always numbered 9–18. Complete the grids at the bottom of the answer sheet for the test where the student response questions appear.

- If your answer is 2/3 or .666 . . . , you must enter **the most accurate value the grid can accommodate,** but you may do this in 1 of 4 ways:

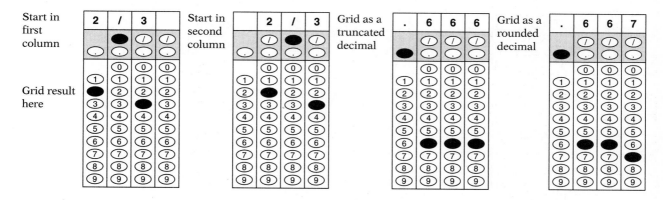

- In the example above, gridding a response of 0.67 or 0.66 is **incorrect** because it is less accurate than those above.

- The scoring machine cannot read what is written in the top row of boxes. You **MUST** fill in the numerical grid accurately to get credit for answering any question correctly. You should write your answer in the top row of boxes only to aid your gridding.

Reference Information

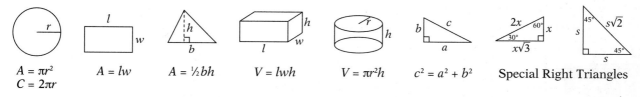

$A = \pi r^2$
$C = 2\pi r$

$A = lw$

$A = \frac{1}{2}bh$

$V = lwh$

$V = \pi r^2 h$

$c^2 = a^2 + b^2$

Special Right Triangles

The arc of a circle measures 360°.
Every straight angle measures 180°.
The sum of the measures of the angles in a triangle is 180°.

Start with number 1 for each new section. If a section has fewer questions than answer spaces, leave the extra answer spaces blank. Be sure to erase any errors or stray marks completely.

25 Minutes

SECTION 3

1. (A) (B) (C) (D) (E)
2. (A) (B) (C) (D) (E)
3. (A) (B) (C) (D) (E)
4. (A) (B) (C) (D) (E)
5. (A) (B) (C) (D) (E)

6. (A) (B) (C) (D) (E)
7. (A) (B) (C) (D) (E)
8. (A) (B) (C) (D) (E)
9. (A) (B) (C) (D) (E)
10. (A) (B) (C) (D) (E)

11. (A) (B) (C) (D) (E)
12. (A) (B) (C) (D) (E)
13. (A) (B) (C) (D) (E)
14. (A) (B) (C) (D) (E)
15. (A) (B) (C) (D) (E)

16. (A) (B) (C) (D) (E)
17. (A) (B) (C) (D) (E)
18. (A) (B) (C) (D) (E)
19. (A) (B) (C) (D) (E)
20. (A) (B) (C) (D) (E)

25 Minutes

SECTION 4

1. (A) (B) (C) (D) (E)
2. (A) (B) (C) (D) (E)

3. (A) (B) (C) (D) (E)
4. (A) (B) (C) (D) (E)

5. (A) (B) (C) (D) (E)
6. (A) (B) (C) (D) (E)

7. (A) (B) (C) (D) (E)
8. (A) (B) (C) (D) (E)

Student-Produced Responses

ONLY ANSWERS ENTERED IN THE CIRCLES IN EACH GRID WILL BE SCORED. YOU WILL NOT RECEIVE CREDIT FOR ANYTHING WRITTEN IN THE BOXES ABOVE THE CIRCLES.

Grids numbered 9, 10, 11, 12, 13, 14, 15, 16, 17, 18.

20 Minutes

SECTION 9

1. (A) (B) (C) (D) (E)
2. (A) (B) (C) (D) (E)
3. (A) (B) (C) (D) (E)
4. (A) (B) (C) (D) (E)

5. (A) (B) (C) (D) (E)
6. (A) (B) (C) (D) (E)
7. (A) (B) (C) (D) (E)
8. (A) (B) (C) (D) (E)

9. (A) (B) (C) (D) (E)
10. (A) (B) (C) (D) (E)
11. (A) (B) (C) (D) (E)
12. (A) (B) (C) (D) (E)

13. (A) (B) (C) (D) (E)
14. (A) (B) (C) (D) (E)
15. (A) (B) (C) (D) (E)
16. (A) (B) (C) (D) (E)

TEST 4 QUESTIONS
SECTION 3

1. If $4a - 7 > 9$, then which of the following cannot be equal to a?

   A. 3
   B. 5
   C. 7
   D. 9
   E. 11

2. $3^{\frac{x}{2}} = 27$, $x =$

   A. 1.5
   B. 3
   C. 4.5
   D. 6
   E. 9

3. $(y + 7) + k = y - 2$, $k =$

   A. −2.5
   B. −4.5
   C. −5
   D. −9
   E. −18

4. Which of the following figures could not be formed when the cone shown below is intersected with a plane?

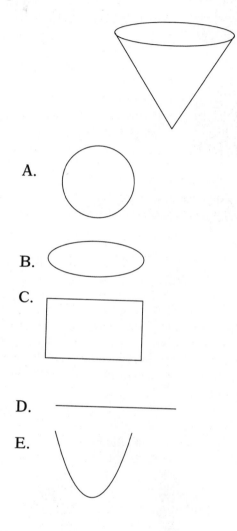

   A.

   B.

   C.

   D. ——————

   E.

5. A complete network of size *n* is *n* points connected by line segments, as shown below. What is the minimum number of segments that must be removed from a complete network of size 5 so that one point has no segments connected to it?

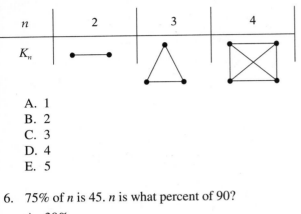

n	2	3	4
K_n			

   A. 1
   B. 2
   C. 3
   D. 4
   E. 5

6. 75% of *n* is 45. *n* is what percent of 90?

   A. 30%
   B. 33%
   C. $33\frac{1}{3}\%$
   D. 50%
   E. $66\frac{2}{3}\%$

7. The figure below is made up of a square and four congruent triangles. The height of each triangle is half the base. What is the probability that a point in the figure picked at random will be inside the shaded area?

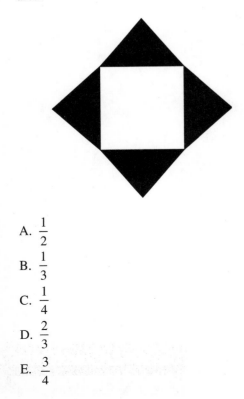

   A. $\frac{1}{2}$
   B. $\frac{1}{3}$
   C. $\frac{1}{4}$
   D. $\frac{2}{3}$
   E. $\frac{3}{4}$

8. Let *a* be an even integer and *b* be an odd integer. Which of the following is odd?

   I. $a + b$
   II. ab
   III. b^a

   A. I only
   B. II only
   C. I and II
   D. I and III
   E. II and III

9. A translation in the *xy*-coordinate plane is as follows: for every positive horizontal move of 4 there is a positive vertical move of 2. Starting at the point (5,7) the translation goes to (*x*,31). What is the value of *x*?

   A. 12
   B. 17
   C. 24
   D. 48
   E. 53

10. $f(x) = \dfrac{x^2 + 8x + 15}{x + 5}$ for $x \neq 5, f(-3) =$

   A. −9
   B. −3
   C. 0
   D. 3
   E. 24

11. In the figure below *x* = 130. Which of the following is not true?

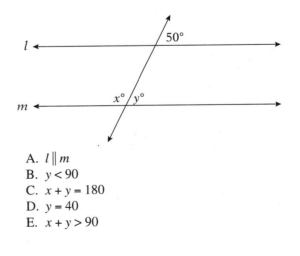

   A. $l \parallel m$
   B. $y < 90$
   C. $x + y = 180$
   D. $y = 40$
   E. $x + y > 90$

GO ON TO THE NEXT PAGE

12. In the xy-coordinate plane which of the following is a true statement about the graph of $f(x) = x^2 - 2x + 2$?

   A. The graph never crosses the y-axis.
   B. The graph crosses the y-axis at $y = -2$.
   C. The graph crosses the y-axis at two points.
   D. The graph crosses the x-axis at $x = 2$.
   E. The graph never crosses the x-axis.

13. The sum of the heights of six people is 336 inches. No two people are the same height. What is the mean height of the third and fourth tallest people if the mean and the median height of all six people are equal?

   A. 84
   B. 67.2
   C. 56
   D. 56.5
   E. 57

14. The figure below is formed by inscribing a square in a circle. If the circumference of the circle is 16π, what is the area of the shaded regions?

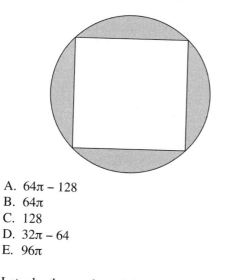

   A. $64\pi - 128$
   B. 64π
   C. 128
   D. $32\pi - 64$
   E. 96π

15. Let c be the number of distinct prime factors of 34. Let k be the number of distinct prime factors of 37. What is the value of ck?

   A. 1
   B. 2
   C. 4
   D. 6
   E. 8

16. Lines p and q are perpendicular. Each line has a y-intercept of -4. If line p crosses through the x-axis at $x = 3$, at which value of x does line q cross the x-axis?

   A. $\dfrac{4}{3}$
   B. -4
   C. $-\dfrac{3}{4}$
   D. $-\dfrac{16}{3}$
   E. $\dfrac{16}{3}$

17. $a\Delta b = \dfrac{a^2 - b^2}{a^2 + 2ab + b^2}$, $x\Delta 4 = \dfrac{1}{5}$, $x =$

   A. 2
   B. 4
   C. 6
   D. 8
   E. 12

18. A copy center charges $0.07 per copy up to and including 100 copies, $0.05 for every copy over 100 up to and including 300 copies, and $0.03 for every copy over 300 copies. How much does it cost to make 500 copies?

   A. $6
   B. $7
   C. $10
   D. $15
   E. $23

GO ON TO THE NEXT PAGE

19. The area of the circle shown below is 81π. What is the length of arc *PQR*?

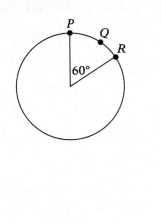

A. 18π
B. 15π
C. 12π
D. 6π
E. 3π

20. Over a 3-year period, a car company manufactured 50% more cars in the second year than in the first year, and twice as many cars in the third year than in the first year. What is the probability that a car produced in this 3-year period was built in the second year?

A. $\dfrac{1}{3}$

B. $\dfrac{4}{9}$

C. $\dfrac{5}{9}$

D. $\dfrac{2}{3}$

E. $\dfrac{2}{9}$

GO ON TO THE NEXT PAGE

SECTION 4

1. $\dfrac{3 + x}{x} = 3$, $x =$

   A. 0
   B. $\dfrac{2}{3}$
   C. 1
   D. $\dfrac{3}{2}$
   E. 3

2. In the figure below if $l \parallel m$, $2x - y$ could not equal which of the following?

   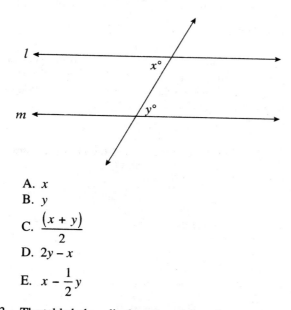

   A. x
   B. y
   C. $\dfrac{(x + y)}{2}$
   D. $2y - x$
   E. $x - \dfrac{1}{2}y$

3. The table below displays the results of a survey given to an equal number of males and females. How many of the females surveyed graduated from college?

	College Graduate	Not College Graduate	Total
Male		7,000	
Female			
Total		17,000	46,000

   A. 29,000
   B. 23,000
   C. 16,000
   D. 13,000
   E. 10,000

4. The weekly profit for a magazine company is given by the function $P(x) = \dfrac{3}{2}x - 300$, where x represents the number of magazine sold. What is the weekly profit if 400 magazines are sold?

   A. $100
   B. $150
   C. $200
   D. $250
   E. $300

5. What is the intersection point for the graphs of the lines $y = 2x + 7$ and $y = 3x + 2$?

   A. (9,25)
   B. (5,17)
   C. (−17,−5)
   D. (17,−7)
   E. (−7,17)

6. The ratio of married employees to the total number of employees at a company is 3 to 5. If there are a total of 1,000 employees at the company, how many are not married?

   A. 300
   B. 400
   C. 600
   D. 700
   E. 800

7. $1 \leq a < b \leq 4$, where a and b are integers. What is the sum of all the unique values of b^a?

   A. 245
   B. 196
   C. 147
   D. 98
   E. 48

GO ON TO THE NEXT PAGE

8. In the figure below, what is the value of z in terms of x and y?

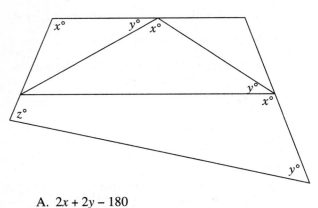

   A. $2x + 2y - 180$
   B. $2x + 2y - 360$
   C. $3x + 3y - 360$
   D. $360 - 2x + 2y$
   E. $540 - 3x - 3y$

9. $3t^7 = 45$, $t^7 =$

10. In the figure below, B is the midpoint of $\overline{AC}$. What is the sum of the x-coordinate and y-coordinate for point A?

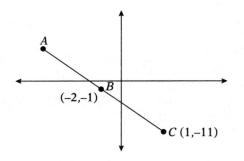

11. In a certain rectangle the length is three time the width. If one side of the rectangle is 9, what is the smallest possible value for the area of the rectangle?

12. $(x^2 - y^2) = 44$, $x + y = 4$, $x - y =$

13. A circle is partitioned into eight unequal wedges having a ratio of $1:2:3:4:5:6:7:8$. What is the median of the central angles of the wedges?

14. A 120-foot-long rope is cut in half. One of those two pieces is cut in half and the process continues. What is the maximum number of cuts so the length of the remaining piece of rope is a whole number?

15. Point F is the midpoint of $\overline{AC}$, and E is the midpoint of $\overline{AD}$. What is the value of $\dfrac{\text{Area of triangle } AFE}{\text{Area of rectangle } ABCD}$?

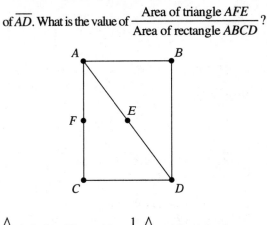

16. $\boxed{x} = 2x^2 + 10x - 42$. $\dfrac{1}{2}\boxed{a} = 15$, what is one possible value for a?

17. The table below gives the speed and time spent running for three different people. If they are all running around a quarter-mile track, how many laps did all three people run?

	Constant speed	**Time spent running**
Josh	6 miles per hour	90 minutes
Rob	7.5 miles per hour	60 minutes
Mike	10 miles per hour	45 minutes

18. A 6-digit security code is made up of four 0s and two 1s. How many security codes of this type can be formed?

GO ON TO THE NEXT PAGE

SECTION 9

1. When a number is increased by 8, the original value is 75% of the new value. What is the original value of the number?

    A. 2
    B. 3
    C. 6
    D. 18
    E. 24

2. Which of the following graphs of a quadratic function has a negative *y*-intercept and positive *x*-intercepts?

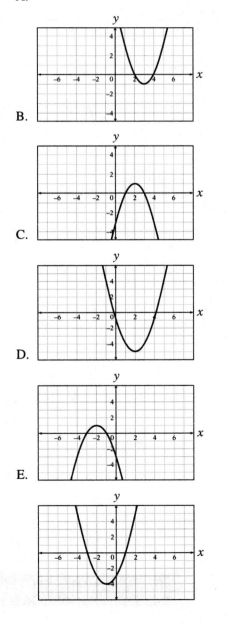

   A.

   B.

   C.

   D.

   E.

3. John traveled 600 miles in 9 hours. Which of the following is John's average speed?

    A. $33\frac{1}{3}$ mph
    B. 45 mph
    C. $66\frac{2}{3}$ mph
    D. 75 mph
    E. 90 mph

4. There are 4 blue, 6 red, and 8 green marbles in a jar. What is the least number of marbles that can be removed, without replacing, to guarantee that a chosen marble is red?

    A. 3
    B. 12
    C. 13
    D. 14
    E. 15

5. In the graph of $h(x)$ below, $h(a) = 1$, which of the following is not a possible value of *a*?

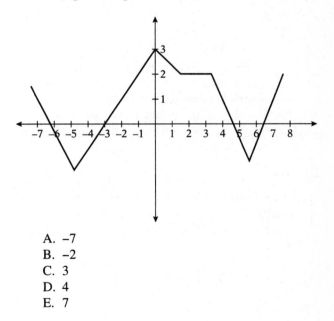

    A. −7
    B. −2
    C. 3
    D. 4
    E. 7

GO ON TO THE NEXT PAGE

6. What is the value of x?

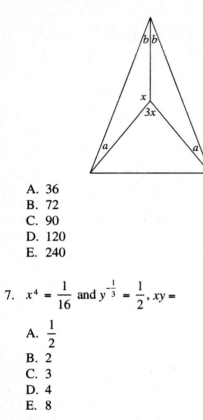

A. 36
B. 72
C. 90
D. 120
E. 240

7. $x^4 = \dfrac{1}{16}$ and $y^{-\frac{1}{3}} = \dfrac{1}{2}$, $xy =$

A. $\dfrac{1}{2}$
B. 2
C. 3
D. 4
E. 8

8. What is the range of the function $f(x) = -(x-2)^2 + 4$.

A. All real numbers less than or equal to 4
B. All real numbers greater than or equal to 4
C. All real numbers less than or equal to -4
D. All real numbers greater than or equal to -4
E. All real numbers greater than or equal to -4 and less than or equal to 4

9. When k is divided by 6 the remainder is 5. What is the remainder when $k + 7$ is divided by 6?

A. 0
B. 1
C. 2
D. 3
E. 4

10. Choose a number and continuously add a constant to form a sequence with an even number of elements. Which of the following lists all the true statements about the sequence?

    I.   The mean is equal to the median.
    II. The mode is equal to the median.
    III. The mean is equal to the average of the smallest and largest number in the set.

    A. I only
    B. II only
    C. I and II
    D. I and III
    E. I, II, and III

11. Which of the following could be the quadratic equation of the graph shown below?

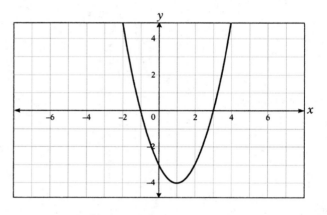

A. $y = -x^2 - 2x - 3$
B. $y = x^2 - 2x - 3$
C. $y = x^2 + 2x - 3$
D. $y = x^2 + 2x + 3$
E. $y = -x^2 + 2x + 3$

GO ON TO THE NEXT PAGE

12. On the graph below point B is symmetric to point A about the y-axis and point C is symmetric to point B across the x-axis. What is the area of triangle ABC?

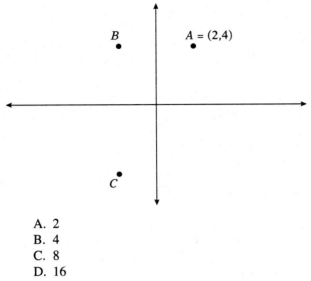

A. 2
B. 4
C. 8
D. 16
E. 24

13. The price of a shirt was discounted by 15%, and then again by 20% to a final discounted price of $27.20. What was the original price of the shirt?

A. $18
B. $32
C. $34
D. $36
E. $40

14. Decreasing the price of an item by 20% is the same as decreasing the price by $14. What would be the discounted price of the item if the original price was decreased by 50%?

A. $33
B. $34
C. $35
D. $36
E. $37

15. The area of a right triangle is 48 square inches, and the longer leg is 4 more than the shorter leg. What is the length of the hypotenuse of this right triangle?

A. $2\sqrt{13}$ inches
B. $4\sqrt{13}$ inches
C. $16\sqrt{13}$ inches
D. $4\sqrt{26}$ inches
E. $16\sqrt{26}$ inches

16. If $x(x - y) > 0$ $(x > 0, y > 0)$, which of the following lists all the true statements?

I. $x > y$
II. $x = y$
III. $x < y$

A. I only
B. II only
C. III only
D. I and III
E. I, II, and III

ANSWERS AND EXPLANATIONS
SECTION 3

1. *Answer:* **A**

   Solve the inequality for *a*.

   $4a - 7 > 9 \Rightarrow 4a > 16$

   $a > 4$. So *a* cannot be 3.

2. *Answer:* **D**

   First find the power of 3 so that $3^x = 27$

   $27 = 3^3 \Rightarrow 3^{\frac{x}{2}} = 3^3$

   $\dfrac{x}{2} = 3 \Rightarrow x = 6$

3. *Answer:* **D**

   Solve for *k*.

   $(y + 7) + k = y - 2 \Rightarrow y + 7 + k$

   $= y - 2 \Rightarrow k = -9$

4. *Answer:* **C**

   Visualize a plane intersecting a cone, which includes tangent to a cone.

   A. Horizontal plane

   B. Plane on an angle

   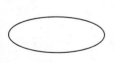

   C. No

   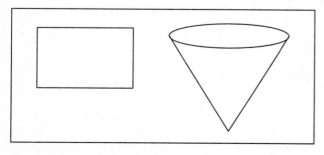

D. Plane tangent to the side

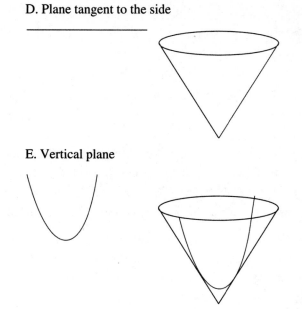

E. Vertical plane

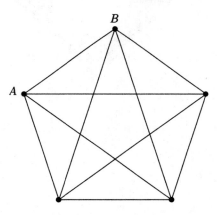

5. *Answer:* **D**

The figure below shows a complete network of size 5. Choose one point to isolate.

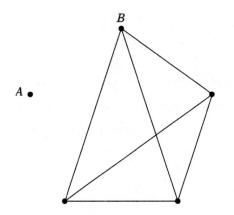

You must remove four segments to isolate the point.

6. ***Answer:* E**

Write an equation and solve for *n*.

$.75n = 45 \Rightarrow n = 60 \Rightarrow 60$ is $\frac{2}{3}$ of 90.

So, *n* is $66\frac{2}{3}\%$ of 90?

7. ***Answer:* A**

The height of each shaded triangle is half the length of the base of the square. Fold the triangles on top of the square, and they cover the square. So the total of the shaded triangles is equal to the area of the square. That means the area of the shaded triangles is half the area of the entire figure. The probability is $\frac{1}{2}$ that a point picked at random inside the figure will be in one of the shaded triangles.

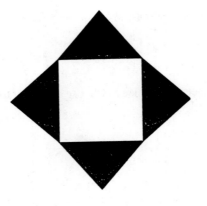

8. ***Answer:* D**

Choose an even value for *a* and an odd value for *b*, say $a = 2$ and $b = 1$.

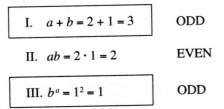

I. $a + b = 2 + 1 = 3$ ODD

II. $ab = 2 \cdot 1 = 2$ EVEN

III. $b^a = 1^2 = 1$ ODD

I and III are correct.

9. ***Answer:* E**

The question indicates point $(5,7)$ translates to point $(x,31)$. The change in the vertical direction is $31 - 7 = 24$.
The vertical (*y*) translation occurs in increments of 2, so there were a total of $\frac{24}{2} = 12$ vertical steps. There must be 12 horizontal (*x*) steps in increments of 4. The total horizontal translation is $12 \cdot 4 = 48$. $x = 5 + 48 = 53$.

10. *Answer:* **C**

It is best to realize that the numerator can be factored.

$$f(x) = \frac{x^2 + 8x + 15}{x + 5} \Rightarrow f(x) = \frac{(x + 5)(x + 3)}{x + 5}$$

Simplify:

$$f(x) = x + 3$$

Substitute -3 for x.

$$f(-3) = -3 + 3 = 0.$$

11. *Answer:* **D**

The diagram shows that x and y are a linear pair.

That means $x + y = 180$. We know $x = 130$ so $y = 50$.

You can notice that D is incorrect because it states that $y = 40$, when you know $y = 50$.

12. *Answer:* **E**

Graph the function $f(x) = x^2 - 2x + 2$ on your calculator, and you can see that the graph of the function never crosses the x-axis.

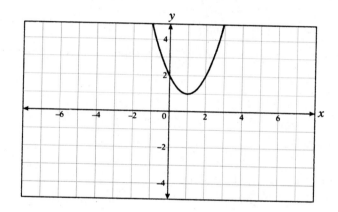

13. *Answer:* **C**

The mean height for all six people is $336 \div 6 = 56$. The median height for all six people is also 56. But the median height for all six people is also the mean height for the third and fourth tallest people; it's 56.

14. *Answer:* **A**

Use the formula for circumference to find the radius.

$C = 2\pi r = 16\pi \Rightarrow r = 8$.

Draw on the diagram.

The radius of the circle is 8. Use two radii to form a 45°-45°-90° triangle. The side of the square as the hypotenuse with a length $8\sqrt{2}$. The area of square is $A_I = \left(8\sqrt{2}\right)^2 = 64 \times 2 = 128$.

The area of the circle is $A_C = \pi(8)^2 = 64\pi$.

Subtract the area of the square from the area of the circle to find the area of the shaded region, which is $64\pi - 128$.

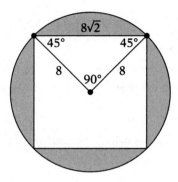

15. *Answer:* **B**

Find the number of distinct prime factors of 34 and 37. Remember, 1 is not a prime number.

$34 = 2 \cdot 17 \qquad 37 = 1 \cdot 37$

$C = 2 \qquad\qquad K = 1$

$C \cdot K = 2 \cdot 1 = 2$

16. *Answer:* **D**

<u>Identify two points on line p to find the slope of line p.</u>

The y-intercept of line p is -4, which means point $(0,-4)$ is on line p.

The x-intercept of line p is 3, which means point $(3,0)$ is on line p.

Use the points to find the slope of line p, $\dfrac{-4-0}{0-3} = \dfrac{-4}{-3} = \dfrac{4}{3}$.

<u>Find the equation of line q.</u>

Since $p \perp q$, the slope of line q is $-\dfrac{3}{4}$ (The product of the slopes of perpendicular lines is -1).

Line q also has a y-intercept of -4. Therefore the equation of line q is $y = -\dfrac{3}{4}x - 4$.

<u>Find the x-intercept of q.</u>

When line q crosses the x-axis, $y = 0$, so $0 = -\dfrac{3}{4}x - 4 \Rightarrow 4 = -\dfrac{3}{4}x \Rightarrow -\dfrac{16}{3} = x$.

The x intercept is $\dfrac{-16}{3}$.

17. *Answer:* **C**

    Notice that both the numerator and the denominator can be factored.
    Fractions can be simplified.

    $$a\Delta b = \frac{a^2 - b^2}{a^2 + 2ab + b^2} = \frac{(a+b)(a-b)}{(a+b)^2} = \frac{a-b}{a+b}$$

    Use the simplified form of $a\Delta b$ from above to rewrite $x\Delta 4$

    $$x\Delta 4 = \frac{x-4}{x+4} = \frac{1}{5}$$

    Cross multiply and solve for x

    $$x + 4 = 5x - 20 \Rightarrow 24 = 4x \Rightarrow 6 = x$$

18. *Answer:* **E**

    Use the information from the question to write an expression.

    $$100 \cdot 0.07 + 200 \cdot 0.05 + 200 \cdot 0.03 = \$23.$$

19. *Answer:* **E**

    Find the radius. The area of the circle below is 81π.

    That means $r = 9$.

    Find the circumference $C = 2\pi(9) = 18\pi$.

    The central angle is $60°$, $\frac{1}{6}$ of $360°$.

    That means the arc length is $\frac{1}{6}$ of the circumference.

    The measure of arc PQR is $\frac{1}{6}(18\pi) = 3\pi$.

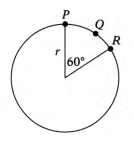

20. *Answer:* **A**

    There were a total of $1 + 1.5 + 2 = 4.5$ cars in 3 years, 1.5 were produced in year 2.

    $$\frac{1.5}{4.5} = \frac{1}{3}$$

    The probability is $\frac{1}{3}$ that the car was produced in year 2.

SECTION 4

1. *Answer:* **D**

   Solve the equation for x.

   $$\frac{3 + x}{x} = 3 \Rightarrow 3 + x = 3x$$

   $$3 = 2x \Rightarrow \frac{3}{2} = x.$$

2. *Answer:* **E**

   $l \parallel m$ means $x = y$ because alternate interior angles are congruent.

   Try any number for x and y to check the answers. We use 60, but you could use any number.

   $$2x - y = 2(60) - 60 = 60.$$

   Substitute 60 for x and y in each answer choice.

   Find the answer where the result is not 60.

   That's choice E.

   A. $x = 60$
   B. $y = 60$
   C. $\dfrac{x + y}{2} = \dfrac{(60 + 60)}{2} = 60$
   D. $2y - x = 2(60) - 60 = 60$

   > E. $x - \dfrac{1}{2}y = 60 - \dfrac{1}{2} \cdot 60 = 60 - 30 = 30$

3. *Answer:* **D**

   Complete the table. We find that number of female college graduates is 13,000.

	College Graduate	Not College Graduate	Total
Male	16,000	7,000	23,000
Female	13,000	10,000	23,000
Total	29,000	17,000	46,000

4. *Answer:* **E**

   $$P(x) = \frac{3}{2}x - 300$$

   Substitute 400 for x and solve for p.

   $$P(400) = \frac{3}{2}(400) - 300 = \$300.$$

5. *Answer:* **B**

   Set the equations equal and solve for x.

   $$y = 2x + 7 \text{ and } y = 3x + 2$$

   $$2x + 7 = 3x + 2 \Rightarrow 5 = x.$$

Substitute 5 for x and solve for y.

$$y = 2(5) + 7 = 10 + 7 = 17$$
$$y = 3(5) + 2 = 15 + 2 = 17$$

It works for both equations the intersection point is (5, 17).

6. ***Answer:* B**

   Let x = number of married employees.

   Write a proportion and solve for x.

   $$\frac{3}{5} = \frac{x}{1,000} \Rightarrow 5x = 3,000 \Rightarrow x = 600$$

   There are 600 married employees, which means that there are $1,000 - 600 = 400$ nonmarried employees.

7. ***Answer:* D**

   $1 \le a < b \le 4$. Write all the possible value of b^a.

   Note that a must always be less than b.

   $$4^1 = 4$$
   $$3^1 = 3$$
   $$2^1 = 2 \qquad \qquad 4^2 = 16$$
   $$3^2 = 9$$
   $$4^3 = 64$$

   The sum of the values is $2 + 3 + 9 + 4 + 16 + 64 = 98$.

8. ***Answer:* E**

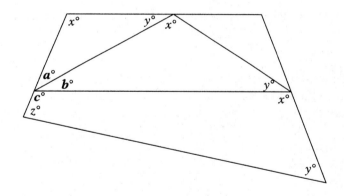

   This is a difficult problem involving many steps and substitutions.

   Angles a, b, and c have been added to the picture to help with the explanation.

   <u>Write an equation for z.</u>

   $z = 360 - c - x - y$ (sum of the angles of a quadrilateral is 360°)

   <u>Write an equation for c.</u>

   $c = 180 - a - b$ (sum of the angles of a triangle is 180°)

   <u>Write an equation for a and b.</u>

   $a = b = 180 - x - y$ (sum of the angles of a triangle is 180°)

   <u>Substitute $180 - x - y$ for a and b in the equation for c.</u>

   $c = 180 - (180 - x - y) - (180 - x - y) = -180 + 2x + 2y$

Substitute $-180 + 2x + 2y$ for c in the equation for z.

$$z = 360 - \left(-180 + 2x + 2y\right) - x - y = 540 - 3x - 3y$$

z in terms of x and y is $540 - 3x - 3y$

9. *Answer:* **15**

   Divide 45 by 3 to find t^7.

   $$3t^7 = 45$$

   $$t^7 = 15$$

10. *Answer:* **4**

    B is the midpoint, so the change in x and the change in y from B to A will be the same as the change in x and the change in y from C to B. The change in x from C to B is -3, and the change in y from C to B is 10. Therefore $A = (-2 - 3, -1 + 10) = (-5, 9)$. The sum of the x and y coordinates of A is $-5 + 9 = 4$.

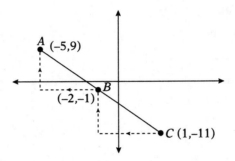

11. *Answer:* **27**

    The smallest rectangle is formed when 9 is the length and 3 is the width. That means the area is 27.

12. *Answer:* **11**

    Factor $x^2 - y^2$.

    $$\left(x^2 - y^2\right) = 44 \Rightarrow \left(x + y\right)\left(x - y\right) = 44$$

    Substitute 4 for $x + y$.

    $$4\left(x - y\right) = 44$$

    Find the value of $x - y$.

    $$x - y = 11$$

13. *Answer:* **45**

    Write an equation to express the ratio.

    $$1x + 2x + 3x + 4x + 5x + 6x + 7x + 8x = 36x$$

    There are 360° in a circle, so $36x = 360$ and $x = 10$.

    The measures of the angles are 10, 20, 30, <u>40</u>, <u>50</u>, 60, 70, and 80.

    The median of these angles is $\dfrac{40 + 50}{2} = 45$.

14. *Answer:* **3**

    $120 \div 2 = 60 \div 2 = 30 \div 2 = 15$. But $15 \div 2 = 7.5$. The length of the remaining piece of rope is a whole number after 3 cuts.

15. *Answer:* $\dfrac{1}{8}$

Because *F* is the midpoint of *AC* and *E* is the midpoint of *AD*, the figure can be split into 4 smaller congruent rectangles. Each of these smaller rectangles has an area $\dfrac{1}{4}$ of the total figure. The area of triangle *AFE* is $\dfrac{1}{2}$ of the area of a smaller rectangle.

That means the area of triangle *AFE* is $\dfrac{1}{2} \cdot \dfrac{1}{4} = \dfrac{1}{8}$ of rectangle *ABCD*.

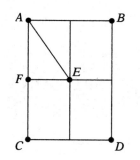

16. *Answer:* **4**

Rewrite as $\dfrac{1}{2}\,\boxed{a} = 15$ as $\boxed{a} = 30$

Because $\boxed{x} = 2x^2 + 10x - 42$ Rewrite $\boxed{a} = 30$ as

$2a^2 + 10a - 42 = 30 \Rightarrow 2a^2 + 10a - 72 = 0$

Factor and solve for *a*

$2(a^2 + 5a - 36) = 2(a + 9)(a - 4) = 0 \Rightarrow (a + 9)(a - 4) = 0$

$a + 9 = 0 \Rightarrow a = -9$

$a - 4 = 0 \Rightarrow a = 4$

17. *Answer:* **96**

Complete the table to show the total number of miles.

	Constant Speed	**Time Spent Running**	**Number of Miles**
Josh	6 miles per hour	90 minutes = 1.5 hours	$6 \cdot 1.5 = 9$ miles
Rob	7.5 miles per hour	60 minutes = 1 hour	$7.5 \cdot 1 = 7.5$ miles
Mike	10 miles per hour	45 minutes = 3/4 hours	$10 \cdot 3/4 = 7.5$ miles

Multiply number of miles by 4 to find the number of laps.

Josh ran $9 \cdot 4 = 36$ laps.

Rob ran $7.5 \cdot 4 = 30$ laps.

Mike ran $7.5 \cdot 4 = 30$ laps.

A total of $36 + 30 + 30 = 96$ laps were run by all three people.

18. *Answer:* **15**

The best way to do this is to focus on the positioning of the ones.

<u>000011</u>   <u>000101</u>   <u>001001</u>   <u>010001</u>   <u>100001</u>

<u>000110</u>   <u>001010</u>   <u>010010</u>   <u>100010</u>

<u>001100</u>   <u>010100</u>   <u>100100</u>

<u>011000</u>   <u>101000</u>

<u>110000</u>

There are 15 different ID numbers.

SECTION 9

1. *Answer:* **E**

Write an equation and solve.

$x = 0.75(x + 8) \Rightarrow x = 0.75x + 6$

$0.25x = 6 \Rightarrow x = 24$

2. *Answer:* **B**

Inspect graphs and notice that in choice B both x intercepts are positive and the y intercept is negative.

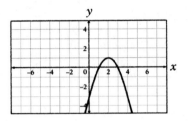

3. *Answer:* **C**

Divide 600 by 9 to find the average speed.

$\dfrac{600}{9} = 66\dfrac{2}{3}$ mph

4. *Answer:* **C**

It is possible that all the blue and green marbles will be chosen before a red marble is removed. Therefore, $4 + 8 + 1 = 13$ marbles must be removed to guarantee that a red marble will be chosen.

5. *Answer:* **C**

Draw the horizontal line $y = 1$. The function $h(a) = 1$, so a could equal -7, -2, 4, or 7. But $a \neq 3$ because $h(3) = 2$.

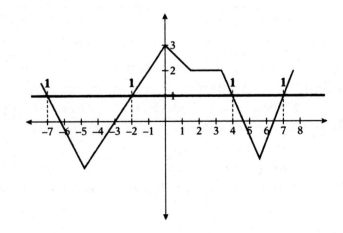

6. *Answer:* **B**

The top two triangles in the figure have two congruent corresponding angles. That means the third angle in each triangle are congruent and the missing measure of the third angle must be x.

The sum of the angles around a point is 360°.

Write an equation and solve.

$x + x + 3x = 360 \Rightarrow 5x = 360 \Rightarrow x = 72$.

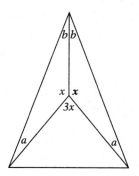

7. *Answer:* **D**

Find the value of x.

$$x^4 = \frac{1}{16} \Rightarrow (x^4)^{\frac{1}{4}} = \left(\frac{1}{16}\right)^{\frac{1}{4}}$$

$$x = \frac{1}{2}.$$

Find the value of y.

$$y^{\frac{1}{3}} = \frac{1}{2} \Rightarrow \left(y^{\frac{1}{3}}\right)^{-3} = \left(\frac{1}{2}\right)^{-3} \Rightarrow y = 2^3$$

$$y = 8.$$

Multiply x and y.

$$xy = \frac{1}{2} \cdot 8 = 4.$$

8. *Answer:* **A**

Below is the graph of the parabola $f(x) = -(x - 2)^2 + 4$. From the graph we can see that the range is all real numbers less than or equal to 4.

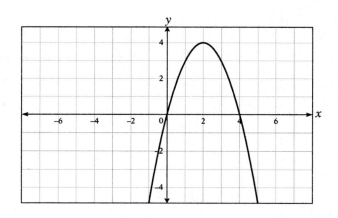

9. *Answer:* **A**

Let $k = 11$. $11 \div 6 = 1$ with a remainder of 5. That means $k + 7 = 18$, $18 \div 6$ has a remainder of 0.
It follows that if $k \div 6$ has a remainder of 1, then $(k + 7) \div 6$ has a remainder of 0.

10. *Answer:* **D**

An example of this sequence is $\{4,9,14,19,24,29\}$. This sequence starts with 4 and the constant is 5.
I.   TRUE—When the numbers are evenly spaced, as they are here, the mean and the median are equal.
II. FALSE—No number repeats so there is no mode.
III. TRUE—When the numbers are evenly spaced, as they are here, the mean is the average of the smallest and largest numbers.

11. *Answer:* **B**

The parabola is "moving up," so eliminate choices A and E. Graph the remaining choices with your graphing calculator to find choice B is correct.

$$y = x^2 - 2x - 3.$$

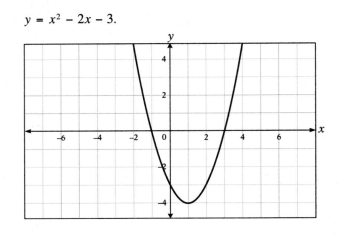

12. *Answer:* **D**

Use the coordinates of the points in the diagram to find the base and the height of the triangle.

base = 4 and height = 8.

The area of the triangle is

$$A = \frac{1}{2} \cdot 4 \cdot 8 = 16.$$

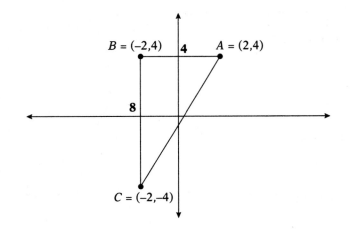

13. *Answer:* **E**

Write an equation to represent the discounted price.

$0.80(0.85x) = 27.20$

Solve for x, the original price.

$0.68x = 27.20$ $x = \$40$

14. *Answer:* **C**

Write an equation to relate the 20% discount and a \$14 price reduction.

$0.8x = x - 14$

Solve for x, the original price.

$-0.2x = -14 \Rightarrow x = \$70$

$0.5(70) = \$35$

15. *Answer:* **B**

Draw a diagram.

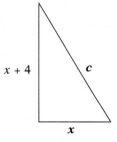

Write a formula for the area and solve for x.

$A = \dfrac{1}{2}(x)(x + 4) = 48 \Rightarrow (x)(x + 4) = 96$

$x^2 + 4x = 96 \Rightarrow x^2 + 4x - 96 = 0$

$(x + 12)(x - 8) = 0 \Rightarrow x - 8 = 0 \Rightarrow x = 8$

The legs of the triangle are $x + 4 = 8 + 4 = 12$ and $x = 8$.

$c^2 = 12^2 + 8^2 \Rightarrow c^2 = 144 + 64 = 208$

Use the Pythagorean Theorem to find the hypotenuse of the right triangle.

$c^2 = 208 \Rightarrow c = \sqrt{208} = 4\sqrt{13}$

16. *Answer:* **A**

   I. $x > y$

       $x = 2$ and $y = 1$

       $2(2 - 1) = 1$ TRUE, Greater than 0

  II. $x = y$

       $x = 1$ and $y = 1$

       $1(1 - 1) = 0$ FALSE, Not greater than 0

 III. $x < y$

       $x = 1$ and $y = 2$

       $1(1 - 2) = -1$ FALSE, Not greater than 0

SCORE ESTIMATOR

Use this sheet to estimate your SAT Mathematics scale score. These scores are <u>estimates</u>, and your performance on the actual SAT could easily fall outside your scale score range for this test. One primary reason for the difference is that you did not take this test in a completely realistic test setting.

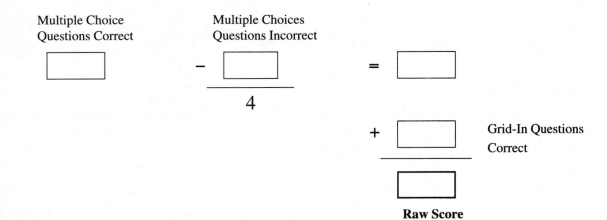

Raw Score	Scale Score Range	Raw Score	Scale Score Range
54	800	27	470–550
53	740–800	26	470–540
52	710–800	25	460–540
51	690–790	24	450–530
50	680–760	23	440–520
49	670–750	22	430–510
48	650–740	21	430–500
47	640–730	20	420–490
46	630–720	19	420–480
45	620–710	18	410–470
44	610–700	17	400–460
43	600–680	16	390–450
42	600–670	15	390–450
41	590–660	14	380–440
40	570–650	13	370–430
39	560–640	12	360–430
38	550–630	11	350–430
37	540–620	10	340–430
36	540–610	9	330–430
35	530–600	8	320–420
34	530–600	7	310–410
33	520–590	6	300–400
32	510–580	5	290–390
31	500–570	4	280–380
30	490–560	3	270–370
29	490–560	2	240–340
28	480–550	1, 0, or less	200–320

CHAPTER 23

SAT MATH PRACTICE TEST 5

Directions for Multiple-Choice Questions

In this section, solve each problem, using any available space on the page for scratchwork. Then decide which is the best of the choices given and fill in the corresponding oval on your answer sheet.

- You may use a calculator on any problem. All numbers used are real numbers.
- Figures are drawn as accurately as possible EXCEPT when it is stated that the figure is not drawn to scale.
- All figures lie in a plane unless otherwise indicated.

Directions for Student-Produced Response Questions

Student Response questions are always numbered 9–18. Complete the grids at the bottom of the answer sheet for the test where the student response questions appear.

- If your answer is 2/3 or .666 . . . , you must enter **the most accurate value the grid can accommodate,** but you may do this in 1 of 4 ways:

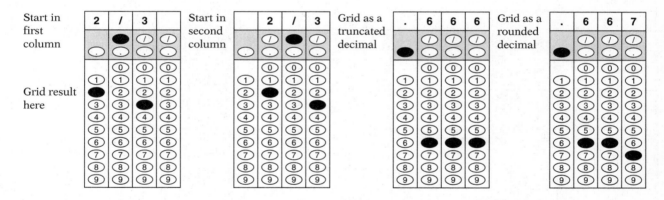

- In the example above, gridding a response of 0.67 or 0.66 is **incorrect** because it is less accurate than those above.

- The scoring machine cannot read what is written in the top row of boxes. You **MUST** fill in the numerical grid accurately to get credit for answering any question correctly. You should write your answer in the top row of boxes only to aid your gridding.

Reference Information

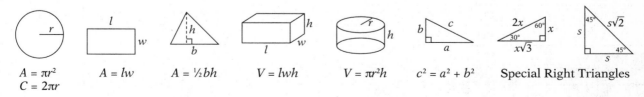

$A = \pi r^2$ $A = lw$ $A = \frac{1}{2}bh$ $V = lwh$ $V = \pi r^2 h$ $c^2 = a^2 + b^2$ Special Right Triangles
$C = 2\pi r$

The arc of a circle measures 360°.
Every straight angle measures 180°.
The sum of the measures of the angles in a triangle is 180°.

Start with number 1 for each new section. If a section has fewer questions than answer spaces, leave the extra answer spaces blank. Be sure to erase any errors or stray marks completely.

25 Minutes

SECTION 2

1. Ⓐ Ⓑ Ⓒ Ⓓ Ⓔ 6. Ⓐ Ⓑ Ⓒ Ⓓ Ⓔ 11. Ⓐ Ⓑ Ⓒ Ⓓ Ⓔ 16. Ⓐ Ⓑ Ⓒ Ⓓ Ⓔ
2. Ⓐ Ⓑ Ⓒ Ⓓ Ⓔ 7. Ⓐ Ⓑ Ⓒ Ⓓ Ⓔ 12. Ⓐ Ⓑ Ⓒ Ⓓ Ⓔ 17. Ⓐ Ⓑ Ⓒ Ⓓ Ⓔ
3. Ⓐ Ⓑ Ⓒ Ⓓ Ⓔ 8. Ⓐ Ⓑ Ⓒ Ⓓ Ⓔ 13. Ⓐ Ⓑ Ⓒ Ⓓ Ⓔ 18. Ⓐ Ⓑ Ⓒ Ⓓ Ⓔ
4. Ⓐ Ⓑ Ⓒ Ⓓ Ⓔ 9. Ⓐ Ⓑ Ⓒ Ⓓ Ⓔ 14. Ⓐ Ⓑ Ⓒ Ⓓ Ⓔ 19. Ⓐ Ⓑ Ⓒ Ⓓ Ⓔ
5. Ⓐ Ⓑ Ⓒ Ⓓ Ⓔ 10. Ⓐ Ⓑ Ⓒ Ⓓ Ⓔ 15. Ⓐ Ⓑ Ⓒ Ⓓ Ⓔ 20. Ⓐ Ⓑ Ⓒ Ⓓ Ⓔ

25 Minutes

SECTION 4

1. Ⓐ Ⓑ Ⓒ Ⓓ Ⓔ 3. Ⓐ Ⓑ Ⓒ Ⓓ Ⓔ 5. Ⓐ Ⓑ Ⓒ Ⓓ Ⓔ 7. Ⓐ Ⓑ Ⓒ Ⓓ Ⓔ
2. Ⓐ Ⓑ Ⓒ Ⓓ Ⓔ 4. Ⓐ Ⓑ Ⓒ Ⓓ Ⓔ 6. Ⓐ Ⓑ Ⓒ Ⓓ Ⓔ 8. Ⓐ Ⓑ Ⓒ Ⓓ Ⓔ

Student-Produced Responses   ONLY ANSWERS ENTERED IN THE CIRCLES IN EACH GRID WILL BE SCORED. YOU WILL NOT RECEIVE CREDIT FOR ANYTHING WRITTEN IN THE BOXES ABOVE THE CIRCLES.

9   10   11   12   13

14   15   16   17   18

20 Minutes

SECTION 8

1. Ⓐ Ⓑ Ⓒ Ⓓ Ⓔ 5. Ⓐ Ⓑ Ⓒ Ⓓ Ⓔ 9. Ⓐ Ⓑ Ⓒ Ⓓ Ⓔ 13. Ⓐ Ⓑ Ⓒ Ⓓ Ⓔ
2. Ⓐ Ⓑ Ⓒ Ⓓ Ⓔ 6. Ⓐ Ⓑ Ⓒ Ⓓ Ⓔ 10. Ⓐ Ⓑ Ⓒ Ⓓ Ⓔ 14. Ⓐ Ⓑ Ⓒ Ⓓ Ⓔ
3. Ⓐ Ⓑ Ⓒ Ⓓ Ⓔ 7. Ⓐ Ⓑ Ⓒ Ⓓ Ⓔ 11. Ⓐ Ⓑ Ⓒ Ⓓ Ⓔ 15. Ⓐ Ⓑ Ⓒ Ⓓ Ⓔ
4. Ⓐ Ⓑ Ⓒ Ⓓ Ⓔ 8. Ⓐ Ⓑ Ⓒ Ⓓ Ⓔ 12. Ⓐ Ⓑ Ⓒ Ⓓ Ⓔ 16. Ⓐ Ⓑ Ⓒ Ⓓ Ⓔ

TEST 5 QUESTIONS
SECTION 2

1. When Mr. Mayer went to the grocery store he spent $5 on grapes and $4.50 on peaches. If grapes cost $2 per pound and peaches cost $1.50 per pound, how many total pounds of grapes and peaches did Mr. Mayer purchase?

   A. 2.5 pounds
   B. 3 pounds
   C. 5.5 pounds
   D. 8 pounds
   E. 8.5 pounds

2. A, B, and C are points on a line, and B is the midpoint of $\overline{AC}$. If $AB = 15$, then $AC =$

   A. 60
   B. 30
   C. 15
   D. 10
   E. 7.5

3. $2x + 4 = 8$, $6x + 12 =$

   A. 2
   B. 4
   C. 8
   D. 16
   E. 24

4 and 5.
The scatterplot below shows the ages of a group of 15 married couples along with the graph of the equation $y = x$, where y represents the husband's age and x represents the wife's age.

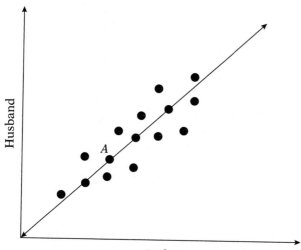

4. The age of the wife is 36 in the married couple represented by point A. How old is the husband?

   A. 37
   B. 36
   C. 35
   D. 34
   E. 33

5. In what percent of the couples is the husband older than the wife?

   A. $26\frac{2}{3}\%$
   B. $33\frac{1}{3}\%$
   C. 40%
   D. 60%
   E. $66\frac{2}{3}\%$

6. Which of the following points on the number line below has the same value as $|x - y|$?

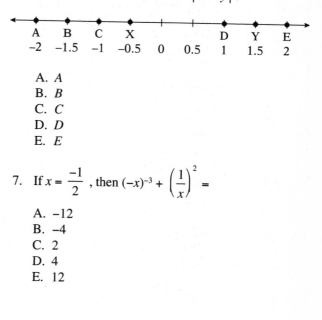

   A. A
   B. B
   C. C
   D. D
   E. E

7. If $x = \dfrac{-1}{2}$, then $(-x)^{-3} + \left(\dfrac{1}{x}\right)^2 =$

   A. −12
   B. −4
   C. 2
   D. 4
   E. 12

GO ON TO THE NEXT PAGE

8. The height and the base ($\overline{AB}$) of triangle ABC are equal and the change in the *x*-value from A to C is one-fourth the base. Which of these could be the co-ordinates of point C?

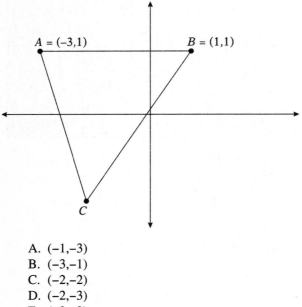

A. (−1,−3)
B. (−3,−1)
C. (−2,−2)
D. (−2,−3)
E. (−3,−2)

9. The table below gives the value of a function, $f(x)$, for a certain value of *x*. Which of the following could be equal to $f(x)$?

x	−2	−1	0	1	2
$f(x)$	−7	0	1	2	9

A. $f(x) = 3x − 1$.
B. $f(x) = 3x + 1$.
C. $f(x) = x^3 + 1$.
D. $f(x) = x^3 − 1$.
E. $f(x) = x^2 − 3$.

10. The square of a number equals the sum of 21 and 4 times the number. Which of the following could be the number?

A. −7
B. −4
C. −3
D. 3
E. 4

11. The diagram below represents the cost to set up a computer network, in thousands of dollars. What is the least amount of money it will cost to guarantee that there will be a connection between each point on the network?

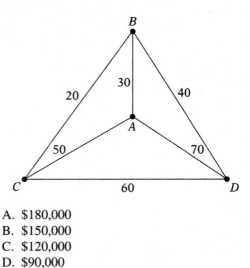

A. $180,000
B. $150,000
C. $120,000
D. $90,000
E. $70,000

12. 648 same-size cubes fill a rectangular box. The dimensions of the rectangular box are 18 inches by 27 inches by 36 inches. What is the length of the side of each cube?

A. 3 inches
B. 6 inches
C. 9 inches
D. 18 inches
E. 27 inches

13. For which of the following values of *x* is the relationship $x < x^2 < x^3$ true?

A. −2
B. $\dfrac{-1}{2}$
C. 0
D. $\dfrac{1}{2}$
E. 2

GO ON TO THE NEXT PAGE

14. What is the average of the lengths of the five segments seen below?

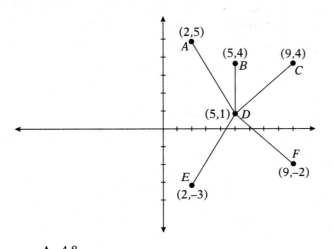

    A. 4.8
    B. 4.6
    C. 3.8
    D. 3.6
    E. 3.4

15. A person's weight on the moon is one-sixth of her or his weight on Earth. If a person weighs 30 pounds on the moon, how much would the person weigh on Earth?

    A. 5 pounds
    B. 30 pounds
    C. 60 pounds
    D. 150 pounds
    E. 180 pounds

16. In the figure below, the two semicircles have centers that are midpoints of the side of the rectangle. What is the area of the shaded region?

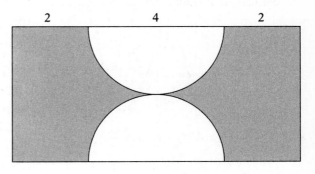

    A. $16 - 4\pi$
    B. $24 - 4\pi$
    C. $32 - 4\pi$
    D. $16 - 2\pi$
    E. $32 - 2\pi$

GO ON TO THE NEXT PAGE

17. The graph of the function $g(x)$ is shown below. Which of the following is the graph of $g(x) + 2$?

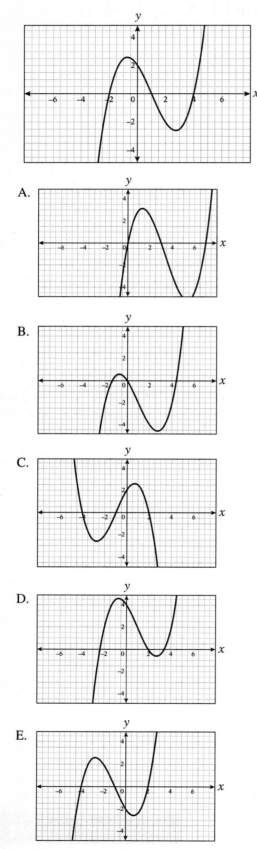

A.

B.

C.

D.

E.

18. Triangle ABC is an equilateral triangle. Rectangle $DEFG$ is inscribed in triangle ABC. What is the value of x?

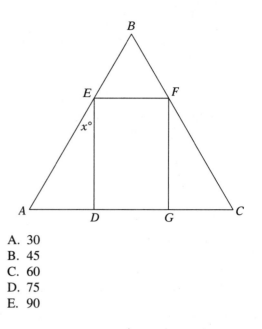

A. 30
B. 45
C. 60
D. 75
E. 90

19. $a : b = c : d$, which of the following is not an equivalent statement?

A. $\dfrac{b}{a} = \dfrac{d}{c}$

B. $\dfrac{a}{c} = \dfrac{b}{d}$

C. $\dfrac{b}{d} = \dfrac{c}{a}$

D. $\dfrac{c}{a} = \dfrac{d}{b}$

E. $\dfrac{a}{b} = \dfrac{c}{d}$

20. For all positive integers x and y, $x \lozenge y = x^2 - 2xy$. $a \lozenge b$ is equal to zero when:

A. $a = b$
B. $a = -b$
C. $a = 2b$
D. $a = -2b$
E. $a = \dfrac{1}{2} b$

GO ON TO THE NEXT PAGE

SECTION 4

1. $2x - y = 4$ and $-x + y = 2$, $x =$
   A. 2
   B. 3
   C. 4
   D. 6
   E. 8

2. Which of the following statements is true about the lengths of the sides of triangle ABC below?

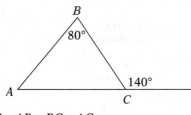

   A. $AB < BC < AC$.
   B. $AB < AC < BC$.
   C. $BC < AB < AC$.
   D. $AC < BC < AB$.
   E. $BC < AC < AB$.

3. The average of six consecutive positive integers is 4.5. What is the median of these six integers?
   A. 3
   B. 3.5
   C. 4
   D. 4.5
   E. 5

4. Let A be the set of all numbers in the form 2^n, where n is an even integer. Which of the following numbers is not in set A?
   A. $\dfrac{1}{4}$
   B. 1
   C. 2
   D. 4
   E. 16

5. The radius of the circle O below is 4. What is the area of triangle AOB?

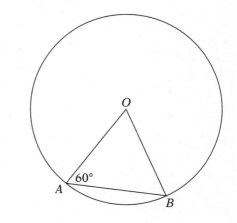

   A. $2\sqrt{3}$
   B. 4
   C. $4\sqrt{3}$
   D. $8\sqrt{3}$
   E. 12

6. There are six soccer teams in a league. Every team must play every other team twice. How many games must be played?
   A. 6
   B. 12
   C. 15
   D. 30
   E. 60

GO ON TO THE NEXT PAGE

7. The radius in the cylinder below is one-fourth the height. Which of the following is a formula for the volume of this cylinder?

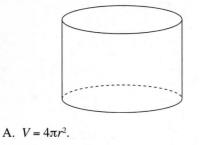

   A. $V = 4\pi r^2$.

   B. $V = \dfrac{1}{4}\pi r^2$.

   C. $V = \dfrac{4}{3}\pi r^3$.

   D. $V = 4\pi r^3$.

   E. $V = \dfrac{1}{4}\pi r^3$.

8. If x and y are positive integers and $\left(x^{\frac{1}{3}}y^{\frac{1}{4}}\right)^{12} = 11{,}664$, what is the value of xy?

   A. 6
   B. 12
   C. 18
   D. 24
   E. 36

9. How many distinct prime factors does 700 have?

10. John exercises 45 minutes a day, 3 days a week. How many hours does John exercise in 8 weeks?

11. The sale price of a television after a reduction of 15% is $357. What was the original price of the television set?

12. The volume of a rectangular prism with a square base is 128 cubic inches. If the height of the prism is 8, what is the perimeter of the base?

13. Tickets at a movie theater cost $5 for children and $7 for adults. A total of 400 tickets were sold for $2,300. How many children's tickets were sold?

14. $x^2 + 2xy + y^2 = 121$, $|x + y| =$

15. A circle with radius 10 has center (9,10). A new circle is formed by reflecting the center of the given circle across the y-axis. How many times do these two circles intersect?

16. The table below shows the results of a survey about high school students' support for reporting class rank to colleges. How many nonseniors do not support reporting class rank to colleges?

	Number of Students	Percent Who Support Reporting Class Rank
All Students	800	60%
Seniors	225	80%

17. A rectangle with height 16 is inscribed in a circle whose area is 100π. What is the area of the rectangle?

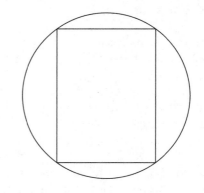

18. In the function $f(x) = |x - a| + b$, $f(9) = f(-3)$, what is the value of a?

 **GO ON TO THE NEXT PAGE**

SECTION 8

1. $n + 5 = 8$, $3(n + 5) =$

    A. 8
    B. 15
    C. 16
    D. 24
    E. 30

2. A certain hat style comes in five different colors and three different sizes. How many different hats of this style are there?

    A. 2
    B. 3
    C. 5
    D. 8
    E. 15

3. The square of the sum of $2x$ and $3y$ is equal to the sum of the square of y and the square root of x. Which of the following represents this statement?

    A. $4x^2 + 9y^2 = y^2 + x^2$.
    B. $4x^2 + 9y^2 = (y + x)^2$.
    C. $(2x + 3y)^2 = y^2 + x^2$.
    D. $(2x + 3y)^2 = y^2 + \sqrt{x}$.
    E. $2x^2 + 3y^2 = y^2 + x^2$.

4. In the figure below, points B and C are on circle O whose area is 81π. $\overline{BA}$ is tangent to circle O at point B and $BA = 12$. What is the length of $\overline{CA}$?

    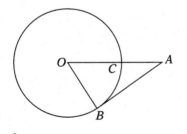

    A. 6
    B. 9
    C. 15
    D. 16
    E. 25

5. $x : 4 = 25 : x$ and $x \leq 0$. Which of the following is equal to x?

    A. −10
    B. −5
    C. −2
    D. 5
    E. 10

6. In the figure below $l \parallel m$. What is the value of $x + y$?

    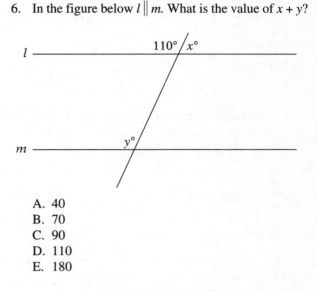

    A. 40
    B. 70
    C. 90
    D. 110
    E. 180

7. In the xy-coordinate plane, line k passes through the point $(2,4)$ and is perpendicular to the graph of the line whose equation is $y = \dfrac{2}{3}x - 6$. Which of the following is the equation for line k?

    A. $y = \dfrac{3}{2}x - 6$.

    B. $y = -\dfrac{3}{2}x + 7$.

    C. $y = \dfrac{2}{3}x + 7$.

    D. $y = -\dfrac{2}{3}x + 7$.

    E. $y = -\dfrac{3}{2}x - 6$.

8. $f(x) = 2x^2 + x + k$ is the equation of a quadratic function with a graph that passes through the x-axis when $x = 3$. What is the value of k?

    A. 21
    B. 18
    C. −21
    D. −18
    E. −3

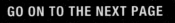 GO ON TO THE NEXT PAGE

9. If $x = -\dfrac{1}{2}$, then which of the following is always positive for $n > 0$?

    A. x^n

    B. n^x

    C. nx

    D. $n + x$

    E. $\dfrac{n}{x}$

10. Five groups of men, 10 men in each group, have the following average ages: 36,42,32,34, and 40. What is the sum of the ages of all 50 men?

    A. 184

    B. 368

    C. 552

    D. 1,840

    E. 3,680

11. Let a represent the arithmetic mean of k numbers whose sum is S. Which of the following is equal to 1?

    A. $\dfrac{a \cdot k}{S}$

    B. $\dfrac{S \cdot a}{k}$

    C. $\dfrac{S \cdot k}{a}$

    D. $S \cdot a \cdot k$

    E. $\dfrac{k}{a \cdot S}$

12. The figure below is formed by two overlapping equilateral triangles, each having area $36\sqrt{3}$. The shaded region is made up of six congruent equilateral triangles. What is the perimeter of the shaded region?

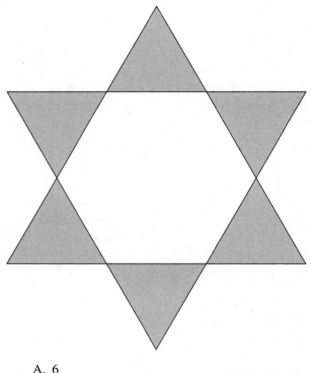

    A. 6

    B. 12

    C. 36

    D. 48

    E. 72

GO ON TO THE NEXT PAGE

13. The graphs of $f(x)$ and $g(x)$ are shown below. What is the value of $g[f(5)]$?

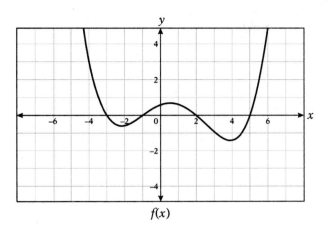

f(x)

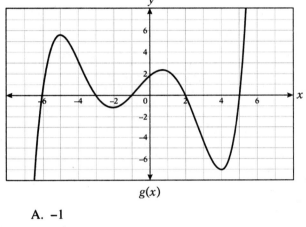

g(x)

A. −1

B. $\dfrac{-1}{2}$

C. 0

D. $\dfrac{1}{2}$

E. 2

14. The product xy equals every value in the interval [−2,4] and no values outside the interval. Which of the following describes possible values for x and y?

A. $-4 \le x \le 8$ and $0 \le y \le 2$.
B. $-1 \le x \le 2$ and $-2 \le y \le 0$.
C. $-2 \le x \le 1$ and $0 \le y \le 2$.
D. $-1 \le x \le 2$ and $-2 \le y \le 0$.
E. $-2 \le x \le 1$ and $-2 \le y \le 0$.

15. In the figure below, what is the value of x in terms of a and b?

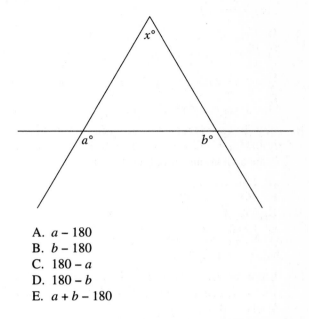

A. $a - 180$
B. $b - 180$
C. $180 - a$
D. $180 - b$
E. $a + b - 180$

16. A network with n points and a segment joining each point to every other point is called a complete network of size n. If k is the number of segments in a complete network of size n, which of the following is the number of segments in a complete network of size $n + 1$?

A. $k + n$
B. $k + n + 1$
C. $k + n + 2$
D. $k + 2n + 1$
E. $k + 2n + 2$

ANSWERS AND EXPLANATIONS
SECTION 2

1. **Answer:** **C**

   Calculate how many pounds of fruit were purchased.

   $\dfrac{5}{2}$ = 2.5 pounds of grapes. $\dfrac{4.5}{1.5}$ = 3 pounds of peaches.

   Mr. Mayer bought a total of 2.5 + 3 = 5.5 pounds of grapes and peaches.

2. **Answer:** **B**

   B is the midpoint of $\overline{AC}$. $\overline{AC}$ is twice $\overline{AB}$. $AB = 15$

   $AC = 2(15) = 30$.

3. **Answer:** **E**

   Factor $6x + 12 = 3(2x + 4)$.

   Substitute 8 for $2x + 4$.

   $3(8) = 24$.

4. **Answer:** **B**

   The equation of the line is $y = x$ and point A is on the line. If the wife's age is 36, the husband's age must be 36.

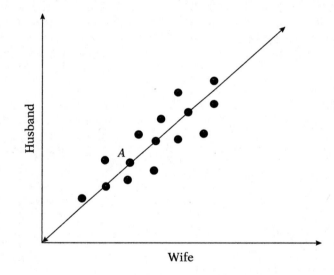

5. *Answer:* **C**

    There are a total of 15 couples; the 6 points above the line $y = x$ represent the couples where the husband is older than the wife.

    $\dfrac{6}{15}$ = 40% of the couples, the husband is older.

Wife

6. *Answer:* **E**

    Find the absolute value of $x - y$.

    $|x - y| = |-0.5 - 1.5| = |-2| = 2$.

    2 is point *E*.

7. *Answer:* **E**

    Substitute $\dfrac{-1}{2}$ for x

    $$(-x)^{-3} + \left(\frac{1}{x}\right)^2 = \left[-\left(-\frac{1}{2}\right)\right]^{-3} + \left(\frac{1}{-\frac{1}{2}}\right)^2$$

    Evaluate the expression.

    $$\left(\frac{1}{2}\right)^{-3} + (-2)^2 = 2^3 + (-2)^2 = 8 + 4 = 12.$$

8. *Answer:* **D**

   Find the x coordinate of point C.

   As the diagram on page 412 indicates, the base (AB) of the triangle is 4.

   The problem also states that the change in x from A to C is $\frac{1}{4} AB$.

   So the change in x from A to C is $\frac{1}{4}(4) = 1$.

   Add to find the x coordinate of C: $-3 + 1 = -2$.

   Find the y coordinate of point C.

   The problem states that the base and height of the triangle are equal.

   The problem also states that the base is 4. That means the height is 4.

   The change in y from A to C is -4 (negative because the direction is down).

   Add to find the y coordinate of point C. $1 + -4 = -3$.

   The coordinates of point C are $(-2,-3)$

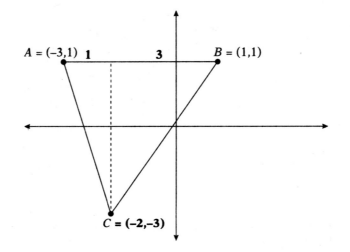

9. *Answer:* **C**

   You can eliminate answers. Substitute -2 for x in each answer choice. That eliminates all answers but A and C. Then substitute -1 for x in choices A and C. Notice that only choice C is correct.

   The function $f(x) = x^3 + 1$ works for all values in the table.

   $f(-2) = (-2)^3 + 1 = -8 + 1 = -7$

   $f(-1) = (-1)^3 + 1 = -1 + 1 = 0$

   $f(0) = 0^3 + 1 = 1$

   $f(1) = 1^3 + 1 = 2$

   $f(2) = 2^3 + 1 = 9$

x	-2	-1	0	1	2
$f(x)$	-7	0	1	2	9

10. **Answer:** **C**

Write an equation to represent the words.

$x^2 = 21 + 4x$

Factor to solve for x.

$x^2 - 4x - 21 = 0 \Rightarrow (x - 7)(x + 3) = 0$

$x - 7 = 0 \Rightarrow x = 7$. This is not an answer choice.

$x + 3 = 0 \Rightarrow x = -3$. This is choice C.

11. **Answer:** **D**

Three segments are needed to guarantee a connection between all points. Start from point A. Look at the diagram below. Pick the least expensive connection from A, and then the other two connections from B. The least amount of money that will guarantee a connection between all points is $20,000 + $30,000 + $40,000 = $90,000.

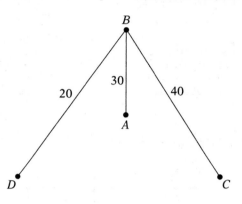

12. **Answer:** **A**

The volume of the rectangular box is $18 \cdot 27 \cdot 36 = 17{,}496$. The volume of each cube is $\dfrac{17{,}496}{648} = 27 = 3^3$. The length of the side of each cube is 3 inches.

13. **Answer:** **E**

This relationship is only true for positive numbers greater than 1.

So $x = 2$

$2 < 2^2 < 2^3 \Rightarrow 2 < 4 < 8$.

14. **Answer:** **B**

Use the distance formula to find the length of each segment. Notice $\overline{DA}$ and $\overline{DE}$ have the same length and that $\overline{DC}$ and $\overline{DF}$ have the same length.

$DA = DE = \sqrt{(2 - 5)^2 + (5 - 1)^2} = \sqrt{(-3)^2 + 4^2} = \sqrt{9 + 16} = \sqrt{25} = 5$.

$DC = DF = \sqrt{(9 - 5)^2 + (4 - 1)^2} = \sqrt{4^2 + 3^2} = \sqrt{16 + 9} = \sqrt{25} = 5$.

$BD = 3$.

$\dfrac{5 + 5 + 5 + 5 + 3}{5} = 4.6$.

15. **Answer:** **E**

Multiply a person's weight on the moon by 6.

$6 \times 30 = 180$ pounds.

16. *Answer:* **C**

    Find Area of Semicircles.

    The radius shown on each semicircle is 2. The area of the two semicircles equals the area of one circle. The area of the semicircles is $\pi(2)^2 = 4\pi$.

    Find Area of Rectangle.

    The width of the rectangle is the twice the radius, or 4. The length of the rectangle is 8. So the area of the rectangle is $8 \cdot 4 = 32$.

    Find Area of Shaded Region.

    The area of the shaded region equals Area of Rectangle – Area of Semicircles, $32 - 4\pi$.

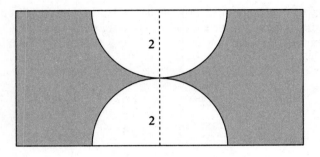

17. *Answer:* **D**

    Adding 2 to the *y* value shifts the graph up two units.

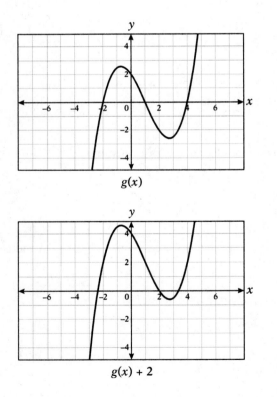

$g(x)$

$g(x) + 2$

18. *Answer:* **A**

Triangle *ABC* is an equilateral triangle, so the measure of angle *A* is 60°.

The measure of angle *ADE* is 90°.

Triangle *ADE* must be a 30°-60°-90° triangle, so *x* = 30.

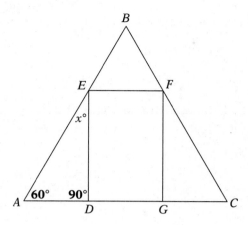

19. *Answer:* **C**

$\dfrac{a}{b} = \dfrac{c}{d}$ ⇒ cross-multiply to find *ad* = *bc* and *bc* = *ad*. Choice C alone does not yield one of these answers.

A. $\dfrac{b}{a} = \dfrac{d}{c}$ ⇒ *bc* = *ad*

B. $\dfrac{a}{c} = \dfrac{b}{d}$ ⇒ *ad* = *bc*

C. $\dfrac{b}{d} = \dfrac{c}{a}$ ⇒ *ab* = *dc*

D. $\dfrac{c}{a} = \dfrac{d}{b}$ ⇒ *bc* = *ad*

E. $\dfrac{c}{a} = \dfrac{d}{b}$ ⇒ *ad* = *bc*

20. *Answer:* **C**

Write an equation for $a \lozenge b = a^2 - 2ab = 0$

Factor and solve: $a(a - 2b) = 0$

There are two possible solutions.

$a = 0$ is incorrect because *a* must be a positive integer (greater than 0).

$a(a - 2b) = 0 \Rightarrow a = 2b$ is the correct solution.

SECTION 4

1. *Answer:* **D**

   Add the two equations to eliminate y.

   $$2x - y = 4$$
   $$\underline{-x + y = 2}$$
   $$x = 6$$

2. *Answer:* **A**

   The angles on either side of point C form a linear pair.

   Linear pairs have an angle sum of 180. So angle ACB measures 40°.

   Angle BAC measures 60° because the angle measures in a triangle total 180°.

   The longest side of a triangle is opposite the largest angle.

   So $AB < BC < AC$.

   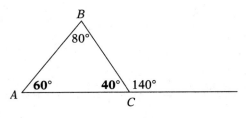

3. *Answer:* **D**

   The median and mean of consecutive integers are equal.

   We know the mean is 4.5, so the median is 4.5.

4. *Answer:* **C**

   $2^1 = 2$. The exponent 1 is not even, so 2 is not in the set A.

5. *Answer:* **C**

   Notice triangle ABO is an equilateral triangle.

   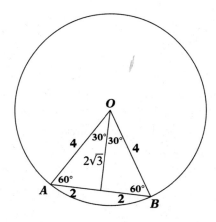

   <u>Find the height of the triangle</u>

   Draw the height, which forms two 30°-60°-90° right triangles.

   The side opposite the 30° angle is 2 so the height of the triangle, which is opposite the 60° angle, is $2\sqrt{3}$.

   The area of triangle $ABO = \dfrac{1}{2} \cdot 4 \cdot 2\sqrt{3} = 4\sqrt{3}$

6. *Answer:* **D**

   Let A, B, C, D, E, and F represent the different teams. There are a total of 15 ways for each team to play every other team, as listed below. Each team plays every other team twice so, $15 \cdot 2 = 30$ is the number of games.

   AB, AC, AD, AE, AF

   BC, BD, BE, BF

   CD, CE, CF

   DE, DF

   EF

7. *Answer:* **D**

   The volume formula for a cylinder is: $V = \pi r^2 h$.

   Notice that none of the formulas contain h.

   The problem states $r = \dfrac{1}{4}h$.

   Solve for h in terms of r.

   $$r = \dfrac{1}{4}h \Rightarrow 4r = h.$$

   Substitute $4r$ for h in the volume formula and solve.

   $$V = \pi r^2 h \Rightarrow V = \pi r^2 (4r)$$

   $$V = 4\pi r^3.$$

8. *Answer:* **C**

   Simplify

   $$\left(x^{\frac{1}{3}} y^{\frac{1}{4}}\right)^{12} = \left(x^{\frac{12}{3}} y^{\frac{12}{4}}\right) = x^4 y^3 = 11{,}664.$$

   The trick to solving this problem is to see that the prime factorization of 11,664 is $2^4 3^6$, so $2^4 3^6 = x^4 y^3$. We can see that $x^4 = 2^4 \Rightarrow x = 2$ and $y^3 = 3^6 = (3^2)^3 = 9^3 \Rightarrow y = 9$. Multiply to find $xy = (2)(9) = 18$.

9. *Answer:* **3**

   $700 = 2^2 \cdot 5^2 \cdot 7$.

   That means, 700 has three distinct prime factors.

10. *Answer:* **18**

    Calculate the number of minutes John exercises each week. $45 \cdot 3 = 135$ minute a week. Convert to hours: $\dfrac{135}{60} = 2.25$ hours a week. John exercises a total of $2.25 \cdot 8 = 18$ hours in 8 weeks.

11. *Answer:* **420**

    Represent reduced price as $0.85x$.

    Write equation and solve.

    $0.85x = 357 \Rightarrow x = \$420$.

12. *Answer:* **16**

    Divide volume by height to find area of the square base. $128 \div 8 = 16$.

    Take square root of area to find length of each side. $\sqrt{16} = 4$.

    Multiply length of side by 4 to find perimeter of square. $4 \cdot 4 = 16$.

13. *Answer:* **250**

    C = Number of children tickets sold.

    A = Number of adult tickets sold.

    Children's tickets cost $5.

    Adult tickets cost $7.

    $5C + 7A = 2{,}300$

    Substitute $A = 400 - C$.

    $5C + 7(400 - C) = 2{,}300$

    $5C + 2{,}800 - 7C = 2{,}300$

    $2C = 500$

    $C = 250$

    A total of 250 children's tickets were sold.

14. *Answer:* **11**

    Factor the perfect square and solve.

    $x^2 + 2xy + y^2 = 121 \Rightarrow x^2 + 2xy + y^2 = (x + y)^2 = 121$

    $|x + y| = 11$.

15. *Answer:* **2**

    The center of the new circle is $(-9,10)$. The graph below shows the original and reflected circles, and we can see that the circles intersect two times.

    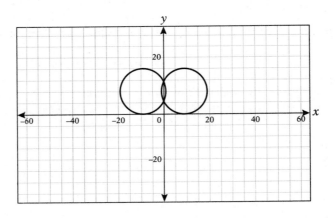

16. *Answer:* **275**

    Find the total number who do not support reporting class rank.

    Because 60% of all students support reporting class rank, 40% of all students do not support reporting class rank. Therefore, $0.40 \cdot 800 = 320$ of all students do not support reporting class rank.

    Find the number of seniors who do not support reporting class rank.

    80% of seniors support reporting class rank, 20% of seniors do not support reporting class rank. $0.20 \cdot 225 = 45$ seniors do not support reporting class rank.

    Subtract the number of seniors who do not support reporting class rank from all the students who do not support reporting class rank.

    $320 - 45 = 275$ nonseniors do not support reporting class rank.

17. *Answer:* **192**

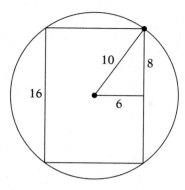

Find the base of the rectangle.

The area of the circle is 100π, so the radius of the circle is 10.

The radius of the circle is the hypotenuse of the triangle, so the hypotenuse is 10.

The height of the rectangle is 16, so the height of the triangle is 8.

Notice that the triangle is a 3-4-5 triangle, so the base of the triangle is 6, and the base of the rectangle is $2 \cdot 6 = 12$.

The area of the rectangle is $12 \cdot 16 = 192$.

18. *Answer:* **3**

Substitute 9 for x: $f(9) = |9 - a| + b$

Substitute -3 for x: $f(-3) = |-3 - a| + b$

The problem states $f(9) = f(-3)$

So $|9 - a| + b = |-3 - a| + b \Rightarrow |9 - a| = |-3 - a|$

Therefore, the two values inside the absolute value signs either equal each other, or one equals the negative (opposite) of the other.

$9 - a = -3 - a$	or	$9 - a = -(-3 - a) \Rightarrow 9 - a = 3 + a$
This is a false statement;		$6 = 2a$
because this would mean $9 = -3$,		$3 = a.$
which is impossible.		

SECTION 8

1. **Answer: D**

   Substitute 8 for $n + 5$.

   $3(n + 5)$

   Multiply.

   $3(8) = 24$.

2. **Answer: E**

   Multiply.

   $5 \cdot 3 = 15$ different hats.

3. **Answer: C**

   Write an equation.

   $(2x + 3y)^2 = y^2 + x^2$.

4. **Answer: A**

   Write on the diagram.

   The area of the circle is 81π. The radius of the circle is 9.

   Points B and C are on circle O. That means $OC = OB = 9$.

   $\overline{AB}$ is tangent to circle O at point B. The measure of $\angle OBA$ is $90°$.

   Use the Pythagorean Theorem to find OA.

   $(OA)^2 = (OB)^2 + (BA)^2 \Rightarrow (OA)^2 = (9)^2 + (12)^2$

   $(OA)^2 = 81 + 144 = 225$.

   $OA = \sqrt{225} = 15$.

   Inspect the diagram to see.

   $OA - 9 = CA$
   $15 - 9 = CA$
   $CA = 6$

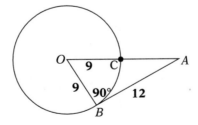

5. **Answer: A**

   Set up a proportion.

   $\dfrac{x}{4} = \dfrac{25}{x}$

   Cross multiply and solve for x.

   $x^2 = 100 \Rightarrow x = \pm 10$.

   The problem states $x \le 0 \Rightarrow x = -10$.

6. **Answer: E**

   $x = 70$ because the sum of a linear pair is 180°.

   $y = 110$ because $l \parallel m$ and corresponding angles are congruent.

   Add x and y: $70 + 110 = 180$.

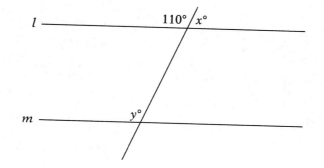

7. **Answer: B**

   Find the slope of k. Slopes of perpendicular lines are opposite reciprocals (the product is –1). So the slope of line k is $-\dfrac{3}{2}$.

   Use the point $(2,4)$ and the slope $-\dfrac{3}{2}$ to find the y intercept of line k.

   $$y = -\frac{3}{2}x + b \Rightarrow 4 = -\frac{3}{2}(2) + b$$

   $$4 = -3 + b \Rightarrow 7 = b.$$

   The equation for line k is $y = -\dfrac{3}{2}x + 7$.

8. **Answer: C**

   The graph crosses the x axis at $x = 3$.

   So the point $(3,0)$ is in the graph.

   That means $f(3) = 0$. Write an equation and solve for k.

   Write the equation for $f(x)$.

   $$f(x) = 2x^2 + x + k$$

   $$f(3) = 2(3)^2 + 3 + k = 0$$

   $$21 + k = 0 \Rightarrow k = -21.$$

9. *Answer:* **B**

Substitute $\dfrac{-1}{2}$ for x in the expression n^x.

$$n^x = n^{-\frac{1}{2}} = \frac{1}{n^{\frac{1}{2}}} = \frac{1}{\sqrt{n}}$$

The problem states that n is always positive, so $\dfrac{1}{\sqrt{n}}$ is always positive.

Below are examples for situations when each of the other choices is negative.

A. $x^n = \left(-\dfrac{1}{2}\right)^1 = -\dfrac{1}{2}$.

C. $nx = 1 \cdot -\dfrac{1}{2} = -\dfrac{1}{2}$.

D. $n + x = \dfrac{1}{4} + \left(-\dfrac{1}{2}\right) = -\dfrac{1}{4}$.

E. $\dfrac{n}{x} = \dfrac{\frac{1}{4}}{-\frac{1}{2}} = -2$.

10. *Answer:* **D**

There are 10 men in each of the 5 groups. The sum of the men's ages in each group is equal to the mean age in each group multiplied by 10.

The sums of the men's ages in each of the five groups are 360, 420, 320, 340, and 400. The sum of all the men's ages is $360 + 420 + 320 + 340 + 400 = 1,840$.

11. *Answer:* **A**

Notice that the sum of the values (S) equals the number of values (k) times to the mean (a).

Written symbolically

$S = ak$

It follows that $\dfrac{a \cdot k}{S} = 1$ and $\dfrac{S}{a \cdot k} = 1$.

Only $\dfrac{a \cdot k}{S}$ is an answer choice.

12. *Answer:* **E**

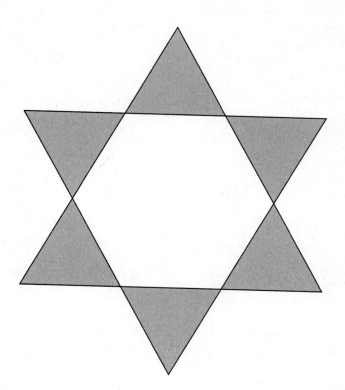

The length of each side of a large equilateral triangle is three times the length of one side of a shaded equilateral triangle. Therefore the length of each side of a large equilateral triangle is equal to the perimeter (3 sides) of a shaded triangle.

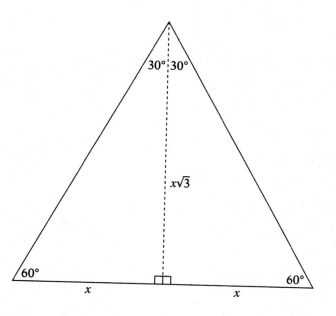

Draw the height of the triangle to form two 30°-60°-90° right triangles, shown above. The area of the triangle is $\frac{1}{2} \cdot (2x) \cdot (x\sqrt{3}) = x^2\sqrt{3} = 36\sqrt{3}$, so $x^2 = 36$ and $x = 6$. Therefore the length of each side is $2(6) = 12$. So the perimeter of each shaded triangle is 12 and the perimeter of the shaded region is $6(12) = 72$.

13. **Answer: E**

Use the graph for $f(x)$ to find $f(5)$.

$f(5) = 0$

$g[f(5)] = g(0)$

Use the graph of $g(x)$ to find $g(0)$.

$g(0) = 2$, so $g[f(5)] = 2$.

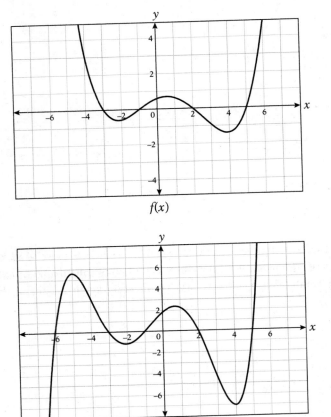

$f(x)$

$g(x)$

14. **Answer: E**

The correct choice must make xy equal only the values in the interval $[-2,4]$.

A. $-4 \le x \le 8$ and $0 \le y \le 2 \Rightarrow -8 \le xy \le 16$

B. $-1 \le x \le 2$ and $-2 \le y \le 0 \Rightarrow -4 \le xy \le 2$

C. $-2 \le x \le 1$ and $0 \le y \le 2 \Rightarrow -4 \le xy \le 2$

D. $-1 \le x \le 2$ and $-2 \le y \le 0 \Rightarrow -4 \le xy \le 2$

$\}$ Choices A–D create values outside the interval.

E. $-2 \le x \le 1$ and $-2 \le y \le 0 \Rightarrow -2 \le x \le 4$

15. *Answer:* **E**

The triangle diagram below shows the angle measures.
The sum of the angle measures in a triangle is 180.
Write an equation and solve for x.

$$x + (180 - a) + (180 - b) = 180 \Rightarrow x + 360 - a - b = 180$$
$$x = a + b - 180$$

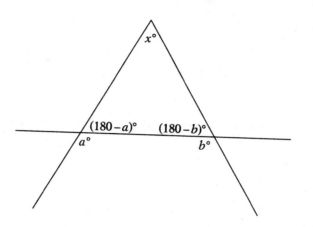

16. *Answer:* **A**

If one more point is added to a complete network of size n, n segments must be added to connect the new point to all existing points. Since k is the number of segments in a complete graph of size n then $k + n$ is the number of segments in a complete graph of size $n + 1$.

SCORE ESTIMATOR

Use this sheet to estimate your SAT Mathematics scale score. These scores are <u>estimates</u>, and your performance on the actual SAT could easily fall outside your scale score range for this test. One primary reason for the difference is that you did not take this test in a completely realistic test setting.

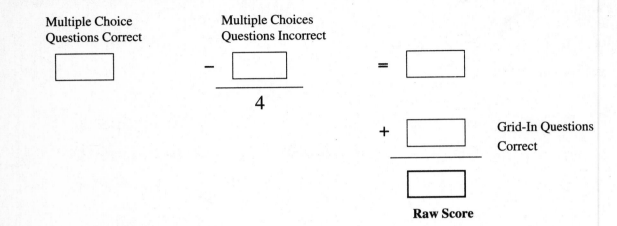

Raw Score	Scale Score Range	Raw Score	Scale Score Range
54	800	27	470–550
53	740–800	26	470–540
52	710–800	25	460–540
51	690–790	24	450–530
50	680–760	23	440–520
49	670–750	22	430–510
48	650–740	21	430–500
47	640–730	20	420–490
46	630–720	19	420–480
45	620–710	18	410–470
44	610–700	17	400–460
43	600–680	16	390–450
42	600–670	15	390–450
41	590–660	14	380–440
40	570–650	13	370–430
39	560–640	12	360–430
38	550–630	11	350–430
37	540–620	10	340–430
36	540–610	9	330–430
35	530–600	8	320–420
34	530–600	7	310–410
33	520–590	6	300–400
32	510–580	5	290–390
31	500–570	4	280–380
30	490–560	3	270–370
29	490–560	2	240–340
28	480–550	1, 0, or less	200–320